FRANCE 1848–1945
INTELLECT & PRIDE

FRANCE 1848–1945

INTELLECT & PRIDE

By
THÉODORE ZELDIN

OXFORD NEW YORK TORONTO MELBOURNE
OXFORD UNIVERSITY PRESS
1980

Oxford University Press, Walton Street, Oxford OX2 6DP

OXFORD LONDON GLASGOW
NEW YORK TORONTO MELBOURNE WELLINGTON
KUALA LUMPUR SINGAPORE JAKARTA HONG KONG TOKYO
DELHI BOMBAY CALCUTTA MADRAS KARACHI
NAIROBI DAR ES SALAAM CAPE TOWN

First published as the first section of France 1848–1945, *volume 2, by the Clarendon Press 1977. First issued, with additional material, as an Oxford University Press paperback 1980*

British Library Cataloguing in Publication Data

Zeldin, Theodore
France, 1848–1945.
Intellect and pride
1. France—Civilization—1830–1900
2. France—Civilization—1901–
I. Title II. Intellect and pride
944.07   DC33.6   79-41397
ISBN 0-19-285096-2

*Printed in Great Britain by
Cox & Wyman Ltd, Reading*

CONTENTS

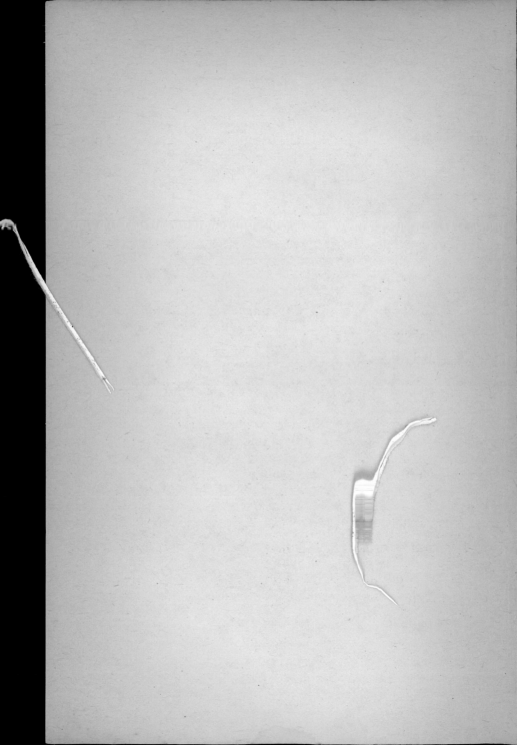

1. The National Identity

In 1864, an inspector of education, touring in the mountains of the Lozère, asked the children at a village school: 'In what country is the Lozère situated?' Not a single pupil knew the answer. 'Are you English or Russian?' he demanded. They could not say. This was in one of the remoter parts of France, but the incident illustrates how Frenchmen only gradually became aware of what it was that distinguished them from other men. The French nation had to be created. The slogan *Vive la France!* was not just a formal salute but a positive assertion of faith in the virtues of patriotism.

Because the spread of this faith was largely the work of the middle classes, it has been said that modern France, as it emerged in this period, was essentially bourgeois. But the bourgeoisie was so varied, and bourgeois ideals were so complex, that no satisfactory explanation of French behaviour can be provided simply in these terms.[1] One should not indeed unquestioningly assume that the French were a single people, clearly defined by their political boundaries. The process by which their unification was attempted continued throughout this period: the resistance that patriotism met, the varieties of allegiance that resulted from the clash of innovation and tradition, exactly what was involved in being French and how the sense of belonging to the nation was spread among different groups, all this is usually glossed over, because the division of Europe into nation-states has been regarded as natural and inevitable. But even the ideals that Frenchmen set themselves, the image of themselves that they formed, were not clear or distinct.

The politicians were the principal architects of national unity: the fact that Frenchmen willingly died for their country in several wars (though not with equal enthusiasm) seems to imply that the politicians were largely successful. However, France's political history also shows that the acceptance of

[1] See Zeldin, *Ambition and Love*, 1979.

common ideals was vigorously denied and that profound differences about what communal life involved continued unabated. I have argued[1] that the French were not only confused about what held them together, but that they consistently exaggerated their differences and that emphasis on diversity was an essential part of their society. One needs to go beyond political history to see the extent and the limits of these divergencies. National unity was fashioned not only by politics but also by the schools. The educational experience of Frenchmen needs to be investigated with care, to uncover the pressures to which they were subject, and to assess just how much they resisted those pressures. Having probed *la France bourgeoise*, it is necessary to analyse *la France*.[2]

In political terms, France was one of the first 'nation-states' in Europe, but for long its unity was felt consciously more by its rulers than by its people. In the seventeenth century, La Bruyère justly pointed out that men served the state from 'interest or desire for glory' and that they considered themselves to be servants of their prince, rather than of the community. The idea of France having a common personality and interest —as distinct from its all being the possession of one king—did not emerge till the eighteenth century, when the word nation first came to be used in a combative sense, to mean the sovereign people, as opposed to its despotic rulers. A despotic country could not be considered a *patrie*—a word adopted almost as a political slogan by the revolutionaries in 1789—a patriot being the opposite of an aristocrat.

Montesquieu had said that love of the *patrie* was the distinguishing mark of republicans, because it meant love of equality. Voltaire, in his *Philosophical Dictionary*, had added that the poor could have no *patrie*, and neither could the philosopher, who

[1] See Zeldin, *Politics and Anger*, 1979.
[2] Carlton J. H. Hayes, *France. A Nation of Patriots* (New York, 1930); W. C. Brownell, *French Traits* (New York, 1888); Vicomte d'Avenel, *Les Français de mon temps* (n.d., about 1900); Barrett Wendel, *La France d'aujourd'hui* (1909); Gustave Rodrigues, *La France éternelle* (1919); E. R. Curtius, *Essai sur la France* (1931); Fortunat Strowski, *Nationalisme ou patriotisme* (1933); Wladimir d'Ormesson, *Qu'est-ce qu'un Français* (1934); Paul Distelbarth, *La Personne France* (1935); Lucien Maury, *Définitions de la France* (1941); Alexandre Eckhardt, *Le Génie français* (1942); Marcel Raymond, *Génies de France* (Cahiers du Rhône, Neuchâtel, May 1942); M. M. Martin, *Histoire de l'unité française* (1949); A. Siegfried, *L'Âme des peuples* (1950); Raoul Girardet, *Le Nationalisme français* (1966); Z. Sternhell, *Maurice Barrès et le nationalisme français* (1972).

loved all humanity—in the same way as Montaigne had said that all men everywhere were his compatriots. The *ancien régime* had failed to instil any real sense of belonging into the country at large. Turgot told Louis XVI that ordinary villagers knew little about their links with the state. 'They are rather badly informed of their family duties and not at all of those which they owe to the state. Families barely know what holds them to this state of which they are part, they do not know in what way. They regard the exercise of authority in the collection of taxes, which serve to maintain order, as the law of the strongest, seeing no reason to yield to it other than their powerlessness to resist, and they believe in avoiding them whenever they can. There is no public spirit, because there is no common, known, visible interest.' When in 1787 the Academy of Châlons-sur-Marne held an essay-competition on 'the best means of giving birth to and encouraging patriotism in a monarchy', it awarded its prize to the entry which said that patriotism was only possible if the monarch pursued the happiness of his people, so that all citizens were satisfied. When the Revolution broke out, different ways of securing this happiness were seen and not all involved national unity. Only 35 per cent of the *cahiers de doléances* demanded a national programme of reform as the solution for France's discontents; 30 per cent looked to the church against the monarchy, to the parishes as defences against the central government, and to class privilege against the idea of the nation; and 34 per cent, though willing to increase the central power to a certain extent, favoured federalism, and the preservation of local privileges.[1] On the whole, it was only the old provinces, around Paris, which identified themselves with France; the frontier ones demanded the confirmation of their ancient prerogatives and Navarre even refused to attend the Estates General on the ground that it was independent. It was only in 1789 that the unity of the country was proclaimed, after the different estates and regions renounced their privileges in 'a heroic suicide of particularism', and that the equality of all was accepted. There were, however, some who rejected this new order: first the Girondin federalists and then the royalist émigrés, who

[1] Beatrice F. Hyslop, *French Nationalism in 1789 according to the General Cahiers* (New York, 1934), 198–228.

even co-operated with the rest of Europe to fight the French revolutionary armies. It was in these armies that patriotism received its baptism, and for long after it remained warlike, 'liberal', implying the liberation of subject peoples from tyrannical rule, and therefore inevitably as much partisan as national.[1] Paradoxically therefore, patriotism and nationalism were things that could divide Frenchmen, as much as expressing what they felt in common.

Nationalism was an ideal as much as a fact, and it is important to distinguish between the two, between the way the nation was idealised and held up as an object of veneration, and the way the people viewed it and responded to it in real life, even though their reactions might be very different in the course of ordinary routine and in times of war or crisis. The idealisers put forward theories as to what France ought to represent, and by force of repetition these theories have sometimes been accepted as descriptions of what France in fact was. Here, too, it is necessary to be clear as to what one is talking about.

The first and most influential theory about France was that it stood for 'civilisation'. To be a Frenchman, in the fullest sense, meant to be civilised, which required that one accepted the models of thought, behaviour and expression held in esteem in Paris. At one level, to accept civilisation meant to accept cultural uniformity and centralisation. By this definition, to be a Frenchman meant more than to be born in France, or to be a mere peasant; it involved adherence to a set of values, but in return one could hope to benefit from all the rewards that the state showered on those who adopted those values. *Civilisation* (like *nation*) was a new word, first used in 1766, and admitted into the dictionary of the French Academy only in 1798 (the year in which the word *nationalism* was first used in France). The idea of course was much older, though it is significant that the word formerly used was *civility*: this implied politeness, urbanity, a rejection of savagery and rurality, aspiration towards justice, order, education.[2] But at the beginning of the nineteenth century civilisation was still a contro-

[1] A. Aulard, *Le Patriotisme français de la renaissance à la révolution* (1921), 39, 102–5.

[2] George Huppert, 'The Idea of Civilisation in the Sixteenth Century', in A. Molho and J. A. Tedeschi, *Renaissance Studies in honour of Hans Baron* (Florence, 1971), 759–69.

versial idea.[1] On the one hand conservatives rejected it, because it seemed to imply change: Montlosier equated it with the Rights of Man, and the public prosecutor in a treason trial in 1822 declared that just as humans perished from excessive plumpness, so societies perished from an excess of civilisation. On the other hand Fourier denied that civilisation could be the ultimate destiny of man and invented a utopia to replace it. A Société de Civilisation was founded in 1832; Lamartine called the journal he founded in 1852 *Le Civilisateur*. The arguments were all complicated by the fact that the romantics— in the tradition of Rousseau who had praised the noble savage— imagined that the 'barbarians', the poor masses, being uncorrupted, were destined to give new life to a civilisation already considered decadent. But the basic idea behind 'civilisation' was that it was a state of movement and development. Guizot was the man who propagated this idea, and who worked out the theory that France was the country which led this movement. 'One can say, without flattery', he declared in his Sorbonne lectures on 'The General History of Civilisation in Europe' (1828), 'that France has been the centre, the home of civilisation in Europe.' 'It would be going too far,' he admitted, 'to pretend that it has always, and in every instance, marched at the head of the nations.' He acknowledged that Italy had at times led the world in art, and England in political institutions, but France possessed certain unique qualities, which meant that 'civilising ideas and institutions born in other lands have been in some way forced to undergo a further development in France whenever they wanted to transplant themselves, to become fruitful and general, to act for the common benefit of European civilisation; and it is from France, as from a second, more fecund and richer fatherland, that they have launched themselves to conquer Europe. There has been hardly any great idea, any great principle of civilisation, which, seeking to spread everywhere, has not first passed through France.' Guizot defined civilisation as the broadening and improvement of life, both by the amelioration of relations between men and by the elevation of the intellectual and moral condition of individuals. Civilisation meant progress in the way society organised itself and

[1] L. Febvre, *Pour une histoire à part entière* (1962), 'Civilisation, le mot, l'idée', 481–528.

behaved, it required an increasingly equitable distribution of goods and enlightenment between men, but it existed only when all the ingredients which made it up were found together. No one factor should be favoured at the expense of the others. Civilisation meant at once the perfecting of the individual and of society. It was therefore something very new, for the ancient world had never succeeded in achieving all of this and had reached a high level only in one particular sphere. Guizot saw an essential link between civilisation and national, representative government: the development of centralised states made possible the introduction of the benefits of civilisation to all classes; the adoption of liberal institutions meant that all classes could participate in deciding the direction civilisation took. Civilisation was a moral idea, and a humane idea, but also an artistic one, because it involved proselytisation. That is why France was at the head of European civilisation, because its instinct for sociability, its sympathy for generous ideas, the clarity of its language, made it best capable of understanding its goals and explaining them to others.[1] One thus became a better man by being civilised—more educated, polite, understanding—and one's country became a better place to live in —with more justice, liberty and prosperity—but acquiring civilisation involved not just receiving advantages but also preaching the gospel and helping others in the same path. Civilisation implied a whole social, economic and political programme, to be carried out in co-operation with like-minded citizens and, inevitably, against those whom one would label as obscurantist and reactionary. It was egalitarian but also elitist. It was universal, but also nationalist. These ambivalences were to remain as a constant feature in the French patriotic ideal.

At different times in this period, different facets of it were stressed more or less. Thus in the Second Empire Napoleon III presented every instance of technical progress, agricultural modernisation or improvement in communications as a triumph for civilisation and France's every political act as proof that it was 'the advanced sentinel and first soldier of civilisation'. Catholics like Veuillot complained that this was too materialist an interpretation of France's mission; the Pope

[1] F. Guizot, *Cours d'histoire moderne. Histoire générale de la civilisation en Europe* (1828), lecture 1.

condemned 'modern civilisation' altogether in 1864; but Catholics were happy to support French colonial expansion, and the conversion and westernisation of their new subjects in the name of civilisation. For a long time this certainty that French values were so superior that they had to be communicated to others possessed even the most liberal thinkers. The republican Edgar Quinet wrote that some other countries had indeed succeeded in acquiring supremacy in one field—Italy in art, Germany in science and religion, Britain in industry, the United States in liberty—but their achievements were always partial. France alone had 'the instinct of civilisation, the need to take the initiative in a general way to bring about progress in modern society. . . . It is this disinterested though imperious need . . . which makes French unity, which gives sense to its history and a soul to the country. This civilising force, this desire for external influence is the best part of France, its art, its genius, its happiness.'[1] The vagueness and variety of these grandiloquent statements meant that people defined civilisation in ways totally unacceptable to many Frenchmen. Adolphe Thiers, who was often regarded as the mouthpiece of the common-sensical, realist bourgeoisie, saw civilisation as the movement 'from the desert to the city, from cruelty to gentleness, from ignorance to knowledge'. But he concluded that its very foundation was private property 'without which there can be no civilisation'. He had no use for generosity and sacrifice in this matter and still less in the preservation of the national interest, which he insisted should be defended by military force, in exactly the same way as the Bourbon kings of the *ancien régime* had done. Important elements of the old monarchical ideals of grandeur and even conquest survived the Revolution, even if they put on new clothes. It was never really clear what aspect of civilisation France represented, or what aspect of France was being vaunted at any particular time. Civilisation was, to some extent, a war cry, preaching peace.[2]

An alternative tradition was that what made a man French

[1] E. Quinet, *De l'Allemagne et de la Révolution* (1832).
[2] R. A. Lochore, *History of the Idea of Civilisation in France 1830–1870* (Bonn, 1935), written by a student of Curtius; P. C. Roux-Lavergne, *De la philosophie de l'histoire* (1850), chapter one on 'Civilisation'; Antoine Arago, *Étude sur le rôle politique de la France* (1859).

was his race. This had a wider and longer vogue than is now generally admitted. It used to be thought that the French were descended from the Franks, who themselves came from Troy, and, until the eighteenth century, genealogies going back to Priam were dutifully memorised by schoolboys. Politics then complicated this theory. The bourgeoisie began to trace their descent back to the Gallo-Roman cities, and to claim the legacy of their liberties and privileges. Boulainvilliers (1658–1722) worked this into a theory whereby the nobles of France were Franks, while the third estate were Gauls.[1] The popularity of this view is seen in the way many people, Siéyès for example, saw the Revolution as a racial victory for the Gauls against the Frankish conquerors.[2] In the eighteenth century the noble Franks claimed to represent the freedom of the German forests against the despotic monarchy, but then in the nineteenth it was the Gauls who stood for democratic freedom. Napoleon, considering himself the heir of both the Roman Caesar and the German Charlemagne, dissociated the Gauls from the Romans and attributed the faults in the French character to the Gallic elements in it; but Augustin Thierry devoted his life to championing the Gallic third estate and his brother Amédée wrote a *History of the Gauls* (1828) which went through ten editions by 1881. The issue was complicated by the discovery of the Celts or Kymris (Bretons), a race less influenced by Rome, more indigenously French, who were praised as endowed with many qualities.

The scientists rallied to the support of the historians and declared that these racial varieties could still be discerned, in the shape of the skulls of living Frenchmen; and phrenology allowed them, moreover, to attribute moral characteristics to each race.[3] Physical anthropology grew into a fashionable and active science from the 1860s, stimulated by the dedication of Paul Broca (1824–80), the Protestant doctor who founded the Anthropological Society in 1859, which at first consisted entirely of doctors of medicine. Broca, who was appointed

---

[1] Boulainvilliers, *Essai sur la noblesse de France* (1732).
[2] Jacques Barzun, *The French Race: Theories of its Origins and their Social and Political Implications prior to the Revolution*, Ph.D. Columbia (New York, 1932).
[3] W. Edwards (founder of the Ethnological Society of Paris in 1838), *Des Caractéristiques physiologiques des races humaines considérées dans leur rapport avec l'histoire* (1829).

professor at the Paris faculty of medicine in 1867 and ended as
a senator of the republic, had originally been watched by the
police, for fear that his materialist doctrines might be dangerous,
but in the 1870s his work was subsidised both by the Paris
municipal council and by the state. He invented a large number
of instruments for measuring men, particularly their skulls, from
which he and his disciples drew varying conclusions.[1] The
disputes about just how many races France contained grew
complicated. Broca studied the height of conscripts and showed
how the inhabitants of Brittany, the Massif Central and the
Alps were between 8 and 17 per cent shorter than elsewhere.
Comparing the heads of doctors and male nurses at his hospital,
he discovered that the former were considerably larger. This
led to more and more skulls being measured. One craniologist
took this to the point of being able to make 5,000 measurements
on a single skull. Bigger heads were sometimes declared to be
better, but then that required the Auvergnats to be placed at
the head of civilisation, while the Corsicans had to be relegated
to the supposedly inferior level of the Chinese and the Eskimos.
But then the theory that protruding foreheads were signs of
civilisation made the Corsicans world leaders by this criterion.
Collignon, a military doctor, interpreted the class struggle in
France as a racial war between narrow-headed 'dolichocepha-
lics'—who had arrived in France more recently, and represented
innovation and adventure—and the round-headed 'brachy-
cephalics' who were conservative peasants. He prophesied the
victory of the latter. He measured the cephalic indexes of
16,000 people, and produced a map of their regional distribution. Professor Tropinard, in the 1880s, examined the colouring
of 200,000 Frenchmen, assisted by a whole phalanx of interested
doctors, and showed that twenty-two departments of France had
a predominance of blonds and twenty-two of dark complexions,
the rest being mixed. Basing himself on these and other
studies, Deniker divided France into six different races; and
Montandon in 1935 summarised all previous work in a new
map, which divided France into three races and seven sub-
races. The simple generalisations about the Gauls were thus

[1] Dr. Samuel Pozzi, *Paul Broca, biographie, bibliographie* (1880); Paul Broca,
Instructions générales pour les recherches et observations anthropologiques (1865), id., *Instructions craniologiques et craniométriques* (1868). Broca's bibliography lists 450 articles.

broken down into patterns too complicated to have more than a negative significance.[1] Science in the end confirmed the view which many people had held in any case, that France was not a unity from a racial point of view.

But this did not end the debate. Theorists argued how these disparate elements ought to be combined. Darwin was used freely to support conflicting arguments. Old Dr. Cabanis had laid it down that the mixing of races produced an improvement. But then the comte de Gobineau (1816–82) started the idea that it was precisely mixture that was ruining French civilisation, for though mixture at first led to the creation of higher qualities, continuation of it produced increasing amounts of the characteristics of the inferior race and the superior race inevitably disappeared. This was his explanation of the rise and fall of civilisations.[2]

The extremes to which these racial theories were taken may be seen in criminal anthropology, which at the turn of the century favoured the view that criminals were a distinct race, recognisable by their long jaws, flattened noses, scanty beard and other peculiarities supposedly denoting a reversion to savagery. The discovery that the shape of the famous murderer Vacher's skull was identical with Gambetta's was not enough to discredit this. In 1915 Dr. Edgar Berillon conveniently 'discovered' that Germans had intestines nine feet longer than all other humans, as well as being prone to polychesia (excessive defecation) and bromidrosis (body odour), by which criteria Berillon was able to uncover German spies and Germans masquerading as Alsatians.[3] However absurd this pushing of racial ideas to their utmost extremes may now appear, it was nevertheless long possible to appear both erudite and scientific

---

[1] P. Broca, 'Sur l'ethnologie de la France', *Mémoires de la Société d'Anthropologie de Paris* (1860), vol. 1 and (1868) vol. 3; Jacques de Boisjolin, *Les Peuples en France* (1878); Gustave Lagneau, *Anthropologie de la France* (1879); René Collignon, 'Étude anthropométrique élémentaire des principales races de France', *Bulletin de la Société d'Anthropologie de Paris* (1883), 3rd series, vol. 6; J. Tropinard, *L'Homme dans la nature* (1891); J. Deniker, *Les Races de l'Europe* (1899–1908); Dr. G. Montandon, *L'Ethnie française* (1935), 168–9.

[2] J. A. de Gobineau, *Essai sur l'inégalité des races humaines* (1853–5); Janine Buenzod, *La Formation de la pensée de Gobineau* (1967); M. D. Biddiss, *Gobineau* (1970); cf. G. Vacher de Lapouge, *L'Aryen, son rôle social* (1899).

[3] Jacques Barzun, *Race. A Study in modern Superstition* (1938), 240. Cf. Jean Finot, *Le Préjugé des races* (1905); Christine Bolt, *Victorian Attitudes to Race* (1971).

with almost any variation on this theme. Taine himself had espoused race as one of the three determining factors behind human behaviour: he had attributed characteristics to different nations on this basis; and his works were standard textbooks in every school. It was on the basis of such respectable authorities, and of all this scientific research, that the nationalist movements of the twentieth century built their theories about the need to exclude foreigners from France and to 'keep the French race pure'.

But the research also fitted an equally powerful tradition, that race played no part in creating French nationality. France would have had to surrender considerable areas on its borders, and perhaps have granted independence to whole regions, if it had been simply racialist. The loss of Alsace and Lorraine, like the annexation of Savoy, made this obvious, and stressed the need to have an alternative theory. It was Ernest Renan who supplied it. In a lecture at the Sorbonne given in 1882, which was much publicised and reprinted, he asked the question, 'What is a nation?'. Race, he declared, was no longer an adequate basis: the French were 'Celtic, Iberic and German', the Germans were 'German, Celtic and Slav'. Race was an interesting subject for historians to investigate but it could have no place in politics. It meant different things in any case, depending on whether one studied it anthropologically or philologically. Neither blood, nor appearance, could describe a man, because men were essentially reasonable and moral entities. The language men spoke did not say what their nationality was, because both English and Americans spoke the same language, and besides Switzerland showed that a common language was not indispensable. It is clear that Renan was arguing not from first premises, but from the nineteenth-century situation: his theory, like the theories of so many historians, was designed to justify the *status quo*. Religion, he went on, was nowadays a personal matter, so it could not make a nation; nor could community of interests: the Zollverein was a commercial, not a national arrangement. He concluded, in a peroration that was to become famous: 'A nation is a soul, a spiritual principle . . . [it is based on] the common possession of a rich legacy of memories from the past and consent in the present, the desire to live together and the will to continue to develop one's heritage.' Nations cannot be improvised: they are 'the result of a long history of effort, sacrifice and devotion'. Nations existed therefore because of the will of their members, reiterated in a silent daily plebiscite: they implied that the members had done great things together, and wanted to do more in the same company. They represented 'a great solidarity, constituted by the feelings created by sacrifices borne together and the wish to bear further ones'. If there were any doubts about their frontiers, they could easily be resolved by asking the people.[1]

Renan's principle, however, was seldom fully accepted, even by himself. He rather contradictorily objected to the annexation of Nice and Savoy, even though these two provinces had voted in a plebiscite to join France: he declared it would have more inconveniences than advantages, and was probably worried that they were clerical and conservative areas. Michelet was likewise uncertain as to what he thought, despite his democratic instincts. He declared that 'France was not a race, as Germany was, but a nation. Its origin is mixture. Individuals in it derive their glory from their voluntary participation in it.' He maintained, however, both that 'the immense majority of Frenchmen are Celts' and that 'language is the principal sign of nationality'.[2] In the same way, Émile Ollivier, who wrote one of the most interesting works on the 'Principle of Nationalities' (1895), argued that any group of people, of whatever number or race, had the right to form independent states if they wished; he did not think nations necessarily had to be large, though he expected that the unification of Germany and Italy would in due course lead to a Confederation of Europe. The racial idea, he said, was 'barbarous and retrograde'. Civilisation consisted in destroying primitive groups so as to form by free will contractual groups which would be far more solidly cemented than those born from chance. But in 1870 he declared war on Germany, on the ground that the whole nation wanted war, implying that free self-determination could be stopped by a foreign neighbour where 'dignity and honour' were insulted by it.[3] Not everyone who believed in nations

[1] E. Renan, *Qu'est-ce qu'une nation* (1882).

[2] J. Michelet, *Tableau de la France* (1875), 1, 14; id., *La France devant l'Europe* (1870).

[3] É. Ollivier, *Du principe des nationalités* (1895), vol. 1 of *L'Empire libéral*, and further references in T. Zeldin, *Emile Ollivier* (1963), 168–72.

based on the popular will accepted that it required only a
plebiscite to set up a new country. Proudhon disliked large
countries and wanted to divide the great powers of Europe into
sixty different states.

Since nationalists were usually imperialists, they were faced
with the problem of reconciling their belief in the superiority
of the French race with a willingness to admit conquered
peoples into the fold of the nation. Some controversy arose about
the extent to which the French were free from racial prejudice.
There were those who claimed French colonisation was marked
by an exceptional readiness to assimilate people of other colours.
It will be shown, in due course, that this was only superficially
true.[1] And when, in 1963, the first scientific inquiry into racial
prejudice in France was carried out, on a sample drawn mainly
from the liberal professions, it was shown that racism remained
very strong, with much use of insult, rejection of contact, and
even violence towards people of other races. Interestingly
enough, it was found that the peasants were the least racist,
particularly in areas which had little contact with foreigners.
In the departments of Lot and Corrèze there was no patois
word for Jew until the Occupation and the peasants there
discovered the Jew only then.[2] After the war of 1914–18, quite
a few Frenchmen rejected the right of the Germans to be one
nation, and twisted their theories so as to justify the setting-
up of a buffer Rhine state.[3] The French law on nationality
certainly never accepted the view that anyone could elect to
be a Frenchman, though, as the number of Frenchmen declined relatively to the population of other powers, naturalisa-
tion was facilitated, and foreigners allowed to enter freely. This
new admixture of alien races, however, stimulated protests
against the 'métèques', who were adulterating 'purer blood'.

Whatever may have been France's racial composition in
the days of Caesar and Charlemagne, in modern times it
was distinguished by the large number of foreigners living
in it. Though it obviously could not be compared with the
U.S.A., France had some of America's problems regarding the

[1] See Zeldin, *France 1848–1945*, vol. 2, ch. 18; Zeldin, *Anxiety and Hypocrisy*,
ch. 5 (forthcoming).

[2] P. H. Maucorps, *Les Français et le racisme* (1965), 155.

[3] René Johannet, *Le Principe des nationalités* (1918); Louis Le Fur, *Races, nationalités, états* (1922); Judith M. Hughes, *To The Maginot Line* (Cambridge, Mass.,
1971).

absorption of newly arrived citizens. The statistics of foreign residents were:

1851	380,000	1901	1,034,000
1861	497,000	1911	1,116,000
1872	741,000	1921	1,496,000
1881	1,001,000	1931	2,613,000
1891	1,130,000		

This, however, does not accurately reveal the total number of foreigners, for naturalised immigrants were deducted. The figures for these latter rose rapidly:

Naturalisations

1851	13,500	1891	170,700
1861	15,300	1901	221,800
1872	15,300	1911	252,000
1881	77,000		

Between 1889 and 1927 1,330,000 foreigners were naturalised, and between 1927 and 1940 another 967,000. So in 1940 it was estimated that 1,750,000 naturalised Frenchmen needed to be added to the 2,600,000 unnaturalised foreigners. But in addition many Frenchmen were the children of mixed marriages. In 1888 (when the first figures on this subject were compiled) there were about 8,000 mixed marriages; in the 1920s there were about 17,000 per annum. Originally, the foreigners who came into France were mainly from border regions, notably Belgians,[1] Italians,[2] Germans,[3] Portuguese and Spaniards. But after the war there was an immense influx of Poles into France —412,000 according to the French statistics and half as many again according to the Polish ones.[4] Half a million Russian, half a million Spanish, and 30,000 Jewish political refugees escaped into France. How many settled is not clear. Perhaps one-third of the Jews stayed on. The Spaniards mainly went back to Spain: in 1951 only 165,000 of them were still in France.[5]

[1] 33 per cent in 1851, 47 per cent in 1872, 24 per cent in 1911.

[2] 16 per cent in 1851 rising gradually to 36 per cent in 1911.

[3] 15 per cent in 1851, 17 per cent in 1861, declining gradually to between 8 and 10 per cent.

[4] S. Wlocewski, *L'Établissement des Polonais en France* (1936); Pierre Depoid, *Les Naturalisations en France 1870–1940* (Études Démographiques, no. 3) (1942); Henri Bunle, *Mouvements immigratoires entre la France et l'étranger* (1943), 70–2.

[5] Guy Hermet, *Les Espagnols en France* (1967).

How quickly those who stayed came to consider themselves and came to be considered as Frenchmen has not been investigated. The Russians certainly formed a separate community for a long time, with their own cathedral and at one stage as many as forty different churches and chapels in the Paris region alone. They had sixty-two newspapers and reviews. The princes (and others) who became taxi drivers were numerous enough to have a Russian newspaper for themselves, *Le Chauffeur russe*, a review (*Au volant*), libraries, garages, canteens of their own. Passy became almost a Russian town. The pretender, Grand Duke Vladimir, lived in Brittany (Saint-Brieuc-sur-Mer) from 1921 to 1944. But many Russians were in varying degrees assimilated, particularly if they entered the service of the French state: Gorky's adopted son, Zinovy Pechkoff, became a brigadier-general; Michel Garder, professor at the School of War, became a leading French strategist; Serge Lifar transformed the art of ballet; two authors, Kessel and Troyat, were even elected to the French Academy. Prince Youssoupoff, one of the murderers of Rasputin, set up as a couturier.[1]

France was considered capable of absorbing such varied populations—not only foreign ones, but also the different types at its extremities—because the possession of French culture was another definition of what constituted a Frenchman. This meant that a peasant, as much as an immigrant, had to be made French, and that it was the inculcation of the traditional values, particularly through the schools and the army, that was primarily responsible for creating the nation. The institution of compulsory, free and lay education was a major step, therefore, in the diffusion of patriotism—which underlines how much effort had to be put to stimulate that sentiment. It will be seen, in the chapters on education, how the teaching of civic and moral duties was an important part of the school curriculum, how love for the nation was preached as something expected of the child, in the same way as love for his mother. It was explained to him how much he owed to France, and how therefore no sacrifice was too great to repay his debt. Now, to acquire French culture meant first of all to obtain mastery of its language, and language, it was believed, contained the key to the art both of

[1] Banine, *La France étrangère* (1968).

behaving and of thinking. No one has given a better statement
of how much was expected of the French language than Joseph
de Maistre, himself of course a Savoyard, for whom therefore
France was a freely chosen ideal. France, he said, may not have
succeeded in dominating the world by force of arms, but it
enjoyed 'another kind of domination, much more honourable,
that of opinion . . . and to exercise this, it has a dominating
language . . . which, even before it made itself illustrious by
masterpieces of all kinds, was recognised as supreme by Europe.
People loved it and considered it an honour to speak it. What
is called the art of speaking is eminently the talent of the French,
and it is by the art of speaking that one rules over men.
Someone has said that an idea is never adopted by the world
until a writer of genius takes hold of it and expresses it well . . .
That is presumably the source of the influence of France: the
good writers of this nation express things better than those of
all other nations, and make their ideas spread throughout
Europe in less time than a writer of another country would
need to get his ideas known in his province. It is this talent, this
distinctive quality, this extraordinary gift that has made the
French the distributors of fame . . . Self-love—more insidious
and stronger than national pride—revealed this truth to all
the famous men of the whole world who had the more or less
open ambition to win the approbation of the French, because
they could not conceal from themselves that they were condemned to a local reputation until Paris consented to make them
famous . . . English literature owes all its celebrity to the French:
it was completely unknown to the rest of Europe until France
took a liking to the literary productions of its rival . . . Perhaps
nothing is properly understood in Europe until the French have
explained it.'[1]

It should not be thought, however, that the interest in language was confined to writers seeking fame. The peculiarity of
the French situation was that, from a very early period, to
speak and write well, according to the manner laid down in
turn by the Court, the Academy, the University, and Paris
became a mark of distinction in all classes. The French language acquired its prestige first of all because it liberated men

[1] J. de Maistre, *Trois Fragments sur la France*, printed in *Œuvres inédites du comte
J. de Maistre* (1870), 7–9.

from isolation, enabled them to get beyond the patois of their families and villages, to mix on equal terms with anybody, to participate in the most sociable and most cultivated of the arts, conversation. It has been seen how to this very day, uneducated workers regret above all that they lack mastery of the language, because they see it as the passport to social intercourse and to full equality.[1] This attitude could probably be found in other countries, but nowhere was language so highly esteemed as embodying the national genius. When Paul Valéry, in 1941, was asked to say what France represented, he replied that 'the first thing to examine if one wants to appreciate the mental life of this people and its evolution . . . is its language, the first intellectual fruit of a nation'.[2] Its literature and philosophy were 'nothing but the exploitation of certain properties' of this language. Even though Saussure pointed out that 'the generally accepted view that language reflects the psychological character of a nation' was not supported by even the most elementary investigation of linguistics,[3] it nevertheless was an ineradicable superstition that by speaking French a man gave expression to the values the country admired. 'Whatever is not clear is not French', Rivarol had said in 1783 in the essay with which he won the competition set by the Academy of Berlin, asking why French was a universal language, why it deserved this status and whether it was likely to keep it.[4] French was then the language of diplomacy and remained so until 1919 when English was admitted as its equal at the Peace Conference of Versailles. That the claims of French were less and less accepted was seen in 1945 when the peace treaties were drawn up in English and Russian, with French being added only after protests from France. When the United Nations planned to have English, Spanish and Russian as its three working languages, French had again to be forced in as a fourth.[5] In the age of the enlightenment, most educated people could speak French, but the advent of democracy ironically revealed

[1] Zeldin, *Ambition and Love*, 273.

[2] Paul Valéry *et al.*, *La France et la civilisation contemporaine* (1941), 8–9.

[3] F. de Saussure, *Cours de linguistique général* (1916), 310–11; cf. Georges A. Heuse, *La Psychologie ethnique* (1953), 39.

[4] A. de Rivarol, *Discours sur l'universalité de la langue française* (1784).

[5] Firmin Roz and Maurice Honoré, *Le Rayonnement de la langue française dans le monde* (1957).

French to be very much a minority tongue. It is wrong to
think that French retained its supremacy as an international
language until the end of this period. In diplomacy it may have
done so, but in other fields, notably in commerce, industry and
outside Europe, English was very often an easily successful
rival. Already in 1859 a French critic was remarking 'in our
generation, dominance is passing more and more to the
English language'.[1]

Nevertheless it was argued that French was unbeatable if
one wanted clarity. The French language was supposed to give
expression to the great French quality of logic. 'Logic governs
our speech,' wrote Jules Simon, 'affecting even the very form
of our periods . . . It is impossible to be unreasonable or equivocal when one speaks French, without it being immediately
obvious that it is not French that one is speaking.' The language
was supposed to reflect the good sense and clarity of mind that
all Frenchmen inherited from Descartes.[2] This myth, as will
be seen,[3] represented some very confused thinking. French, as
the Danish linguist Otto Jespersen pointed out, was not a particularly logical language by any professional test—Chinese
and English were both more logical.[4] But what Frenchmen
stressed was that the order of words in French was governed by
strict rules, in contrast with German where the weight of words
counted for more than meaning in determining order. Subordinate clauses had to be introduced by definite conjunctions,
unlike English which allowed greater freedom, so that the
links between phrases were less clearly defined. It was claimed
that in French it was impossible to lapse into Germanic
'verbal diarrhoea'. What this meant was that French had
rules which were more clear-cut, defended on the ground that
they represented the triumph of reason, taste and art over
chaos. These rules encouraged people to order their ideas in
a certain way, to classify them according to a set pattern, and
to present them with a due degree of abstraction. The conclusion was rather hastily drawn that other nations lacked the

[1] J. Lemoine, *Nouvelles études critiques et biographiques* (1863), article on 'Grandeur
et décadence de la langue française' written in 1859, 362–71.

[2] *Alliance Française*, pamphlet in British Museum, 1601/193 (1889), 29.

[3] See chapter 5.

[4] Otto Jespersen, *The Growth and Structure of the English Language* (1938, New
York reprint), 1–16. Cf. N. Chomsky, *Cartesian Linguistics* (1966), 28–31, 93–5.

French power of abstraction. To many people, form was all important; the way a man expressed himself mattered almost as much as what he said. Politicians were admired for their oratory quite as much as for their principles, and some quite second-rate people with beautiful voices could, largely on the ground that they could roll out harmonious periods loaded with the right allusions and rhythm, reach the highest positions in the state. Viviani, who became prime minister in 1914, took lessons at the Comédie-Française in the art of declamation and used to spend long hours practising his parliamentary speeches, as though they were songs. To be able to classify material in an orderly, traditional manner often appeared as the sign of intellectual superiority, even when it only involved the application of old rules. Pedantry, as opposed to efficiency, could thus often become the ideal of junior employees in the civil service and the rising mass of clerks who mistook the form for the essence.

To those who had acquired mastery of the French language only by personal effort, in family surroundings where patois was supreme, French did indeed represent more than a means of expression. Jean-Paul Sartre recalled how his grandfather Charles Schweitzer, an Alsatian, was 'still amazed by the French language at the age of seventy, because he had learnt it with difficulty and had not quite made it his own; he used to play with it, he enjoyed the words and liked saying them, and his merciless diction did not spare me a syllable.' He and his grandson wrote to each other in verse: 'bound by a new link, they talked, like Indians or the pimps of Montmartre, in a language forbidden to women'. Sartre has shown the effects of this on behaviour. He had discovered the world through language and so 'for a long time I mistook language for the world. To exist was to have a registered trade-name somewhere in the infinite Tables of the Word.' Observing the world meant not investigating it, but 'catching living things in the trap of phrases', imposing names on them, and taking pleasure above all in words.[1] In politics, the tendency to confuse words with action, to think one had dealt with a situation by making a fine speech about it, by defining it precisely in a beautiful piece of prose, was an inevitable consequence of this attitude.

But not all Frenchmen spoke good French or fulfilled the

[1] J.-P. Sartre, *Les Mots* (1964); Penguin translation *Words* (1967), 89, 115.

ideals of the grammarians. Linguists showed that almost every village had its own peculiarities of style, vocabulary and pronunciation.[1] Pronunciation certainly long remained very diverse. In the 1930s to say *cinq* francs was considered vulgar and men of distinction still did not do it. At the end of the nineteenth century people used to pronounce *sept* francs *sè* francs, differentiating it from *c'est franc* only by spelling. Popular pressure fought against such ambiguities imposed by formal rules, but also created ambiguities of its own which the rules forbade. Uniformity in speech had not even been established among the most highly educated élite of the country at the turn of the century, so that they could hardly set a model to others. A German linguist had the idea of recording phonetically the speech of a number of eminent writers in Paris, and he was amazed by the wide discrepancies in their pronunciations.[2] The way most Frenchmen pronounce *r*, which appears as one of their most characteristic idiosyncrasies, is quite a recent phenomenon. The *r* used to be pronounced in a full, rolled way (with the point of the tongue in the same position as for *l*, but with a vibration of both tongue and vocal chords). The Parisian *r* (with the back of the tongue against the palate) appeared only in the eighteenth century, as an urban phenomenon. It came to be used independently at the same time in the city of Marseille, so that in a vaudeville played in Toulouse in 1850, an actor who had the part of a Marseillais used the guttural *r* to show his origin. This pronunciation spread to other towns and to the northern part of France in the course of the next century under the joint influence of women and education, but without being totally victorious; and the regionalist movement may well halt it in its tracks. All the while professors of singing continued to teach their pupils to pronounce *r* in a rolled way, so that, for example, Edith Piaf, born and bred in Paris, sang as though she came from Carcassonne. But until the 1890s, the majority of Frenchmen still used the rolled *r*. In the same way the pronouncing of both consonants where two are found side by side,

[1] J. Gilliéron and E. Edmond, *Atlas linguistique de la France* (1902–20); on patois, see below, chapter 2, and M. de Certeau, D. Julia and J. Revel, *Une Politique de la langue: La Révolution française et la langue. L'Enquête de Grégoire* (1975).
[2] Eduard Koschwitz, *Les Parlers parisiens* (1893). Cf. Marguerite Durand, *Le Genre grammatical en français parlé à Paris et dans la région parisienne* (1936) for changes in popular speech in the previous fifty years.

as in *grammaire*, was a development of this period, stimulated partly by teachers, who liked to enunciate clearly in order to help their pupils in dictation, partly by the snobs of the Second Empire, copying the Italian singers, fashionable then, and finally by the radio announcers, who, as one chansonnier said, even put three *t*s in *attendre*. This again was a form which was developed mainly in the north.[1]

If French was a logical language in the fullest sense, it could have adapted its spelling to changes in pronunciation. Because it is a language which has experienced rapid evolution, the discrepancy between the two is considerable. But the Academy has been reluctant to modernise spelling: it once agreed, for example, under the influence of Émile Faguet, to replace the plural ending *x* by *s* and to return to the medieval simplicity of *chous*; but it never implemented its decision. Spelling survives therefore which is antiquated and complicated by the pedantry of Renaissance rhetoricians who introduced parasitic letters to satisfy the demands of false etymologies and by legal bureaucrats who added double letters and multiplied *h* and *y* in order to make words look more beautiful in their fine script. Illogicalities like *honneur* and *honorer* remain. How difficult the Academy itself finds it to be logical was shown when it debated the question of whether *automobile* should be masculine or feminine—genders in French are of course unreasonable, the neuter has illogically been allowed to die. The Conseil d'État, which needed to issue a decree using the word, was inclined to make *automobile* masculine, which is what it was in popular parlance at first, but the Academy decided it was a *voiture* and should therefore be feminine, which people gradually accepted.

The slowness with which the Academy has revised its dictionary and the way it has resisted change should not be taken at their face value. In eighteenth-century France, inventing new words was considered acceptable. It was only in the nineteenth century that the French Academy became timid about neologisms, so that when it produced a new edition of its dictionary in 1835, critics complained that it had left out about one-third of the spoken language. Littré, whose dictionary (1863–72) remained the standard authority for nearly a hundred years, gave himself the objective of producing a record of

[1] A. Dauzat, *Le Génie de la langue française* (1943), 37–9.

'contemporary' language and he added vastly to the Academy's vocabulary, not only technical terms but also words from daily speech, including dialects (and particularly the dialect of Normandy). But he interpreted contemporary to mean France since the beginning of the seventeenth century and he also inserted older words left out of the Academy's dictionary; his examples were drawn very largely from authors before 1830. Under Louis XVI, d'Alembert protested against dictionaries laying down the law; but now the major ones were generally accepted as authoritative.[1] However, the language continued to change all the same. Argot as well as patois survived and both developed actively in this period. The rules of style and even of grammar have been broken, on the one hand, by successive literary movements, so that the ideal of classical abstraction has long been challenged, even though it still retains certain well-entrenched positions, and on the other hand by journalists, scientists and travellers, who have introduced modes of speech which have never won literary admiration, but have been used none the less. English has made deep inroads into French. Philosophers have borrowed heavily from German, and a certain kind of obscurity has become fully accepted, despite all the traditions against it. In 1937 the leading linguist in the country, Ferdinand Brunot, assisted by many dignitaries like Paul Valéry, established the Office of the French Language to 'prevent the nomenclature of new things being left to the arbitrary decision of individuals, especially at a time when pedantry and pretentiousness are supreme'. The French language, the Office declared, 'because of the fantasies of certain industrialists, engineers, merchants and journalists, is in the process of becoming a ridiculous carnival'. This body of course had no effect. Archaism was not a characteristic of the French language in this period; the language was in constant movement; and that is why the notion that it gave expression to French nationalism was either naïve or too complicated to be useful.[2]

The principles of civilisation, the bonds of race and the

---

[1] Georges Matoré, *Histoire des dictionnaires français* (1968); Eugène Ritter, *Les Quatres Dictionnaires français* (Geneva, 1905), 24-5.

[2] Michel Bréal, 'Le langage et les nationalités', *Revue des Deux Mondes* (1 Dec. 1891), 615-39; Henri Bauche, *Le Langage populaire* (1920); F. Brunot, *La Pensée et la*

French language as an expression of these, were put forward
as the main factors which made the inhabitants of France into
Frenchmen, conscious of their nationality. French 'nationalism',
as a creed, went far beyond this. Paradoxically, nationalism
was a source of division among Frenchmen, because it became
the instrument through which quite different political ideas
were propagated. Thus on the one hand, nationalism was at
first equated with liberalism or revolution: it was the Jacobin
doctrine of the emancipation of oppressed peoples; the leaders
of the Third Republic, from Gambetta to Clemenceau, proclaimed themselves heirs of this tradition, and the conservatives attacked them. On the other hand, nationalism, at the
turn of the century, emerged also as a reactionary doctrine,
protesting against the way French life was developing: Barrès
found in anti-Semitism a passion around which Frenchmen
could reunite, against what he called decadence; Maurras
was anxious that his generation should not be 'the last of the
French'. All the different varieties of nationalism therefore
aroused bitter hostility among Frenchmen, for they always
emphasised only one aspect of the nation's values. The League
of Patriots was strongly opposed by the League of the Rights
of Man. Neither of these, however, involved more than small
minorities.[1] The most important kind of nationalism was that
which gave no reasons. Michelet had defined it as a new religion.
That was in effect what the schools preached, when they urged
children to love France 'with an exclusive and jealous affection'.[2]
General de Gaulle explained what this meant when he defined
his own nationalism as being essentially sentimental, based on
the 'instinct' that Providence meant France to enjoy an eminent and exceptional destiny. France was not itself except when
it was in the first rank: it could not exist without 'grandeur';
and if it ever fell into mediocrity that was an 'absurd anomaly'

langue (1922); Charles Bally, *Le Langage et la vie* (1952); Georges Matoré, *Le Voca-
bulaire et la société sous Louis-Philippe* (1951).

[1] The League of Patriots (founded in 1882) had at most 100,000 members in
1888–9. Peter M. Rutkoff, 'The Ligue des Patriotes', *French Historical Studies* (Fall,
1974), 585–603. See also Eugen Weber, *The Nationalist Revival in France 1905–14*
(U. of California Press, 1959), 9–10, 58, 89. For the development of nationalism,
see below, ch. 23.

[2] Pierre Nora, 'Ernest Lavisse: son rôle dans la formation du sentiment national',
Revue historique (July 1962), 99.

due to the faults of individuals, and not to the 'genius of the fatherland'.[1]

One needs to explain how this state of mind could develop; and one needs to balance the loyalty people felt to the nation against their other loyalties. The nation, of course, meant not only grand principles, great literature and art but also taxation, compulsory schooling, military service. It was no easy matter judging the benefits that membership of the nation bestowed against the price that had to be paid. What ordinary citizens thought about this is very difficult to discover, because nationalism, like religion, was something which they seldom analysed. The history of nationalism is still in the state that the history of religion was before the sociology of religion was invented, to ask not what doctrines churches proclaimed, or how governments and bishops quarrelled, but how religion affected the masses and was felt by them. However, two eminent sociologists did direct their attention to the problem of the ties that held the people together. The relations of the individual and the community had of course been a principal object of interest to most political thinkers, but they had hitherto examined it from the point of view of rights and obligations, law and morals. Durkheim, while not indifferent to these considerations, concentrated on what the bonds between the individual and other groups actually were, regarding them simply as a sociological phenomenon. Durkheim's conclusions should have worried the nationalists, if they had not written him off as a Jewish socialist. He maintained that the old loyalties of the village, the family and the province were withering away and had ceased to awaken any 'profound sentiments'. 'The provincial spirit has vanished without hope of return; local patriotism has become an archaism which cannot be restored at will.' Local government interested people only in so far as it affected their personal concerns. Society had become 'an infinite powder of unorganised individuals which a hypertrophied state tries to contain and to hold in check'. But the state was too far away from the individual and had contacts with him which were too intermittent to be able to 'penetrate much into their consciences and to socialise them internally'. Moreover, as society developed, individuals increasingly freed themselves from the collective

[1] C. de Gaulle, *Mémoires de guerre*, vol. 1 (1954), 1–3.

personality and their diversities increased. Durkheim noted that the fraternity and solidarity which the Revolution and the republic had stood for had not been achieved in practice. He diagnosed, at the turn of the century, what men like Comte and Tocqueville had argued, with less elaboration, some time before, a widespread state of *anomie*. Comte's solution had been a strong government to produce the missing unity, particularly by means of moral education and the inculcation of altruism. The Third Republic to a certain extent tried to implement these ideas. Durkheim on the one hand believed in them too, and wrote a book on moral education to develop them; but he also noted the failure of fifty years of effort to produce a harmonious nation by this means. He advocated the additional use of social institutions, notably professional corporations, to diminish the individual's isolation. But alienation became an increasingly frequent theme among commentators in France as in the industrialising nations.[1]

At about the same time, Gustave Le Bon, in his *Psychology of Crowds* (1895), argued that it was necessary to distinguish between what people believed as individuals and the views they expressed when they formed groups. The nation was therefore far more than the sum of its parts. Crowds gave the individual a sense of invincible power, which allowed him to yield to instincts he forcibly repressed when he was alone; they allowed him to lose his sense of responsibility; they diminished his critical powers, aroused the intolerant, authoritarian and conservative elements in him, increased his suggestibility and made him an easy prey for leaders with skill at repeating slogans and formulas. The key to understanding national behaviour was therefore to be found in the unconscious 'collective soul': it was only when an idea penetrated into the unconscious that it could lead to effective action.[2] Nations thus became considerably more mysterious, but also much more influential. This was a conclusion very different from Durkheim's. Le Bon, however, did not provide much detailed evidence to support his theory: he was one of the pioneers of social psychology, but he was also an old-fashioned polymath doctor, who was interested

---

[1] É. Durkheim, *De la division du travail social* (1902, 2nd edition with a new preface), XXXII, 341.
[2] G. Le Bon, *La Psychologie des foules* (1895).

in almost everything, from atomic energy, photography and sound recording to the dangers of smoking and the training of horses, and it was on the basis of his observation of horses that he developed his views on crowds. Durkheim, for his part, supported his theory with a study of suicide, which, though it was of seminal importance in the development of sociology, left a great many questions unanswered.[1] Both of them in fact offered methodological guidelines more than conclusions based on a thorough investigation of anything like all the loyalties that were influential in the society of their day.

It is not enough to quote the opinion poll, held in April 1945, asking Frenchmen what nationality they would choose, if they were free to: 74 per cent said they would still like to be French.[2] How nationalism was seen in practice, how a national way of thinking was propagated, and indeed, how far it ever existed, need further examination. And to begin with, one can look at the contrast between Parisians and provincials, and between the provincials of different parts of the country.

[1] Steven Lukes, *Émile Durkheim* (1973), 191–226.
[2] H. Cantril, *Public Opinion 1935–46* (Princeton, 1951), 508. Three per cent said they would like to be American, 2 per cent English, 2 per cent Russian, 9 per cent Swiss, 1 per cent Swedish.

2. Provincials

THE inferiority complex of provincials in this period is one of the most important and deceptive factors in the image that France had as a nation. It is as a result of this complex that historians have been able to present France as a single unified entity, assuming that what happened in Paris was decisive in the country as a whole. The self-flattery of governments has been accorded the status of accepted truth. Governments liked to believe that their laws would be obeyed throughout the land, and that they represented the whole nation. This was, of course, to a considerable extent, wishful thinking. Historians, by concentrating on the doings of these governments, have strengthened the myth. Though the history of governments tells one a great deal about the country, and even more about the mentalities of politicians, it is important to supplement one's investigation of them by asking how far and in what variety of ways their laws were implemented, and how much national uniformity there really was.

This chapter will attempt to delve beneath the nationalist platitudes to assess the survival of regional individuality. The contempt Parisians have shown for the whole idea of 'provincialism', and the oblivion to which they have attempted to condemn this, cannot be dissociated from the fact that most Parisians in this period had been provincials only a generation or two before. Throughout this period, as will be shown in due course, less than half of Parisians had been born in Paris. Provincialism is therefore an idea full of ambivalence.

Balzac can be used to illustrate the condemnation of the provinces which has done so much to sap their self-confidence. Balzac described provincials as dominated by routine and monotony; their small towns 'apart from a few usages, are all the same'. Provincials were like moles burrowing about in their little plots, or frogs at the bottom of their puddles, engaged in sordid, trivial rivalries, moved by petty jealousies, avarice and material interests. Since they do not think about anything

serious, 'the passions shrink while getting excited about tiny
things. That is the reason for the greed and gossip which plague
provincial life.' There was gossip in Paris too, but provincial
life was so narrow that gossip assumed far greater importance
there. Provincials had to 'live in public'; they could have no
secrets. 'In the provinces, you are not allowed to be original,
because this means to have ideas others cannot understand,
and people want similarity of minds as well as similarity of
manners.' So the main activity must be to live as your father
did, to eat four meals a day and watch over your property.
Morals are stuffy, dictated by interest and fear of what others
will say rather than by virtue. So the monotony can be relieved
only by faction and malice.[1]

Over a century later, in 1951, a public opinion poll revealed
that, to a considerable extent, this view was still accepted.
Forty-six per cent of the Parisians questioned reproached
provincials for these same faults: narrowness, meanness,
hypocrisy, prejudice, avarice, backwardness, too much interest
in others' private lives, and lack of elegance. Forty-five per
cent of Parisians, it is true, did not support these accusations.
But then only 24 per cent of provincials criticised Parisians (for
pretentiousness, superficiality, egoism, noisiness, cynicism,
loose morals and wasting money), while 64 per cent spoke well
of them. The majority of provincials accepted their inferiority:
64 per cent said they would like to live in Paris, and 50 per
cent thought they would improve personally and in terms of
education, and broader outlook, if they did. It is true provincials
had a limited knowledge of what Paris represented: thus only
42 per cent of them (as opposed to 79 per cent of Parisians)
knew who J.-P. Sartre was—others described him variously
as a street, a deputy, a painter and a dress designer.[2] But a
constant feature of modern French history is that provincials
have tried to turn themselves into Parisians.

The peculiarity of France is that people migrated from the
countryside to Paris far more than to local regional capitals.
This at once destroys part of the image of the provincial as one
who stays put where he was born. The population of the pro-

[1] Jared Wanger, 'The Province and the Provinces in the Work of Honoré de
Balzac' (Princeton Ph.D. thesis, 1937).
[2] *Sondages* (1951), no. 2, 3–42.

vinces was far from being static. If one takes, for example, the
villages of the canton of Confolens (Charente), one finds that
between 1900 and 1967, 3,233 people born there died. Of these
only 797 died in the commune where they were born. 585 died
in the same canton, but outside their commune; 360 died in
communes bordering on their canton; and 530 in rural areas of
neighbouring departments. 359 died in towns in neighbouring
departments, 227 in Paris and 372 in the rest of France. Thus
about 30 per cent of the children in these villages abandoned
their province altogether; but the town which attracted the
largest number among them was Paris. Only 98 went to Limoges,
only 84 to Angoulême, 57 to Bordeaux, 47 to Poitiers, even
though Paris was 375 kilometres away. People born in small
towns migrated to Paris in even larger numbers. Thus of the
3,078 deaths of natives of Châtellerault (Vienne) between 1901
and 1967, only 31 per cent occurred in that town; 12 per cent
were in the department of Vienne, 12 per cent in neighbouring
departments, 25 per cent in Paris, and 18 per cent in the rest of
France. Thus only 128 died in Poitiers, even though it was ten
times nearer than Paris, where 788 people ended their days. In
the canton of Castries (Hérault) twice as many left for Paris
as for Marseille, even though the latter was five times nearer.[1]

Because of this polarity, it has always been common to make
blanket generalisations about the provinces as a whole. François Mauriac, in a book written between the two world wars,
and which he reprinted in 1964, considering it still to be true,
showed that the contrast of Paris and the provinces continued
to be seen very much to the disadvantage of the latter, even
when analysed with profound psychological insight. Mauriac
saw provincial life, first of all, as incompatible with intelligence.
'The horror of the provinces', he wrote, 'consists in the certainty that we can find no one who speaks our own language,
and at the same time in the fact that we cannot spend a single
second unobserved.' An intelligent provincial was plagued by
loneliness, 'neither intelligence, nor wit, nor talent counting
for anything . . . Conversation is a pleasure the provinces do not
know. People get together to eat, or to play cards, but not to
talk.' Provincial hostesses do not know how to bring together

[1] Jean Pitié, *Exode rural et migrations intérieures en France. L'exemple de la Vienne et
du Poitou-Charentes* (Poitiers, 1971).

men who otherwise would not meet. The reason was the
'terrible law that one can only accept a politeness which one can
return', with the result that social life and conversation were
killed. Men were devoured by their professions and very seldom
avoided being forced to play the roles which these imposed on
them. They moved therefore in definite and limited circles.
They hardly ever invited people from outside their own *milieu*
or *monde*. In Paris, the artist or writer was welcomed everywhere; he could enjoy as much isolation as he wanted, but
could emerge from it when he felt like it; he was not constantly
watched, nor forced into hypocritical conformity. He was not
sat upon by his family as he would be in the provinces, where
the family was all-powerful. There, individuals were worth
only what their family was worth. Families intermarried and
so were able to suffice unto themselves, killing true social life,
and setting up stifling controls on their members. 'What is
known as family life often comes down to every member of the
family being watched by the others, and shows itself in the
passionate attention with which they spite each other.' Their
furious internal rivalries—as to who could marry his daughters
quickest, who could find the richest spouse, who could keep his
servants longest—were what preoccupied them. Their meals
were the main events of the day. The kitchen was the most
important room in the house, to the extent that the rich had
two kitchens, one for the cook and one for the mistress of the
house, where she could make her *terrines* and *confits* and receive
her sharecroppers. Secondly, therefore, Mauriac saw provincial
life as an almighty barrage of obstacles set up against the
passions. It was based on envy, repression and hypocrisy.
Religion and social hierarchy restrained the expression of greed,
hate, love and pride, which accumulated bitterly. The provinces knew how to hate as no one else, and they passed their
hates on to their children. 'The French provinces are peopled
by young beings consumed by unsatisfied appetites. All these
repressed ambitions, decupled in intensity by their repression,
ensure that later these provincials win the first places in politics,
literature and business. . . . The provinces are a nursery of
ambitious people, so starved that they can never be satisfied
in later life.' Emma Bovary lived in many a soul. The result of
this was that the provinces could create deep animosity against

virtue and religion, because they produced such awful carica-
tures of them. Paris got its population from the provinces, but
gave it back its worst features—like its fashions—and kept for
itself everything worth keeping, like painting and music.[1]

In 1934 *L'Avenir de l'Yonne*, a regional newspaper, carried
out an inquiry into intellectual life in the provinces, seeking
out the opinion of writers, teachers and notables all over France.
Though many of them voluntarily preferred to live in the
country, they were nevertheless often scathing about its satisfactions. They were very much influenced by the fact that the
state system of promotion sent the junior members of the civil
service to the most distant posts, with least population, and
then gradually promoted them to larger towns, before giving
them the crowning glory of a Parisian appointment. This
implied that anyone who stayed in the provinces all his life was
incompetent. Even writers who devoted themselves to singing
the praises of their region admitted the 'obsessive tyranny of
the capital which thinks it is the unique brain of the country'.
There were intelligent men who devoted themselves to local
causes and local studies, which gave them much satisfaction;
and many said they could keep up with new developments,
in Paris and elsewhere, perfectly well by reading books and
reviews. Some nationally famous authors were able to ply their
trade without difficulty from obscure provincial retreats. But
very few lesser intellectuals were able to view the world independently of Paris. Many, while enjoying the countryside,
condemned regionalism as absurd or anachronistic. Maurice
Grammont, for example, professor of phonetics at Montpellier
(and therefore very much the sort of man who might be expected
to become a self-conscious advocate of his regional dialect) said
he took his job because he liked the climate and he had never
responded to the advances of the regionalist movement. A
provincial town like Montpellier, he said, had the disadvantage
that an expert like himself had no one to talk to about his
subject. Those bourgeois who wanted to occupy their leisure in
an intellectual way usually studied history, 'one of the domains
in which one can most easily give oneself the illusion of writing
remarkable books', but they were amateurs without training and 'what they produce is usually without value'. Most

[1] François Mauriac, *La Province* (1964 edition).

provincial literature was 'worthless'. Jean Azais, a judge of the peace in the Haute-Garonne, said regional pride was good in theory but in practice it expressed itself in boring and ridiculous little societies, inadequate libraries, symphonic associations producing bad music, and periodical reviews with less than a hundred readers. Jean Dayma, though he devoted himself to salvaging Gascon dialect and tradition, lamented the indifference he encountered. Daniel Bourchenin, the president of the Academy of Mountauban, one of the founders of the Society of Popular Traditions (1882), a member of the Feminist Federation of the south-west, of the Society of French Folklore, of the Society of Writers, of the Historical Society of Niort (where he was born), placed limits on what the provinces should claim: he said he was against their developing an 'excessively proud consciousness of their originality and respective merits'; he was against regional *fanfaronnade* or autonomy. Paul Cazin, who lived in Autun, translating Polish literature, reiterated the old criticism that the provinces 'lacked altruism'. 'The clan and the tribe still survive in small towns and in the countryside ... People entrenched themselves in their little properties, with their petty interests, and petty grievances ... mistrustful of young talent ... oblivious of the great problems of the world.' It was no wonder the young fled to Paris.[1]

Such opinions were banal, but they were not the whole truth. The attacks on provincial life came from a certain kind of person, who was involved in the political or cultural climb to Paris, or regretting in some way that he was not. The tentacles of the capital did not reach everywhere, however, and one finds an extremely rich variety of thought and feeling, which deserves independent study. One reason why the capital ignored this was that knowledge of France—in the simplest geographical sense—was still astonishingly primitive, even at the end of the nineteenth century. It should not be taken for granted that most people had any clear idea of what the rest of the country, outside their own part of it, was like. The first complete and accurate map of France was made only in 1750–89 by Cassini, and some of it remained unpublished till 1815 because Napoleon

[1] Ch. J. Millon, *La Vie intellectuelle en province* (Sens, 1934), 10–16, 42, 94, 71–2, 101.

considered it a military secret. It suffered from a rather elementary depiction of relief, in that little dells were indicated with
the same marks as the deepest valleys and abysses; and its
scale was only 1:86,400. A new map, attempting greater legi-
bility and capable of being used by all the public services, was
produced between 1818 and 1866, but it was still on the scale
1:80,000. (A one-inch Ordnance Survey map is on the scale
1:63,360.) Despite the consciousness of the need for more
detailed maps, even a 1:20,000 map was considered too expensive to contemplate, and by 1914 only a few sheets of a new
map, coloured and contoured, at 1:50,000, had appeared.[1]

During the Second Empire, the study of geography was
still largely historical, concentrating on the frontiers and
administrative divisions of ancient Persia, Rome or Byzantium.
Geography at school meant essentially the memorising of
place-names; and the best introduction to it was still Jules
Verne, which is partly why he was so popular. Only in 1872,
when Émile Levasseur was appointed to the Collège de France
as professor of geography, history and economic statistics (the
breadth of his scope shows how limited was that of geography),
did the study of modern France acquire the status of an academic subject. At first the emphasis was statistical, digesting
the results of the government's demographic statistics, and
industrial, agricultural and social inquiries.[2] It was still possible for Élysée Reclus (1830–1905), when not active as an
anarchist agitator, to write almost single-handed a *Universal
Geography* in nineteen volumes (1876–94). Reclus had been
virtually forced to travel abroad, because he was expelled for
political reasons from France, first by Louis Napoleon in 1851
and then in 1871 for his part in the Commune. His monumental
work is important because it attempted to go beyond description, and to produce general explanations. This approach was
taken further by Paul Vidal de la Blache (1845–1918), who,
after starting as an ancient historian, began teaching geography at the École Normale in 1875 and was professor at the

---

[1] See the history of French map-making in the appendix to Jean Brunhes,
Géographie humaine de la France (1920), 2. 617 ff.

[2] B. Gille, *Les Sources statistiques de l'histoire de France: Des enquêtes du 17ᵉ siècle à
1870* (1964); É. Levasseur, *L'Étude et l'enseignement de la géographie* (1872); id.,
Précis de la géographie physique, politique et économique de la France et de ses colonies (1886);
P. Joanne, *Dictionnaire géographique et administratif de la France* (1888–1905).

Sorbonne from 1899 to 1909. His *Historical and Geographical Atlas* (1894) was the first which did not concentrate on place-names. He founded the tradition of walking as a means of learning about geography. His method was to collect facts, group them, show how various factors combined to produce the total result, making geography a science which sought to generalise and explain. He was attacked by students of other subjects who claimed there was no room for geography; Durkheim, for example, battled with him, claiming that 'social morphology' should replace geography. Vidal de La Blache was highly influential in developing first 'general geography' (based on the view that all lands belong to a 'type') and in urging his pupils to embark on 'regional geography'. How much still needed to be accomplished, however, may be seen from the way he purposely excluded the study of social and economic factors from geography, on the grounds that they were controversial and therefore difficult to be impartial about. He gave greatest weight to politics as the factor which determined the extent of a region.

In his *Portrait of the Geography of France* (1903) which was published as an introduction to Lavisse's multi-volume history of France, he devoted 180 pages to the Paris region, because that was where 'national history essentially took place', but only 27 pages to the Massif Central, and 15 to the Mediterranean South. Regional geography had still to be created. Adolphe Joanne's famous series of department geographies (1868-9) were mainly lists of railway stations and rivers. Geographical theses had till then usually been historical. This marriage of history and geography has remained one of the strongest features of the French approach to geography, but it was only at the turn of the century that the decisive alliance with economics and social studies was effected. The outstanding theses of Jules Sion on Normandy[1] and Albert Demangeon on Picardy,[2] which gave a total picture of society, linking human activity with physical features, for the first time brought out the profound originality of different regions of France. Instead of simply trying to categorise each region, as an example of a

---

[1] J. Sion, *Les Paysans de la Normandie orientale: étude géographique* (1909).
[2] A. Demangeon, *La Picardie et les régions voisines* (1905); cf. id., *Les Sources de la géographie de la France aux Archives nationales* (1905).

type within a framework provided by general geography, they studied each for its own sake, investigating whatever special problems each presented. Some of the most original thinking about France has been embodied in these regional geographical theses, which revealed the country in a new light, making correlations and distinctions where none had been suspected. André Siegfried analysed the links of politics and geography, Albert Demangeon showed the contribution geography could make to economics and to planning.[1] Geographers thus looked beyond the artificial administrative divisions of the country, and sought to delimit real entities, with a uniform mode of life. A vast number of theories followed as to how France could most satisfactorily be divided, and as to what elements created it. In 1912 a chair in human geography was founded at the Collège de France for Jean Brunhes (1869–1930), one of its most active popularisers. In 1928 the *Annales* review was started by a group of geographers and historians, which did a great deal to broaden the sort of question that was asked by both.

There were certainly gaps in this discovery of France. How much remained to be done was shown by the outpouring of theses on regions still unstudied after 1945. Thus urban geography was slow to develop. Demangeon's thesis on Picardy gave Amiens only one page, and in 1929 Pierre Denis in his geography of South America gave no more to Buenos Aires or Rio de Janeiro. Raoul Blanchard's pioneering work on Grenoble (1912) was followed by only a few between the two World Wars. Rural problems tended to preoccupy the geographers, perhaps because they knew more medieval than modern history. Morphology, because it seemed more scientific, turned many geographers away from human problems altogether. Emmanuel de Martonne (1873–1955), La Blache's son-in-law, led this reaction with his *Treatise of Physical Geography* (1908–9). As a result the important review *Annales de géographie* (founded 1891), which in 1902–11 had only 44 per cent of its articles devoted to morphology, printed 57 per cent on it in 1912–21 and 80 per cent in 1922–31. In 1928 the International Congress of Geographers, attended by 547 specialists, included 42 French representatives; ten years later, 147 out of the 1,217 participants were French. The way French geographers altered their

[1] On Siegfried, see Zeldin, *Politics and Anger*, 3–10; A. Demangeon, *Le Déclin de l'Europe* (1920).

countrymen's self-consciousness and awareness of their complicated heritage deserves further study. They included an exceptionally large number of outstandingly able men. But the
'French school' of geography, which has won international
admiration for its breadth and liveliness, itself contained
diverse elements, and it should no more be regarded as mono-
lithically uniform than should the France whose diversity they
revealed.[1]

It was easy for Parisians, and for reluctant provincials, to
decry the intellectual life of the provinces, and to suggest that
nothing original or interesting happened there, but this was not
true. The provincial academies and learned societies, whose
importance in the *ancien régime* is generally conceded, were
indeed temporarily abolished at the Revolution, but they
quickly revived, and by the end of the century there were
roughly three times as many societies in the provinces as in
Paris: about 1,100 as opposed to 375 in Paris. Almost every
town which could claim that title had some kind of intellectual
activity. Mâcon, for example, (population 18,000) had in
1903 an Academy, known also as the Society of Arts, Sciences,
Belles-Lettres and Agriculture of Saône-et-Loire, with 347
members and an uninterrupted history dating back to 1805. It
also had an Agricultural Society (founded 1880) with 450
members, a Natural History Society (founded 1893) with 140
members, a Horticultural Society (1841) with 450 members;
and all of these produced publications and journals. In Agen
(population also 18,000) the Society of Agriculture, Sciences
and Arts of Agen (founded in the Year VI) issued three different
periodicals. A city like Lyon had about 30 different more or less
intellectual societies in 1903 which are worth listing to show
the kind of activities that were popular.

Society	Founded	Members
Academy of Sciences, Belles-Lettres and Arts	1700	232
Society of Agriculture, Sciences and Industry	1761	173
Literary, Historical and Archaeological Society	1778	94
Medical Society	1789	76
Pharmaceutical Society	1806	67
Linnean Society	1822	95
Architectural Society	1830	182

[1] André Meynier, *Histoire de la pensée géographique en France* (1969) is an invaluable
starting-point.

Society	Founded	Members
Educational Society	1830	80
Society of Practical Horticulture	1843	609
Pomological Society (publishing *La Pomologie française*, monthly)	1856	450
Society of Medical Sciences (*Lyon-Médicale*, weekly)	1861	211
Book-readers Society	1862	406
Rhône Society for Professional Education	1864	800
Society of Political and Social Economy	1864	385
Viticultural Society (*La Vigne américaine*, fortnightly)	1870	372
Horticultural Association	1872	1,050
Botanic Society	1872	154
Lyon section, French Alpine Club	1875	605
Geographical Society	1875	626
Association of Steam Engine Owners	1876	850
Architectural Union	1879	86
Anthropological Society	1881	218
Bibliophiles Society (limited membership)	1885	20
Provincial Association of French Architects	1886	597
Society of Fine Arts	1887	1,000
Photo Club	1888	100
Cercle Pierre Dupont (artistic and literary)	1894	403
Rhône Pedagogical Union	1896	450
Society of Veterinary Sciences	1898	510

It is true that gardening emerges as the most popular society, and that some societies had less than a hundred members, but they all busily published proceedings, bulletins and reviews, at annual, monthly or even fortnightly intervals.[1]

No one has gone through all these publications systematically to assess their worth, partly perhaps because the encyclopedic knowledge required is beyond the modern specialist. In the eighteenth century, one of the sources of the importance of the provincial academies had been that they were privileged to print without permission from the Censor. In the nineteenth century their publications became even more numerous, more bulky and more regular than in the eighteenth. They still offered prizes which were sought out by the young: Léon Faucher, Thiers, Guizot, Mignet and Louis Blanc were among the prizewinners who were thus launched on the path to fame. Though the academies had lost a great deal of their property at the Revolution, they had accumulated more from new donations and from local subsidies, and they were therefore patrons of learning on a substantial scale. The Academies of Lyon, Bordeaux, Rouen, Caen and Marseille were able to

[1] H. Delaunay, *Annuaire international des sociétés savantes* (1903).

offer a large number of prizes. The subjects they set for competition not only reveal what they were interested in, but also directed research into these fields. Thus the Academy of Lyon managed a prize of 1,500 francs established by Arlès-Dufour for an essay on the amelioration of the lot of women. It also had an income of 1,800 francs, bequeathed by the scientist Ampère, to enable a young man of talent to complete his education. Besançon had a similar one, founded by Suard, from which Proudhon benefited. The Academy of Caen awarded a prize of as much as 4,000 francs for an essay on botany. There were some who thought that all this provincial activity ought to be organised, to form a counterweight to Paris. In 1833 Arcisse de Caumont, a wealthy nobleman who devoted his fortune and forty years of activity to this cause, attending more learned society meetings probably than anyone ever has, held the first Congress of Provincial Societies and in 1839 founded the Institut des Provinces. This, however, appeared to be a challenge to the national and official Institut de France, particularly since Caumont was constantly attacking the latter for supporting the centralisation of the country and for refusing to put itself at the head of the provincial intellectuals. In the eighteenth century there had been close ties between the Paris and provincial academies: individual members of the Académie française or (in the case of Montpellier and Bordeaux, which specialised in medicine and physics respectively) the Académie des Sciences constituted themselves protectors of the provincial academies, which for their part were given the right to send deputies to Paris, to report on their work and to receive comments and compliments on it. The sense of isolation which the provinces felt in the nineteenth century was partly the result of the ending of this tradition. The Congress of Learned Societies, which Caumont also started in 1850 (with 120 participants, rising to 200 in 1875), was designed to remedy this, but the large academies boycotted it, because it was open to all, and did not seek to be exclusive as they were. They claimed that only second-rate scholars attended, and that since papers on any subject under the sun could be presented, there was no possibility of useful discussion.

The government too was jealous of this independent body, and so founded a similar one of its own, with an identical title, but crowned by official prizes awarded by the ministry of education in an annual ceremony at the Sorbonne. This second and official Congress of Learned Societies was an outgrowth of the Historical Committee Guizot had established in 1833 when he was minister of education, to publish historical records. It had doled out subsidies to local scholars who spent lifetimes editing medieval manuscripts for publication, at a snail's pace, for forty years later only 258 volumes had been published at a cost of 130,000 francs a year. During the Second Empire this subsidy system was reorganised, so that it could be spread out more thinly to more people: other subjects apart from history were encouraged. The competition for these grants kept quite a lot of provincials busy; it also stimulated bitter antagonisms, because the grants and prizes tended to be given out on a geographical basis, with special favour shown to new and as yet undistinguished societies. Eminent scholars and the more ancient academies resented that they were not justly recognised. This effort to bring provincial intellectuals closer to the government, through the bait of honours and decorations, was hardly successful. The really active provincial scholars were stimulated to stress their independence. An academician of Lyon, when told off by the minister of education in 1857 for criticising the government's policy towards the provinces, replied that he had no need of ministerial permission, he could speak as he pleased, for the academies were 'little republics which administered themselves . . . living off their own income, and once instituted by decree of the head of state, they were no longer subject to anybody'.[1]

There were plenty of bookshops, journals and newspapers in the provinces to allow them an independent life. In 1860 there were 622 bookshops in Paris (publishers and booksellers being combined in this figure), and about 1,180 printing firms of all kinds. Marseille, which had a population of 233,000 compared to Paris's 1,500,000, had at least 33 bookshops, and 65 printers. Proportionately, Paris had about three times as many bookshops and publishers, but Marseille had enough, in however modest a way, to have a personality of its own. Moreover, every town in the surrounding department of

[1] F. Bouillier, *L'Institut et les académies de province* (1879); E. de Robillard de Beaurepaire, *M. de Caumont* (1874).

Bouches-du-Rhône had its own bookshops too. Aix, with only 26,000 inhabitants, had five bookshops, Arles (population 24,000) four, Tarascon (13,000) three, Salon (7,000) two, Gardane (2,700) one, etc., and there were in addition fifteen printing firms in these towns. Lyon (292,000) had at least eighty bookshops and publishers and eighty printers. The sub-prefecture of Baume-les-Dames (2,615) had three bookshops and one printer. The distribution was unequal. The department of Morbihan for example was underprovided: Vannes (14,000) had four bookshops and three printers, while Beauvais, with the same population had twice as many of each.[1] Some authors claimed that unless their books were published in Paris, they could not regard themselves as successful, but that was because they demanded a certain kind of success. In 1934 there were a very substantial number of provincial publishers to produce their works. Paris now had around 800 publishers, but the provinces had almost 400. Paris had about 3,700 printers, but the provinces had about 3,800. Paris had 820 bookshops, and the provinces 3,250.[2] An *Annuaire des poètes* produced in 1935 listed 800 people claiming to be poets, most of them living and writing in the provinces. Massive local bibliographies testify to the productivity of authors whom neither Paris nor posterity noticed. The single arrondissement of Le Havre, for example, counted 2,038 writers publishing between 1850 and 1900. They were men of all professions: the director of the Havre branch of the Bank of France, the chaplain of the hospital, the conductor of the orchestra, many doctors, teachers, solicitors, a 'poète géologue', a clerk in the navy, etc.[3] Between 1918 and 1936 the publications of Alsace were voluminous enough to require a bibliography of six bulky tomes just to list them.[4] A list of Breton authors published in 1886 included 915 names under the letter A, and seems to have petered out, because of the immensity of the task of producing a full catalogue, halfway

---

[1] Jules Delalain, *Annuaire de la librairie, de l'imprimerie, de la papeterie* (1860); *Recherches statistiques sur la ville de Paris, d'après les ordres de M. le baron Haussmann*, vol. 6 (1860).

[2] *Annuaire-agenda des auteurs, éditeurs, imprimeurs, etc.* (1934). These are very rough statistics, and include many publishers who only issued reviews.

[3] A. Lechevalier (instituteur), *Bio-bibliographie des écrivains de l'arrondissement du Havre* (Le Havre, 1902–3).

[4] *Bibliographie alsacienne*, published by the Faculty of Strasbourg (1918–36).

through the letter B.[1] The town of Mulhouse produced over
3,000 works about itself between 1870 and 1960.[2] In addition
to all this, there was the immensely active local newspaper
press, which will be discussed separately.

As an example of what a provincial intellectual could do,
one can look at the career of Raoul de la Grasserie (1839–1914).
Born in Rennes, he spent the whole of his life in Brittany, as a
judge, mainly in Rennes and in Nantes. He published over 360
books and articles. The range of his interests and his competence
is astounding. He wrote about psychology (social, ethnic and
religious), sociology (theoretical, political and criminal),
linguistics (comparative, semantic and North American), law,
literature, politics, 'anti-feminist prejudices', 'sexuality in
language'. There was almost no contemporary social or theoretical issue on which he did not have something—and often
something interesting—to say. He belonged to many learned
societies and corresponded with some foreign ones. He showed
a knowledge of the latest trends in European scholarship far
superior to many a Paris professor. He was making use of
Frazer's *Golden Bough*, for example, within a few years of its
publication, to analyse the religion of the Bretons.[3]

Provence

The most obvious division of France was between north and
south. When Mérimée came down the Rhône to visit Provence
for the first time, and got off his boat at Avignon, he declared
that he felt as though he was landing in a foreign country.[4]
The language of the people, indeed the landscape, the climate,
the way of life were all in marked contrast to the north, whereas
the links with Italy and Spain were striking. The economic
unity of France was only in the process of being achieved in

[1] R. Kerviler, *Répertoire de bio-bibliographie bretonne* (1886).

[2] Denise May and Noë Richter, *Bibliographie mulhousienne 1870–1960*, published
by the municipal library of Mulhouse (1966); cf. Ed. Vimont, *Catalogue des livres
imprimés de la ville de Clermont-Ferrand . . . relatifs à l'Auvergne* (Clermont, 1878), with
3,419 items; Académie Nationale de Metz, *Bibliographie lorraine*, vol. 1 (Metz,
1970), lists 654 authors whose names begin with the letter A.

[3] The municipal library of Rennes has the fullest collection and bibliography
of his works.

[4] P. Mérimée, *Notes d'un voyage dans le Midi de la France* (1835), 131; Stendhal,
Mémoires d'un touriste (1838).

the second half of the nineteenth century. While the north of the country exported wheat and sugar, the south imported it. Protection was bitterly opposed by Marseille, which regarded it as a sign of its oppression by the northerners. The Mediterranean trade gave the south an outlook towards Africa, the Levant and the Far East. This was even accentuated after 1870, when Marseille lost its position as the busiest port of the continent to Rotterdam, Hamburg and Antwerp, for it then became an industrial city specialising in producing for markets in underdeveloped countries. Politically, the south had a distinctively revolutionary character, supporting radicals, socialists and communists in turn.[1] Psychologically, it constantly complained of being underprivileged, even though it paid less taxes than the north and had a disproportionate share of representatives in parliament.[2] The political leaders it produced in great numbers were, rather vaguely, seen as orators and operators who typically embodied its faults—though there was not all that much in common between Guizot of Nîmes, Thiers and Émile Ollivier of Marseille, Gambetta of Cahors, Paul Reynaud of Barcelonette and Daladier of Carpentras.

The belief that the people of the south were a different kind of people, with a distinct mentality, was widely held and actively propagated by the southerners themselves. The man who perhaps more than anybody made the southerner a distinct type was Alphonse Daudet, with his novels *Tartarin, Numa Roumestan* and *L'Arlésienne*. Daudet popularised the notion that the southerners were above all people of unbridled imagination, as though the sun, which dominated their civilisation, created mirages for them. According to him, they were not so much liars as exhibitionists, who deceived themselves, who were carried away by their own inventions and ingenuity and who found in their exaggerations a necessary *bouquet* to season reality. They loved the theatrical stance; they liked giving themselves up to passion, eloquence 'with short and terrible rages, ostentatious and grimacing, always a little simulated even when they were sincere, making tragedy or comedy of everything', then relapsing into indolence and torpor. They

[1] See maps in Zeldin, *Politics and Anger*, 3–5.
[2] *Questions du Jour* (July 1935), special number on regionalism, gives figures 167–75. Cf. also Zeldin, *Politics and Anger*, 346.

were men of words and gestures, who had a great need to communicate their feelings and who never fully experienced an emotion unless they told others about it. 'When I do not speak, I do not think,' said Numa Roumestan. Their words, however, always said more than they meant. They regarded the idea of a home as a northern one, for they lived out of doors, but they were also devoted to family and tradition, 'resembling Orientals in their fidelity to the clan and the tribe, in their taste for sweet foods and in that incurable contempt for women, which did not stop them being passionate and voluptuous to the point of delirium'. They were superstitious and idolatrous while also vigorously anticlerical; they forgot their gods in daily life but ran back to them in sickness or misfortune. They loved gaiety and laughing though they were also malicious; they were optimistic even though they had an exaggerated fear of death and illness. Alphonse Daudet came from a ruined family of silk weavers in Nîmes; he made his fortune in Paris and stayed there. His portrait of the south was that of an émigré who had escaped. He declared that he mocked the south because that was his way of loving it. Southerners complained that he had caricatured them, so that no one could take them seriously any more.[1]

However, writers about Provence developed this idea that the people of the south had a distinct psychology. One, J. Aurouze, obtained a doctorate of letters in 1907 from the Faculty of Aix (which had established a chair of Provençal history in 1894) by putting these claims into scientific jargon and proving them with Taine's theory of race, milieu and moment. Even if the Provençals were not biologically a race, he said, 'centuries of peculiar habits had been building up in their brains and souls' to produce a 'psychological alluvium', which made them unique and distinct. It was the beauty of the landscape which had developed their 'noble and harmonious gestures'; the fact that their agriculture consisted principally of fruit and vine, and so did not require hard work from them, made them gay and happy; the warmth of the climate explained their great powers of perception

[1] Alexander Krugicoff, *Alphonse Daudet et la Provence* (1936); Louis Michel, *Le Langage méridional dans l'œuvre d'Alphonse Daudet* (1961); Jean Camp, 'Le Midi dans l'œuvre d'Alphonse Daudet', *Nouvelle Revue du Midi* (1924), 65–84; A. Daudet, *Numa Roumestan* (1881), postscript.

and sensation and their curiosity.[1] He, and many others, protested against the feelings of inferiority which had been instilled into provincials, because they could not speak properly, because they were not Parisians. In a reaction against this, the peculiarities of southerners were dissected, explained and turned into positive advantages. Self-denigration was replaced by pride in those very traits which had formerly been held against them. It used to be said that patois was incapable of expressing ideas, or thought, and was only useful for the farmyard and practical daily life. Now Provençal was exalted as being the only medium by which the 'true emotions and obscure sentiments' of the Provençals could develop and express themselves.[2] Such ideas were paradoxically strengthened by the realisation that the Provençals were racially one of the most mixed regions of France. The birth-rate was comparatively low, emigration was frequent, and there was a great deal of immigration.[3] The Provençal mentality thus emerged as similar in kind to the American one, imposed, as a rather clever book by a doctor argued in 1883, by neighbours more than inherited from ancestors. This book suggested that most Provençals did not have the mentality in any full sense because they had not had time to acquire it. However, immigrants were quick to call themselves Provençals. So there were many varieties of the mentality, and Provençals could be divided into three generations. The first had immigrated from the French Alps (65 per cent) or the Italian Alps (Piedmont and Genoa, 20 per cent), the Cévennes and Pyrenees (5 per cent), the centre or north of France (5 per cent), Corsica (2 per cent) and other countries (3 per cent). A quarter of them were foreigners, and 90 per cent of them men from mountainous regions, poor, seldom very successful, but hard-working, respectful towards authority, thrifty and prolific of children. Only in the second generation did they develop their ambition and imagination and begin to talk more. It was the third generation, consisting

---

[1] J. Aurouze, *Histoire critique de la renaissance méridionale au XIXe siècle* (Avignon, 1907), 1. 53.

[2] Cf., e.g. Émilien Cazes (inspecteur d'Académie à Marseille), *La Provence et les Provençaux* (n.d., about 1895), 192; Abbé J. Mascle, *La Provence et l'âme provençale* (Aix, 1911), discours prononcé à la distribution des prix du Collège Catholique d'Aix.

[3] Cf. Pierre Merlin, *La Dépopulation des plateaux de Haute-Provence* (1969).

of only 25 per cent of the population, which exhibited the psychology popularly attributed to the typical Provençal. It was these men, who had made good, who were loquacious and conceited and who constantly felt the need to tell and show everybody how clever and beautiful they were. They now sought to solve their difficulties not by hard work but by wit, imagination and family relations: they gambled, drank, confided in anyone willing to take them seriously, in order to conceal their troubles and maintain a superficial decorum. They sought to stupefy their neighbours by acts of incredible bravura like giving fantastic banquets, with food brought from Paris by express railway. They mocked and criticised their compatriots a lot, so it was difficult for them to become prophets in their own part of the country, but they had a great enthusiasm for causes, and because they loved attracting attention, politics played a great part in their lives. After politics, they gave their energy to societies of all sorts, and for preference musical ones, which, like politics, they valued because these gave splendid opportunities for exhibitionism, the wearing of decorations and the waving of flags. They seized on every occasion—marriage, burial, promotion—to parade, to play music, to hold enormous processions with ribbons and fanfares.[1]

Though the majority of Provençals continued to take the well-known path of careerism towards Paris, and assimilated themselves as Frenchmen, a small but increasingly vocal minority stressed their affinities with other Mediterranean peoples, rather than with the French. They expressed pride in traditions they claimed to have inherited from the Arabs, and the Spaniards, and sang the praises of Raymond Lull, the prolific thirteenth-century Catalonian author, whom they portrayed as a Mediterranean man, uniting the races, religions and philosophies of its two coasts.[2] They claimed that their love of poetry, for example, had more in common with that of Arabs, such as Ibn Dawoud or Ibn Hazm, than with Ovid, and criticised Renan for saying that there was an unbridgeable abyss between Roman and Arab literature. They saw themselves

---

[1] L. J. B. Bérenger-Féraud, *Les Provençaux à travers les âges* (1900); id., *La Race provençale* (1883); cf. Lucien Duc, *En Provence, études de mœurs* (1895).

[2] See the thesis by J. H. Probst, *Caractère et origine des idées du bienheureux Raymond Lull* (Toulouse, 1912).

as heretics in Christendom, heirs of the Cathar creed of the twelfth and thirteenth centuries which France had brutally repressed but which still survived among them. They argued that the Manichaean heresy accurately embodied the deepest and continuing inclinations of the Provençals. Provençals, they claimed, did not see good and evil as contradictory; they had no hierarchy of values, no moral imperatives; they saw life as an art, to be played with coquetry and dilettantism; they did not judge other people on the basis of the qualities they had, but accepted their right to be what they were, and appreciated an individual in proportion to the extent that he lived up to his own ideal. They did not judge the ideal. Unlike the northerner who believed in absolute truth, they valued men for the way each one lived with himself and coped with his characteristics. Thus they identified themselves with Ulysses, whom they saw as the eternal prototype of the Mediterranean man, and whose essential quality was ambivalence. Ulysses might be considered a liar, but lying was not disapproved of in the Mediterranean. Lying indeed was neither a game nor a psychosis, but a rite and a ceremonial. Ulysses coloured reality, because he liked to see himself as its creator. He did not fear death, because Mediterraneans did not think about death, but only about funerals, as Mediterranean cemeteries showed. They did not live in order to obtain rewards in the next world, but sought to enjoy the present, to please themselves, to create an image of themselves as agreeable, noble, beautiful. Love in the south was different from what it was in the north. Provençals did not condemn passion; they did not hold up faithfulness to one woman as the supreme virtue; they stressed man's superiority over woman, respecting her above all as Mother. All this, they claimed, made the 'Occitane genius' and the Mediterranean mind totally different from that of Paris, with its rules of taste and of reason. They had a different philosophy, poetry, religion. They had a different way of feeling. Their culture was based on oral tradition, not on literature.[1]

In the nineteenth century, the richness of the Provençal inheritance was rediscovered, partly by foreign scholars who

---

[1] 'Le Génie d'Oc et l'homme méditerranéen', *Cahiers du Sud*, special number 249, Aug.–Oct. 1942. For legal peculiarities, see Charles Tavernier, *Usages et règlements locaux ayant force de loi dans le département des Bouches-du-Rhône* (Aix, 1859).

took an interest in it before the Parisians, and partly by southern erudites, many of them amateurs but with the leisure to devote a whole lifetime to local study.[1] The discovery of the poetry of the Troubadours revealed Provence as the seat of one of the most magnificent literatures of medieval Europe, expressed in a language which could now be seen to be no mere dialect, or corruption of French, but its equal, developing simultaneously with and independently of French. This medieval lyricism appealed strongly to the romantics. Augustin Thierry presented French history as a clash of north and south, with the south as the home of liberty, envied for its rich fields and large towns, crushed by the military despots of the north, whose language the Provençals had once likened to the barking of dogs. In Guizot's histories, too, Provence emerged as a conquered land. In 1831, when Fauriel was appointed professor of foreign literature at the Sorbonne, he lectured on the history of Provençal poetry and published a book about Southern Gaul dominated by the conquering Germans.[2] In 1851, when Hippolyte Fortoul of Digne, professor at Aix, became minister of education, he sent emissaries into the provinces to collect popular songs and ballads, which 'literature' had so far disdained.[3] François Raynouard, a barrister of Aix and Brignoles (1761–1836), published a dictionary, a compendium of laws and an anthology of the poetry of Provence.[4] Louis Méry protested against 'the Parisianisms which are infecting the Provençals'.[5] Dr. S. J. Honnorat of Digne, who had been brought up to speak Provençal, and who had then taught himself French, produced a dictionary of Provençal five times larger than any previously available.[6] All this was on a small scale: Honnorat's dictionary was remaindered, even though the ministry of education bought a hundred copies. It was only

[1] For example, A. Bruce Whyte, *Histoire des langues romanes et de leur littérature depuis leur origine jusqu'au 14ᵉ siècle* (3 vols., 1841).

[2] C. C. Fauriel, *Histoire de la Gaule méridionale sous la domination des conquérants Germains* (4 vols., 1836); id., *Histoire de la poésie provençale* (3 vols., 1846).

[3] F. Mistral, *Un Poète bilingue, Adolphe Dumas* (1927).

[4] F. J. M. Raynouard, *Choix des poésies originales des troubadours* (6 vols., 1816–21); id., *Lexique roman ou dictionnaire de la langue des troubadours, comparée avec les autres langues de l'Europe latine* (6 vols., 1838–44).

[5] Louis Méry, *Histoire de Provence* (1830–7).

[6] S. J. Honnorat, *Dictionnaire provençal-français ou dictionnaire de la langue d'oc. ancienne et moderne* (4 vols., Digne, 1846–9).

a modest counter-attack against the far more numerous works
which sought to make the Provençals abandon their dialect
and to teach them how to pronounce and speak French
'correctly'.[1] It was essentially erudition, and only when this
erudition was popularised did it produce really significant
results.

This popularisation was above all the work of Frédéric
Mistral (1830–1914) whose lyrical genius gave Provençal
poetry an international status. In 1905 Mistral was awarded the
Nobel Prize. One is immediately led to ask why the Provençal
regional movement, of which he was the head, never got much
success beyond its poetry, by contrast with that of Catalonia,
with which for a while Mistral maintained close relations, and
whose literary festival he attended in 1868. The answer is that
the Catalan movement had a backing of economic forces which
the Provençal one never did. Catalonia was in the forefront
in the industrialisation of Iberia; but its businessmen and commercial leaders also took an active part in its literary renaissance. The secretary of the Metallurgical Employers Union
was a poet; philologists were also engineers. It was the adoption of Catalan by the upper classes, and their total rejection
of Spain, which made Catalan particularism so powerful—a
condition never attained in Provence. Catalan was thus installed as the first language of all classes, but Provençal never
had the same status against French.[2] The Provençals continued
to seek their fortune in Paris or in the civil service. When industrialisation finally did come to the south, it was largely with
capital from outside and with managers drawn from other
regions. The railway network of the PLM made it easy to go
north, but difficult to move across the south. The leaders of the
Provençal regionalist movement were survivors of the old
economy, looking backward to a glorious past. Mistral was the
son of a *ménager*, that is a small landowner halfway between a
peasant and a bourgeois, and he inherited just enough to
enable him to live modestly. After obtaining his degree in law at
Aix, he devoted himself to poetry. He made friends with young

[1] For example J. F. Rolland, *Dictionnaire des expressions vicieuses et des fautes de
prononciation les plus communes dans les Hautes et les Basses-Alpes, accompagnées de leur
correction* (Gap, 1810).

[2] Pierre Vilar, *La Catalogne dans l'Espagne moderne. Recherches sur les fondements
économiques des structures nationales* (1962), 1. 30 ff.

men of similar status, who met to read their poems to each other, and in 1854 seven of them, meeting at Font-Ségugne, founded the Félibrige, a society for the propagation of Provençal. Their creed was populist and linguistic. They believed that the people's patois had wrongly been considered fit only to express 'low or droll subjects'. There had been numerous popular poets in the south, before the Félibres—men like Pierre Bellot, the stocking manufacturer of Marseille, whose Provençal tales, in four volumes, had sold 2,000 copies in 1840. He had made his characters speak each in his own tongue, Provençal, Gascon, Italian and various degrees of French. Victor Gelu (1806–85), son of a baker of Marseille, had sung realistically about the troubles of his fellow citizens, a southern version of Bérenger. Mistral continued and expanded this popular literature, but with a skill unequalled before, and with a youthful zest which makes him a precursor of the modern popular American singers and musicians who have likewise expressed a whole way of life. He announced his programme in the first issue of the *Provençal Almanach* (1855), which contained new poems by him and his friends:

> Nous sommes des amis, des frères,
> Étant les chanteurs du pays!
> Tout jeune enfant aime sa mère,
> Tout oisillon aime son nid;
> Notre ciel bleu, notre terroir,
> Sont pour nous autres, un paradis.

Refrain:

> Tous des amis, joyeux et libres,
> De la Provence tous épris,
> C'est nous qui sont les Félibres,
> Les gais Félibres provençaux.

The Almanach's first edition consisted of only 500 copies, but it later sold about 10,000 copies a year, which Mistral claimed meant that it had about 50,000 readers.[1] However, the aim of the Félibres was not simply to give expression to popular feelings in the language of the people, but also to reform, improve and standardise Provençal. This was a major purpose of

[1] Frédéric Mistral, *Mémoires et récits; correspondance*, ed. Pierre Rollet (1969), 463.

their congresses, and also a major stumbling-block to harmony.
Provence had some twenty different variants of its dialect,
and this was itself different from that of other southern provinces—Toulouse, Béarn, Languedoc, Auvergne, Limousin,
etc. In view of this, it was amazing that the Félibres won so
much support over so wide an area. In old age, Mistral
became a kind of patriarch, almost a king, surrounded by a
court, treated with veneration by disciples who came long
distances to pay him homage. In 1876 a Félibre constitution
divided up the south into regions or 'maintenances', each
with its own dignitaries, reviews, periodical meetings and
squabbles. A history of literature names over 500 writers in the
Oc dialect, as being particularly noteworthy, and there were
many more.[1]

However, the Félibres remained a small minority and failed
to acquire mass influence, because they were torn by fundamental disagreements which paralysed them. Mistral himself
was not content to be simply the poet of Provence. He always
had an eye on Paris. It was indeed Adolphe Dumas, Fortoul's
emissary in the search for popular songs, who discovered him,
invited him to Paris and introduced him to Lamartine. Mistral
published his first masterpiece, *Mireille*, with a French translation which was as carefully worked at as the Provençal.
Lamartine hailed it as a new *Iliad* and Mistral as a new Homer.
Mistral was never able to resist these blandishments. He lacked
the resolution or vigour to be a party leader. He was at first
a republican and appreciated Proudhon as a federalist; but
after the defeat of 1870 and the Commune, he was frightened
into dropping his support of Provençal autonomy, and became
the poet of tradition, and the old provincial life, even going so
far as to favour Catholicism (though never practising). With
time, the delirious enthusiasm people felt for him waned. He was
accused of singing only about Provence in the sunshine, about
its rural beauties, about his own feelings, ignoring the problems
of industrialisation and never speaking of Marseille. It was
said that he made Provence into a folkloric curiosity—and
indeed he used his Nobel prize money to start a museum at
Arles in which he collected and catalogued the dress and tools

[1] Robert Lafont and Christian Anatole, *Nouvelle Histoire de la littérature occitane*
(2 vols., 1970), is an excellent guide.

of the peasantry, as though he was an ethnographer. He did not in fact know much about the south beyond the district immediately around where he lived: for his poem on the Rhone, he read tourist books and then took a steamboat excursion to collect further detail. His retrospective idealisations prevented him from becoming more than a poet. In the end his message appeared negative: his search for the ideal, for perfection, which is the constant theme running through his poetry, was a search which he declared wellnigh impossible to complete. He created illusions in order to take refuge in them. As he said, he had 'a violent distate for the artificial world in which I was shut up' and he was drawn to 'a vague ideal I saw distantly blue on the horizon'.

Mistral's friends were considerably more reactionary than he was. Joseph Roumanille (1818–91), the son of a poor gardener, was a teacher and then a printer's proof-reader. He had been destined for the priesthood and remained religious; his inclinations were conservative, pious, virtuous, moralising; the Catholic polemicist Veuillot acknowledged him as an ally. Théodore Aubanel (1829–86) was also pious, son of the Pope's well-to-do official printer at Avignon, although his autobiographic love poem, about his hopeless love for a poor girl who ended up as a nun, was condemned as obscene by the clergy. Aubanel was very much an urban poet, describing the sordid side of life, rejecting the Félibres' idealisation of Provence; he was a sort of provincial counterpart to Baudelaire. He was the most professional of the Félibres, making friends with the leading Parisian writers of his day. When Mistral and Roumanille united in a conservative front in 1876, Aubanel emerged as the leader of a liberal, anti-provincial movement centred round the young Félibres of Paris, for there was also a school of provincials who rejected provincialism or who wanted to combine it with what was best in French culture. These few tergiversations give only a small idea of the constant disagreements which divided individuals, towns and regions, in an infinite variety of ideological positions. Marseille and Montpellier, for example, had strongly anticlerical branches of the Félibre movement which contradicted many of the master's teachings. The Montpellier Reds were led by L. X. de Ricard (1843–1911) who was the son of a marquis and general of Napoleon III's reign, and who had rebelled to republicanism at the age of twenty. Victor Gelu, the popular poet of Marseille, despised the Félibres as pretentious and preferred to show provincialism as dying, doomed in the age of industrialisation. Another tendency was to promote the 'Latin idea', in which Italians, Catalans and Romanians were united; this was launched with a Festival at Montpellier in 1878.[1] But the unity of the south was never established. Roumanille's langue d'Oc, which Mistral adopted, was only one dialect; they claimed it should be the national language of the south, but it was not. Mistral, who in 1892 had combined with Maurras and Amouretti to launch a federalist manifesto for France, typically retracted during the Dreyfus Affair and formed the Ligue de la Patrie française. When the vinegrowers of the south revolted in 1907,[2] he refused to put himself at their head. He disliked the dynamism of the young men who came forward to head the movement at the turn of the century, like the Protestant Paul Devoluy. The traditional divisions of the south, expressed with their usual vigour, were all reflected in the Félibre movement. It could not decide what precisely it represented.[3]

The Bretons

The national self-consciousness of the Bretons has been considerably more forceful. It has carried separatism to the point where some Bretons in 1939 refused to fight for France against the Germans and it has produced the only autonomist movement using violence. This independence has a long history. Under the *ancien régime* Brittany succeeded in resisting centralisation and modernisation more effectively than most provinces; and it was hit all the more noticeably by the reinvigorated centralisation of the nineteenth century. It stood out in France as the most steadfastly religious province, and it was regarded with particular fear by modernisers, who attributed this piety to its economic backwardness. Breton religion was something few outsiders understood. It was quite different, for example, from that of Spain. Its strength came from the reinforcement of

[1] See *La Revue du Monde latin*, 1883–6 and *Le Félibrige latin*, 1890.
[2] See Zeldin, *Politics and Anger*, 342–3.
[3] Émile Ripert, *La Renaissance provençale 1800–60* (n.d., about 1917); Beatrice Elliott, *Émile Ripert* (Avignon, 1938).

Catholicism by much older pagan beliefs and practices. The basis of Breton religion was superstition and magic, against which the Catholic clergy had at first fought hard, but which it had usually been forced to incorporate into its own system. Thus the ancient magic fountains were turned into objects of Catholic pilgrimage. Magic became an inferior demoniac religion. Fairies survived: 'the Bretons speak of them with complaisance as though they were a delicious forbidden fruit.' The Church tried to condemn them as evil spirits but the peasants refused to believe this and continued to use them. The worship of saints (after whom most Breton villages are named), though given an external Catholic respectability, continued in forms which were barely Christian. Most of the saints were local ones, unknown to Rome. Every parish had at least a couple of chapels in their honour, often as many as six: Plouaret (population 3,300) had twenty-four chapels. Each saint had a particular and definite purpose. Religion was powerful here because it was useful and practised from self-interest. Each saint could grant specific favours and each required different rewards. St. Onenne cured dropsy, St. Trémeur cured neuralgia, St. Brandon cured ulcers. Every species of animal also had its own saint. St. Avoye required white hens before he would do anything, St. Majan (who cured headaches) accepted hair as his offering. And when saints refused to grant their favours, they were forced to. Renan tells how his father went to a saint to cure a fever: he took the village blacksmith with him, complete with his tools; the blacksmith heated up an iron till it was red hot, held it up to the saint's face and said, 'If you do not cure this child of this fever I shall shoe you like a horse'. The saint obeyed. The Bretons did not communicate with God except through saints, and indeed had no dealings with God, but only with the saints, with whom they were involved in a ceaseless commerce, exchanging services. The Christian God was turned into a kind of constitutional monarch, above the details of daily life. The saints, unrecognised elsewhere, gave the Bretons a provincial allegiance; because there were so many of them, the individualism of the Bretons was respected; because they provided opportunities for so many social activities, they were valued for the fun as well as for the consolation they provided. The Breton 'pardons' and pilgrimages were outings on a mass scale carried out long before the holiday excursion. But this religion turned the Bretons always towards their past; every ceremony was linked with the worship of their ancestors, to the extent even of holding funeral memorial services as part of wedding celebrations. Breton piety was not exempt from doubt. The three great writers of nineteenth-century Brittany—Chateaubriand, Lamennais and Renan—were all involved in doubt or unorthodoxy. This doubt was all the more disconcerting because it was countered with sentiment rather than reason. There was thus a mysterious element at the bottom of Breton religion, and the Bretons were religious in an original way.[1]

The Breton language distinguishes this people still further, since it is a Celtic tongue totally incomprehensible to Frenchmen and having much more in common with Welsh and Gaelic. It has been estimated that in 1806 one million people normally spoke Breton, in 1886 1,300,000, and in 1970 about 600,000 to 700,000 used it daily. In the course of the nineteenth century in this province as in others, it became a mark of education and progress to forget Breton, which disappeared most rapidly in the towns. More recently, since 1920, Breton has been taken up again with pride by intellectuals, so that it is no longer simply a language for peasants. Its importance can be seen from an inquiry conducted in 1927 which revealed that out of 635 communes questioned, 474 had sermons entirely in Breton and 397 taught the catechism in Breton. Seventy had sermons mainly in Breton, 21 in both languages, 21 mainly in French and 49 entirely in French.[2] Religion and language combined to produce another distinctly individual tradition—that of an extremely vigorous popular theatre. In 1929 there were still over a hundred theatrical troupes in Brittany, performing plays which were at once traditional and demanding of imagination. These were not the hobby of middle-class people with leisure, but the recreation of men of all classes and all ages. (Women were allowed to act only in the towns.)[3]

[1] Cf. Émile Jobbé-Duval, *Les Idées primitives dans la Bretagne contemporaine* (1920).
[2] The figures for catechisms mainly in Breton are 72, in both languages 30, mainly in French 33, entirely in French 103. P. Sérant, *La Bretagne et la France* (1970), 205.
[3] A. Le Braz, *Essai sur l'histoire du théâtre celtique* (1904), doctoral thesis by a lecturer at the University of Rennes who became a leading advocate of the language.

Celtic literature had been as brilliant and as individual as that of Provence in the Middle Ages, and in the nineteenth century its traditions were revived by a large number of writers who, for obvious reasons, have not reached the French textbooks. In 1879 the Society of Breton Bibliophiles published a list of nineteenth-century Breton poets which contained over 200 names. By 1914 there were about fifty associations in Brittany devoted to Breton art and literature, and some thirty more in Paris.[1] All this activity allowed Arthur Le Moyne de La Borderie to say in his inaugural lecture, when taking up the chair of Breton history in 1891, that Brittany had all the bases of national originality—a language, a national character, a history and a poetry of its own.[2]

This view could be challenged. Brittany had four, if not five, different dialects. Part of the province, Basse Bretagne, was largely Francised, or at least spoke French—though it was significantly here that the Breton separatist movement made most headway. The juxtaposition of these two cultures was comparable to that prevailing in Belgium. But the province was exceptionally divided geographically and economically. There were very different conditions on the sea coast and in the interior the former having a density of population twice that of the latter. The Bretons' political and religious behaviour was by no means as uniform as appeared at first glance, so that there were exceptions to almost every generalisation about them. The intense mistrust and rivalry between the villages, which often broke out into bloody battles, made united action difficult. Though the Bretons had a very high birth-rate, they appeared to be a vanishing race, because they emigrated in such enormous numbers, providing Paris with its prostitutes and the army with its private soldiers: no province lost as many men in 1914–18 as Brittany did. Émile Souvestre wrote a book about them in 1836 entitled *The Last Bretons*, as though they were disappearing like the Amerindians. But very little was really known about Brittany then. Souvestre claimed that travel books about it simply copied from each other, all of them written in a style reminiscent of Christopher Columbus's

---

[1] Camille Le Mercier d'Erm, *La Bretagne vue par les écrivains et les artistes* (1929).

[2] Cf. A. Le Moyne de La Borderie, *Histoire de Bretagne* (6 vols., 1896–1914).

discovery of an unknown race of savages.[1] The self-consciousness of the Bretons had to be created by intellectuals and this is what happened, even while—and perhaps because—the province was exporting its children to the rest of France to the extent that no city in Brittany contained anywhere near as many Bretons as did Paris. And the Bretons outside Brittany, despite the nostalgia which they exhibited in the early years of exile, quickly assimilated themselves to their new surroundings: they were not nearly as active as, for example, the Auvergnats, in keeping together and preserving the memory of their homeland.[2] The Breton revival of this period has been likened to Zionism in its early years. Both movements were an answer to maltreatment in various degrees, for Brittany resented its poverty and its neglect by the government. Both were the creation of determined and able individuals.

In 1870 the Army of Brittany, under the command of Kératry (a great-grandson of a president of the Estates of Brittany), formed to repulse the Prussians, had so frightened the republican leaders, as potentially a dangerous and alienated force, that it was left virtually without arms. 'I beg you', telegraphed Freycinet to Kératry, 'to forget that you are a Breton and remember only that you are French.'[3] There were a number of people who refused to forget their origins and rejected assimilation.

The man who put Brittany on the map as a nation with a distinguished past, at a time when it was considered a backward and bigoted bogland, was Théodore Hersart de La Villemarqué (1815–95). In 1839 he published *Barzaz-Breiz* which purported to be a collection of the popular songs of Brittany collected by himself. He seems in fact to have contributed a lot to their composition, so that it was more creative poetry than folklorism (the word folklore, it might be added, was first used in 1846, by an Englishman). His book was written for Parisians, and he himself was a Breton émigré to Paris, who had become interested in Brittany only after he had settled in the capital.

---

[1] Émile Souvestre, *Les Derniers Bretons* (1836, new larger edition 1854).

[2] The *Annuaire des Bretons de Paris* (1911) said that only 2 per cent of Bretons in Paris were members of Breton associations: its list of Breton addresses in Paris contained only 3,600 names out of an estimated 200,000.

[3] C. Le Mercier d'Erm, *L'Étrange Aventure de l'armée de Bretagne* (first published, privately, 1935, reprinted 1970), 110.

A year before, the minister of education had given him a grant of 600 francs to attend the Eistedfodd at Abergavenny and to search the library of Jesus College, Oxford, for historical records. Such places, and the École des Chartes in Paris, which he attended, were paradoxically the most convenient sources from which one could obtain the information needed to re-create the idea of Breton nationality. La Villemarqué's book came out looking very much like the *Popular Songs of Modern Greece* which Fauriel had published in 1824. Only 500 copies were printed, and, over the century, no more than an average of 25 copies were sold each year. But George Sand declared after reading it that no one could henceforth pass a Breton in the street without taking his hat off to him. It made a very considerable impression on a few influential people. La Ville-marqué was elected to the Institut and he became the centre of a Bretons-in-exile fraternity, devoted to reviving the use of the ancient language. Already in 1841 the *Dictionnaire encyclopédique* talked of the 'Breton nationality'.[1] Le Gonidec's Breton–French dictionary, published posthumously in 1847, was the work of an exile too, who managed to compile its 835 double-columned quarto pages without setting foot in Brittany between 1804 and his death in 1838. Joseph Loth, another of the pioneers of the study of ancient Breton literature, went to learn Gaelic in Wales, married a Welsh girl, and only then, in 1884, started lecturing on Celtic literature at the Faculty of Rennes. There a whole line of distinguished pupils were to continue his work.

The Breton movement had three different strands in it. The first was Celtic, erudite, essentially interested in the study of the past, and principally linguistic. An *Association bretonne*, founded in 1834, was suppressed by Napoleon III who, how-ever, did not obstruct the Académie bardique (1855), which was purely cultural. The College of Druids, founded at the end of the century, modelled its statutes on those of its Welsh counterparts, and held annual competitions in the same way. Later it organised examinations in Breton for children and even offered prizes for Breton advertising slogans. By the 1930s, however, its activities were scorned by the younger genera-tion, who criticised the Druids for dressing up for the benefit

[1] Francis Gourvil, *T. C. H. Hersart de La Villemarqué (1815–95) et le 'Barzaz-Breiz'* (Rennes, 1960), 21, 28, 77, 147.

of tourists, for closing their minds to changing economic conditions and even for being hypocritical, when the Grand Druid Taldir, who wrote a celebrated anti-alcoholic tract, was revealed to be a cider merchant. The scholarly side of the Celtic movement, however, had some very formidable men in it, who in 1898 founded the Breton Regionalist Union. This included the leading Breton authors of the day—Anatole Le Braz, Charles Le Goffic, Camille Vallée, with the marquis de L'Estourbeillon as president. Its main interest was the teaching of the Breton language in schools, and up to *baccalauréat* standard, arguing that Breton had as much right to be officially recognised as Arabic, Annamite and Malagache, which were optional parts of the syllabus. Its slogan was 'Children: speak Breton to your parents'. It also pressed for the economic development of Brittany, but it abstained from any serious political activity and so had comparatively little influence.

The really important development in the revival of Breton was the foundation of Gwalarm (meaning north-west), which lasted from 1915 to 1940. This was a publishing house, directed by Roparz Hemon, a teacher of English at Brest. Its achievement was to turn Breton into a modern language, in the way that Hebrew was later revived in Israel. It published a large number of books, novels, poems, plays and, not least, works on every subject including science—all in Breton. It arranged for numerous translations of European classics into Breton, from Aeschylus to Alexander Blok. It commissioned a new history of the world in Breton, as well as physics and geometry textbooks. It was particularly successful with Breton children's books, with stories generally derived from Irish or Danish sagas, or definitely non-French sources like Finnish. It supplemented its publishing by language classes, correspondence courses and a summer university. It paid no royalties, and all the work, which made Breton into an authentic and modern vehicle of self-expression, rather than a folkloric survival, was done by amateurs.[1] At the level of the primary schools, Yann Sohier, the communist *instituteur* of the village of Plourivo, in 1928 began

---

[1] Roparz Hemon, *Les Mots du breton usuel classés d'après le sens* (Brest, 1936); id., *Petit Dictionnaire pratique breton–français* (Brest, 1928); id., *L'Orthographie bretonne* (Brest, 1929); id., *Dictionnaire breton–français* (second revised edition, La Baule, 1948).

speaking to his pupils in Breton and corrected their mistakes in Breton as severely as those they made in French. He discussed current events with them in Breton and sought to end their feelings of guilt about using a language normally associated with the uneducated and the poor. The School Inspector could do nothing about it because the pupils were the best in the canton in French, and Sohier won the approval of their parents. In 1933, together with some other primary teachers, he founded *Ar Falz* (*The Sickle*), a review and a movement which spread this new method widely in the schools of the province.

The second strand in the Breton revival was that of the conservative aristocrats. Little is written about this, though the influence normally attributed to the aristocrats would make their activities worth investigating. The paradox of their situation was that though they favoured greater autonomy for the Bretons, they also wanted to change the Bretons, to reform them, so that they would accept their dominance. The comte de Lantivy-Trédion, who was a disciple of La Tour du Pin, and who wrote a book on 'The Breton Question' in 1909, was severe in his criticisms of the Breton peasants. He castigated them for being egoistic, anarchistic, irrational, only superficially religious, attending *pardons* simply in order to get drunk. He feared the Druids because they were pagan and because they had links with Protestant England. He denounced that wayward Breton imagination which had led men like Lamennais on the dangerous paths of heresy. La Tour du Pin's efforts to establish the Free Estates of Dauphiné had failed because they had lacked popular support. The lesson was to form the masses into professional corporations who, it was hoped, would accept an aristocratic constitution. Something of this kind was mooted again under the Vichy régime. But it was never a powerful trend.[1]

What attracted more public attention was the third, more violent and demanding aspect of the Breton movement. In 1911 Camille Le Mercier d'Erm founded the Breton Nationalist Party, which asked for national independence. It declared that Brittany was an enslaved nation, like Ireland and Poland, and only independence could free it. His was a party of young men, ready to go to prison for their beliefs. At the unveiling

[1] Comte de Lantivy-Trédion, *La Question bretonne* (1909).

of a new statue in Rennes in 1912 commemorating the union
of Brittany and France, Le Mercier d'Erm organised the first
public demonstration of separatist protest against France, and
was himself the first Breton to be arrested for his nationalism.
His party and his paper *Breiz Dishual* (*Free Brittany*) disappeared
with the war of 1914. But immediately after this, *Breiz Atao*
(*Brittany Always*) was founded, a review which grew into a
movement. Its programme was to fight tuberculosis, alcoholism and French domination, the three scourges of Brittany.
In 1927 it started the Breton Autonomist Party; in 1929 the
review became a weekly; in 1930 it put up a candidate for
parliament, unsuccessfully. The review normally sold about
5,000 copies, though occasional issues were five times as large.
It tried to be neutral in social and religious questions. Its
slogan was: 'Neither red nor blue'. It adopted the Celtic cross
as its symbol, signifying peace and union (until Hitler's demonstrations caused it to abandon this, in favour of the flag of nine
black-and-white stripes—standing for the nine *pays* of Brittany). It expressed itself in very strong language, which worried some of its supporters, on the evils resulting from French
imperialism in Brittany. Its stickers, bearing slogans about how
Bretons were discriminated against, how taxes they paid were
used to develop other regions, etc., spread its message beyond
the faithful who read the review. It had some difficulty, however, in deciding what tactics to follow. For a while it steered
clear of separatism, merely talking about autonomy. It was
rather vague for a few years about what kind of federation it
wanted, suggesting occasionally that Brittany should be part
of a reorganised Europe as much as of a decentralised France.

Though its emphases were modified from time to time, its
1929 Manifesto gives the best idea of its general line of attack.
This began by insisting that it was not retrograde. Old Brittany had gone for ever, and it did not want to resurrect it,
though it respected it. It denied being anti-French, but it
declared that French rule was illegitimate, contrary to the
wishes of the Bretons and in violation of the Treaty of 1532,
which had united them to France on condition that their
customs were respected. It opposed French centralism and
French imperialism 'which exposes us to new wars for interests
which are not ours. We are rising against France's indifference

towards our economic needs, its inability to understand our
cultural and moral aspirations, its militant animosity against
our language. We note France's inability to accord with the
rhythm of the world's general evolution. We think that what it
is usual to call France is not a Nation, but a State, containing
a certain number of nationalities, and we cannot accept that
our demands should be opposed by the mystical dogma of a
Nation "one and indivisible", which is today left way behind
by all the enlightened people of the globe.' Breiz Atao was
the first movement to denounce French 'imperialism' within
metropolitan France itself, and to coin the slogan which has,
since the 1960s, been widely adopted by other people. 'Brittany', it declared, 'has been an exploited colony.' Brittany was
a nation born of events entirely foreign to the history of France,
as a result of emigration from Great Britain. It was a nation
'and every nation which does not administer itself rapidly falls
into decadence'. This had happened to Brittany, and that is
why it now demanded its own parliament, controlling its own
executive, with particular concern for the organisation of
education and the revival of the arts 'in conformity with our
Western and Nordic genius, to expel the Latin obscenities
with which the novels, songs, theatres and newspapers of Paris
poison us'. It wanted a religious settlement 'in accord with the
wishes of our people', social legislation adapted to their needs,
the abolition of France's prefectoral and departmental system
which was out-dated in an age of improved communications,
to be replaced by communes free from administrative inter-
ference. France would lose nothing if it granted all this, because
its centralisation had paralysed it: it was outdistanced in social
legislation, economic equipment, education, dramatic and
architectural production, hygiene and urbanisation by many
other countries, notably Germany, England, Switzerland,
Holland, Czechoslovakia and Scandinavia. The interesting
feature of this programme was the way it looked to Europe,
beyond France (rather than the U.S.A.). As a model for
federalism it sometimes quoted Switzerland; for its cultural
inspiration it looked to a wide variety of Nordic countries.
'We believe', it declared, 'that Europe is destined to form,
sooner or later, an economic unity', which was the only way to
stop it fighting. 'But this unity will not be constituted by a

federation of the present states, which are arbitrary aggre-
gations, the products of chance, violence and guile, and
which are not as eternal as the politicians so emphatically
claim.'[1]

How to deal with this problem of federalism produced
divisions and resignations. Some—'the federalists'—wanted
to make Brittany a general international question, while 'the
nationalists' wanted to concentrate on the internal problems
of Brittany itself. In 1936 the latter set up a *Front Breton* to
support candidates for parliament who would accept the
Breton demands: forty-one did accept and of these fifteen were
elected, constituting a 'committee for the defence of Breton
interests'. But the government got worried by this agitation,
and in 1938 the Breiz Atao leaders, Michel Debauvais and
Olier Mordrel, were arrested and put on trial at Rennes, and
in 1939 their party (now called the Breton National Party)
was banned. The demands of the Breton movement were thus
completely rejected by the French. When a young Breton
heckled Daladier, at a public meeting about this, Daladier
scornfully replied: 'Do you want us to go back to the Gauls?'
The Breton programme was too savage an attack on France's
pride in its achievements and on the progress it claimed to
incarnate. So as soon as war broke out in 1939, Debauvais and
Mordrel went to Berlin and issued a manifesto inviting the
Bretons to remain neutral in a war that did not concern them.
They believed that by this bold gesture they could turn Brittany into a second Ireland, and that it required only a few hundred determined men to bring this about. It was a complete
miscalculation. This was because, first of all, the Breton movement had been too divided and ambivalent about its attitude
to France to allow any enthusiastic and widespread support for
such a drastic course. Secondly, Pétain presented an apparently
viable alternative—he was a regionalist peasant, in his own way.
The Bretons at first got no response from him to their requests
for autonomy, but in 1942 a Lorrainer, Jean Quenette, became
regional prefect of Brittany, and created a Breton Consultative
Committee—the first recognition they had ever had. This
appears to have given some satisfaction; it made Breton a
subject in the primary school-leaving certificate and increased

[1] René Barbin, *L'Autonomisme breton 1815–1930* (1934, no place of publication), 136.

the teaching of the language. Thirdly, the Germans, though they allowed Mordrel and Debauvais to try and form (without much success) a Breton Corps from Breton prisoners of war, who were segregated into a special camp, had their own plans for dealing with France. The 'reconciliation' of France and Germany was a greater prize, so they could not offend France by dismembering it. Otto Abetz, who was married to a Frenchwoman, effectively killed the hopes of Mordrel: he thought the best that should be done for him was to offer him a professorship in Celtic at the University of Tübingen.

Olier Mordrel, twice condemned to death for treason, in 1940 and 1946, published his memoirs in 1973, after twenty-two years of exile in Argentina. He was just eighteen when he helped to found Breiz Atao and he shows how it needed only a few young men to produce and maintain the agitation. In 1927 the movement had only about 100 active members; in the 1930s, they never even dreamed of having more than 20,000 'potential supporters'; and in 1938 their congress at Guincamp was attended by only 1,500 people. They were not pro-German and still less Nazis: their contacts with Germans had been with outsiders and eccentrics like themselves, who proved powerless to obtain official aid for them. If they had a foreign model, it was rather the Irish Republican Army, from which they got some arms. They had a small dissident faction, which formed a tiny 'army', determined to use violence, and this was particularly active during the war. Mordrel took the risk of going to Berlin, conscious that he would be called a traitor if he failed, but convinced that the Bretons' only hope of success was to seize the opportunity presented by France's involvement in war. His memoirs are written with a remarkable serenity and modesty, which contrasts strangely with his inextinguishable optimism.[1]

The Bretons were torn by the war in a particularly acute way, because while many joined the Resistance, a small group of antagonists waged war against these, and a series of bitter reprisals followed. In 1944–5 many Breton autonomists were arrested, which hardened their hostility to the French, turning moderates into separatists. After a lull of some years, the Breton movement revived with considerably greater popularity, and

[1] Olier Mordrel, *Breiz Atao: Histoire et actualité du nationalisme breton* (1973).

more will no doubt be heard of it.[1] But a good many years will
elapse before enough historians will have had the time to work
through the vast amount of material that needs to be looked at.
A bibliography of Breton periodical publications, published
in 1898, shows that in Nantes alone there were 60 journals produced before 1848 and about 130 between 1848 and 1896. The
list for the single department of Loire-Inférieure was 583 items
long.[2] It is not surprising that the French never became aware
of all this literary activity, which was essentially local, particularly because the more independent reviews were not sold
openly at railway stations, but went straight to subscribers,
and the really Breton bookshops were obscurely tucked away
in back streets. It will be interesting to see in due course how the
'Breton character' is redefined, whether melancholy and taci-
turnity—even in love—obstinacy, indolence, asceticism, violent
alternations between gravity and drunken festivity, religiosity
and anarchism, continue to be regarded as basic traits, or
simply the product of a poor and isolated civilisation. In 1905
Raoul de La Grasserie claimed that the Breton character was
inseparable from its surroundings and collapsed in emigration.
It is curious that when a national public opinion poll asked
people what made them feel attached to their native province,
the Bretons stressed the 'temperament' of their people less than
others, but laid twice as much emphasis as others did on 'folkloric
traditions'. But the factor stressed more than any other was the
same with them as with all the Frenchmen: having been born
in Brittany or having many relations there. The increasing
mobility of labour no longer takes the form of onion sellers
coming to England seasonally (the Bodleian Library has a
drawing of one of these dated 1753), nor adventure beyond the
seas (there is a colony of 90,000 Bretons in New York). Bretons
have sought work all over France for many generations now and
have become assimilated there. There are about 600,000 today,
born in Brittany, who live elsewhere in France, and there are
200,000 natives of other regions of France living in Brittany.[3]

[1] The best accounts of it are in P. Sérant, op. cit., Barbin, op. cit. A vigorous
contemporary document is Morvan Lebesque, *Comment peut-on être Breton?* (1970).
[2] René Kerviler, *Essai d'une bibliographie des publications périodiques de la Bretagne*
(Rennes, 1884–98).
[3] Poll in Sérant, 166. For Bretons abroad, see Olivier Vincent Lossouarn, *Les
Bretons dans le monde* (1969) and Jean Choleau, *Les Bretons à l'aventure* (1950). For

That is why the new generation of autonomists is redefining what it stands for, in a wider European context which must have more general relevance.

The Auvergnats

It would take too long to list all the regional parties and groups, seldom mentioned in French national histories, which flourished with more or (usually) less success in these years. However, they raise some important general questions about the degree to which French culture was assimilated. The regions were of two kinds. Some were frontier regions, whose inhabitants shared a non-French language with people living under other governments—like the Basques, the Flemish, the Alsatians, the Catalans, the Corsicans. The central regions of France were not subject to this tension, but they showed strong signs of independence and individuality all the same, though in different ways. Thus the Auvergnats had a distinctive consciousness both of the outside world and of their own poor province. They had fewer illusions about themselves. They admitted the accusation, which seems to have been almost universally made, that they were above all interested in making money. They prided themselves on being honest, hard-working, thrifty, persevering and practical. Their ideal was the man who showed good judgement, who gave sensible opinions, who always kept practical aims in view, and who concentrated on amassing money and land. Even one of their most venerated writers, Ajalbert, talked of their 'absolute contempt for anything which was not money'. At most, they enjoyed music and dancing, but had little use for art and less for utopianism. Jules Romains, another of their sons who had made good in Paris, lamented that they 'did not contribute enough to the expression of the national genius' or 'make their weight felt in the common consciousness of the country'.[1]

'Breton psychology', see Raoul de La Grasserie, *Essai d'une psychologie du peuple breton* (Nantes, 1905); Anatole Le Braz, *La Bretagne* (1925) and Stéphane Strowski, *Les Bretons, essai de psychologie et de caractérologie provinciales* (Rennes, 1952); Marquis de L'Estourbeillon, *L'Immuabilité de l'âme bretonne* (1914); Charles Le Goffic, *L'Âme bretonne* (1902–8); Y. Le Febvre, *La Pensée bretonne* (1914); M. Duhamel, *La Question bretonne* (1929).

[1] Max Giraudet, *Les Auvergnats découverts et jugés par un Parisien* (1912); Joseph Desaymard, *L'Auvergne dans les lettres contemporaines* (1943); Vercin-Rhétorix,

They had a long tradition of emigrating, usually for about twenty years of their adult life, to make their fortunes. Already in the seventeenth century, the French ambassador in Madrid reported that there were at least 200,000 of them in Spain. They worked as merchants, usurers, pedlars in Andalusia and Castile. They were bakers in Madrid. In 1936 their factories in Valencia and Candette were still responsible for importing half the jute used in Spain to make the soles of espadrilles.

The Auvergne's most respected modern poet, Arsène Vermenouze (1850–1910), came from a family which had long had a small business in Illescas. Each member of the family usually went there for two years at a time, known as a 'campaign', and then came home for ten months. Young men would spend their first six or eight years of work as itinerant pedlars until they were admitted as full members of the company at around the age of thirty; they then spent most of their time in the shop. (The smuggling of goods into Spain was a specialised trade.) Most Auvergnat papers usually had a regular column of news about Spain. Vermenouze himself spent his youth reading not just Hugo, but Calderón, Cervantes, Moratín and Lope de Vega, and when he finally brought his profits home to settle in Auvergne, he still treasured his memories of Spain as 'his second fatherland'. But this migration to Spain diminished considerably in the nineteenth century and had largely dried up by 1875.[1] Instead the Auvergnats made their way to Paris, whither they had long travelled, first as chapmen and water-carriers, but increasingly as building workers, coal dealers, café and hotel keepers. They provided a lot of the labour which rebuilt Paris, and many of the hotels which its rapid growth necessitated. They specialised in buying up crumbling houses, refitting them and turning them gradually into respectable and highly profitable businesses. Paris became the city in France with most Auvergnats, who were all the more noticeable because they became famous for the way they stuck together

L'Auvergne aux Auvergnats (Clermont-Ferrand, 1969); Dr. A. Béal, Passe-temps d'un practicien d'Auvergne. Causeries sur l'hygiène et autres sujets joyeux (1900), interesting on Cantal cheese, among other things.

[1] M. Trillat, 'L'Émigration de la Haute-Auvergne en Espagne du 17ᵉ au 20ᵉ siècle', Revue de la Haute-Auvergne (1954–5), vol. 34, 257–94; Société française de littérature comparée, Actes du quatrième congrès national: Espagne et la littérature française (Toulouse, 1960).

and helped each other out. By the Second World War, there were 147 friendly societies for Auvergnats in Paris, some general ones, but most of them for individual villages, cantons or departments. In 1927, for example, the Friendly Society of Parisians from Cayrol (Aveyron) held a banquet attended by 227 people, followed by a ball to which 350 others came. Cayrol itself then had a total population still living there of only 646. The banquet was presided over by the mayor of Cayrol, aged 80, who came to Paris for the purpose and recalled how he had lived in the capital from 1887 to 1915, before retiring with his profits from the wine trade. The Auvergnats had their own newspaper in Paris (*L'Auvergnat de Paris*) founded in 1882 by Louis Bonnet, who also started the *Trains-Bonnet*, cheap special transport to allow his countrymen to spend the summer at home. Every new arrival in Paris, if he did not have relatives or friends, could go to what called itself the Auvergnat Embassy—a wine merchants' shop in fact—which issued references or 'passports', and gave help. All this organisation was designed, as one of its leaders said, 'to stop the Auvergnats being treated as pariahs in the capital', to ensure that the government recognised their importance, and to arrange that when a man set up a business or entered the liberal professions, he should be provided with Auvergnat clients to start him off. Any one of them who succeeded in national terms was invited to preside over their banquets (which sometimes had over 1,000 diners) and to use his influence on their behalf. The community life of the Auvergnats was essentially practical, though it also manifested itself in sport and dancing.[1]

However, there was also a literary side to their particularism, which had some curious characteristics. The first writers in Auvergnat patois were priests, like the abbé Courchinoux (1859–1902), professor of history at the seminary of St. Flour (whence he visited Jerusalem), subsequently promoted director of studies at the École Gerson in Paris, and abbé Pierre Gérand, professor of sciences and English at the seminary of Pléaux,

[1] Antoine Bonnefoy, *Les Auvergnats de Paris* (1925); Roger Béteille, 'Les Rouergats à Paris, aux 19ᵉ et 20ᵉ siècles. Le rôle du clergé dans l'émigration', *Études de la région parisienne* (Jan. 1972), 9–18; cf. Marcel Berthou, *Les Associations professionnelles et ouvrières en Auvergne au 18ᵉ siècle* (Clermont-Ferrand, 1935, Poitiers law thesis).

tutor successively to the princes of Bavaria, the French ambassador in Madrid and the prince of Romania. Auvergnats
travelled far. Other notable pioneers were J. B. Veyre (1798–
1876), an *instituteur*, who was the first major poet in Auvergnat,
until he died of drink, and Auguste Bancharel (†1889), who
founded a newspaper, *L'Avenir du Cantal*, to publish the works
of these men. In 1894 a correspondent of *La Dépêche de Toulouse*
at Aurillac got the Auvergnat writers to affiliate themselves
to the Southern Félibrige, and a new paper, *Lo Cobreto*, was
founded to spread the word. It is significant that this was set on
its feet by a banquet held in Paris (attended by 1,200), as a
result of which the director of the *Auvergnat de Paris* promised to
take 6,000 copies, out of the 7,000 it printed for his subscribers.
Considerable contact with the Félibres of other regions followed, and pious pilgrimages to Mistral.[1] The outstanding
lyrical poetry of Vermenouze gave national recognition to the
individuality of Auvergnat literature. It is not surprising that
this poetry, though all in praise of the beauty of the Auvergne
forests and mountains, was not the product of a solitary or
withdrawn backwoodsman. Vermenouze, as has been mentioned, had spent his youth in Spain. He then set up as a
liqueur and lemonade manufacturer in Aurillac. He did his
commercial travelling in the surrounding regions, taking with
him his dog and his rifle, for hunting was another of his passions; he brought back business orders, game and poems at the
same time. He travelled also to Italy, to Algiers to see his
brother, to Normandy to see a cousin, to other provinces to
partake in Félibre banquets, to Paris to advance his literary
fame, and after his retirement at the age of 50 (by which
time he had converted his 10,000 francs investment into
60,000 francs) to numerous spas where he met other ageing
dignitaries. Another side of his life was his political activity.
Though a republican in the early 1870s, he was alienated by
the regime's anticlericalism, and wrote a great deal of polemic
against freemasons, against Jews, against England, and in
praise of General Boulanger and Joan of Arc, urging revenge
on Germany. He was one of the principal writers for *La Croix
du Cantal*, the weekly local supplement of the virulent Catholic

---

[1] Duc de La Salle de Rochemaure, *Régionalisme auvergnat* (Aurillac, 1909) and
Régionalisme et Félibrige (Aurillac, 1911). Rochemaure was a Papal Duke.

newspaper. His anti-Semitism was of long standing, and was noteworthy because the Auvergnats engaged in precisely the same commercial and social activities for which the Jews were criticised. He worked hard to become famous, and a whole network of compatriots was got busy in Paris to propagate his name among the literary establishment. He put in several times for the prizes of the French Academy and eventually won one. Coppée deigned to express a wish to see 'this peasant, this savage'. Vermenouze's friends obtained long reviews for him in the Paris press. In time, he graduated to becoming a literary glory, and was invited to make speeches at school prize-givings. Auvergnat regionalism was thus no challenge to French unity in any way. Vermenouze's career was a literary counterpart of the Paris business success-stories of his region. But it shows how the Auvergnats stuck together and worked for their success. They were a powerful element in French life.[1]

The Normans

As one examines in turn the image which each province had of itself, it becomes clear that 'French culture', or the French ideal, as presented by the most celebrated national writers, is not the sum total obtained by adding up all the regional variations, and that it is not even a reconciliation of them. This can be seen once again if one looks at the Normans. They too had a region-alist movement, though it was not influential. A speaker at a banquet held by the Old Boys' Association of a school at Flers in 1911 (and this kind of occasion is one of the best sources of banal opinions, on which everybody agreed) lamented that even in the single department of the Orne, there was no 'fusion of ideas or of manners, no conformity of religious habits or social relationships'. The idea that the provinces were each more of a moral unity than the country as a whole was also a myth, the creation of men who sought something greater than their own village to attach themselves to. To the local inhabi-tants, the Pays d'Auge, the Pays Bas and the Perche appeared quite distinct in their attitudes. Nevertheless, it was claimed

---

[1] Jean Marzières, *Arsène Vermenouze (1850–1910) et la Haute-Auvergne de son temps* (1965); A. Vermenouze's *Œuvres complètes* (published in 1950–1 in four volumes); H. Pourrat, *Ceux d'Auvergne, types et coutumes* (1928).

that over and above these differences, the Norman could be
distinguished by the energy and skill with which he pursued
his own interest. Prudence was his favourite virtue. He had cold
common sense, practicality and repugnance for risky theories;
he avoided all extremes in politics; he respected the past; he
was cautious towards the future, and 'without committing himself, he drew the best he could out of the present'. He had a
reputation for being quibbling and litigious, but that was
because he had a 'refined sense of law and of mine and thine'.
He liked the rules to be followed always.[1]

More gifted regionalist writers elevated these mundane
attributes into much more exciting qualities. La Varende made
much of the Normans as descendants of the Vikings, and if
Scandinavian beauty could not always be recognised in them,
this was because they had an admixture of Andalusian and
Castilian blood. It was the Vikings, searching for a better life,
who explain why the Normans were keen on money and good
living; if the Normans were often miserly, this was because
their ancestors were poor. What gaiety they had owed nothing
to the Gauls; and conversely the melancholy everybody saw as
one of their characteristics was German in origin. This melancholy nevertheless had its individuality. It was not avowed; it
was not the result of disillusionment, but of the acceptance of
the world as it was. Thus Norman funerals were seldom emotional and death was accepted readily. Religion, when it
existed, was combined with materialism, with a barter system
carried on through local saints, with superstition and devil
worship. Melancholy therefore remained reasonable, and it did
not lead to sterile romanticism. If there was an internal conflict
among the Normans, it was between their passion for the land
and their love of adventure: the heirs of the Corsairs were the
Norman businessmen. But it could be argued that compromise,
which is what the Normans had settled for, was the result of
the clash between their Viking desire for action, and French
centralisation, which frustrated it. That was a good regionalist
explanation, which kept hope and idealism alive. But then
that was one of the functions of regionalism. La Varende even

[1] S. Guesdon, *Toast à l'occasion du millénaire de la Normandie, prononcé au banquet de
l'association amicale des anciens élèves de l'Immaculée-Conception à Flers* (15 June 1911,
pamphlet), 8–10.

managed to sing the praises of the rain of Normandy, so preferable, he declared, to the 'stupid and stupefying sun' of the south. He even defended the high illegitimate birth-rate in Normandy, by saying that, though he had a profound respect for Christianity and the family, bastardy was a most valuable element in Norman society and a condition of its success, because it was the product of vigorous blood, rather than marriages of convenience fixed by old notaries. This kind of regionalism was a protest against the oecumenical character of the French culture, which sought to appeal throughout and beyond the frontiers of the country, which imported and exported values. France, as Montherlant was to say, represented a 'great conspiracy against the naïve and the natural'. The regionalists claimed that they wished to preserve the 'real' personality of the people, as against the model and the ideal invented by Paris.[1]

The Savoyards

In 1860 Savoy, which was then part of the kingdom of Piedmont and Sardinia, became French, as part of the deal by which Italy was unified with Napoleon III's help. This event gives one an opportunity to study how France absorbed a hitherto foreign province, how French culture penetrated, how the natives reacted, and what vestiges of particularism survived. But France had already spread its influence over Savoy long before annexation. The language universally spoken was French; the leisured classes were imbued with French culture; Joseph de Maistre, the political philosopher of Chambéry, though he was not a French citizen, though he was educated at Turin and though he did not visit Paris till he was 73, was very much absorbed by French problems and thought that the dismemberment of France would be a great calamity.[2] Bishop Dupanloup, a major French Catholic leader, and Buloz (1803–77), a key figure in the French literary world as editor of the *Revue des Deux Mondes*, were both Savoyard by birth. At a humbler level, Paris, Lyon and Marseille each had some

[1] Jean Datain, *La Varende et les valeurs normandes. Essai régionaliste* (Saint-Lô, 1953); J. de La Varende, *Pays d'Ouche 1740–1933* (1934); R. Lelièvre, *La Varende* (1963).
[2] J. de Maistre, *Considérations sur la France* (1797).

10,000 Savoyards for at least part of the year (as did Geneva also), for in many mountainous regions, up to 50 per cent of the young men migrated seasonally in search of supplementary income. The sense of belonging to a separate 'nation' existed—for that word was used of Savoy—but subject to two qualifications. First, it was the well-to-do rather than the masses who ever thought about Savoy in this general sense. They were involved, as electors and as civil servants, in dealings with Piedmont, and their main aim was to preserve their independence and their privileges. It was partly because Piedmont adopted an anticlerical and Italian policy that these men were alienated from it and supported annexation by France. The change in their attitude came with the revolutions of 1848, which threatened their aristocratic rule. In a united Italy, Savoy would be an appendage, speaking a different language, whereas in the original kingdom of Piedmont, presided over by the House of Savoy, it could be certain of a large influence. Secondly, the idea of the Savoyard nation was modified by very strong local particularisms within it. Savoy became two departments when it was annexed by France because Chambéry contained a wealthy aristocracy, which made its contempt for the petty bourgeoisie of Annecy too evident. Annexation by France gave equality at last to the latter, and made their town into a departmental capital. And again beyond this rivalry in the bourgeoisie, each village had a very strong sense of its own independence and, apparently, even a particularity of dialect which enabled it to be distinguished from all others. The result of this was seen in Paris, where the Savoyard colony was divided into no less than forty different societies, one, more or less, for each village or groups of villages. These societies maintained a strong sense of loyalty between the émigrés in Paris and those who had remained at home, and they regularly sent donations and gifts to help the villages whenever they suffered from fire, flood or other misfortune. This particularism should not be exaggerated, however, for the Savoyards still met as such; 6,000 of them celebrated the anniversary of the union of Savoy and France in 1910 at the Trocadéro. Those who had emigrated to the U.S.A. had a single society, Les Allobroges de New York, founded in 1901, and maintained in some prosperity through the generosity of J. B. Martin, owner of one of the city's largest French cafés, which was said to employ some 400 Savoyards.[1] The paradox of Savoy was that it contained a mass of isolated and inaccessible valleys but that it also had a tradition of migration, so that Savoyards often had more contact with distant cities than with their own immediate neighbours.

The Savoyards voted to join France overwhelmingly in the plebiscite held in 1860. They believed that they would benefit from the union by the abolition of the customs barriers of France; imports would be cheaper and they would have good markets for their own produce; the jobs of the massive French civil service would be opened to them; they would have a shorter military service (seven years, as opposed to eleven years in Piedmont). But before the plebiscite the local leaders visited Paris and extracted assurances that their own positions and their special usages would be respected. Savoy thus entered France rather like the old provinces, with guarantees, though the world noticed only the plebiscite. France did start by trying to honour its undertakings. Missions were sent to study local usages. But after a few months in which every care was taken to tread carefully and tactfully, the French centralising machine began to knock everything down, as it had always done, because it could not easily behave in any other way. There was no question of giving Savoy any autonomy. It soon became clear that France would not give all the best jobs to Savoyards (who, by the unofficial agreement, had a right to the same jobs as they had held in Piedmont, or their equivalent). Disillusion rapidly set in; there was much haggling over claims and endless delays while 'notables' sought compensation. Most of the Savoyard 'syndics' were kept on as mayors, but when they proved unsatisfactory instruments of the French bureaucracy, French *instituteurs* were sent in, with special additional training in administration, to serve as secretaries to the mayors. Schooling cost more, the French forest administration was more severe, and the new roads, which were perhaps the most striking visible sign of French rule, failed to bring prosperity. Napoleon III, who seems to have appealed to the Savoyards and whose personal prestige seems to have played some part in attracting them into France, was soon replaced by anticlerical

[1] Alphonse Buinoud, *Les Savoyards à Paris* (1910), 267.

republicans who seemed as bad as Cavour and Garibaldi—
exactly what the Savoyards had tried to escape. Emigration
increasingly emptied the region, until Savoy was saved by an
unforeseen boon—the tourist trade—which gave it a new role
to play in France and indeed in Europe. Just when Savoy became French, the first Englishmen were arriving to climb the
mountains. Savoy then had at most 20,000 tourists a year. The
largest single group went to Aix-les-Bains, which had only
ten hotels and eight pensions, accommodating about 5,000
bathers, 3,000 of them French. These numbers increased
rapidly, and when watering-places lost their attractions,
skiing became fashionable, so that by 1960 at least one and a
quarter million tourists visited Savoy annually. Even with the
change of tastes, Aix in 1934 still had 45,000 bathers, and
Évian 30,000. Savoy thus became one of France's playgrounds
and in this cosmopolitan and changing function, there was no
longer cause to ruminate about whether it was a separate
nation. By 1925, 26 per cent of the permanent residents had
been born outside the region. Formerly, Savoyards had intermarried so closely that, stricken by thyroid hypertrophy,
cretinism and goitre, they showed in their physical appearance
pronounced signs of backwardness. In 1800 35 per cent of
Savoyards were under 5 feet tall (150 cm) and 20 per cent
were even under 4 feet 10 inches (145 cm). In the years 1800–
1850 they gained on average 2 inches in height, and between
1850 and 1950 another 2 inches. St-Jean-de-Maurienne, in
1925, still had some of the smallest men in France, and still
had the highest amount of consanguinity, but such villages
were now the exception. Savoy as a whole was absorbed into
France, and found a function to fulfil, in its leisure activities, as
respectable as Paris or any other region had in its own speciality. This is an instance of economic and social change making
regionalism irrelevant.[1]

[1] Ginette Billy, *La Savoie, anthropologie physique et raciale* (1962, Paris thesis for
the doctorate in natural sciences); Jacques Lovie, *La Savoie dans la vie française de
1860 à 1875* (1963); Charles Montmayeur (an *instituteur*), *Choses de Savoie vers 1860*
(1911), 28, 30; *Mémorial de Savoie: le livre du centenaire 1860–1960* (Chambéry and
Annecy, 1960, with a preface by Henry Bordeaux), 125, 313, 366; Henry Bordeaux,
Portrait de la Savoie par ses écrivains (1960). For regionalist feeling see the *Revue
Savoisienne*. For other regionalisms see Roland Moreau, *Histoire de l'âme basque*
(Bordeaux, 1970); Émile Coonaert, *La Flandre française de langue flamande* (1970).
For an instructive comparison, H. J. Hanham, *Scottish Nationalism* (1969).

Alsace

In the case of Alsace-Lorraine, however, regionalism became an important political issue, because when the provinces, which the Germans annexed in 1871, were recovered in 1918, it was too easily assumed that they would welcome the restoration of French sovereignty without reservations. In fact forty-eight years of German government had brought about profound changes in a territory which in any case had only just started to become French when it was lost. Alsace-Lorraine was ceded to France in 1648, with reservations, and finally only in 1697. In the eighteenth century it enjoyed much autonomy and no attempt was made to incorporate it systematically into France —its legal and customs arrangements remained peculiar to it. Voltaire visiting Colmar in 1753 described it as 'half German, half French and totally Iroquois'; eighty years later Michelet still could not decide whether it was French or German. Its patriotic attachment to France was greatly stimulated during the Napoleonic wars, to which it contributed a large number of soldiers and a quite exceptional proportion of generals and marshals; and in the nineteenth century nowhere did the Napoleonic cult flourish more vigorously. However, French culture had made but slight inroads.[1] In 1870 only the bourgeoisie habitually spoke French; most of the peasants spoke Alsatian, which is a German dialect; and German was the language in which both Catholics and Protestants (a minority of about 20 per cent) were taught their religion. There were small areas, particularly around Metz, which spoke French, but it was only at the close of the Second Empire that an attempt was made to make French the principal language taught in schools. In 1871, 12·5 per cent of the population opted to keep their French nationality and to migrate to France: these were mainly members of the middle classes, and so the provinces lost precisely those elements who were most French. After 1871 the Germans systematically pursued a policy of 'deforeignisation'. German became the sole official language; and the spread of French was halted and indeed reversed. By 1918 it could be said that five-sixths of the population normally

[1] Paul Leuillot, *L'Alsace au début du XIXe siècle* (1959); F. L'Huillier, *L'Alsace en 1870–71* (Strasbourg, 1971).

spoke German; and three-quarters had done their military service in the German army.

However, the Germans made the mistake of pursuing their national aims too vigorously, without tact or consideration for the traditions and interests of the natives. Alsace-Lorraine was made a Reichsland—subject directly to the emperor, and not an equal of the other members of the federation, like for example Bavaria. It was in effect Germany's first colony, and it was treated as a colony. It was administered by a civil service composed very largely of Prussians. Power was concentrated in the hands of a nominee of the emperor; the local assembly was without influence and when in 1911 a new constitution estab-lished a Landtag this turned out to be an empty sham, for the ministers continued to be responsible to the emperor.[1] The Germans certainly brought efficient administration (even if it involved little popular participation), the most advanced social security system in Europe and reasonable economic prosperity.[2] But this was not enough to win the Alsatians' loyalty. It is true that in 1914 there was little enthusiasm amongst them for reunion with France;[3] and the Ligue Patriotique had only a few hundred members. During the first fifteen years of German rule, the Alsatians merely sent opposition deputies to the Reichstag, but after that a movement for local autonomy won increasing influence, until it obtained almost universal support. It demanded more jobs for natives, the use of the local dialect by the civil service, the expenditure of locally levied taxes for Alsatian purposes, the reintroduction of French teaching in schools and the elimination from textbooks of deprecating reflections on the ancestors of the new generation of Alsatians. 'Français ne peux, Prussien ne veux, Alsacien suis.' The Germans made the Alsatians a self-conscious nation, aware of their unique position, and anxious to remain in cultural con-tact with both their neighbours. This movement was not so much directed at Germany as against the arrogance and

[1] Jean-Marie Mayeur, *Autonomie et politique en Alsace: la constitution de 1911* (1970).

[2] Joseph Weydmann, ancien député, 'L'Évolution de la législation sociale en Alsace-Lorraine de 1870 à 1918', *L'Alsace contemporaine: études politiques, économiques et sociales*, published by the Société savante d'Alsace et des régions de l'est (Strasbourg, 1950).

[3] Coleman Phillipson, *Alsace-Lorraine. Past, Present and Future* (1918), 198, a valuable impartial study of the German period.

persecuting spirit of the conquerors (for there were sons of German immigrants among the autonomists); a change of regime might well have satisfied them.

The idea that Alsace-Lorraine wished to be fully absorbed into French life was largely the creation of the Alsatians who emigrated to France after 1871. These formed an important pressure group in French politics—emerging into the limelight in the Dreyfus Affair.[1] Their departure had created a vacuum of power in Alsatian politics, and the leadership of the people was assumed in their stead by the clergy. Under Germany the Catholics were a minority in a Protestant country; after 1918 they were an anomaly in a France that had adopted anti-clerical principles. In 1918 Alsace was still subject to the Concordat, the clergy were paid by the state, the Loi Falloux was still in force and members of religious orders taught in schools, where religious education was compulsory. The French realised that serious problems would be created by reannexation, so they promised full respect for Alsatian traditions. The French armies were therefore received with great enthusiasm, as liberators.

This enthusiasm soon disappeared, for the French made the same mistakes as the Germans and possibly even more. They wrongly assumed that the autonomists were pro-German and gave them no sympathy. They did not keep their promises for long. Millerand, appointed Commissaire général de la république for Alsace-Lorraine, introduced a bill to give the two provinces a regional council: this might both have satisfied the Alsatians and prepared the way for a general decentralisation of French administration, in fulfilment of the ideas of the regionalists who were pressing for a drastic revision of the Napoleonic system. But parliament rejected this, as it rejected anything which appeared too radical.[2] Millerand's successor Alapetite (1920–4) instead achieved the full reintegration of the provinces into France and in 1924 his post and the Consultative Council (which was a kind of regional parliament) were abolished. Alsace was ruled once more from Paris—

[1] On the Alsatian clique, see e.g. Paul Appell, *Souvenirs d'un Alsacien* (1923); his brother Charles, leader of the Alsatian pro-French party, spent ten years in prison.
[2] A. Millerand, *Le Retour de l'Alsace-Lorraine à la France* (1923), particularly the introduction.

though until 1940 the three prefects remained responsible to the prime minister instead of the minister of the interior, and a special department was established in his office to supervise Alsatian affairs. This was largely because the incorporation of Alsace presented very difficult problems. French law could not be reintroduced at once and in 1940 there were still numerous legal differences—for example, in local government, public health, civil law, in addition of course to the special pre-1870 religious laws. The province's laws—a mixture of German, French and Alsatian—were a veritable labyrinth of confusion.[1] Disillusionment with the French regime was rapid. The provinces were invaded by French civil servants, as they had previously been flooded by Prussian ones. The misfortune of the Alsatians was that very few of them had obtained senior administrative experience under German rule, and they seemed unfitted to take over the running of their country. They found they were paying far higher taxes than the rest of France because their municipal system involved local taxes four or five times greater than French ones; the French state elsewhere paid for services which in Alsace were the responsibility of the communes.[2] German property was confiscated and sold at fantastically low prices, with a great deal of corruption and profiteering, which seems to make previous financial scandals pale into insignificance.[3] The Alsatian railways, which had till then been making a profit, were taken over by the French state, with an agreement by which most of those profits went to help the French railways. The potash mines were also bought by the state at a very low price, and only a fraction of the profits were ploughed back into Alsace. The autonomists claimed that twenty-five milliard francs disappeared through corruption. All but one of the local Alsatian banks were taken over by the large French ones in the economic crisis of 1928–32, and it was claimed that Alsatian money deposited in them was used elsewhere: the banks were said to have refused to help out

---

[1] Jacques Fonlupt-Esperaber, ancien secrétaire général du Haut Commissariat de la république à Strasbourg, *Alsace et Lorraine: Hier, aujourd'hui, demain* (1945), 39–125.

[2] Georges Lasch, 'Politiques municipales', *L'Alsace depuis son retour à la France*, published by the Comité Alsacien d'études et d'information (Strasbourg, 1932–3), 1. 277–88.

[3] See Cluzel's report, *Journal officiel*, 1928.

the local textile firms when they got into difficulties, so that they collapsed or were absorbed by French concerns. Alsace, it was said, became a colony of France, exploited for French ends, in the same way as it had been of Germany. Certainly the prosperity of the provinces declined. They had been in the van of progress before 1870, but the readaptation to the German market had slowed down growth, and again in 1918 the attempt to find a place in the French market proved very difficult. Political uncertainty had greatly reduced investment. Between the wars this once flourishing province was economically almost stagnant.

Even more important, the French aroused the hostility of the clergy, who had consolidated their hold on the masses by closely linking religious and social activities in the village. They insisted on making French the primary language everywhere and on teaching it by the direct method, so that there should be no interposition of German. German was maintained but only as a secondary language, which was not taught to the very young. This was to attack the language of prayer, as well as the mother tongue of the majority. The clergy protested under their leader abbé Haegy, the editor of the *Elsässer Kurier* of Colmar and inspirer of many other Catholic journals (whose vigour and number were a further element in the clergy's power). Abbé Haegy, it has been written, 'succeeded in exercising over the militant clergy of the Union Populaire Républicaine (the Catholic party) a veritable dictatorship. Already under German rule he had the reputation of an obstinate member of the opposition. He always placed the interests of the Church, as he understood them, above the national interest, which he had never tried to understand. Ignorant of all things French, with which he deliberately avoided making contact, abbé Haegy was haunted by the idea of a Jacobin France having no aim but to laicise Alsace.'[1] In 1924 Herriot, ignoring the strength of the Alsatian Catholics, announced his intention of introducing the republic's lay legislation into Alsace. This led to violent agitation and to the foundation, in

---

[1] Albert Wolff, *La Loi Falloux et son application en Alsace et Lorraine* (1939), 128–9 n. A thorough piece of work. On the clergy's power see also Odette d'Allerit, 'Une enquête de sociologie religieuse en milieu rural', *Paysans d'Alsace*, published by the Société Savante d'Alsace et des régions de l'est (Strasbourg, 1959), 523–57.

1927, of an Autonomist Party. The government replied by twenty-five arrests and a dramatic trial for plotting against the safety of the state. It was said that the autonomists had clandestine depots of German arms and a plan for armed insurrection. Certainly the Germans were active and generous in their support of the autonomists, flooding the provinces with cheap literature and subsidising the autonomist press.[1] But the autonomist movement was no puppet of the Germans; and the trial was unable to prove anything much; most of the accused were acquitted; and two of the four imprisoned were immediately elected to parliament. The election results in the interwar period confirmed the strength of the autonomists. They obtained few concrete gains from their agitation beyond thwarting an attempt by Blum to keep Alsatians at primary school for an additional year so as to improve their knowledge of French. Successive governments in Paris showed a complete inability to understand autonomism: they did not realise that there were several different attitudes concealed behind this general label. The separatists, who wanted a return to Germany, were a small minority, confined to some Protestant rural districts, led by Lutheran pastors trained in Germany, but including also some workers who refused to learn French. There were others who wanted to erect the provinces into a buffer Rhineland state, and demanded equality between the *Muttersprache* and French. The vast majority were however simply regionalists, wishing to maintain local traditions against French centralisation, as they had opposed German centralisation. The radicals and socialists, who were firm believers in centralisation, had no sympathy for this view, and they therefore lost most of their influence and votes. The communists profited a little from this, and by taking up the autonomist programme, they were able, with the assistance of the Catholics, to elect a communist mayor of Strasbourg. But the main result of the republic's hostility was that Alsace-Lorraine became largely 'Christian democrat' and 'Centre'.[2] Ultimately, this was to be the way that it came to be integrated

---

[1] Édouard Helsey, *Notre Alsace. L'Enquête du* Journal *et le procès de Colmar* (1927).

[2] F. Eccard, Sénateur du Bas-Rhin, in *L'Alsace depuis son retour à la France* (Strasbourg, 1932–3), 164; Jean Dumser, *Confessions d'un autonomiste alsacien lorrain* (1929), on the press; François G. Dreyfus, *La Vie politique en Alsace 1919–1936* (1969).

into France. The M.R.P. and Gaullist movements were the natural heirs of this political nuance, which came into its own after 1945. They ended the identification of France with anti-clericalism and the provinces could therefore at last find a satisfactory place, and no longer a marginal one, in French politics. The rise of Nazism was decisive too, for it dealt a mortal blow to autonomism: Hitler did more for the French cause than two centuries of French rule had done; he was much more savage in his repression of Alsatian particularism. In 1945, therefore, the government was able to have only French taught in the primary schools, to the exclusion of German, even though it supported its legislation by an advertising campaign with the slogan 'It is *chic* to speak French'. However, the linguistic problem remained: knowledge of German declined among the young generation, but in 1952 German was restored as an optional subject: about 85 per cent of parents declared their wish that their children should study it. A new *modus vivendi* has developed. It was fitting that Strasbourg should have been chosen as the seat of the Council of Europe.[1]

The movement to decentralise France and to give these regions a greater share and independence in its administration has a long history, which is worth mentioning even though it had no significant results till the 1960s. At first decentralisation was principally a royalist doctrine, by which the nobles expected to regain their waning influence. This was one reason why it was so vigorously resisted not only by those in power, but also by many republicans who were willing to sacrifice their liberal principles to keep the royalists out. But during the Second Empire an important breakthrough occurred when some liberals agreed to join people of all but the Bonapartist party in a manifesto, known as the Programme of Nancy (1865), which demanded that at least a beginning should be made in reducing centralisation. In 1870 a certain Charles de Gaulle (a schoolmaster, uncle of the general), together with the comte de Charencey and H. Gaidoz, petitioned parliament

[1] Paul Sérant, *La France des minorités* (1965), 312; Pierre Pflimlin and René Ulrich, *L'Alsace, destin et volonté* (1963); Pierre Maugué, *Le Particularisme alsacien 1918–67* (1970). For a German view, see Dr. Christian Hallier, *La Lutte de l'élément ethnique allemand d'Alsace et de Lorraine pour son existence 1918–40* (Brussels, n.d.).

asking that chairs of regional languages and literatures should be established in the provincial universities, that teachers in schools should have the right to teach in the local dialect, and that in future all new teachers should have to prove, in an examination, their knowledge of the local language. Governments, however, still feared these languages as instruments of reaction and resistance to progress, maintaining the belief expressed by Barrère during the first Revolution that they represented 'superstition and error'. The commissions which were set up by Émile Ollivier's liberal empire in 1870 and by Ribot in 1895 came to nothing, any more than did the twenty-five different bills introduced into parliament between 1887 and 1910. Briand, when he became prime minister in the latter year, promised that he would take up the cause—but without result. The cause was certainly winning increasing support from many moderate republicans, including a considerable number who had no special reason to be personally dissatisfied with things as they were, like Paul Deschanel and Paul-Boncour. By 1903 the *Figaro* could say that regionalism was 'a sort of new faith', or, as another journal put it in 1906, 'today the question is no longer whether one is a regionalist, but how'. That was the problem. Each proposal offered a different solution. No agreement could be reached as to what should constitute a region. The National Regionalist League founded in 1895, the Regionalist Federation founded in 1900 and its review *L'Action régionaliste*, started in 1907, aired the issues without making much progress. There was division even on whether local languages should be encouraged, for those who spoke nothing but French opposed the revival of obstacles to mutual comprehension. J. Charles-Brun (1870–1946), who was the most active organiser of the federalist movement, liked to link his views with those of Proudhon. He lectured on the Serbo-Croats to show, as he thought, how people of different languages could live together. Jean Hennessy of the Cognac family, ambassador at Berne (1924), minister of agriculture (1928–30), a deputy, who was also active in support of the League of Nations, and who in 1940 advocated Franco-British union, was another leading advocate of regionalism: he saw Switzerland as a model. He, Étienne Clémentel (minister of commerce 1915–20) and the historian Henri Hauser were among the few who were conscious of the importance of having economic bases for regional decentralisation, but this was an aspect which was widely and more fully studied only after the Second World War. It will be seen how the Vichy regime tried to do something about regionalism, because by then it was generally accepted as a necessary reform, but of course war-time was hardly propitious for such experiments.[1] Only in 1951 did the Loi Deixonne allow the teaching of local languages—optionally—in schools and provide for their examination in the *baccalauréat*, but it did not make any arrangements for the teaching, so the law was largely a dead letter. It was in the 1960s that regionalism finally became a live issue, but in new conditions, and it is too early to assess its consequences.[2]

[1] F. Jean-Desthieux, *L'Évolution régionaliste, du Félibrige au fédéralisme* (1918); J. Charles-Brun, *Le Régionalisme* (1911); Jean Hennessy and J. Charles-Brun, *Le Principe fédératif* (1940); François Prevet, *Le Régionalisme économique* (with a preface by E. Clémentel), 1929; H. Hauser, *Le Problème du régionalisme* (1924).

[2] R. Lafont, *La Révolution régionaliste* (1967); J. F. Gravier, *La Question régionale* (1970); T. Flory, *Le Mouvement régionaliste français* (1966); M. Philipponneau, *La Gaule et les régions* (1967); K. Allen and M. C. MacLennan, *Regional problems and policies in Italy and France* (1970).

3. Attitudes to Foreigners

FRANCE was defined as a nation not only by the policies of its rulers—or, alternatively, by the peculiarities of the provinces from which it was formed—but also by the way it distinguished itself from the nations that surrounded it. To understand France, one must appreciate the complexity of its attitudes towards foreigners.

Travel

The first question is, what did Frenchmen know of foreigners? They could claim that they had no need to go abroad, because their country was the centre of the world, which everybody who mattered was obliged to visit. A very large number of people did indeed visit France in this period. As soon as statistics of tourism began to be kept, France was revealed as the country which was almost the major tourist attraction in Europe.[1] Already in 1910 it was estimated that France was earning 350 million francs from its tourists compared to the 200 million francs earned by Switzerland and the 318 million francs by Italy. International travel appears to have roughly doubled in the 1920s: 1929 was the peak year, after which travel collapsed back to its 1920 level. In 1929 the credit and debit account in tourism showed France as a country which imported far more tourists than it exported. France earned £80 million from tourists, while its nationals spent only £12 million as tourists abroad. The U.S.A. received £37 million from visitors, but spent £178 million. Britain earned £22 million and spent £32. Germany earned £8·8 million and spent £14·6 million. Visitors to France, moreover, spent more money there than they did elsewhere—on average £40 a head, compared to only £21 spent in Italy; and the American visitor spent £120 a head in France. The British were probably always the most numerous visitors to France, as these figures for 1929 show:

[1] The Italians started keeping statistics in 1899, but comparative figures for Europe are available only after 1919.

Visitors to France (1929)

From		
	Britain	881,000
	Spain	350,000
	U.S.A.	296,000
	South America	150,000
	Netherlands	55,000
	Switzerland	45,000
	Belgium	38,000
	Germany	35,000
	Austria	30,000
	Other countries	30,000
	TOTAL	1,910,000

France in 1929 had more visitors than any country except Switzerland, which had 2,154,000; it had more than Austria's 1,849,000 and was far ahead of Italy, which had 1,290,000. But the balance of curiosity between France and its visitors was far from being reciprocal. Thus in return for the 881,000 British visitors to France, France sent only 55,000 visitors to Britain: though it is fair to add that, even so, the French were the second most numerous tourists in Britain (representing 13·6 per cent of the total who visited Britain), coming after the U.S.A. (33·7 per cent, or 137,000 people), but ahead of the Germans (49,000, 12·1 per cent) and the Dutch who came fourth (8·2 per cent, 33,000). When the great depression reduced American visitors to Britain to 66,000 in 1933, the French still continued to come at the same rate: 55,000 in 1933. France was the favourite country for British travellers, but when the French travelled abroad, they preferred first of all Switzerland and then Italy.

Comparison of travel abroad by the British and the French (1929)

		British Travellers	French Travellers
To	Switzerland	204,000	104,000
	Italy	132,000	97,000
	France	881,000	..
	England	..	55,000
	Norway	28,000	3,136
	Japan	6,391	883

One striking feature in these unequal exchanges is that the French barely visited Germany, and few Germans came to

France. In 1929, 297,000 Italians visited France, but only 35,215 Germans. Seventeen per cent of visitors to Germany were Americans, 11 per cent were British, only 2·6 per cent were French. The Germans preferred to go to Italy, 313,000 of them in 1930, accounting for 24·3 per cent of all tourists in Italy, whereas the French comprised only 7·6 per cent.

Visitors to Italy (1930)

Germans	313,000
Swiss	148,000
Austrians	143,000
Americans	133,000
Britons	132,000
French	97,000

The Germans also dominated tourism in Switzerland, where in 1929 38·8 per cent of tourists were German, 13·7 per cent British, 13·2 per cent American and only 9·4 per cent French. The statistics are too imperfect to make a map of European travel possible, but they reveal enough to show that the political alignments did not necessarily reflect popular knowledge or taste.[1]

They show also that the French did travel to a considerable extent, even if not on the same scale as the British. There certainly were far fewer Frenchmen abroad than there were Britons; but their numbers were not insignificant. French emigration has a long history. Without going back to the 60,000 Normans who are said to have invaded England in 1066, and the even larger number who settled in Spain between the sixteenth and eighteenth centuries, one has around half a million Huguenots leaving France in 1660–1710. Many Frenchmen went to fight in foreign armies: the Prussian army is said to have contained 25,000 Frenchmen in 1773. Between three and four hundred thousand may have emigrated at the Revolution (1789–95) though many of them later returned. Only some 25,000 had left for Canada by the time it became British, but at the end of the *ancien régime* it was estimated that there were about 230,000 Frenchmen abroad: 90,000 of them were in Europe, and 74,000 in French colonies. The total increased

[1] A. J. Norval, *The Tourist Industry* (1936); F. W. Ogilvie, *The Tourist Industry. An Economic Study* (1933).

rapidly during the century covered by this book (as shown in the accompanying table).

Frenchmen Abroad

In	1861	1881–6	1901	1911	1931
Britain	13,000	26,600	22,450	32,000	15,000
Jersey	2,780	?	8,100	8,500	7,000
Belgium	35,000	52,000	56,580	80,000	80,000
Russia	2,479	5,760	8,000	12,000	1,500
Germany	6,429	1,756	20,480	19,000	15,000
Switzerland	45,000	54,260	58,520	64,000	40,000
Italy	4,718	10,900	6,950	8,000	9,000
Spain	10,642	17,600	20,560	20,000	20,000
TOTAL EUROPE	128,000	185,000	220,000	269,000	220,000
Egypt	14,207	15,700	10,200	11,500	18,000
Asia (mainly China)	4,000	5,000	7,000	10,000	11,000
U.S.A.	108,870	106,900	104,000	125,000	127,000
Canada	3,173	4,400	7,900	25,000	21,000
Mexico	—	8,800	4,000	4,000	6,000
Argentina	29,196	60,000(?)	94,100	100,000	80,000
Brazil	592	68,000	10,000	14,000	14,000
Chile	1,650	4,198	7,800	10,000	6,000
Uruguay	23,000	14,300	12,900	9,500	8,000
TOTAL FOR SOUTH AMERICA	56,000	92,000	130,000	138,000	113,000
TOTAL FOR WORLD	318,000	426,000	495,000	600,000	535,000

Source: État Français, Service National des Statistiques, *Études démographiques* no. 4, *Mouvements migratoires entre la France et l'étranger* (1943) [by Henri Bunle], 33–4.

The figures give only a very rough and general idea of the extent to which the French moved around the world, for the statistics are, as usual, unreliable. Many people left France without any government department knowing: emigration was most active in the frontier regions which had strong traditions in smuggling and in the evasion of military service, and where Frenchmen participated to some extent in the large-scale movements which drove so many Italians, Germans and Spaniards to the new world. Thus Alsatians went to America with the assistance of the German businessmen who specialised in transporting their own countrymen; the Savoyards emigrated as part of the Italian exodus, and the Basques travelled to South

America through Spain. In 1857 the department which had the highest rate of emigration was the Basses-Pyrénées (the second was Paris). By 1860 emigration had become so active that France had no less than thirty-one authorised emigration agencies. The major shipping lines which linked France with the U.S.A. (there were ten of them by the end of the Second Empire) co-operated with these, since they wanted passengers to fill up their boats, sent out to fetch American cotton. The government, however, tried hard to restrict and obstruct emigration, because it was keen that if any Frenchmen did leave, they should go to Algeria. But France's emigration was difficult to control, because it was somewhat different in character to that of the rest of Europe. The people who went out from France were in general not driven out by poverty or unemployment; many of them were enterprising individuals, making their own choice, rather than participating in a mass movement; they were often artisans or even professional men anxious to make a fortune and to use their skills in a new environment. In 1858–60 only 21·2 per cent of passports issued for emigration were granted to peasants. The people who went to Algeria were of a special kind, and (apart from 1848, when some 13,500 Parisians went out—and quickly returned—and from 1871, when some Alsatians tried it) generally from southern France. The Bretons, by contrast, went to Paris for the most part. No accurate figures are available for emigration from France: in 1860–70 four times more Frenchmen arrived in the U.S.A. than were supposed to have left France. About 7,000 appear to have left for the U.S.A. in, for example, 1840, but 20,000 in 1846; more or less this level may have been maintained till 1860, despite the supposed prosperity of the Second Empire. In 1871–6 about 8,000 or 9,000 went each year to the U.S.A. (and 4–5,000 to Argentina); in 1888 the figure was 17,000, in 1889 27,000, in 1890 17,000. But the departures for the new world were probably considerably less frequent than emigration, permanent or temporary, to Europe, where the French presence was always more consciously felt, instead of being absorbed.[1] It has been estimated that between a third and a half of French emigration was to Europe. That to the colonies accounted for between one- and

[1] L. Chevalier, 'L'Émigration française au dix-neuvième siècle', *Études d'histoire moderne et contemporaine* (1947), 127–71.

two-fifths.[1] After the exodus to South America (highest in 1875–87), the colonies and Europe thus attracted the largest share of French emigrants.

The French often liked to make a virtue of the supposed fact that they seldom travelled abroad, but the stay-at-home Frenchman was something of a myth. The French were quite active travellers even in the nineteenth century. Already in 1864 a doctor writing a medical guide for travellers (and many such were published) declared that one of the most noticeable characteristics of the century and indeed one of its 'most intense and active passions' was the desire to travel.[2] It is true there were also moralists, and particularly clergymen, who considered this a dangerous development. The timid abbé Hulot—who was worried by every new or old amusement, from dancing to novel-reading—published little books to urge people to stay at home, rather than face the hazards of corruption in public carriages full of strangers: and if you absolutely had to travel, he advised, pretend to be asleep, so as to avoid conversation.[3] As late as 1878 a travel guide urged men who ventured on trains alone to arm themselves with a revolver or cane.[4] Some young women long continued to express terror at the idea of travelling by train as they later feared aeroplanes; some doctors claimed to share these fears, for they reassured their patients that travel was not dangerous provided it was endured under medical supervision. Commercial travellers had special diets composed for them because of the troubles their constant movement produced. But, though dangerous, travel was also highly valued as a cure for many diseases. A doctor writing in 1864 described it as 'a fashionable remedy', and there was indeed a whole science behind the different prescriptions of it which could be issued. Climate, it was agreed, had direct influence on temperament and a change of climate could therefore modify temperament. Italy was thus recommended for the cure of 'moral diseases, profound sorrows, hallucinations and monomania', though it

[1] 27% (1851–60), 19% (1861–90), 30% (1891–1900), 13% (1901–20), 35·6% (1921–30), 43% (1931–5).

[2] Dr. Émile Decaisne, *Guide médical et hygiénique du voyageur* (1864), iii, vii.

[3] Abbé Hulot, *Instructions sur la danse* (1821), *Instructions sur les spectacles* (1823), *Instructions sur les mauvaises chansons* (1824), *Instructions sur les romans* (1825), *Instructions sur l'abstinence* (1830).

[4] Eugène Chapus, *Voyageur, prenez garde à vous* [1878], 51.

would not help nervousness. Obesity could be cured by travel,
in the case of lymphatics, though those of sanguine temperament were made worse by it. 'Thin women with disordered
imaginations, unbridled passions, jealous characters and worried dispositions', and indeed the vast number of people of both
sexes who plagued doctors with complaints about nervousness
and headaches—'nothing is more common than the complaint
J'ai mal aux nerfs'—were recommended to travel, because medicine could find no other cure.[1]

Travel for one's health did not necessarily mean travel
abroad. Very often it meant going to a watering-place. The
fashion for this was one of the major reasons that kept the
French in their own country, and brought foreigners to France.
Interest in mineral waters for medical purposes was of course
very old, and a French author who produced a work on them
in 1785 was able to list no less than 1,140 titles in his bibliography. At that date, Parisians could take the waters at Passy
and a whole host of little resorts in what are now the suburbs;
Plombières was then beginning to rival Baden, offering, it was
said, much better food at half the price. Voltaire and Saint-
Simon went to Forges, the rising rival to Bagnères-de-Bigorre
which was the most fashionable French resort of the eighteenth
century, with thirty-two different springs and over 10,000
visitors a year. But it was during the Second Empire that taking
the waters became a widespread middle-class recreation and
also the subject of a new and vigorous medical science. In 1853
Dr. Isadore Guitard founded the Société de Médecine du Midi
appliquée à l'Hydrologie, and in the same year the Société
d'Hydrologie médicale de Paris was established, producing
learned annual publications. In 1858 the bi-monthly *Gazette des
eaux*, which in the next century was renamed the *Presse thermale
et climatique*, started a flood of periodicals devoted exclusively to
this subject. By 1871 it was such a busy industry that a Mineral
Waters Agency was set up in Paris, publishing the *Conseiller des
villes d'eaux*. In 1886 the first international congress of hydrology
was held at Biarritz, to be followed by about a dozen more. In
1887 'hydrological caravans' were started by Dr. Carron de la
Carrière (and long continued by such eminent doctors as

[1] J. F. Dancel, *De l'influence des voyages sur l'homme et sur ses maladies. Ouvrage
spécialement destiné aux gens du monde* (1846), viii, 186–7, 482.

Landouzy and Laignel-Lavastine), by which interested doctors travelled around the resorts examining their merits. In 1891 the first chair of medical hydrology was founded at Toulouse for Félix Garrigou (born 1835), one of the pioneers of 'hydrochemistry'; by 1928 all faculties of medicine had similar chairs; in 1933 the *agrégation* in hydrology was established. The speed at which taking the waters became popular may be seen from a few statistics. In 1822 about 30,000 people visited spas; in 1852 the figure was 93,000; in 1855 140,000. This sudden increase in a few years was related partly to the building of the railways and partly to the development of the spas on an ambitious commercial scale. Vichy, which had belonged to the state since Francis I, was now suddenly made one of the great attractions in the country by lavish building and by the opening-up of new springs. In the 1850s, second- and third-class bathing establishments were built there to draw a far wider clientele. Napoleon III transformed the town with splendid boulevards; he built himself a private chalet, to use during his repeated visits. Magnificent and huge hotels appeared, and innumerable doctors set up private clinics offering as many varieties of treatment. The municipality then acquired an energetic mayor in a pharmacist who specialised in embalming the corpses of foreigners who died in the town, for dispatch to their native countries; between them, the doctors, pharmacists and hoteliers formed a powerful lobby, which knew both how to advertise their services and how to obtain subsidies from the state. In 1903 the crowning glory of Vichy, a new first-class bathing house, replaced the old one which had itself been greatly admired. The number of visitors, which had been a mere 575 in 1833 and 2,543 in 1840, rose to around 20,000 in 1860 and perhaps 100,000 by 1890. The attraction of Vichy of course was not simply medical, or perhaps even predominantly so, for the great watering-places were beautiful towns, offering amusements and a social life which even Paris could barely rival. The basis of their prosperity was the decree of 24 June 1806 which forbade gambling houses in France but exempted those in wateringplaces, and gambling drew hordes of idle rich, and so hordes of mothers and daughters in search of husbands. The best resorts organised a wide variety of entertainments, excursions and concerts: one of the most successful *coups* carried out by Vichy was to entice Isaac Strauss from Aix in 1853 to conduct its symphony orchestra.

But the craze for taking the waters would not have been particularly important if it had affected only fashionable people, even though the number of those who aspired to be so was constantly rising. There were several hundred spas, each of which came to attract a different kind of clientele. It was not just that each claimed different medicinal virtues: an enormous literature poured forth analysing these, making elaborate recommendations about where to go, and what to do, for every kind of complaint. Sets of people got into the habit of meeting in a particular resort in the summer; fashions were established and then waned. Thus Cauterets, though an old established resort, had only a small clientele until in the latter years of the century it was 'discovered' as a place where people who were 'really ill' could go and be very well looked after. Then many actors and actresses, including Sarah Bernhardt, took to going there, since it claimed to cure throat troubles, and it attracted as many as 25,000 visitors a year. Eaux-Bonnes and Mont-Doré were frequented by actors and singers, and also many priests, for the cure of sore throats too. Saint-Sauveur specialised in aristocratic ladies with neuralgia, hysteria and hypochondria, and Plombières acquired a reputation for treating other female diseases. Luchon by contrast was a gay gambling place, which had the advantage, as had Aix-les-Bains also, that its public baccarat rooms were open to both sexes. Royat, owned by the chocolate manufacturer of that town, had not only two casinos but also an English church. And depending on one's taste, one could choose between the grape cure, the milk and whey cure, the earth cure (for gout, particularly good at Arcachon and Dax), or one could be massaged under a shower at Aix and then carried home in a basket, wrapped in a warmed blanket.

In 1882 France had no less than 1,102 mineral sources. Prices suited all pockets, and they remained relatively stable till 1914. Thus at Flourens, near Toulouse, board and lodging could be had at the hotels for 4 francs a day, eating at the 'best table', 3 francs at the 'second table' and 2 francs at the servants' table. One could spend a month at Cauterets for 65–70 francs, but many people, for whom even this was too much, brought their own food with them. Foreign guides suggested 10 francs a day as the minimum and foreigners were no doubt often charged much more. A lot depended on which doctor one chose. Increasingly, fashionable doctors set up practices in the fashionable resorts, and even famous Parisian ones opened clinics there for the season, because there were such enormous profits to be made.

The trade in bottled mineral waters rose constantly. It had already been big business in the eighteenth century, but in the nineteenth shops selling them issued catalogues listing as many as 300 different types, each with its own elaborate medical analysis. But in the 1890s, four-fifths of all the bottled water consumed in France came from Saint-Galmier: it cost only 30 centimes a bottle, whereas Vichy cost 70 centimes. The label on a bottle however meant little in itself: in 1908 an industrialist was found guilty of having taken three million litres of Paris tap water and selling it fraudulently as Vichy water.

Bottled mineral water continued to increase in popularity, and to become an important industry, but by the turn of the nineteenth century the visiting of watering-places had reached its peak and after 1914 they went into rapid decline. If they had been popularised by the railways—and they had been very good at getting special cheap excursion tickets from the railway companies—the bicycle and the motor car offered people a wider choice of recreation. The seaside and sports of all kinds provided alternative attractions. But the decisive factor in their downfall was that they failed to win a place in the social security system of the new welfare state. The law of 1893 did not include water cures among the free medical assistance it offered. Instead, a law of 1907 levied a 15 per cent tax on gambling in casinos, which yielded 6·8 million francs. The railway companies took to offering very cheap excursions to the seaside, but offered only minimal reductions for trips to watering-places, and in the case of the Est and PLM railways, no reductions at all. The rise of the Côte d'Azur has something to do with this. The final blow came after 1958 when the social security system, which had hitherto subsidised 75 per cent of patients at the watering-places, greatly reduced its grants. So, when figures were compared in 1965, France was shown to have only half a million people taking the waters in that year, representing only 1 per cent of its population. By contrast the Federal Republic of Germany had 2·2 per cent, Czechoslovakia 5 per cent and Hungary 6 per cent. It was not simply that the seaside and warm sun were now preferred: Italy had one million visitors to its watering-places. Foreigners almost ceased to come: their numbers fell from 500,000 in 1952 to 17,000 in 1970. In the latter year, 'thermalism' was an industry with a turnover of 750 to 1,000 million francs a year, which was still a little more than the cinema industry, but a little less than the jewellery industry. But the production and distribution of bottled water had reached a figure of 1,400 million francs a year.[1]

The French tourist industry developed along lines which were slightly different from those of its neighbours. There were few large hotels in France at the beginning of the period, and though an increasing number were built after 1860, they were long confined to a few tourist towns and were designed as much for foreigners as for Frenchmen. To stay in a hotel was still something of a luxury in 1900 and to a certain extent it remained so till the 1960s. In 1961 only 22 per cent of French holiday-makers in France stayed in hotels or boarding-houses; 12·5 per cent rented houses or rooms, but 45 per cent lodged with their families or friends; 10 per cent stayed in second homes owned by themselves, 10 per cent went camping. By contrast 45 per cent of British holiday-makers stayed at hotels and boarding-houses, 8 per cent in rented accommodation, 26 per cent were with family or friends, and 17 per cent camped. In 1967 France still had only 13,000 approved hotels (giving only 350,000 rooms) and 50,000 unofficial hotels. But 950,000 people had second homes in the country or at the seaside. In Lille, 30 per cent of employers and members of the liberal professions had a second home and 3 per cent of the workers, but the poor were not always as underprivileged as this might suggest, for many had family homes (even if they did not own them) in their village

[1] E. H. Guitard, *Le Prestigieux Passé des eaux minérales. Histoire du thermalisme et de l'hydrologie des origines à 1950* (1951); Dr. Grelletty, *De l'importance sociale des villes d'eaux* (Mâcon, 1895); Marcel Craponne, *Les Neurasthéniques aux villes d'eaux* (1914); *Troisième Congrès des villes d'eaux, bains de mer et stations climatiques tenu à Paris du 11 au 14 décembre 1911, rapports et comptes rendus* (1912); François Delooz, *Le Thermalisme à Néris-les-Bains* (unpublished mémoire, Institut d'Études politiques, Paris, 1971); E. Decaisne and X. Gorecki, *Dictionnaire élémentaire de médecine* (1877); F. Engerand, *Les Amusements des villes d'eaux à travers les âges* (1936); M. L. Pailleron, *Les Buveurs d'eaux* (Grenoble, 1935); Thomas Linn, M.D., *The Health Resorts of Europe* (7th edition, 1899); A. Mallat and J. Cornillon, *Histoire des eaux minérales de Vichy* (Vichy, 1906); A. Mallat, *Histoire contemporaine de Vichy de 1789 à 1889* (Vichy, 1921).

of origin. Many of these second homes were let to holiday-makers. Money thus went into homes rather than into hotels. At La Baule, for example, in 1900 there were 2,300 hotel rooms but 7,000 villas. The point made by these figures is that there was a strong tendency to confine one's movement between the place where one lived and the province from which one came; and to save up to buy a house to which one could retire. This basic travel was supplemented by relatively short trips to the seaside or other resorts, and by the occasional pilgrimage. In 1867 the railway network reached Lourdes; by 1872 100,000 pilgrims were visiting it and in the jubilee year of 1908 no less than 300,000 pilgrims were counted. The Touring Club de France, founded in 1890, had 20,000 members in 1895 and 100,000 members by 1905, so that there was quite a large minority keen on travelling from the beginning of the twentieth century. It is true the club's publications warned members that prices were high in England, that 'the food does not always suit stomachs accustomed to French cuisine' and that hotel accommodation in many countries was primitive; and there were also organisations set up in the 1900s to urge Frenchmen to spend their honeymoons in France rather than be charged fancy prices in Switzerland.[1] It is true also that it was easier to travel in France than abroad because the foreign holiday with all accommodation arranged in advance was almost unknown, while on the contrary there were innumerable reduced-price tickets offered by the French railway companies. There was nothing to compare with the low-cost tours organised for Englishmen by Thomas Cook, who in 1867 was able to offer four days in Paris for only £1·80, and who in that year transported over 12,000 Englishmen to the Paris exhibition, lodging half of them in special accommodation he had built in Passy.[2] The French

---

[1] Touring Club de France, *Annuaire des pays étrangers* (1912), 1. 25; *Le Compagnon de voyage*, published by the Société Anonyme pour la propagation des voyages en France (1909). *L'Indicateur du tourisme*, published by the Office central des voyages et excursions (first issue 1910), encouraged travel in France by producing very good maps, with suggested routes and excursions. For an early example of a practical travel magazine, see *Revue des voyages* (started April 1852), for which Jacques Offenbach wrote the gossip column.

[2] Thirty-six shillings is the price quoted by W. Fraser Rae, *The Business of Travel* (1891), but Thomas Cook and Son, *Cook's Tours* (1875), *Cook's Guide to Paris* (1878), 101, give the normal 4-day tour to Paris as costing between £4·55 and £5·35.

preferred, or had, to make their own arrangements. Whereas
Thomas Cook advised his customers to save money by sharing
one meal between two—for good meals, he said, could be got
only at the top restaurants, the others being 'varied and showy
rather than wholesome'—the French seemed to have tried to
economise by renting very cheap accommodation in the country,
often of a primitive kind, and they usually did not go very far.

There was, moreover, no dramatic change in travelling habits
produced by longer holidays. The rich had long spent part of
the year on their country estates and part in town. The poor
went away when they were out of work. The idea of the 'holiday'
was slow to penetrate. In 1900 in the Paris department stores,
employees had a right to seven days of unpaid leave every seven
years, if they preferred to accumulate it this way, rather than
have one day off a year. The working class won the right to paid
holidays in 1936, but they were too poor to take advantage of
this and the number of long-distance tickets sold in the years
following increased by only 10 per cent (it was the number of
weekend tickets which doubled). The idea of the holiday spread
slowly from the schools. Education had for long been seasonal
and irregular, particularly at the primary level. However, the
secondary schools, which were more serious, had tried to limit
holidays to the very minimum, because they believed in controlling the whole life of their pupils; they provided recreation in
the form of military exercises. But in the course of the nineteenth
century, a reaction set in against 'overwork' in schools (*surmenage*). In 1834 school holidays were fixed at only six weeks a
year. In 1894 they were increased to eight weeks. They were
put up to two and a half months in secondary schools in 1912
and in other schools in 1935. The notion of the 'holiday' can
perhaps be dated to around 1900. In 1912 an article on this
subject said that fifty years ago, to take a holiday was very odd,
but now not to take one was odd. (This of course referred to the
bourgeoisie.) But it took another half century for new habits to
develop in regard to what one did on holiday. In 1961 still
14 per cent of holidays were taken abroad; in 1966 18 per cent.
These years mark the beginning of the democratisation of
foreign travel.[1]

[1] Françoise Cribier, *La Grande Migration d'été des citadins en France* (1969); Henri
Boiraud, *Contribution à l'étude historique des congés et des vacances scolaires en France du*

However, the statistics of railway travel show France lagging far behind England.[1]

Railway Passengers (in millions)

	France	England
1870		336
1880		603
1884	211	
1890		817
1894	336	
1900	443	1,142
1913	547	1,549
1924	796	1,746
1933		1,575
1935	585	
1937		1,819

The number of people able or anxious to travel in the first and second class in France fell very significantly after 1900; the increase in third-class passengers, though continuous, was not large enough to raise France, in the 1930s, even to the level of England in 1890.

Travel by classes (million passengers)

	First Class	Second Class	Third Class
1884	16	71	124
1894	20	106	210
1900	22	148	271
1910	22	109	378
1935	11	83	490

Nor did France compensate by writing more letters. In the 1880s, Englishmen were posting almost exactly twice as many letters as Frenchmen and four times as many postcards. English

Moyen Âge à 1914 (1971); Victor Parant, *Le Problème du tourisme populaire* (1939); Albert Dauzat, *Pour qu'on voyage. Essai sur l'état de bien voyager* (1911).

[1] Based on *Statistiques des chemins de fer français* (to be found, incomplete, in the offices of the Ministry of Transport, Paris). English figures from H. J. Dyos and D. H. Alcroft, *British Transport* (Leicester, 1969), 148, and P. S. Bagwell, *The Transport Revolution* (1974), 253: English figures to 1912 exclude season ticket holders. A comparison made in 1905, of 'kilometre-travellers per inhabitant' showed 250 as the average for Europe, 539 as the figure for England, 477 for Switzerland, 427 for Germany and 370 for France. É. Levasseur, *Histoire du commerce en France* (1912), 2. 689 n.

figures are not statistically comparable in the 1920s, but German ones are and they show the Germans exchanging twice as many letters as the French and fifteen times more postcards (1927). But for letters sent abroad, France was, interestingly, less far behind:[1]

Number of letters sent per inhabitant

	1882	1892
France	16	16
England	40	51
Germany	17	24
Switzerland	25	29
Italy	7	6
Spain	5	5

Letters sent abroad (1927) in millions

	France	Germany	England	Italy	Japan	Russia
Letters	122	152	174	51	69	12
Postcards	14	55	6	10	48	2
Printed papers	81	109	131	14	36	1

France and England

The odd thing about the relations of France and England in this period is that at no stage was there a war between them. It was the first time they had spent a whole century at peace. The explanation is to be found partly in the growth of new circumstances in international relations, but partly simply in accident. For the animosity, rivalry and incomprehension between them was not extinguished, as will be seen. On several occasions they were on the very brink of war. The phrase Entente Cordiale was first coined in the early 1840s, in a reaction to the crisis of 1840, when Thiers had wanted to fight England over Egypt, but new sources of conflict quickly arose. The Entente Cordiale of 1904, again, was not the solemnisation of a friendship but the settlement of a few colonial disputes, at a time when the two countries were almost ready to fight each other, but felt they would rather

---

[1] *Statistique générale du service postal dans les pays de l'Union postale universelle*, publiée par le bureau international des postes (1882, 1890, 1927).

settle with other enemies first. They quarrelled vigorously even
as joint victors at the end of the 1914–18 war, and in 1940, when
France signed the armistice with Germany, the entente cordiale
reached its lowest ebb. Though General de Gaulle revived it,
there was no love lost between the governments of the two
countries, even when they were supposedly allies. However,
there were two main reasons why animosity never went further
than words in this century. First, the rise of Germany altered
the balance of power so drastically that both England and
France were equally menaced by it and had to co-operate to
keep it in check. Secondly, there grew up, from around 1815,
a notion that England and France represented liberalism in a
world threatened by the despotic governments of Russia, Austria
and Prussia, and that there was therefore an ideological cause
in which they were, more or less, brothers. This was a rather
woolly notion, because Napoleon III could hardly qualify as a
liberal monarch in English eyes, and yet England was willing to
have his help in the Crimean War. The liberal–autocratic divide
in Europe was a little like the Catholic–Protestant, or Christian–
Muslim one of former times, which people used when it suited
them.

Nevertheless, this sense of possessing a common ideology did
have a basis in fact. In the eighteenth century France had discovered the English constitution and a fashion of Anglomania
was firmly established, to last, among a certain class, ever since.
In the fight against the absolute monarchy of the *ancien régime*,
England's parliamentary government was held up by people
like Voltaire, Montesquieu and Mounier as the ideal; and then
after the restoration in 1815, liberal royalists like Guizot and
even extreme ones like Polignac argued that France needed to
learn from England if it wished to enjoy the political stability
and freedom, which, they believed, flourished as nowhere else
on the other side of the Channel. Their political heirs continued
this tradition well into the 1870s. Charles de Rémusat declared
in 1865: 'I confess willingly that the dream of my life has been
the English system of government in French society.'[1] The
'republic of dukes' of 1871–9 was deeply impregnated by Anglophilism, as were also liberal Catholics of the school of Montalembert, Orleanists like Passy and Odilon Barrot, and liberal

[1] C. de Rémusat, *L'Angleterre au 18e siècle* (1865), I. 11.

economists like Leroy-Beaulieu and Michel Chevalier.[1] The snag about a lot of the Anglophilism, however, was that it involved admiration for aristocracy, in one form or another, and that was difficult to reconcile with democracy. Most of the admirers of England were not democrats. Guizot, who considered that fourteenth-century England provided a model for representative government, was careful to point out that he did not wish to copy nineteenth-century England, because by then the king had lost too much of his power to parliament, and Guizot was hostile to parliamentary rule, as he was to popular sovereignty. All these people agreed that what gave England its stability was its gentry, controlling local government with disinterested 'public spirit'. Many of them therefore suggested that France should try and replace its decayed nobility by a new class of local notables, who should be given considerable power in a reorganised, decentralised constitution. The appeal of this programme was inevitably limited to men who considered themselves to be notables. Even Guizot found it too much, for he said that England had achieved liberty, but not equality, and he laid much stress on that also, as he did on the rule of merit. So, though Anglophilism was bolstered by a whole philosophical apparatus, and by the raising of moralists like Reid and Dugald Stewart to the rank of major thinkers (with Cousin, who could recite whole works of theirs by heart, recommending them for study in schools), in the end England remained a model for only a small class of snobs.[2]

The English dandy became a model in France in the early nineteenth century. It became fashionable to wear English

---

[1] G. Bonno, *La Constitution anglaise devant l'opinion française de Montesquieu à Bonaparte* (1931); L. de Carné, *Du gouvernement représentatif en France et en Angleterre* (1841); D. Nisard, *Les Classes moyennes en Angleterre et la bourgeoisie en France* (1850); Paul Leroy-Beaulieu, *L'Administration locale en France et en Angleterre* (1872); C. de Franqueville, *Les Institutions politiques, judiciaires et administratives de l'Angleterre* (1863); Victor de Broglie, *Vues sur le gouvernement de la France* (2nd edition, 1872); O. Barrot, *De la centralisation* (1861); C. de Montalembert, *De l'avenir politique de l'Angleterre* (3rd edition, 1856); Michel Chevalier, 'La Constitution de l'Angleterre', *Revue des Deux Mondes* (1 Dec. 1867), 529–55.

[2] F. Guizot, *Histoire des origines du gouvernement représentatif en Europe* (1820–2, revised edition 1851), 2. 264; id., *Mélanges politiques et historiques* (1869), 47, 74–5; id., *Mémoires pour servir à l'histoire de mon temps* (1858–64), 1. 110–11, 171, 318–22; 5. 8; 8. 3–5; M. de Barante, *La Vie politique de M. Royer-Collard* (1863), 1. 215–19; 2. 232–3; Theodore Zeldin, 'English Ideals in French Politics', *Cambridge Historical Journal* (1959), 1. 40–58.

clothes, and a whole host of French garments began to be called spencers, jerseys, waterproofs, machintoshes, and macfarlanes. 'High life' now involved tying one's tie in a special way, holding one's cane and mounting a horse as, supposedly, the English did. French courtesy was disdained in favour of the frigid haughtiness of the English gentleman. Anglo-American taverns sprang up all over Paris. A new race of sportsmen appeared, copying first the aristocratic English pastimes of horse-racing and then pretty well every other English game (on which more below). The Jockey Club was founded in Paris in 1833. The jargon of the English turf was taken over, clubs and whist drives were organised. French children began to be dressed up in 'Queen Anne' clothes, based on the highly popular fashions set by Kate Greenaway.[1] The romantics introduced Shakespeare, Milton, Ossian, Byron and Walter Scott. The last had numerous imitators in French as well as being a best seller. Seven translations of Scott were published in the years 1830–5 alone. In 1832 there was already a Paris bookshop and lending library which claimed in its advertisements that it received 140 English newspapers and had 40,000 volumes, mainly in English. After 1848, Dickens succeeded Scott in popularity, but obscure women novelists like Miss M. S. Cummins and Mrs. Elizabeth Wetherell went through edition after edition during the Second Empire.[2] 'Humour' was added to wit in social intercourse. Strong spirits and beer became fashionable drinks.[3] The dates at which *franglais* words were first used in French provide an archaeology of the new mixed culture that was growing up: bifteck (1786), fashionable (1803), lunch, dandy (1820), corned beef (1826), pyjama (1837), high life (1845), baby (1850), shirting (1855), cocktail (1860), breakfast (1877), flirt (1879), five o'clock tea (1885), smoking (jacket) (1889), grill room (1893), lavatory (1902), shorts (1933).[4] By the end of the nineteenth century, there were Frenchmen who argued that, despite the pre-eminence of French culture, the English system of education,

---

[1] Ruth Hill Viguers, *The Kate Greenaway Treasury* (1968). Between 1878 and 1905 932,100 copies of her books were produced.

[2] M. G. Devonshire, *The English Novel in France 1830–70* (1929), 67, 327, 395.

[3] Georges Renard, 'L'Influence de l'Angleterre sur la France depuis 1830', *Nouvelle Revue* (1885), vol. 35. 673–715, vol. 36. 35–76.

[4] R. Leslie-Melville, 'English Words in French', *Notes and Queries* (28 Sept. 1940), 225–8, (5 Oct. 1940), 246–8.

which trained character, had much to be said for it and deserved to be imitated.[1]

Though it was regretfully concluded that England could not be copied politically, given the inalterably different conditions of France, nevertheless admiration for England continued in modified form, following a new approach to the question inaugurated by Hippolyte Taine. He more than any man created the image of England held by Frenchmen between 1870 and 1939. His *History of English Literature* (1863–9) claimed to be based on a scientific analysis which distilled the essential character of the English 'race', though in fact, and significantly, it was based almost entirely on book reading. Though he did visit England for six weeks, he did so only after he had worked out his theories, and he was happy to note that observation confirmed them. His theories were influential not only because they were 'scientific' but also because they were systematic and clear. It was a part of them that books were an excellent instrument for understanding a civilisation and 'almost always capable of replacing the actual physical sight of it'. (His pronunciation of English was so bad that when he ordered potatoes, he got buttered toast.) Politically, Taine admired English self-government, the justices of the peace, private philanthropy and the educational system—he claimed an Eton schoolboy knew more about politics than most French deputies. But though he admired the aristocracy, he contradictorily could not stomach the 'humiliating inequality' which went with it—to the extent even of disliking the distinction between nobles, commoners and scholars at Oxford, each wearing a different gown. Though an unbeliever, he loved the broad church of England and thought —without much hope—that France would be transformed by Protestantism of this kind. These institutional observations were however impractical and irrelevant, because his view was that there were distinct English and French characters, which naturally developed the institutions that suited them. He therefore tended to stress the differences between the two countries. He distilled their peculiarities into two distinct 'types'. The English type was incarnated in the gentleman. He had pride, but also tenacity, practical business sense and the ability to concentrate on his ambitions and achieve them. That is why

[1] É. Desmolins, *A quoi tient la supériorité des Anglo-Saxons?* (c. 1897).

England had become a great industrial and colonial power. It represented will power, but it lacked the capacity to form abstract ideas, to converse pleasantly and wittily, which was where Frenchmen excelled. This is not to say that he saw England as simply a nation of shopkeepers and squires. Far from it. England, he said, had the best poetry in Europe and its prose equalled that of France—though it was weak in criticism and in art. To admire English literature—as opposed to English ideals—thus became fashionable.[1]

Taine's theories were elaborated by Émile Boutmy, the first director of the Paris School of Political Sciences, which Taine helped to found, to remedy France's inferiority to Eton schoolboys, and which became one of the mainstays of this new kind of Anglophilism. Using the same positivist methods of analysis, Boutmy argued that the grey and misty climate of England encouraged vigorous action, morose thoughts and an ardent imagination feeding itself on internal reverie rather than observation. But the most interesting statements by Boutmy are the ones he makes, by way of contrast, about France, which show how the French sense of national identity was developing, or rather was consolidating itself in its traditional mould. In France, he said, the air is limpid, the light is brilliant and varied, so sensations are extremely distinct and infinitely diversified. The French therefore have clear ideas: 'these classify themselves automatically in the brain, which enjoys reviewing them, and expressing them in polysyllabic, joyous and sonorous words, pronounced slowly in a warm air which carries them back whole to the ear. Thought and speech are in France naturally analytical; both are at once a representation of reality and a source of enchantment; they absorb, like a theatre stage, the successive march, the ordered deployment of ideas and images; they become in some way part of the external world.' Words thus become objects. 'Enjoying himself amid so many varied and delicate impressions, the Frenchman only regretfully tears himself away to act, and he hastens to return to the animated spectacle that nature and his own intelligence provide him with at all times.' From this contemplation come the abstract ideas at which the French were said to be so good and the English so hopeless.

[1] F. C. Roe, *Taine et l'Angleterre* (1923); H. Taine, *Notes sur l'Angleterre* (1872).

The English have therefore failed to satisfy what is most basic in man, to dissipate the sadness with which their heavy clouded sky oppresses them. They have gross humour, but not delicate wit. They are more poetic than the Latins, more creative, but less artistic, because they have too much arbitrary freedom in the way they express themselves; they disdain clarity, harmony, plausibility, without which (to a Frenchman believing in classical rules, as Boutmy does) art is impossible. Thus he criticises the English novel for trying 'to portray life in all its infinite variety, in contrast to French novels which restricted themselves to studying two or three characters, around whom they arranged the other characters hierarchically, in a gradually diminishing order of importance'. Art for the Frenchman meant rules, ordered development, crisis and solution, because art was inspired by the desire for clarity, order, unity. Boutmy saw the French as trying to order the world in their ideas, loving to contemplate beauty, while the English were filled with a desire for action and efficiency, because they felt the need to master themselves: Protestantism was the religion of internal self-government. Thus, he said, English puritanism concealed a deep and violent sexuality. 'Anyone who has lived long in England knows the bestiality of the majority of the race. Sport, gambling and drunkenness are among the pleasures the English appreciate most. In sexual relations, they are interested in the direct satisfaction of the senses ... The Englishman goes straight to the object of his desires, instead of combining love-making with light entertainment and with the pleasures of conversation. The sensuality of the upper classes is concealed by a heavy hypocrisy . . . the lower classes can amuse themselves only grossly and violently.'

The result of this was, on the one hand, that English literature provided marvellous insights into the emotions, but, on the other hand, the English were able to show 'unequalled inhumanity' in dealing with colonial peoples. The English had not learnt how to enjoy themselves, because they did not know how to 'enjoy the superfluous, which gives charm to life, and which the French cultivated'. The English succeeded in business and industry because they were always direct, practical and concentrated on definite aims. By contrast, in France, action was the result of abstract ideas, which were complicated and involved many problems which needed discussion. So the French were likely to stop half-way and to move constantly from one novelty to another. 'That is why the French are revolutionaries, while the English do not go beyond eccentricity.' That, too, is why the English were the 'provincials of Europe', self-sufficient, suspicious of continental ideas, unaffected by what they saw abroad, and incapable of intermarrying with any other race. They were the most solitary and unsociable of people, the very opposite of the French, and, as Montesquieu said, 'The French cannot make friends in England'. The English were not naturally polite, as the French were: 'it is because the Englishman is not naturally a gentleman that England has a class of gentlemen'. Gentility represented the result of hard effort over many generations to overcome a natural boorishness: the masses realised how difficult it was to achieve and most did not aspire to so exalted a state. The French by contrast were 'poets and orators by birth', who were naturally graceful and who, with only a few months of acclimatisation, could modify their manners to make them equal to those of any class. That is why they were egalitarian.

The English got a lot of satisfaction from their work, even the most lowly of them, because of their passion for action, and that was another reason why the poor did not revolt, even though English employers were unequalled for their 'brutal insensitiveness'. The English had a 'slow intelligence' which 'rarely gave itself the time for profound deliberation'. Politics therefore was not about issues, but trials of strength, and since the English believed that will-power triumphed (rather than ideas) the aristocracy readily yielded. The masses willingly accepted the constant changes of their position, however contradictory, provided such changes did not appear to show weakness of will in the leaders. Rapid change was possible in England, because the rich were very rich and therefore able to take risks, and the poor, having nothing to lose, took risks too. The spirit of initiative was partly the result of the 'scandalously disproportionate distribution of property'. Boutmy concluded that though England was changing, it remained and would always remain individualist, incapable of feeling sympathy for others and not caring about whether it had the sympathy of others, very proud, contemptuous of other races and incapable of mixing with them, unable

to unite ideas into syntheses, preferring to follow a great states-
man rather than principles, having no revolutionary spirit but
many individual eccentrics. Boutmy's ingenious arguments thus
end up with admiration for England whittled down to virtues
which France is shown as being better without. Even this Anglophile concludes that the two countries are incompatible, and
that ultimately he prefers to be French.[1]

This conclusion is important, because it meant that the pro-
English party in France, aside from its superficial snobbery,
ultimately came to adopt many of the criticisms of the anti-
English, who were more numerous and had a longer tradition.
Even among conservatives, England was far from being universally accepted as a model. Joseph de Maistre had said in 1814:
'In philosophy, wisdom begins with contempt for English
ideas.'[2] Most conservatives abominated England's Protestantism, its Civil War, its empiricism: they insisted that a French
constitution should be based on French, not foreign, traditions,
and that truth came from God, not from Bacon or Locke. The
abbé de Genoude, one of the legitimists' leaders, was not even
impressed by England's prosperity, for, he said, it was based on
commerce, whereas that of France was founded on glory: 'In
England power and intelligence are very developed, but the
heart is arid . . . Cupidity is the universal motive. The question
everybody asks about a man is, How much is he worth? Even
the aristocracy has prostrated itself at the feet of the golden calf
. . . The arts are a nullity.'[3] This materialism was frequently
stressed, until it was transferred as an accusation against the
Americans: it is striking that the two countries were disapproved
of for the same reasons. The desire to make money, said the
journalist Alphonse Esquiros, whose descriptions of England
were widely read during the Second Empire, was not simply
universal in England, but particularly characteristic, because
men obtained not only comfort from it but also consideration.[4]
England's industrialisation aroused more repulsion than wonder: the quality of life had been ruined, and the destruction of
agriculture meant that England was far more vulnerable than

---

[1] Émile Boutmy, *Essai d'une psychologie politique du peuple anglais au 19ᵉ siècle* (1901);
cf. É. Levasseur, 'Boutmy et l'école', *Annales des sciences politiques* (1906), 141–79.

[2] F. Holdsworth, *Joseph de Maistre et l'Angleterre* (1935), 26.

[3] M. de Genoude, *Lettres sur l'Angleterre* (1842), 26.

[4] Alphonse Esquiros, *L'Angleterre et la vie anglaise* (5 vols., 1869), 4. 174.

a balanced country like France.[1] Léon Faucher, who wrote one of the most detailed descriptions of English society in the mid-nineteenth century, painted a horrific picture of poverty and crime in cities like Liverpool and Birmingham, and vigorously attacked the upper and middle classes for inhumanity and selfishness. Though he wrote generously in praise of English liberty, he argued that the French were generally misinformed about this and did not see the vices which accompanied it. Political liberty was balanced by severe moral intolerance, equality of rights by the most extreme economic inequalities. Love of money was supreme, and went hand in hand with a deep religiosity, but there was no real stability or unity as a result, as outsiders imagined. The inequalities of wealth were driving the poor to emigration, but agitation among them was increasing. So, though the aristocracy was omnipotent, it was unable to sleep in peace. Faucher's remarkable criticism was reproduced in many other attacks on the dangers of following England's course. An early decadence was predicted for England.[2] Edgar Quinet declared that though he breathed more freely in England, he would not advise emigration to it. To crown all its political and economic faults, England was boring: it was the home of spleen. Even the poorest Corsican was happier than the worker of Birmingham. The slave-like conditions in the factories, the endless hard labour, represented France's revenge for Waterloo. If Merry England ever existed, it must have been a very long time ago.[3]

All these old views and prejudices survived into the twentieth century and indeed to 1939. Complaints that Taine's views were out of date had little effect.[4] The translation of Bernard Shaw, who was not only popular but even adopted as a set book in the official school syllabuses, showed that wit, paradox, play with ideas and advanced socialist doctrine could all come from this supposedly decadent country, but the result was only to raise

[1] Boucher de Perthes, De la suprématie de l'Angleterre et de sa durée (1862), 19, predicted that Australia would replace England as leader of the empire; id., Voyage en Angleterre, Écosse et Irlande en 1860 (1868), 66.

[2] Léon Faucher, Études sur l'Angleterre (1843–4, 2nd edition, expanded, 1856); A. A. Ledru-Rollin, De la décadence de l'Angleterre (1850).

[3] Pierre Reboul, Le Mythe anglais dans la littérature française sous la restauration (Lille, 1962) is an excellent guide, unfortunately for only a limited period.

[4] P. Mantoux, A Travers l'Angleterre contemporaine (1909).

still further the prestige of English literature rather than the image of the English people. By 1914, indeed, knowledge of English literature was regarded as essential to anyone claiming to be cultured. Gide, Proust and Claudel were among the leading writers who published translations from English. But the idea the French had of England's way of life remained almost static. It is true that there were a few historians—notably Élie Halévy and Paul Mantoux—who made important contributions to understanding English society and a few minor authors who observed England with accuracy. Pierre Hamp, for example, who worked as a cook at the Savoy Hotel under Escoffier, and Louis Hémon, who sold electric lamps in England (1903–11), produced vivid descriptions of working-class life. However, the authors who were regarded as the main experts on England were interested much more in the aristocracy, Oxford and that old-world England which was blown up into an ideal all the more as it ceased to have any basis in the new democratic age. France thus had pumped into it a fairy-land dream of England which could have little relevance in the inter-war years. Paul Bourget wrote some of his novels in the Randolph Hotel, Oxford, but his first visit to England was in 1880, his last in 1897, and yet his novels long continued to be accepted as though they were about real life. Abel Hermant was another popular novelist, who again loved Oxford, though he also penetrated as far as Newcastle where one of his stories takes place. The most successful Anglophile novelist of all was André Maurois, who fell in love with England during the war when he was a liaison officer with the British troops in France, and who then visited England regularly; but his most famous books were about the old Victorian England, about elegant and proper officers with their good-humoured batmen, and though he knew about it, he seldom referred to unemployment or slums. There were many minor novelists who wrote about England as though it was an island of poetry, aesthetes and athletes, beautiful young men and no women: in Paris, Oscar Wilde was its representative, and when English females did appear in French novels, they were usually simply governesses, the 'miss'. This kind of England enabled Frenchmen steeped in the classics to reconstruct a sort of mirage of ancient Greece. Behind the pastoral calm, many authors also found a fascinating but un-French eroticism:

even Maurois's Dr. O'Grady confesses: 'Englishmen are more bashful because their desires are more violent. One finds even in the most austere of them, crises of sadism which astound one, considering how carefully their souls are cleaned.' *Mœurs oxfordiennes* became synonymous with homosexuality. *Lady Chatterley's Lover*, for the translation of which André Maurois wrote a preface, served to bring out from under Victorian England the bestiality Frenchmen had always claimed existed beneath the surface; and it was more mysterious than attractive, because, as Gide said, 'the more their ideas become emancipated, the more they stick to their morals, to the point that no one is more puritan than some English free-thinkers'. François Mauriac wrote: 'I do not understand and I do not like the English, except when they are dead and a thousand commentators, a thousand published letters, intimate diaries, information supplied by Maurois and good translations finally convince me that they are not Martians but brothers.'[1]

The inter-war writers on England were largely second rank. The most admired French authors drew no inspiration from English life, even if, like Gide, they read a lot of English literature; they were more interested in Russia and the East. The impressions of those who did visit England were superficial: Maurras went only to look at the Parthenon (Elgin) marbles: Jules Romains noticed only the 'chic' of London. The cult of the English gentleman was losing its appeal in a world preoccupied with Marxism, conscious of the decay of imperialism and the strains of capitalism. French books hostile to England were far more numerous than the favourable ones. The treatment of the Irish and the Indians was denounced as proof of English inhumanity and hypocrisy: Pierre Benoit and Henri Béraud wrote best-selling attacks on England, the latter declaring, 'I hate this people, as much from instinct as by tradition'.[2] What is most striking is that, despite the fact that so much was written by Frenchmen about England, they remained profoundly ignorant of how life was changing in it and of how complex its problems and aspirations were. The few carefully documented studies of contemporary conditions—and there were some very perspicacious ones—were little read and made far less impression than

[1] F. Mauriac, *Journal* (1937), 2. 16.
[2] Henri Béraud, *Faut-il réduire l'Angleterre en esclavage?* (1935), 19.

the old stereotypes, reproduced from Bourget to Maurois. One
of the most popular of English novelists in France was Charles
Morgan, because he wrote of the only England the French
wanted to hear about, with its country-houses, its humour and
its vicarage tea-parties. The English for their part translated
Maurois's *Silences of Colonel Bramble*, but they paid no attention
to Pierre Benoit's *Châtelaine du Liban* (1924), a violent attack on
them which had far larger sales.

There was thus a rather curious situation in 1939. English
literature was better known in France than it had ever been
before, and greatly admired, but the French as a whole thought
of England as Victorian, out of date, with nothing new to say
about the urgent problems of the world. All the ancient animosities, far from dying, were sharpened by the numerous conflicts
between the two governments. One can understand therefore
why, during the 1939–45 war, Vichy's hostile attitude to England was possible and popular to such an extent that de Gaulle,
even while benefiting from English aid, kept up a very reserved
attitude towards his ally. In July 1940, it has been said, 90 per
cent of Frenchmen hated the English. The navy, which had
considerable influence under Vichy, was anti-English by tradition and had more recent scores to settle. Many thus felt that
England had abandoned and betrayed France, in the old per-
fidious style. The Resistance was far from being entirely pro-
English: careful archival study has revealed how much variation
there was on a regional basis, the west and north-east being most
favourable to England, while parts of the south-west remained
hostile. The Resistance movement itself, carrying out an inquiry
in November 1943 in the Saint-Étienne region, found that only
40 per cent were pro-English, 30–35 per cent opportunistic and
25–30 per cent anti-English. Young people in general everywhere and in all classes seem to have been more favourable to
England. Perhaps half of the petty bourgeoisie were indifferent
as to whether England or Germany should win the war; but
they were most hostile of all to Russia. Feelings towards the
different powers changed a lot in the course of the war, so no
simple generalisation is possible, except that, for the majority,
to be pro-English meant above all to be anti-German. The
memories of old colonial rivalries were still powerful. The quip
in the manifesto of 8 March 1942 signed by well-known writers

rang true to many: 'Great Britain . . . the country of millionaires and the dole . . . always shows the most profound contempt for the colonial peoples it conquered, remains faithful to its view that the niggers begin at Calais.' Ideologically, the U.S.A. seemed the more dynamic ideal of democracy, and those who thought otherwise turned to Russia rather than to England. But at one time or another probably most people hoped for an English victory and to that extent there was a collective feeling in favour of England. The ambivalence of this conclusion summarises the attraction, the animosity and the mystery inspired by France's ally and oldest enemy.[1]

France and Germany

France's involvement with Germany was much more intense, more important to France, more complicated. It manifested itself in a love–hate relationship which continually tormented and frustrated Frenchmen. If France was married to any country, it was to Germany. The three wars they fought in this period did not end their fascination with each other. The French interest in England was, by comparison, not much more than a flirtation or an affair. When France became really interested in Anglo-Saxon civilisation, it was the U.S.A. that attracted its attention, in a way much more profound than England did. But Franco-German relations reveal best of all the complexity of France's position in Europe. This is a particularly striking case, in which the study of these relations in purely diplomatic terms gives a positively misleading picture of what went on in the minds of people outside the political arena. Germany was the land of Kant, Goethe, Wagner, Marx and Nietzsche to more people than that it was that of Bismarck and Hitler.

France's interest in Germany was from the beginning passionate. It was kept alive by a constant sense of discovery, and a

[1] Marius-François Guyard, *La Grande Bretagne dans le roman français 1914–40* (1954), one of the best works in comparative literature; Manuela Semidei, 'La Grande Bretagne dans l'opinion française pendant les années de guerre 1940–4' (typescript doctoral thesis in the Paris School of Political Sciences library, 1960), based on much original material; Pierre Bourdon, *Perplexités et grandeur de l'Angleterre* (1945); Pierre de Coulevain, *L'Île inconnue* (1906); F. Delattre, *Dickens et la France* (1927); G. Tabouis, *Albion perfide ou loyale* (1938); A. Siegfried, *L'Angleterre d'aujourd'hui* (1924); id., *La Crise britannique au 20ᵉ siècle* (1931); P. Morand, *Londres* (1933); F. Crouzet, *Revue historique* (July–Sept. 1975), 105–34.

sense that these discoveries were immediately relevant and important. Little was known of Germany, and little interest shown, until Madame de Staël suddenly found in Germany the land of liberty, in contrast with France oppressed by the despotism of Napoleon, who promptly banned her book, *De l'Allemagne* (1810). What was particularly attractive to her, and others after her, was that Germany accorded an unusually large role to writers and philosophers, since politically the country was still dismembered and of the second rank. Madame de Staël—who in fact saw very little of Germany and could not speak the language—proclaimed that here at last was a country where men's minds were free, where 'there was no fixed taste on anything, where everything is independence and individuality'. Almost every peasant was musical; the humbler villages had people who loved literature and philosophy: 'they argue in the domain of intellectual speculation, and they leave the realities of life to the great of this earth'. They were primitive, spontaneous, emotional, sociable. Whereas the proud Englishman considered his dignity and the vain Frenchman wondered what others would think, the German gave himself up to reverie and to science. Germany was seized on as the country which would liberate France, from classicism in literature, from materialism in philosophy, and in general revivify it with the qualities that it lacked. The irony of it was that the Germany the French discovered had largely ceased to exist just when they began praising it, so that to a considerable extent the Germany they admired was their own creation. On the theoretical plane, that did not matter, because the influx of ideas proved immensely stimulating, but in practical terms it repeatedly presented French intellectuals with terrifying situations, in which the object of their interest behaved in a way totally different from what they expected. These sudden revelations of unsuspected reality created moral crises as profound as the discoveries they repudiated.

In 1826 Victor Cousin wrote to Hegel: 'Hegel, tell me the truth. I shall pass on to my country as much as it can understand.' Hegel said derisively: 'M. Cousin has taken a few fish from me, but he has well and truly drowned them in his sauce.' Despite all rebuffs, French fascination with German philosophy continued throughout this period. Kant, whom Cousin proclaimed to be one of the origins of the French Revolution, became one of the tutelary dignitaries of French thinking, not merely because he was a set book in the schools, but because he was a decisive influence on most philosophers, from Renouvier onwards, so that he held second place only to Descartes. Marx, Hegel and Nietzsche were a major source of inspiration, particularly between the two world wars; Freud, though long resisted—as is shown in another chapter—finally invaded France after 1945. It is barely possible to disentangle the German contribution to French philosophy—in the widest sense of that word—because it is so universally pervasive. It was much more important than that of England—whose presence was felt more in literature—because it penetrated to the very roots of French attitudes. The philosophical marriage was so close indeed that some French writers, from the 1930s, even lost their taste for clarity, and tortuous obscurity became fashionable—and remains so—in some circles. When the French tired of one German influence, they replaced it by another German one, even though they sometimes disguised the fact. Thus around 1900 Nietzsche became the symbol of liberation from Kant, and people claimed that though he might be German by nationality, his education and his ideas were French.[1] Jaurès wrote his thesis on German socialism and while the republican politicians declared Germany to be the enemy, the socialists proclaimed them allies.

Just how deep this involvement with Germany went can be seen by the way even defeat at Germany's hands was unable to end it. It was to a considerable extent the French intellectuals who stopped France from obstructing the unification of Germany. Germany was seen as one of the pillars of the cosmopolitanism so fashionable in 1848. Traditionally French policy towards Germany had been to keep it disunited. Under the Second Empire, Thiers was one of the few politicians who still believed that this was the right attitude. He looked on Prussian ambitions simply in terms of power and military advantage. Edgar Quinet, once Cousin's pupil, translator of Herder (though significantly he translated it from the English translation), had once said that to study philosophy meant to study Germany, but he had with time become disillusioned and complained of the

[1] G. Bianquis, *Nietzsche en France* (1928).

'unanimous servility with which Frenchmen bow before German doctrines, without discussion or precision, to the point of completely exaggerating and distorting them'. He had spent longer in Germany than most of his colleagues, and had seen the identification of German philosophers with a narrow nationalism, which other Frenchmen did not want to notice, because it contradicted their view that the Germans were, as Flaubert said in his *Dictionary of Received Ideas*, a 'people of dreamers'. But Quinet's protests against 'Teutomania' and Heine's satire of it in his book *On Germany* (1835) completely failed to change the image Madame de Staël had created. Lamartine proclaimed: 'My policy is eminently German: it is the only one that suits this age dominated by the eastern question.' Russia was the great barbarian enemy, and, as Émile Ollivier said, 'the land of Mozart and Beethoven . . . democratic, liberal, cultivated', was France's natural ally against Russia, 'our rampart, our veritable avant-garde'. Michelet talked passionately of 'my Germany, the scientific power that alone has made me study questions deeply, and given me Kant, Beethoven and a new faith'. Victor Hugo wrote of it 'No nation is greater'. Renan declared, 'I studied Germany and I felt as though I was entering a temple; everything I have found there is pure, elevated, moral, beautiful and touching. Ah! How sweet and strong they are! . . . I considered that this advent of a new spirit is a fact analogous to the birth of Christianity.' German idealism had saved French philosophy from English empiricism, which reduced 'all to the miserable level of pleasure and utility'. The romantics saw Germany as rejuvenating the world. A *Revue germanique* was founded in 1857 to 'build a bridge across the Rhine', and many eminent writers contributed to it. The co-operation of the countries which had produced the two greatest movements in modern history, the Reformation and the Revolution, the union of their different talents, was seen as the herald of immense progress. The days of narrow nationalism were declared to be over.[1] Taine wrote in 1867: 'The Germans are the initiators and perhaps the masters of the modern spirit', and he wanted the French, who specialised in making ideas clear, to co-operate to spread it so that it became 'the universal spirit'. He had some doubts about how far this supremacy extended beyond science and

---

[1] Charles Dollfuss, *De l'esprit français et de l'esprit allemand* (1864).

philosophy: during a visit to Germany in the spring of 1870 he was dismayed by the regimentation, and declared that Germany was 'ready for slavery'. But it was considered illiberal to oppose German unification, which many in any case considered to be a necessary preliminary to the confederation of Europe. So it was only when France's 'honour' was slighted that Napoleon III declared war on Prussia.[1]

The defeat—on one level—shook the whole country profoundly. Revenge and the recovery of Alsace-Lorraine became a principal object of French policy for the next forty years. That Germany was France's enemy became the basic fact of international relations. The cosmopolitan, fraternal aspect of France received a crushing blow—though the socialists revived it—and a new strident, inward-looking nationalism developed, demanding rearmament if not war. The liberal illusion appeared to have been unmasked and a return to the chauvinist, power-conscious, egocentric traditions of the old monarchy was demanded. And in due course France fought Germany again and having defeated it, tried to dismember it, or at least to exact savage reparations from it—with a bitterness unequalled by any other belligerent. There is a vast amount of evidence on the animosity that estranged the two countries.

But—at another level—France recovered from its humiliation with astonishing speed, perhaps because it saw it as a justified humiliation at the hands of a country whose superiority in certain fields was manifest and inescapable. So, though French tourists kept away from Germany, co-operation between the two countries was not only resumed in practical terms, but vastly increased. Their economic and financial relations became closer and more extensive, at the same time as the two governments hurled insults at each other. The Paris Universal Exhibition of 1900 publicly revealed this. More Germans attended it than all other foreigners put together, far outnumbering the English and the Russians; and they were awarded nearly 2,000 prizes for their exhibits, their leadership in the electrical, chemical and optical industries being internationally acclaimed. The

[1] Michael Howard, *The Franco-Prussian War* (1961) for the war. For opinion before it, E. Quinet, *La France et l'Allemagne* (1867); L. A. Prévost-Paradol, *La France nouvelle* (1868); E. About, *La Prusse en 1860* (1860); A. Dumas, *La Terreur prussienne* (1867).

nationalist politicians issued cries of alarm about the penetration of German capital into France, but when one looks at this impartially, as an economic historian has recently done in an important thesis, one sees it as part of a co-operation which businessmen and investors found mutually advantageous. The French in fact invested about three times as much in Germany as the Germans did in France, because the investment opportunities were so attractive. In 1914, 445 million francs' worth of shares owned by Germans were sequestrated in France, while Frenchmen owned about 800 million francs' worth of German shares, plus 480 million francs' worth of Alsatian shares. French property in Germany—of all kinds—was worth 3,000 million. What raised the alarm was that the French policy of protection meant that subterfuges had to be found by the Germans to make trade easier. Between 1893 and 1913 French imports from Germany increased threefold and exports to Germany doubled. In the 1890s, a quarter of the beer consumed in France was produced in Germany; the bulk of textile dyes used in France came from Germany; the Lorraine metallurgical industry imported 39 per cent of its fuel from Germany (in 1891); Germany was France's main supplier of coke (whereas England supplied coal). In return, French exports to Germany were raw materials (one-third of the total) and agricultural produce (another third). Though in the statistics of around 1900, England appears still to buy more from France than from any other country, many German goods travelled to England through the Low Countries, so that in fact the figures were about equal. The economic rivalry between France and Germany was blown up out of proportion by the politicians, even though it was true that France lost ground to Germany in world trade. But the two countries were to a considerable extent active in different parts of the world. Thus French investments were predominantly European (see table). This uses official figures: investments in Germany were obviously higher; those in Spain are also estimated to be nearer 5,000 million; those in Egypt nearer 2,700 million. Germany had something like 2,500 million francs more invested in the U.S.A. than France had, and more also in Central America, especially Mexico. In South America, the two countries were roughly equal, notably in Argentina, but Germany had more in Chile and Venezuela, and France more in

Brazil and Colombia. In Africa, Germany concentrated on southern Africa, France on Egypt. The French interest in Turkey was older and therefore larger than Germany's. Germany tended to invest in industry, and outside Europe, while France bought up the state bonds particularly in Europe.

French investments abroad (1902)

French invest-ments in	Million francs	French invest-ments in	Million francs
Russia	6966	China	651
Spain	2974	Turkey in Asia	354
Austria–Hungary	2850	Russia in Asia	60
Turkey in Europe	1818	British Africa	1592
Italy	1430	Egypt	1436
England	1000	Tunis	512
Portugal	900	Argentina	923
Belgium	600	Brazil	696
Switzerland	455	U.S.A.	600
Romania	438	Mexico	300
Norway	290	Colombia	246
Greece	283	Chile	226
Serbia	201	Uruguay	219
Netherlands	200	Canada	138
Monaco	158	Venezuela	130
Denmark	131	Cuba	126
Sweden	123	Peru	107
Germany	85	Haiti	78
Luxembourg	62	Bolivia	70
Bulgaria	48	Central America	42

There was certainly industrial rivalry, as for example in Bulgaria, where Krupp and Schneider fought for military contracts, and in Morocco, where imports from Germany quadrupled between 1894 and 1898; but there was also a lot of financial co-operation between the banks. They collaborated, for example, in the Crédit Foncier Égyptien, apparently an eminently French bank, but in 1908 this had three German directors on its board. The Crédit Lyonnais was represented in Brazil by the German–Brazilian Bank; and here even Cail and Schneider got themselves represented by German firms. Though the Baghdad Railway was an instrument of German expansion, which produced bitter political rivalry, the Germans had French help in financing it: the hostility came from the French government, not the French banks. The German government

forbade the establishment of a German Chamber of Commerce
in Paris for political reasons, and in 1911 financial co-operation
was virtually halted. But in the preceding decade, the Germans
had been buying themselves into French industry, particularly
with a view to ensuring their supplies of iron ore from Normandy
and Lorraine, while the French steelmakers were buying a stake
in the German coalfields. The concessions bought by the Germans frightened public opinion, but not the industrialists, who
had plenty of iron and wanted coal in return. Germany was an
increasingly serious competitor in world trade, but that was
partly because the French were so notoriously inefficient as
salesmen. In many regions, French banks had helped Germany
expand, though after 1910 the Germans got the feeling that the
French were putting obstacles in their way. Till then, there
were strong pressures for an economic rapprochement between
them.[1]

In the same way, at the intellectual level, Germany continued
to be a source of inspiration, even though there was also widespread bewilderment and uncertainty as to how to deal with it.
There were always academics and writers who denounced the
Germans as brutal barbarians—men as distinguished as Fustel
de Coulanges and Émile Durkheim, both of whom owed a lot
to German thought, wrote violent polemics against the German
in war-time.[2] Instead of admitting that they had failed to study
Germany carefully enough, they castigated the Germans as
hypocrites. In some circles it became fashionable to condemn
Germans as barbarians. The generation which had preached
Franco-German friendship up to 1870 was terribly shaken.
Some took up the attitude that the defeat marked the end of
France as a leader in Europe. Taine had already written in
1867: 'Our role is finished, at least for the time being. The
future rests with Prussia, America and England.' French hegemony in Europe, as a result of which the principle of equality
had been introduced, was over, just as Italian hegemony had
ended in the sixteenth century. Taine now gave his life to

[1] Raymond Poidevin, *Les Relations économiques et financières entre la France et l'Allemagne de 1898 à 1914* (1969), a masterly study. For a description of German activity
in France, see Louis Bruneau, *L'Allemagne en France: enquêtes économiques* (1914).
[2] Fustel de Coulanges, *L'Alsace est-elle allemande ou française. Réponse à M. Momm-
sen* (1870); É. Durkheim, 'L'Allemagne au dessus de tout', *La Mentalité allemande
et la guerre* (1915).

studying French history so as to discover the reasons for this defeat, and he found it in what he considered to be the poisoning influence of French classicism and Jacobinism. France was at fault and his belief in German relativism, traditionalism, Protestantism and science thus remained undamaged. The effect of his *Origins of Contemporary France* was thus not to turn Frenchmen against Germany, but to urge them to move on the same conservative, indeed reactionary, path that Germany was following. The new French nationalism did not simply reflect hostility to Germany; in many cases it was also imitative of Germany, which was seen as leading a new, inexorably successful march in the direction of traditionalism. Renan likewise turned conservative, even monarchist, though he also became more critical of Germany, criticising even the values he had once praised, saying that Germany was 'heavy and obstinate'. Younger people did not even need to make Germany their scapegoat: they put the blame for the defeat on Napoleon III and condemned not Germany, but war itself. Many of them, after an initial revulsion against the victor, declared that it was the Second Empire, not France, that had been defeated, or alternatively that it was 'science' that had triumphed, and the answer lay in more education. Socialism, with its international ideals, was an alternative to nationalism, and many people thus revived the old cosmopolitanism of the romantics, in which German ideas kept pride of place alongside French ones. The notion that there were two Germanies was popular: the left admired liberal, intellectual anticlerical Germany, and regretted only that this was unfortunately balanced by the Hohenzollern, despotic Germany. The right admired its monarchist power, and regretted that it was materialist and Protestant. The school manuals did not become anti-German: most denounced war, they preached patriotism but within the context of humanitarianism, in the tradition of Kant.

Germany perhaps was no longer admired so blindly: the historian Seignobos in 1881 suggested that praise of German universities was exaggerated; Durkheim in 1887 was also, to a certain extent, critical of German philosophy; Lucien Herr declared that Germany was living on its past; but nevertheless the intellectuals continued to visit Germany, to write reports on it, and the prestige of its science, its education, its music and

its socialism survived. Even Barrès, who attacked French
schoolmasters for spreading the doctrines of Kant, got some of
his own ideas from Hartmann's *Philosophy of the Unconscious*,
which was translated into French in 1877, and he praised
Wagner in whom he thought he could find his own doctrine of
the Cult of the Ego. It is true that in course of time Barrès
became increasingly anti-German, but he never completely
abandoned the French tradition of universality. It was Maurras
who finally carried egoism to its ultimate conclusion and urged
the purging of all foreign influence from France. When in 1895 the
Mercure de France held an inquiry on Franco-German intellectual
relations, practically all the Frenchmen it questioned said they
were in favour of more contact and exchange of ideas. Another
inquiry in 1902–3 was considerably less enthusiastic: many
people were following the same path as Barrès. As the threat
of war grew, books and novels appeared in increasing numbers
saying that to be pacifist was to play into the hands of a
Germany which hated France; and even people like Péguy
joined those who demanded a victory over Germany, to put
right the insult to French supremacy.[1] But not all people
reacted in this way, for not all were worried in the same way
by the notion of France in fact (as opposed to ideally) being
inferior. As Germany's population, which had been equal to
that of France in 1870, reached 68 million in 1913, and as its
industrialisation was accentuated, some people saw Germany
as the herald of a new kind of civilisation, with urbanisation,
efficiency and a new kind of wealth, in direct contrast to the old
romantic, pastoral myth. And Romain Rolland spent twelve
years writing a long novel, *Jean-Christophe* (1904–12), studying
the question of Franco-German relations, with the conclusion
that both countries had faults and virtues. He wanted them to
combine to create something better than either; his hesitations
about the war, which he ultimately accepted as inevitable,
show how divided the French intellectuals were about patriotism. In 1869, when Sarcey was lecturing on Horace at the
Collège de France, he illustrated his argument about families
being separated by war, by asking his audience to imagine what
would happen if war should break out between France and

---

[1] e.g. Marcel Prévost, *Monsieur et Madame Moloch* (1906); André Lichtenberger,
Juste Lobel, Alsacien (1911); Agathon, *Les Jeunes Gens d'aujourd'hui* (1913).

Germany. The audience protested, and a man shouted, 'The supposition is impious . . . it is unpatriotic'. That attitude never quite died.[1]

During the 1914–18 war, and as a result of it, there was a widespread, deeply felt desire to solve the German problem by destroying Germany. War propaganda portrayed the 'Boches' as violent, inhuman barbarians. Clemenceau incarnated this total opposition to them. But it should not be forgotten that he had to lock up Caillaux, one of the country's leading politicians who enjoyed much support and who wanted an amicable settlement of differences between the two countries. It is striking that while France was trying to force the rest of Europe to take extreme measures against the Germans in the 1920s, the intellectuals once more took up their role as advocates of conciliation and spiritual union. There was a great increase of interest in German literature between the wars, with numerous translations in particular of the German romantics. In 1927 *La Revue d'Allemagne* was founded, supported by Jean Giraudoux, Lévy-Bruhl, Paul Langevin, Jules Romains, as well as Robert Curtius and Thomas Mann, to stimulate friendly discussion about the arts and literature. The years 1926–9 were notable for many congresses and meetings arranged between writers of the two countries. In 1929 the École Normale Supérieure petitioned for a united, disarmed Europe. The surrealists took their hate of French bourgeois culture to the point of shouting 'Down with France, Up with Germany'. Such attitudes were stimulated by the belief that sentimental, cultured Germany, discovered by Madame de Staël, and brutal Prussia, revealed by Bismarck, were neither of them the 'real' Germany. Rather it was argued that Germany had no unalterable character, but was malleable, educable, and that precisely was its charm and the source of its youth; whereas by contrast classical France was inescapably satisfied with itself and immobile. Giraudoux, who had studied German literature at the École Normale Supérieure, and who soon recovered his optimism about Germany after the war, particularly urged this view; in 1928 he staged a play, *Siegfried*, which advocated reconciliation and which was well received. He said the Germans

[1] Claude Digeon, *La Crise allemande de la pensée française 1870–1914* (1959) is the essential guide to this question, with a full bibliography.

were not warlike: 'it was the desire to travel that excited them all into war'. This showed just how full of energy they were; their own Kultur was a failure; but they had irreplaceable characteristics which Europe should value. Jacques Rivière likewise published his memoirs of his prisoner-of-war days without bitterness, arguing that Germans were neither poets nor barbarians but characterless people, unable to distinguish between truth and falsehood, between right and wrong; they were capable of making of themselves anything they pleased, by an act of will. They had no innate taste for war. So they should be used to create a new Europe, since co-operation with them was preferable to fighting them. It is not clear how far Rivière distinguished between romanticism, which he hated, and the Germans, whom he criticised as so confused that their Kultur simply represented an inability to think clearly: they thought of ideals as things to be realised, and therefore had only practical goals. Their domination would destroy the individual and the arts. He saw them not as barbarians but as a flabby, over-emotional people, who needed to be taken in hand. Rivière said in 1923: 'Germany continues to attract and repel me in equal measure.' He refused to reject all things German, or to make French interests the sole guide of policy. Peace could only be obtained by co-operation; Germany should therefore not be frustrated, but made into the industrial region of Europe. Even Barrès, who in 1919 was one of those who warned against forgiving the Germans, came to distinguish between good and bad Germans: he very conveniently produced the theory that the good ones lived mainly in the Rhineland, where they had the benefit of Latin influence, and which should now become France's buffer against bad Germany. His solution was therefore to take over part of Germany.

The 1930s showed how the French tended to look at Germany in ways which suited their ideology. Thus Alain, the philosopher of the individual against authority, wrote on 25 June 1933: 'I have not reacted much in face of the Hitler crisis. Distant events do not move me much. From my very youth, Germany has always been painted as . . . guilty of threats, ruses, lies and torture, given to singing and gorging itself with beer. I believed none of this, and I hope our rulers will free themselves of these phantoms. On the contrary, in every German I have seen, I have promptly recognised the man.' A lot of confusion followed, as people tried to decide whether Nazism should alter their attitude—a confusion which will be studied in another chapter. Left and right, it will be seen, reversed their positions: many pacifists now wanted war, many nationalists now talked of peace with Germany. The net result was that once again France was divided about its attitude to the Germans. But once again there were enough influential people, sufficiently certain of their attitude, to risk co-operating with them.[1]

The belief in France's intellectual superiority did not die. In the interwar period there was a lot of discussion of this matter. French and Germans wrote books about each other's civilisation, translated them and debated them. Both sides ended up with a feeling that their own was, ultimately, best. The Germans accused the French of being static, basically hostile to real innovation, deriving their ideas from Rome—whereas the Germans represented revolt and dynamism. To a considerable extent the French accepted this. The attacks on them made them rise in defence of what were considered their traditional attributes. They replied that their function had been to impose rules of taste, based on reason, upon the chaos of life; that they saw the need to reinvigorate their civilisation, but they were unwilling to make any drastic changes in it. Change, wrote even the future collaborationist Louis Reynaud, should always be carried out 'within the iron framework of certain forms which represent conquests of proved value, which are above argument, and outside which there is only chaos, individual arbitrariness, bad taste and barbarism'. He said Germany also had important qualities: 'a powerful and obscure understanding of the deeper needs of life', of instinct and emotion, and an ability, because their thought was so chaotic, occasionally to produce unexpected truths by putting things together which no one had joined before. They were capable of dealing with the indistinct, the uncertain, and the idea of development was one of their great discoveries; but they also had an unrivalled ability to collect facts, which they combined to produce great speculative edifices. In this way they had renewed European scholarship, and also triumphed as business-men and industrialists. France and Germany thus had different priorities but their views were not necessarily antagonistic. It could be claimed that they should complement each other, and that though they would always have difficulty in agree-ing, it was not impossible for them, meanwhile, to reconcile their immediate practical interests. But it was only when the grandiose ideas of absolute supremacy which both countries held, finally became too unreal after 1945 that they were able to do this.[1]

Paris still has no German restaurants (they call themselves Alsatian). In a poll held in 1966 the French still thought of the Germans as disciplined, proud, romantic, heavy and bellicose and of themselves as elegant, individualistic, logical, frivolous and vain. The Germans agreed about French elegance but not about French logic; German girls, however, while condemning wars, said they liked officers and uniforms. Twenty years of a new kind of propaganda had failed to alter the stereotypes.[2] But perhaps now these mattered much less, because the decisive criteria were no longer spiritual, but economic.

France and the U.S.A.

France was very conscious of America throughout these years. Diplomatic history perhaps inevitably sees France as a Euro-pean power and its relations with America as of secondary importance. But reflexion on the American experience, which was so different to that of France, caused many Frenchmen to redefine their own culture, to stress its originality and to defend it more self-consciously in the face of the power which by 1940 was clearly surpassing it in an increasing number of fields. The new attitudes which appeared in France in the 1950s, and made possible its rapid economic expansion and the unprecedented growth in its population, were, to a considerable extent, prepared by this reflexion.

[1] Louis Reynaud, *L'Âme allemande* (1933)—who was then a professor at the aculty of Lyon; Alexandre Arnoux, de l'Académie Goncourt, *Contacts allemands. Journal d'un demi siècle* (1950), an enlightening and honest personal history.

[2] Yvon Bourdet, *Préjugés français et préjugés allemands* (n.d., about 1967), 29, 38, 41.

Talk of the Americanisation of Europe began very early. Philarète Chasles in 1851 was already saying that 'American ideas are invading us'. The constitution of 1848 had brought the American political model to the highest degree of popularity it was ever to enjoy. But in 1855 Baudelaire, in a much wider context, referred to 'this century americanised by its zoocratic and industrial philosophers'. The fears were certainly premature. In 1850 France and England were still both ahead of the U.S.A. as commercial powers, though the latter's merchant fleet was already second only to England's. In the 1851 Universal Exhibition, England exhibited as much as all the other nations put together, and it won seventy-seven of the medals for outstanding originality, compared to fifty-six given to France and only five to the U.S.A. America was noted then, from the technical point of view, largely for its agricultural machines.[1] Though Singer invented the sewing machine in 1851, Bell the telephone in 1876 and Edison the electric lamp in 1891, the great industrial power was still England. It was only in 1887 that the U.S.A. produced more steel than England, 1890 that it produced more iron and 1899 more coal. By 1890 it had more steam horsepower than England. In 1901 for the first time England received an American loan. In 1891 the U.S.A. produced as much wheat as France and Russia combined. While England was the leading industrial nation, France maintained a very active intellectual resistance to industrialisation, though this did have many French admirers. But it was much more the U.S.A. that finally convinced France that it should abandon its protest and at least some of the values, which, paradoxically, the Americans had admired more than any other nation.

At the beginning of the nineteenth century the French still had rather elementary ideas about America. They relied on such books as those of the abbé Raynal (1770), Volney (1802) and Chateaubriand (1827), and argued about such questions as whether the American climate was conducive to civilisation or was bound to create degeneration. They read unflattering works by English writers such as Mrs. Trollope (1831) which the

---

[1] H. Koht, *The American Spirit in Europe. A Study of Transatlantic Influences* (Philadelphia, 1949); cf. Crane Brinton, *The Americans and the French* (Cambridge, Mass., 1968).

eminent philosopher Jouffroy took seriously enough to devote
three long articles to them in the *Revue des Deux Mondes*. French
emigrants had very little notion of America's size and some
imagined it to be no bigger than a French department. The
President of the Chamber of Deputies himself in 1834 described
Pennsylvania as a desert. Ostensibly respectable French guide-
books thought Boston was the capital of Virginia. But all this
was rapidly changed in the course of the July Monarchy and
the years following it. Between 1815 and 1852 between eight
and ten books on the U.S.A. appeared in France each year—
three to four hundred in all. Benjamin Franklin's *Way to
Wealth* was translated into French, went through fifty editions
by 1852 to become perhaps the most popular foreign book in
France, probably as widely read as La Fontaine and certainly
one of the most widely accepted guides to conduct, because it
was acceptable to all parties. Fenimore Cooper came to live in
Paris 1826–8 and 1830–3 and his highly successful novels gave
Frenchmen a concrete, even if misleading, picture of the new
world, to be complemented in due course by *Uncle Tom's Cabin*,
of which eleven different French translations were published in
ten months. Michel Chevalier spent two years in the U.S.A.
before writing his book on it (1834) which also appeared in the
Journal des Débats, so reaching a wide audience. Tocqueville's
Democracy in America (1825) made the U.S.A. immediately
relevant to anyone interested in France's post-revolutionary
development. Democrats made Washington one of France's
heroes, to counter the autocratic Napoleon. The American
constitution, which the republic of 1848 partly copied, might
well have exerted great influence if that republic had not
collapsed so catastrophically. Frenchmen quickly became
aware of America in economic relations because trade increased
rapidly, American cotton being exchanged for silk and wine
and also—for the French did not always disdain to adapt their
products—such things as wallpaper with special 'American'
scenes. The export of French paintings to America was already
active under Louis-Philippe and soon became important to
both 'academic' and 'modern' artists. In the course of these
years, therefore, the image of America in France changed
from being the land of the eighteenth-century noble savage
into one of a commercial power. But as it was studied more,

criticism increased and people began to see the two countries as representing opposing kinds of civilisation. There were some who praised Americans for their inventiveness, their enterprise and common sense, for incarnating the ideal of the self-made man who would also be a philanthropist. But it became rather more fashionable to caricature Americans as coarse, materialist bores, interested only in making money, narrowly puritan, incapable of conversing in a polished way. That is why the French identified rather with the southern states, which seemed to value aristocracy, leisure and pleasure more, though they disliked the way the southerners treated the Indians and Blacks and deplored the extravagance of their religious sects.[1]

The characteristic feature of America which struck the French most powerfully was perhaps its women. Tocqueville's book on Democracy was complemented by a novel, *Marie* (1835), by his friend Beaumont, and this was only one of a whole host of others discussing the strikingly different relations between the sexes across the Atlantic. The professor of comparative legislation at the Collège de France, Édouard Laboulaye, who had never visited the United States but who was regarded as France's greatest expert on it, likewise complemented his lectures on the American constitution by a novel, *Paris in America* (1862), which went through eight editions in its first year and had been reprinted thirty-five times by 1887.[2] Many other novels appeared in the 1860s which showed American girls in casual clothes and shorter skirts, never troubled by modesty and never lowering their eyes, not voluptuous but simply straightforward. Maurice Sand, in *Miss Mary* (1867), thought this placed an almost unbridgeable gulf between them and Frenchmen. Alfred Assollant, in *Un Quaker à Paris* (1866), depicted American women dominating over the males. Mario Uchard, in *Inès Parker* (1880), which was serialised in the *Revue des Deux Mondes*, claimed that the American principle was that every woman was sovereign, while the French held that every woman was prey. His conservative conclusion was that women needed to be protected by barriers because they were creatures of instinct, not of reason. But there

---

[1] There is an excellent survey of this early period by René Rémond, *Les États-Unis devant l'opinion français 1815–52* (2 vols., 1962).

[2] Laboulaye was also the translator of Channing.

were also others who spoke in favour of American girls, like the French consul in San Francisco, Paulin Neboyet, in *L'Américaine* (1875), who held them up as an ideal, because they were free of preciousness, prudery, superstition, feebleness or puritanism. Just how quickly the debate became active even outside the circles which read books may be seen from the 1852 vaudeville, *The Bloomerists or The Reform of the Skirts*, and from Sardou's highly successful play *Strong Women* (1860) which satirised 'Americomaniac' women with masculine ambitions. In his *The Benoiton Family* (1865), which had 300 consecutive performances, Sardou makes a French father forbid his two girls to go on a walk alone: they reply: 'Oh! What a French papa! Why not alone, like in America?' Sardou kept up his attack on this, saying 'This America I attack has invaded us so successfully that I am very fearful I shâll be defeated in the struggle I am undertaking'.[1] The arguments about this continued for a whole century, so the battle was by no means decisive. But when Simone de Beauvoir said she had identified herself with Jo, the intellectual in *Little Women*, she probably was speaking for many other girls whom the American example urged on the path of greater independence.

The American male was for a long time denigrated as being coarse and clumsy, above all inadequate as a lover, in which role the French imagined themselves to be supreme. Novels often portrayed him as a self-made millionaire, rapacious, exclusively practical, with a commercial attitude even towards religion. One novel, entitled *Miss Million* (1880), by Alphonse Brot, described the sordid squabbling of American oil magnates to produce as the hero a French engineer who eventually succeeds in building the pipe-line. Detective stories about New York started appearing as early as 1877 and the cowboys of the Far West became famous after 1889, following their personal appearance, complete with Indians, at the International Exhibition. Jules Verne was the first novelist to introduce Americans regularly into his works: in about twenty of his novels, Americans have important roles. Verne liked their ready enthusiasm for even the maddest and most dangerous schemes. He portrayed them as having a passion for action, and believing that anything was possible to achieve; but they also

[1] S. Jeune, *Les Types américains dans le roman et le théâtre français 1861–1917* (1963).

had sound common sense, and they relied not simply on human energy but also on technical progress. Verne, who appeared to be one of the great advocates of the indefinite improvement of the world by machines, was perhaps the novelist who was most sympathetic to the Americans, and his enormous sales throughout this period made his sympathy worth a lot. It is true he also admired the English, whom he considered to be equally determined, pursuing their aims with obstinacy and cold passion, but after the increase in Anglo-French colonial rivalry, the English sometimes began to appear a little as villains, too proud, and too certain of their superiority. But this did not mean Verne denigrated his own countrymen: he still praised their wit, intelligence, good humour, elegance, love of glory, and their contempt for material gain.

The opposition between French and American attitudes to life was skilfully analysed by the philosopher Émile Boutroux in 1912, during a series of lectures organised by the France–America Committee in Paris. France and America, he said, both started with the view that all men were equal; that, as Descartes said, common sense was the best shared thing in the world. But the French believed that man needed to be perfected by culture, and as Pascal had pointed out, though man had natural instincts for good, these were often repressed by blind impulses and disordered passions. Art was needed to impose rules and discipline on man, but art by itself was not enough, because it could too easily take itself as its own end and so become artificial. Perfect culture came from the union of art and nature, of mind and heart. But this again was not an aim in itself. The French had an ideal of man with certain qualities which could be developed only in social intercourse, 'that habitual meeting of a certain number of chosen people, where each one tries hard to think and speak in a manner that will win the approbation of all . . . to surpass himself in order to be heard, and where distinction, delicacy, ingeniousness, fine judgement and wit are imposed'. It is in surroundings of this kind, in effect the *salon*, that the French had created the ideal man. They expected from him first of all reason, which could apply all the faculties to understand anything, and this meant taste and sensibility as well as intelligence; secondly, the cult of 'simple and natural sentiments', notably love of the family and of humanity, so that he naturally sided with the weak; thirdly, generosity, devotion to disinterested ends, glory, the honour of France and the good of humanity. The French language had been developed in *salons* of this kind to give expression to the ideals that were valued in them: clarity, precision, elegance. Boutroux argued that the Americans shared the French concern for democracy, humanity, simplicity, cordiality; they had remarkable public spirit and generous philanthropists, who used their millions for cultural purposes. But he felt that they had not quite understood what the perfect man should be like. They sought each of his characteristics independently, they saw the ideal as a synthesis, whereas the French viewed it as a creation.[1]

This was a condescending conclusion, but it showed how far the Americans had risen in the esteem of the French by the First World War. The image of the brutal millionaire was rapidly displaced as the French became increasingly aware of America's cultural achievements, and got to know more of its distinguished people. Bourget, after visiting the U.S.A. for eight months, published a highly successful book on it, *Overseas* (1895), which praised it for reconciling Christianity, democracy and science. He declared that the American businessman was an 'intellectual force' as remarkable as any traditional hero, and that the prejudice of the *lettré* against him was unjustified. Jules Cambon, French ambassador in Washington 1897–1902, could not speak English, but his successor J. J. Jusserand (1902–20) knew it so well that he wrote his memoirs in English, to record the important work he had done to bring the two countries closer together.[2] In 1896, Gabriel Hanotaux, the minister for foreign affairs, had talked about the American menace to Europe, as had also quite a few others, urging European union as the answer;[3] but by 1913 he had changed his attitude completely. In 1895 a meeting was held in Paris, at the house of T. E. Evans, the famous American dentist, of American and French scholars, including the poet Mallarmé,

[1] E. Boutroux, *Les États-Unis et la France* (1914), 10–21.

[2] J. J. Jusserand, *What Me Befell* (1933).

[3] G. Hanotaux, 'Le Péril prochain: l'Europe et ses rivaux', *Revue des Deux Mondes* (1 Apr. 1896); Octave Noël, 'Le Péril américain', *Le Correspondant* (25 Mar. and 10 Apr. 1899); Augustin Leger, 'L'Américanisation du monde', ibid. (25 Apr. 1902); D'Estournelles de Constant, *Les États-Unis d'Amérique* (1913), with a preface by Hanotaux.

to discuss how cultural contacts could be improved. In 1897 the French established the *doctorat d'université*, to provide an equivalent to the Ph.D. In 1898 Harvard established a visiting lectureship to enable it to invite distinguished Frenchmen, using a benefaction from James H. Hyde (once owner of the Equitable Insurance Company), who had settled in France. Exchanges of scholars were arranged, and people as eminent as Émile Boutroux and Gustave Lanson went to lecture in the U.S.A. The interest in America at this time is revealed by the success of E.-M. de Vogüé's novel *The Master of the Sea* (1903) about the struggle between a Frenchman and an American, which went through twenty editions in three months, and was placed by the critic Faguet on the same level as *War and Peace* and *The Red and the Black*. The characters were apparently based on Colonel Marchand and Pierpont Morgan, and the thesis behind it taken from W. T. Stead's *The Americanisation of the World* (1901). Vogüé showed his millionaire as a Homeric hero, whose wealth in no way made him despicable; he seemed to be arguing that the American achievement was compatible with intelligence and generosity, and that economic progress benefited not just the rich but all men.[1] André Tardieu's *Notes on the U.S.A.* (1908) said that America was interesting for its industry but no less for its intellectual and moral life: America was not just a piano factory.[2]

France indeed began receiving numerous benefactions from American millionaires to preserve its cultural heritage: Edward Tuck made possible the restoration of Malmaison in 1911–12, Rockefeller bought Pasteur's house in Dôle and donated it to the town. French noblemen had for some time already been marrying American heiresses: a book published in 1898 listed no less than thirty-two such marriages as having taken place since 1875; and it should be added that there were also three prime ministers who married Americans: Clemenceau, Waddington and Ribot.[3] What was seen as even more significant was

[1] E.-M. de Vogüé, *Le Maître de la Mer* (1903); cf. Paul Adam, *Vues d'Amérique* (1906) and *Le Trust* (1910); Georges Ohnet, *Mariage américain* (1907); Henry Gréville, *Roi des milliards* (1907), all favourable.

[2] For a favourable view of American industry see E. Levasseur, *The American Workman* (Baltimore, 1900, based on a visit in 1893).

[3] F. E. Johanet, *Autour du monde millionnaire américain* (1898); L. de Norvins, *Les Milliardaires américains* (1900).

that Frenchwomen began marrying Americans. The Americans in Paris became numerous enough for the American Express to open its Paris office in 1895; the colony in France was large enough in 1905 to produce a directory.[1] Direct observation of America by French travellers was not inconsiderable, for between 1765 and 1932 no less than 1,583 books were published by such visitors.[2] The French could hardly take no notice of a country in which cultural appreciation has reached such a point that New York itself had become an important centre for the French theatre: in each of the years 1900, 1904 and 1907, thirteen new French plays were staged there, and in 1909 and 1910 no less than eighteen.[3] But Henry Van Dyke was right to say in 1910 that, despite all this, Americans still tended to look on France as the 'home of the Yellow Novel and the Everlasting Dance', while Frenchmen as a whole still thought of the United States as a country of 'skyscrapers and the almighty dollar'.

The study of America in French universities had got off to an early start. There was little room in the school syllabus for American history or literature, but already in 1840 the 'independence of the U.S.A.' was introduced as a subject in the *baccalauréat*; in 1843 the 'history of the United States from the beginning of colonisation to the death of Washington' was set as the examination subject in the history *agrégation*. In 1864 Washington Irving's *Sketch Book* became a set text for the *agrégation*; between 1884 and 1914 American subjects were set in the geographical examination for this degree eleven times, and ten times in history; in English there was one American book set almost every other year. Forty-three doctorates about America were awarded 1887–1918. This compares with nineteen theses on American literature—and eighty-two on Shakespeare—passed in Germany, 1898–1918. The number of people who had a thorough knowledge of American life was still insignificant, but already many courses had been set up on different aspects of it, and many English departments in universities had American sections: only Germany and Switzerland had anything to compare with

---

[1] Alden Hatch, *American Express* (New York, 1950).
[2] Frank Monaghan, *French Travellers in the U.S. 1765–1932* (New York, 1961).
[3] Hamilton Mason, *French Theatre in New York, a List of Plays, 1899–1939* (New York, 1940), 9. For American views of France see Elizabeth Brett White, *American Opinion of France, from Lafayette to Poincaré* (New York, 1927).

France's achievement, and in France American studies were probably better established as a normal part of the university curriculum. In 1917 France was the first European country to establish a specialised university post in American literature and civilisation; in 1922 Anglo-Saxon was dropped as a compulsory subject for a degree in English and a more detailed examination in American literature introduced. Between 1920 and 1934, 118 doctoral theses on American subjects were written. But in 1952, when the Sorbonne had 16,000 students, 1,400 of them were doing English and of these 650 tried for the American certificate. In 1954 only 10 per cent of teachers of English had been to the U.S.A. Despite the introduction of some American studies, the French educational system was still very traditional. The opportunities for reading about America, and indeed about foreign countries in general, remained distinctly limited. Thus the English department of Bordeaux University in 1954 had only 400 English books in its library and very few on America. Lille had about 900 American books, half of them donated by the U.S. Information Library. Perhaps the most influential discovery of America took place outside the classroom, with the advent of the American film and novelists like Faulkner, Dos Passos, Hemingway, Caldwell and Steinbeck.[1]

Though America enabled France to emerge victorious from the First World War, the political relations between them were not always friendly. Napoleon III had won a bad name for himself by interfering in Mexico and by supporting the South. In 1870 President Grant congratulated Prussia on its victory. After 1918 disillusionment set in rapidly, particularly because the French failed to pay their war debts. In 1940, the United States maintained relations with the Vichy government and was slow to accept de Gaulle.[2] So in the first half of the twentieth century, the French still had many causes for suspicion. There were Americanists who pointed out the virtues which were the counterpart of the faults the French complained about: thus when American children were said to have little respect for their parents, it was answered that they were also remarkable for their initiative; it was agreed they lacked

[1] Sigmund Skard, *American Studies in Europe. Their History and Organisation* (Philadelphia, 1958), 131–208.
[2] D. C. McKay, *The United States and France* (Cambridge, Mass., 1951).

intellectual discipline of the French kind, but then they were better informed about politics, economics and sociology than their French counterparts. American universities had weaknesses, but they did much more for society than the French ones, educating not just future teachers; Harvard was said to have a larger annual budget than the whole higher education system in France. Mass production did not necessarily produce shoddy goods. For all their supposed coarseness, the Americans published more books on religion than novels.[1] Paul Morand wrote in praise of the U.S.A. in 1930 in a way which showed that some Frenchmen at least were very conscious that Paris was no longer the centre of civilisation. 'I love New York', he said, 'because it is the largest city in the universe and because it is inhabited by the strongest people in the world, the only one which, since the war, has succeeded in organising itself, the only one which does not live off credit from its past, the only one, apart from Italy, which is not demolishing but on the contrary has been able to construct . . . Everyone adores victory.' It was a double-sided compliment, but he added that New York was now to young artists what Rome had been to Corot and Poussin. 'Only New York offers the superfluous, and the superfluous is father of the arts.' One could no longer understand the world unless one visited New York. He praised even the New York lunch.[2]

Others took up opposite positions. Robert Aron and André Dandieu attacked *The American Cancer* (1931); anarchists and socialists attacked American capitalism.[3] Above all, Georges Duhamel in 1930 produced one of the most all-embracing attacks on American civilisation ever made, in beautiful prose, which showed that the old conservative French bourgeois was still very much alive. He complained angrily of the insufferable bureaucracy of the U.S. immigration authorities; the obsession with calories; the canned music; the illiterate cinema—'I would not exchange one play by Molière, one picture by Rembrandt, or one fugue by Bach for the whole of this celluloid

---

[1] Charles Cestre, *Production industrielle et justice sociale en Amérique* (1921); id. *Les Américains* (1945); E. Servan-Schreiber, *L'Exemple américain* (1917).

[2] Paul Morand, *New York* (1930), 51, 257–81.

[3] R. Aron and A. Dandieu, *Le Cancer américain* (1931); L. F. Céline, *Le Voyage au bout de la nuit* (1932); V. Pozner, *États désunis* (1938). Cyrille Arnavon, *L'Américanisme et nous* (1958) is a useful history, by a professor of English studies at Lyon and Lille, who had also been a visiting professor at Harvard and Columbia.

production' which, because it required no effort from the audience, could not claim to be an art. He objected to controls on the drinking of alcohol—would they propose to control his love-making next? He found that their liberty was superficial, for they were slaves to hygiene, to puritanism, and to experts. The women had identically beautiful legs but laughed identically like Hollywood stars. The motor car was used as the 'revenge of the vain and the incapable'. Everybody was in a hurry; the countryside was being ruined. What artists there were fled the country. Omnipresent advertising was an insult to the public. Their idea of sport was a joke, since it culminated 'in twenty-five boys playing, watched by 40,000 immobile louts smoking and catching colds'. The U.S.A., he concluded, had not made a contribution to European civilisation, but represented deviance and a break from it. That was to him condemnation in itself.[1]

In 1953 a public opinion poll was held asking Frenchmen what they thought of America. To the question 'What foreign country do you like most?' 19 per cent answered Switzerland, 16 per cent answered the United States, 13 per cent the Benelux countries, 11 per cent Britain, 9 per cent the U.S.S.R., 9 per cent Italy and Spain. Thirty-nine per cent thought that the Americans were uncultured, but 43 per cent said they were not; 66 per cent thought they were interested only in money, but 22 per cent disagreed; 46 per cent thought they had bad taste, but 31 per cent did not. 38 per cent said they would use American methods if they were running a business or factory, 21 per cent said they would not, 41 per cent did not know. Only 2 per cent of those questioned had been to the United States—which must be an exaggeration; 56 per cent said they would like to visit it, but 22 per cent said they definitely did not want to. When asked what they liked about the United States, these rather striking replies were made:

Do you like	Very much	Quite	Not at all	No answer
Jazz	12	29	54	5
American films	6	38	43	13
Coca-cola	5	12	61	22
American cigarettes	23	33	36	8
American household appliances	52	21	9	18

[1] G. Duhamel, *Scènes de la vie future* (1930).

It is perhaps this last answer which is significant.[1] In the 1950s the other-wordly values of the intellectuals, heirs of the clergy, had ceased to hold unchallenged sway. The Americans knew how to make life more comfortable, and comfort was not necessarily incompatible with culture. Perhaps the new direction of French behaviour after 1950 came from the feeling that culture by itself had not produced the promised utopia and that the priorities should now be altered.

The contrast of Frenchman and foreigner was thus by no means one of direct opposition. The national identity was not an exclusive one. It may seem, however, that if one considers the matter at a humbler level, in the schools, for example, one will find a simplified and standardised version of it, which could win acceptance from the masses. This is an illusion. Education only looks as though it conveys a simple message if it is viewed superficially, or from the vantage point of the politicians who direct it. It is necessary to examine what the schools did in fact achieve in some detail, for their history reveals that the national message was understood and transmitted in different ways by the different levels in the educational system. The schools were indeed almost as much a divisive as a unifying force. They show that the French way of thinking—if that is what the schools ultimately sought to instil—had many varieties to it.

[1] *Réalités* (September 1953), no. 34 'America as the French see it'. Cf. the Harvard thesis of Charles W. Brooks and the Oxford thesis of Thomas A. Sancton.

4. Education and Hope

AMONG the labels by which one can, summarily but not too inaccurately, characterise this century, one undoubtedly is the Age of Education. It was in this period that Frenchmen were made universally literate; it was in this period that the solution to practically every problem was widely believed to lie in the spread of education. Schools came to be considered indispensable amenities, which every state must provide for all its citizens. Five, then ten and ultimately as much as twenty years of people's lives were, partly by developing usage and partly by governmental sanctions, devoted to supervised study. Education assumed a place second only to that of earning one's bread. Education seemed to hold the key to social prestige, wealth, wisdom, and, some even claimed, happiness.[1]

But it is not satisfactory to examine the history of education simply as one manifestation of Progress. This is perhaps one sphere of life where the historian finds it particularly difficult to detach himself from his subject, for he is usually both a product and a servant of that educational system, which—for all the changes it has undergone—remains omnipresent today, accepted almost as part of the natural order of things. Since the results of education are so difficult to assess, and since the precise details of its work are susceptible of infinite variation, controversy about syllabuses and organisation, about what schools should and should not attempt, have absorbed the attention of most writers on it. So though there are a vast number of books about education, they are virtually all by participants: pretty well every author has been to school. It is impossible to find independent, outside observers or critics, as one can in, for example, activities like coalmining (where the trouble is the opposite one, that there are not enough accounts from inside). The history of education is usually presented in an institutional way, beginning with the chronicle of a particular school by an old boy and ending with the narrative, in

[1] The best bibliography is in Antoine Prost, *Histoire de l'enseignement en France 1800–1967* (1968), which is itself an excellent survey.

much the same way, of the growth of national systems which gradually obtain universal acceptance and practise more and more advanced methods. These may be criticisms or apologias but the focus of attention tends to be the school and the materials put into it—buildings, textbooks, teachers—rather than the mentality of the child who is the victim of these attentions or the adolescent who emerges scathed or unscathed from them. How different did people become as a result of going to school?

This is a key question in the history of France, because there education became almost a substitute for religion; belief in its virtues reached exceptionally high levels. The Third Republic prided itself on its educational achievement as much as or more than on anything else, and the appellation *la république des professeurs* was neither scorned nor unjustified. It becomes all the more important, therefore, to establish precisely what the role of teachers in this society was, what cause exactly they thought they were serving, and how far this image corresponded with the reality. Placing education at the very centre of national preoccupations highlights an essential trait of the period, but it also distorts history. Just as in politics, the proclamation of grand principles and the formation of parties were usually purely superficial, at best a sublimation of other concerns, external to most men's lives and to the vast bulk of intrigues and relationships, so at least to an equal extent in education there was an enormous gap between the legislation, pedagogic theories and changes in official programmes, on the one hand, and what, on the other hand, actually happened. By itself, the history of the instructions issued is profoundly misleading. The instructions tell one about a certain class of men. The history of the masses must be written, for the most part, from other sources.

Mass education had results which were of three different kinds. First, it altered the character of politics. It made it possible for democracy and universal suffrage to function with greater reality; it vastly increased the possibilities of communication between the government and the people; it enabled the masses to watch over those whom they appointed to administer the country. But it also made them even more subject to propaganda and to brainwashing, and to persuasion that they should sacrifice their immediate interests and desires

to supposedly more important national causes—such as glory
or war—which their teachers had the task of enlightening them
about. It increased their articulacy, but it also increased
the power of the press, which simultaneously told them what to
think and spoke in their name. It was in principle egalitarian,
but in practice the very opposite, because there were so many
different gradations in education that the possession simply of
'primary' education came to be held as a mark of inadequacy.
The kind of education that was dispensed was in any case not
necessarily democratic, for though the paternalist reformers
who universalised it claimed they were doing so in order to
educate the electorate—their new masters—the values preached
by the teachers were not on the whole values inspired by the
masses. Rather, mass education could be seen as an attempt by
the élite to avoid a mass civilisation, and to impose aristocratic
values on the people. The political significance of the Age of
Education is thus ambiguous in the extreme and needs careful
analysis.

Secondly, the spread of education had a profound influence
on social relationships. It was one of the greatest stimulants of
national uniformity, while at the same time, to a certain
extent, it also heightened contrasts between Frenchmen and
other people. It represented an organised onslaught on regional
and local eccentricity, in the name of good taste and higher
culture. Just as monetary inflation could suddenly undermine
the economic power of a whole class, so education created a
sudden appreciation of the value of certain literary and verbal
skills. Birth or wealth, by themselves, no longer sufficed to
ensure consideration or influence. New dividing lines cut across
old social barriers. A new mandarinate emerged with a complicated hierarchical organisation, and a largely self-recruiting
membership. Public examinations and school certificates
became a new way of judging people, clashing with the
traditional and still powerful systems of nepotism and clientele.
The irony of it all was that the teachers were not the beneficiaries of this cultural revolution they carried out. One needs
to discover who was.

Thirdly, important psychological consequences followed
from the transformation of a largely illiterate nation into one
in which the written word became the key to many activities.

The usual assumption is that education stamped out superstition, that what the schools stood for—science, progress, rationalism—replaced traditionalism and routine as the ideals of society. In some vague way, these changes are linked up with industrialisation, which makes the change from the old to the new appear complete. But one needs to look more carefully at the changes in mentality that the schools brought about. One needs to investigate the contrast between rural and urban mentalities. Education was, to some extent, a conquest of the countryside by the towns; but the victory was not as total as is usually thought. The schools attempted to discredit certain ways of thinking and of behaving but they were by no means successful in abolishing them. This is a problem which needs to be linked with the debate about the distinction between oral and literate cultures, which unfortunately has generally been confined to 'primitive' tribes. In France, the fact that literature enjoyed such prestige did not mean that another world with different rules did not coexist beside it. When judging the results of literacy campaigns, it is not enough to consider simply the direct benefits in reading skills, nor to establish that literate factory workers have higher productivity levels than illiterate ones (which is by no means always the case).

The demand for education did not originally come from the masses. There was no pressure for it, as there was among the landless for land, or among the workers for economic independence. In 1833, when inspectors were sent round the country to investigate the state of the schools and popular attitudes towards them, they were almost unanimous in being struck by the indifference of parents. They were often greeted, as one of them reported, in the same way as tax-collectors come to inspect the wine-sellers' stocks of bottles. They were told: 'You would do better to turn your attention to the state of the roads. We are not much interested in schools. Our children will be what our fathers were. Look at so-and-so who can read: he is no richer than us who cannot.' The inspectors attributed this inability of the illiterate to appreciate the benefits of education to the combined influence of ignorance, poverty and self-interest. Children were economic assets from the age of five or six; they could earn sums which, though small, were indispensable to the balancing of the family budget. 'Weighed down under the yoke of poverty, they have no worry but that of their subsistence.' The rise of factories could, at first, be a direct hindrance to the spread of education. The better-off classes were in general doubtful or suspicious: they feared that once the children of the peasantry could read, they would desert the countryside; it would be impossible to find labourers or share-croppers. The political consequences were also frightening. Several mayors of the Gironde said that education for all would produce peasants who would be 'indocile, fainéant et raison-neur'. The notaries of the Corrèze, reported another inspector, were preventing grants of public money being given to schools because 'when everybody could sign, they would have fewer powers of attorney and fewer documents'. Mass education was an obvious challenge to many vested interests; but those at the bottom of the social scale generally did not see in it an obvious remedy for their troubles.[1] But there were two exceptions to this attitude.

In 1789 the north and east of France had far more schools, far higher attendance and far greater literacy than the rest of the country. The accompanying map illustrates this clear division, which reflected both a different history and a different pattern of settlement. The basic fact about education is that schools existed originally in towns, and it was still the towns which were best provided with them. This meant not simply the main cities but also small conglomerations, which were more than simply agricultural. In purely rural areas, the school was situated in the *bourg*, and, as Roger Thabaut recounted in the case of his village of Mazières-en-Gâtine, it was the trades-men and artisans, living right next to the school, who sent their children to it, while the peasants in their isolated farms re-mained suspicious and indifferent. The north-east of France began with the advantage that its inhabitants lived in com-pact villages, as distinct from scattered hamlets, and this made the spread of literacy much more rapid. But the arrival of a teacher in a village at all has still to be explained. A decisive factor was religion: the Protestants laid great stress on education

[1] The essential works on primary education are M. Gontard, *L'Enseignement primaire en France de la Révolution à la loi Guizot 1789–1833* (1959) and *Les Écoles primaires de la France bourgeoise 1833–75* (duplicated, Toulouse, 1964). See also A. Léaud and E. Glay, *L'École primaire en France* (1934).

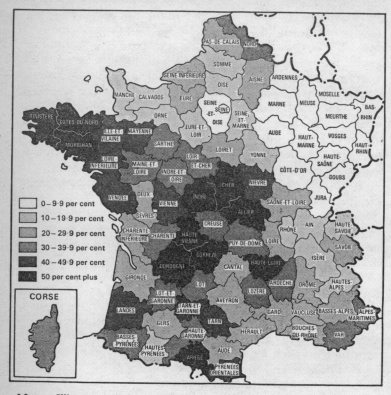

Map 1. Illiteracy (1862) Men aged twenty unable to read or write. Based on
J. Simon, *L'École* (1865), 219.

and on teaching the truth as they saw it to their adherents. The
Catholics, in areas where they were thus challenged, replied by
founding rival schools of their own. Literacy was the fruit of
these quarrels. In the late nineteenth century a new attack on
the Catholic Church, this time by the republicans (many of
them Protestants), repeated the process in areas where the
Church had hitherto been supreme. Till then, popular education had been basically religious, the concern of the Church,
and it was very much in keeping with this tradition that the
republicans made their primary schools concentrate on morals.
But the Church cannot be held to have generally failed in its
mission of rescuing the poor from their benighted ignorance.
People on the verge of starvation had no leisure for useless learning. But in certain regions it was precisely learning which was
discovered to be a possible escape from poverty. On some arid,
overpopulated soils, where tillage and cattle could not keep the
inhabitants alive all the year, the peasants sometimes turned to
artisan activities like weaving, or to seasonal migration. On the
isolated slopes of the Alps and the Pyrenees, the people chose
learning as the source of their supplementary income, and in
winter migrated to supply the plains of southern France with
its teachers. Each of these different reasons for going to school
implied a different attitude to education. Much more still needs
to be discovered about the origins of popular attitudes in this
matter; but these instances are enough to confirm that the
poor viewed it in their own—and varied—way.

The second major exception to the general indifference
towards education was the peculiar and complex attitude of the
leaders of the working class. In the mid-nineteenth century
the skilled Paris artisans often demanded education as a right,
in the same way as they demanded the right to strike, to form
unions and to earn a decent wage. Universal education meant,
for them, the establishment of true equality, the necessary
complement to universal suffrage, the ending of invidious
distinctions, the 'fusion of classes'. But their attitude towards
learning was ambiguous and often even hostile; and there was
considerable uncertainty among them as to what kind of
education they wanted. Thus even the supposedly democratic
idea that all children should be given the opportunity to
develop their individual talents did not receive anything like

universal assent. Fourier was the great advocate of individuals being allowed to express themselves freely, but Proudhon did not like the idea of vocation. He dismissed this as a petty bourgeois dream. 'The masses do not believe in the reality of what you call *vocation*', he wrote. 'They think that every man who is sound in mind and body and who is duly taught, can and ought to be capable, with a few natural exceptions, of doing everything . . . Genius . . . was a halting of natural growth rather than an indication of talent. Children must accustom themselves to eat everything: that is the first parental lesson a poor child receives.' The artisan-politician Corbon, who had himself worked in about five different trades, was likewise a believer in general rather than specialised professional training. (He made a distinction between artists and scientists—whom he called *fantaisistes* and *précisionnistes*—which he saw running right through every form of labour, depending on how much 'geometrical skill' was needed. The making of fashionable objects, decoration and jewellery, for example, was in the first category, carpentry and mechanical trades in the second.) The workers were not necessarily interested in an education which would enable them to escape from their artisan condition, for, as even Corbon said, 'I like my trade; I like my tools as much as my books and even if I could live by my pen, I should not want to stop being a locksmith'.[1] Their discussions of education were very largely concerned with professional, technical training. For them, public schools teaching practical skills meant above all the ending of the secrecy surrounding artisan activity, with a master confiding his special knowledge to a chosen apprentice. They had to establish democracy within their own class before bothering about the bourgeoisie. They were keen on physical education, because they were conscious that the poor were often physically inferior. They had no wish to be turned into 'artists' by the schools; and they often had a certain contempt for the schoolmaster. The idea of a teacher appointed by the state was anathema to Proudhon, who wanted education to be as much as possible a family affair: bachelors—still less nuns—were unfit to teach. The demand was for straight-forward scientific information, but there was also deep suspicion of the technical schools. The remedy for 'secrecy' was

[1] A. Corbon, *De l'enseignement professionnel* (1859), 69.

often just as bad as the disease. The Arts and Crafts Schools were criticised for being too theoretical; conservatives and revolutionaries agreed about this. Blanqui said the technical schools were 'seminaries to produce Chinamen', with the 'fixed idea of incarcerating the workers in a trade and so returning to the system of castes'; Thiers said they 'were good only for producing little Americans'. It was the factory workers, as opposed to the artisans, who were interested in this kind of specialised training. The artisans, moreover, were by no means hostile to Latin or the traditional upper-class syllabus. The autodidacts among them loved the classics: Perdiguier wanted every journeyman to read Homer and Virgil and produced a list of some fifty works from every century as an ideal workers' library, which barely differed from what a good *lycée* pupil would choose. They deplored only the brutality and rigour of the state's schools, and saw the wage earner and the secondary schoolboy united by the link that they were both oppressed. But these were views held at a distance, for the workers had little to say in general about the education of the bourgeoisie, which was too remote from their preoccupations. It was not with the university that they had dealings, neither with its professors nor its textbooks. They got their ideas above all from the newspapers, the journals popularising knowledge and cheap novelettes—that side of bourgeois activity which was officially despised and to which the university turned a blind eye. The workers would not be the first recruits of the educational reformers: they were in many ways—in their attitude towards school discipline for example—deeply conservative.[1]

Education was offered to the people from above, and then enforced upon them. This was done in the name of a variety of ideals, often contradictory, so that though more or less the same subjects were taught at school, the purpose of all the effort varied very considerably. The increasing provision of schools should not be seen as constant evolution in the same direction. It is important to be clear at the outset, therefore, about the deeper motives of the advocates and legislators of education.

The Catholic Church knew exactly what it was doing, though it aroused so much animosity against itself that many otherwise

[1] G. Duveau, *La Pensée ouvrière sur l'éducation pendant la seconde république et le second empire* (1947).

intelligent men got strangely muddled about what this was. As Pius IX put it in his Syllabus of 1864: 'The schools for the masses are established principally with a view to giving the people religious instruction, to bringing them to piety and to a truly Christian moral discipline.' The function of Catholic schools, which before the nineteenth century, meant virtually all French elementary schools, was essentially religious and moral, to produce Christians and to teach whatever was needed to effect this. It laid great stress on the catechism, to the extent of insisting that children should memorise it even if they did not understand it. It sought to cultivate a pious and receptive attitude, to prepare children above all for their first communion, which if received in the right spirit, could, it was thought, be the decisive event in their lives. It treated education as a battle of good against evil, designed to instil horror of ill-doing, consciousness that duty and happiness were inseparable, that the origin of sin was human and that service of God was the prime purpose of life. For long the church schools dispensed education as though it was a mystic initiation into sacred truths. As one textbook said, 'In order to teach letters properly, children must first be taught to make the sign of the cross.' Though children were allowed to keep their hats on during writing and arithmetic classes, they were forbidden to read unless they were bare-headed, as they had to be at prayers also. It was this reverence for books—which the Church treated almost as holy—that explains the acceptance of the Index, the horror of 'evil books', the constant denunciation of sacrilege by modern authors who did not respect Christian dogma. Traditional Catholic teaching was designed not to awaken the child but to teach him that desire could never be satisfied, except in the next world. It sought to fill him with humility, to warn him of God's severity as well as of his justice and mercy. But because Catholic schools tended to use very old textbooks, which were often difficult to understand, their pupils probably absorbed only parts of what they were taught, and invented their own meaning, and often a different meaning each time, for the edifying exhortations they had to spell out. These methods aroused the scorn of lay reformers, who accused the Catholics of standing in the way of enlightenment and progress. Such attacks were only partly justified. There is no doubt that the Church, under attack, tended to entrench itself in the repetition of its dogmas, to divert its efforts to the organisation of spectacular pilgrimages and charitable works, so that the majority of its clergymen were unable to participate on equal terms in intellectual debate with their enemies. But the Church also had some quite outstanding teachers, whose ideas were influential on the whole field of education, lay as well as religious. These included men who were remarkable defenders of the 'rights of the child', as one of them, Bishop Dupanloup, put it. Catholic education was not necessarily more oppressive than that with which the republic tried to replace it. A Catholic manual of 1868 listed nine different reasons why the teacher should *respect* the child, who should not be regarded as an object to be brainwashed.[1] Bishop Dupanloup was one of the first writers on education to protest against the repression of children by over-affectionate mothers and over-ambitious fathers.[2]

The Church held the monopoly of education for so long and kept its teaching at such an elementary level, because the notables on the whole considered that it was providing exactly the service demanded of it. Richelieu had warned against the dangers of having too many learned men in the country, who would be too proud and presumptuous to be obedient. The Parlement of Aix, just before the Revolution, instructed the church schools to limit their admissions and under no circumstances to teach the sons of peasants, for fear that agriculture would lack an adequate labour force. Voltaire ended up by agreeing, saying that the populace 'had neither the time nor the capacity to acquire learning': they should be satisfied with modelling themselves on the example of their superiors. It was only the bourgeoisie, he thought, who ought to be educated. La Chalotais, when drawing up his *Essay on National Education* (1763), agreed with him. Destutt de Tracy insisted that every civilised society necessarily had two classes, living respectively from manual and intellectual labour. The working class needed little knowledge, and could afford little time to obtain it, for parents required the assistance of their children and the children had to be accustomed early to the habits necessary in the

---

[1] J. B. Furet, *Sentences, leçons, avis* (1868), 464–8.
[2] See Zeldin, *Ambition and Love*, 323; and Pierre Zind, *L'Enseignement religieux dans l'instruction primaire publique en France de 1850 à 1873* (Lyon, 1971).

'painful work to which they were destined'. This was a situation 'which no human will could change, following necessarily from the very nature of men and societies'. So it was right that there should be two entirely separate systems of education— one very brief and elementary for the masses, and a fuller one confined to the élite which had the leisure and the need for it.[1] Such views continued to be held well into the nineteenth century, and by men who were politically known as liberals. It should not be forgotten that many of these were religious men, and that the university was firmly Catholic at least until the 1880s. Thus Eugène Rendu, a leading inspector and administrator of primary education during the Second Empire, while urging universal education, insisted that its purpose should not be intellectual but moral. It did not matter very much whether the masses could read or not, for civilisation with large-scale illiteracy had proved possible in the past. What worried him was that the Church was losing its grip on the people, materialism was advancing, and something had to be done to provide the moral and religious education which children were no longer getting from the church or from their parents. The main purpose of primary schools should be not just to teach arithmetic but to 'purify the sentiments' of the poor, 'to give them some dignity'.[2] The liberals often simply wanted to do what the church used to do or was failing to do.

Those who advocated education frequently did so with very conservative or reactionary ends in view. Guizot considered that 'ignorance renders the masses turbulent and ferocious; it makes them an instrument to be used by the factions'. When passing his law requiring every village to have a primary school (1833) he told his prefects: 'We have tried to create in every commune a moral force which the government can use at need.' He wanted the teacher to preach submission, respect for the law, love of order in exactly the same way as the church had done, though perhaps even more explicitly, and indeed he wanted the education dispensed by these schools to be essentially religious.[3] His purpose was not diabolically political. He

---

[1] Destutt de Tracy, *Observations sur le système actuel d'instruction publique* (1800).

[2] E. Rendu, *Mémoire sur l'enseignement obligatoire* (1853).

[3] F. Guizot, *Essai sur l'histoire et sur l'état actuel de l'instruction publique en France* (1816), 5.

genuinely wanted to increase the happiness of the masses, and he believed that this could best be attained by teaching them to accept their lot in life, and to see in the regular fulfilment of their painful daily tasks the source of their contentment.

Against such people, it is natural to contrast those who believed that education would solve most human problems and lead to a better world, though these optimists, like the pessimists, completely misjudged the effect of their proposals, and neither the one nor the other in the end obtained what they wanted. Education was not only one of the causes which raised the highest hopes, but one which has disappointed the reformers most constantly. The real leader of all those who expected education to achieve utopia was Condorcet. His doctrines were the inspiration of many generations of republicans. He believed that mass education would ensure the indefinite progress and happiness of humanity. Liberty and democracy would follow from it, because enlightened citizens would know how to order public affairs; equality would be advanced, because the hidden talents of the poor would be revealed; morality would be perfected, because intelligent men would no longer feel the boredom which led the ignorant to distract themselves 'through sensations as opposed to ideas'; family life would be strengthened, because women would be able to share in their husbands' interests. These facile expectations were raised into dogmas and endlessly repeated throughout the century. Napoleon III, who had a talent for turning into original-sounding slogans the commonest platitudes of his time, laid it down that the nation with the most schools would be the first nation in the world, in its enjoyment of material prosperity, order and liberty; and that by spreading education he was winning 'to religion, morals and comfort' that enormous part of the population 'that barely knew the precepts of Christ'. The victory of the Germans over France in 1870 was held to be due above all to the work of the Prussian schools. Zola repeated, 'France will be what the primary teacher makes it'. This became one of those fundamental truths which, like proverbs, were on everybody's lips, though no one completely believed them in practical life.

It inspired the Education League (Ligue de l'Enseignement), founded in the 1860s by Jean Macé, joined by people of all classes, and ultimately one of the most active pressure groups in the country. Macé became an official hero of the Third Republic, symbolising the struggle of the humble to acquire knowledge. His life, and that of his society, deserve to be better known, because the hagiography surrounding them has obscured the disagreements behind their demands and the complexity of the whole movement for popular education. Macé was the son of a carrier or cart-driver and called himself a *camionneur d'idées*. He was taught to read by his *curé*, and won a scholarship to the Catholic College Stanislas, while his sister went off to be a nun. Because his League came to support lay education, the fact that he was a religious man has been overlooked. He always insisted that the great plague of the century was the lack of religious beliefs and of awareness of God : the soul had its needs as well as the body and Sunday rest was essential to enable one to think of higher things. What he objected to was the incompetence of the clergy, who were not implementing the true spirit of their Church. Macé was always very much a man of 1848, in whom religiosity, emotion and politics combined in the belief that the great need of the time— and of himself—was to love and be loved. His frustration expressed itself in a marriage with an illiterate worker, thirteen years older than himself, who became both a mother and a wife to him, and in a vocation, to which he devoted his life, for teaching girls. He had won top prizes at Stanislas, but rejected a career in the university; 'his independent temperament and his need of an open-air life', as he himself wrote, 'led him to spend the first years of his youth obscurely in adventures'. He was a poor boy who had made good (disproving yet again the view that the poor were cut off from secondary education), but he felt ill at ease in the establishment, and too emotionally hungry to be respectable. He became a Saint-Simonian and then a Fourierist. As a schoolteacher at Mademoiselle Verenet's boarding establishment for girls at Beblenheim, where he continued to teach even when he had acquired national fame, he dispensed a very unorthodox form of education, of Fourierist flavour, totally different from that of the regimented primary public system he worked so hard to spread. The traditional schools, he said, gave their pupils very little knowledge, and a disgust for studying which they would retain all their lives. Macé, in his own teaching, avoided memorising, dryness, overwork; he introduced intellectual work only 'as a second string, in hours of rest' after physical and manual education. He abolished compulsory homework; he used feasts, the theatre and country walks as ways of arousing the individual interests and talents of his pupils, who organised their own discipline and who were not forced to live in drab uniforms. 'Coquetry' was accepted, in keeping with Fourier's opposition to repressing natural instincts. Girls should have the same education as boys, so that they could be true companions to men, who were incomplete without them. He became a best-selling author with chatty little books he wrote for the girls, explaining the facts of life and of science, which Hetzel published side by side with the novels of Jules Verne. The purpose of all this was to give dignity and self-respect. Macé did not wish to end economic inequalities: 'What the poor man has the greatest difficulty in forgiving the rich man for is not his wealth, but his contempt.' For Macé, the republic's main function was to end this contempt. That was what his educational campaigns were for and he stressed that his league was essentially political. He had been terrified by the proclamation of universal suffrage, which he had considered dangerous. He wanted to stop the masses from being surly people who provided fodder for barricades. His aim was 'the embourgeoisement of the masses'.[1] He admitted this in precisely these words; but it is important to realise all the ambiguity contained in the idea of embourgeoisement, as revealed in Mace's own career, which in many ways defied the bourgeois order.

Moreover, the Education League became very different from what Macé had intended it to be. His skill had shown itself in deliberately linking the league to the Freemasons, as a result of which he soon had a nationwide organisation. He had a friend in the Havas news agency, which he was able to use as an advertising medium. The Eastern Railway gave him a free pass to travel on its lines. Napoleon III's prefects gave him their blessing. A Fourierist philanthropist, Faustin Moigneau, provided him with funds. There was a very strange combination of forces behind the league. That did not worry Macé, who was all in favour of each locality enjoying complete autonomy in the running of its educational programme. But the Paris

[1] Letter to Buls, 11 January 1868.

branch of the league, to his consternation, then began assuming leadership of it. Its secretary was a commercial traveller, Emmanuel Vauchez (1836–1926), who gave up his lucrative occupation to devote himself completely to the cause. This man had a passion for organisation, administration and centralisation. He personally wrote 7,000 letters and sent out 80,000 circulars in a campaign lasting fifteen months, as a result of which he collected 1,267,000 signatures for a petition in favour of more education. However, even he could not escape the fact that the league's supporters were divided about exactly what they wanted. Only 348,000 were signatures in favour of free, compulsory and lay education; 383,000 wanted it to be compulsory and free but not lay, and 116,000 wanted it to be simply compulsory.[1] It was Vauchez who made the league adopt laicisation as its demand, then add military training as a supplement to education. Macé was opposed to both of these. Vauchez turned the league into a far more militant, anticlerical, centralised, patriotic organisation than its founder had intended. Having succeeded in getting lay education established, he concentrated its efforts on encouraging those things that the government was not doing, particularly distributing suitably republican books to local libraries, stimulating nationalism through shooting clubs, giving scholarships to primary teachers and turning its attention to adolescents over the compulsory school age. In 1907 the league bought up a dissolved abbey off the rue de Sèvres and built itself a magnificent headquarters.[2] By then it had become part of the establishment, with men like Leon Bourgeois at its head. Increasingly the professors of the university took it over and turned it into a 'cultural centre', where they met to discuss the benefits of keeping the church out of education. Benevolent merchants bequeathed sizeable gifts to it. But it is curious that this temple of reason was in its early years supported by the Kardec sect of spiritualists, and Vauchez, in his retirement, devoted himself to the study of the esoteric. It is important not to take its rationalist proclamations too literally.[3]

The administrators and ministers who set up and ran the

---

[1] The details of the remaining signatures are not known.
[2] Later to become the Récamier Cinema and Theatre.
[3] Édouard Petit, *Jean Macé, sa vie, son œuvre* (n.d.) [c. 1922], is the best, but

primary education system in this period represented two
additional approaches, which were different once again. One
was Protestant, the other was positivist. There was a surprisingly large Protestant group, who naturally recruited like-
minded assistants, at the head of the republic's primary schools.
Their leader was Ferdinand Buisson (1841–1932), director of
primary education from 1879 to 1896, editor of the *Dictionnaire
de pédagogie* (1882–93), which was the *instituteurs'* principal
guide for several generations, president of the Radical Party's
executive committee, president of the League of the Rights of
Man, president of the Education League, and winner of the
Nobel Peace Prize in 1926: his accumulated honours show how
high a place mass education held in the priorities of his day.
Buisson was a Protestant who attempted to reform and update
the religion of his fathers, in a way which combined revolt
against the domination of the past and of traditional institutions with acceptance of their moral doctrines and of their
approach to life. Taking refuge in Switzerland during the
Second Empire, he wrote in favour of a *Liberal Christianity*
(1865); he presented a doctoral thesis on Sébastien Castellion,
the sixteenth-century Protestant divine whom he hailed as a
pioneer of toleration and true religion combined. He distinguished between the body and soul of religion, arguing that the
institutions, hierarchy and dogmas of the church were oppressive, but that its ethics were an indispensable basis of society.
Religion—which he thus equated with morality—needed to
be preserved and the battle for laicisation which he led was
therefore a purely political one. The church should be deprived
of control of the schools so that its doctrines, duly purified and
reformed, could be taught to children as they should always
have been. He deliberately called what he hoped to instil into
them *la foi laïque*—a new kind of religion. Though, as a passionate believer in the principles of the revolution of 1789, he
had infinite faith in the progress of humanity, he was, as a
Protestant, also deeply conscious of man's imperfections and

little-known, biography. Paul Lachapelle, 'Le Cercle parisien et la Ligue française
de l'enseignement de 1866 à 1958', *Cahiers laïques* (Sept.–Dec. 1958), nos. 47 and
48. For other republican institutions and societies supporting education, see Abel
Lefèvre, *Où nous en sommes. L'Enseignement populaire dans le département de l'Eure*
(Évreux, 1899).

of the presence of evil. He combined the two ideas by a definition of religion as that which leads man towards perfection,
towards the true, the good and the beautiful, but through
rational not mystical processes, not by grace but always by
protracted personal effort. Religion was the sentiment that
gave man, though conscious of his weakness, the strength to
undergo the sufferings necessary to improve himself and to
advance progress. He added patriotism as its necessary corol-
lary, for this was a respectable and natural manifestation of
human solidarity, but in no way incompatible with belief in
peace and international arbitration. In this neo-Protestant
doctrine, Buisson also incorporated Kantism. The philosopher
Renouvier (1815–1903) had shown how the mixture could be
carried out. Renouvier was another Christian heretic who spent
his life attacking the Church and writing textbooks of republican morals for teachers, but he was constantly obsessed by the
problems of religion: in 1873 he declared his conversion to
Protestantism and set up a journal, *La Critique philosophique*
(1872–89), to argue that the conversion of France to Protestantism would solve its problems. With the help of the doctrines
of Kant, who henceforth became one of the main sources of
republican inspiration,[1] he developed a *Science of Morals* (1869)
independent of religion. The educational implication of this
was the training of will-power and self-control above all else.
But paradoxically, Renouvier felt dissatisfied with his intellectual creation and in 1894 disowned it: 'Everybody seems to
believe in progress, despite everything,' he wrote. 'I no longer
do. In our time, it is preferable to try to believe in another world
better than this one.'[2] One constantly finds this kind of hesitation among the more thoughtful educational theorists; but the
simplification of their doctrines should not be regarded as the
inevitable result of popularisation. Many teachers, though with
less complicated arguments, seem to have been conscious of
these philosophical difficulties. The educational system gave
the impression, in its slogans, that it had a coherent doctrine
but the reality was more uncertain.

Positivism provided another inspiration of the reformers.
Jules Ferry declared his allegiance to it; and it was the schools

---

[1] J. Benda, *Kant* (1950).
[2] Marcel Méry, *La Critique du Christianisme chez Renouvier* (1952), 2. 15.

which did as much as anything to preserve Comte's popularity, by giving him a prominent place in the syllabus.[1] The education theory of Comte was never succinctly formulated, and, as is known, Comte's ideas developed considerably during his lifetime, so here again theoretical guidance could be very diversely interpreted. What was indubitable was that education held a very high place in his system, and the teacher too, though Comte wanted the teacher to be the mother in early childhood; after that, an independent, autonomous corporation of intellectuals should take over. (That was the theoretical justification of Ferry's making the University a self-governing body, instead of a government department as Napoleon had it.) Comte stressed the importance of emotional and aesthetic education, the need to teach the observation of concrete phenomena, using active methods: he called Froebel 'the only pedagogue who understood the need for harmony between individual education and activity in social life'. Comte wanted great attention to be paid to the development of sentiments of sociability. He greatly admired the Jesuits' educational skills; he wanted his teachers to instil 'active and voluntary submission' as opposed to 'sterile or disorganised discussion'; but he criticised the Jesuits for cutting off their schools from the real world. Comte was not interested in vocational or technical education (as the Saint-Simonians were) and insisted on the primacy of moral education, to be achieved through general studies, as opposed to the acquisition of particular scientific skills.[2] Durkheim repeated Comte's views that education 'must be essentially a matter of authority', but he concentrated his attention on discipline, self-control, effort, duty, in an intellectualist way which was narrower than that of Comte, who was very conscious of the importance of emotionality. For Durkheim, the family was a failure, and the school must replace it.[3] It was against such doctrines that the *École Nouvelle* movement, to be discussed later, rebelled, proposing an approach to education from the very opposite angle, that is, from the needs of the child rather than of society. The disagreements about

[1] On Ferry, see Zeldin, *Politics and Anger*, 257–268; on positivism see Zeldin, *Taste and Corruption*, ch. 5 (forthcoming).

[2] Paul Arbousse-Bastide, *La Doctrine de l'éducation universelle dans la philosophie d'Auguste Comte* (1957) is the fullest account; L. Legrand, *L'Influence du positivisme dans l'œuvre scolaire de Jules Ferry* (1961).

[3] É. Durkheim, *L'Éducation morale* (1925).

what schools should do were thus very considerable indeed. And since it was difficult to study just what effects they did in fact have, the theoretical basis for education was always controversial, uncertain and vague.

The Instituteurs

This review of some of the main ideas which inspired the advocates of popular education points to one obvious reason why the movement bred so much frustration and disappointment, even though it succeeded in bringing all children into schools. The ideas themselves were too varied, if not contradictory, for it to be possible even to find a common criterion by which to judge its consequences, beyond the mere enumeration of examination results. At the same time, the basis of these ideas was a holistic view of man, an expectation that there was one fundamental need in everybody, which schools could satisfy, and that they alone could provide a unique and necessary preparation for life. Just how divorced these notions were from reality may be seen by examining the growth and development of the profession of primary-school teachers. Even they implemented the ideas of the philosophers only very partially and with infinite modifications. The way they fulfilled their function of intermediaries of this new culture illuminates its complex character, and also brings one nearer the actual, practical manifestations of culture in daily life.

The history of the *instituteurs* is one of dedication and struggle. The *instituteurs* came to be seen as symbols of all that was noble and idealistic in the work of the republic; they were praised as the missionaries of its anticlerical doctrines (and vilified by Catholics for the same reason). They came to form an enormous, apparently uniform army: 150,000 in the first decade of the twentieth century, 120,000 after 1918. It is only recently that the full significance of their experience has begun to emerge from the polemic surrounding them. One can see now that too much was expected of them. The elementary schoolmaster at the beginning of the nineteenth century was still, as he had been under the *ancien régime*, a very humble man indeed. Far from having any professional status, he was very often an unemployed peasant or artisan, a 'pedlar of participles' who might hawk pots and pans one year and offer to teach another. He wore one, two or three quills in his hat, to indicate that he could teach reading, writing and arithmetic; and there were few who could manage all of these. His wife might be a washerwoman or keep a grocer's shop, for he could seldom live on the pittance he earned. As soon as spring arrived, his pupils would desert him to help their parents in the fields and he would have to seek another occupation till the winter. Only in the towns could he hope to get a regular clientele. Often families carried on the trade of teaching from father to son. A lecturer at the University of Paris–Nanterre recently unearthed the papers of his ancestors who had been teachers in this way. The first had taken up teaching after failing in trade in 1833. His son opened up a school of his own in 1845, in a stable. He left a pathetic account of his troubles, of poverty so extreme that his children died of starvation or grew up deformed.[1] Other memoirs confirm that this was in no way exceptional—hunger, atrocious living conditions, bullying by the village notables and the *curé*, who used them as jacks-of-all-trades—which they had to be, to get enough to survive on— this was their regular lot. The teacher was poorer than a labourer: Michelet said a baker might be six times richer. In 1840, the minimum salary of a village teacher was 200 francs a year (£8) and 23,000 communes paid precisely that amount. In addition the teacher could expect a small sum (of between 30 centimes and 2 francs a month) for each child who came to school, but he had much trouble in collecting this, and the poor were in any case exempted from paying at all. This poverty was something the teachers never escaped from. Even when they were made civil servants and the state took to paying them salaries, they were the lowest paid of all civil servants. In 1914, teachers in Alsace–Lorraine (under German sovereignty) received twice as much pay as their French counterparts and in an international survey French primary teachers were classified as the worst paid in Europe, coming twenty-fifth, equal with those of Montenegro. The result was that people generally became teachers to escape from something worse or as a stepping-stone to other things. They were sometimes weakling or deformed peasant children, who had to

[1] Yves Sandré, *Marchands de participes* (1962).

use their wits to make up for their physical defects, or they saw in education a means of avoiding the grinding labour of the fields. Few saw it as lifetime's career. One of the ways the government attracted recruits was to offer exemption from military service, provided ten years were spent in teaching. The teacher was very often therefore a young man, waiting to enter the lower ranks of the civil service, through examinations for which his education fitted him. There were of course also teachers who had retired from other occupations—such as the army; and others still whom family tradition kept in the profession. But increasingly, the sons of *instituteurs* attempted to become secondary-school masters; and their sons might aspire to become professors. But this was for long an over-ambitious dream. A survey of kindergarten teachers in the department of the Seine in 1959 showed that 45 per cent of them had grandfathers who had been *instituteurs*, and 25 per cent of these had sons who became *instituteurs*. More often it was the *instituteurs'* daughters who followed them in the same job, while sons moved on to higher things.[1] The teacher training colleges were always definitely proletarian: in Saint-Lô, in 1880–4, 53 per cent of the students were sons of peasants, 28 per cent sons of artisans and shopkeepers, 3·4 per cent sons of workers and clerks. Forty years later peasants no longer found it worth while—9 per cent were sons of peasants, 12·5 per cent sons of artisans and shopkeepers, and 49·5 per cent sons of workers. Between the wars, girls who took up teaching were of slightly higher social origin, but generally they had not gone through the training colleges: they were drop-outs from higher education who had failed to obtain degrees (22 per cent in Ida Berger's survey). When questioned, almost a half of the primary teachers in Paris said they would prefer to teach in more senior schools, even if there was no difference in pay or conditions. Elementary teaching was thus not made attractive as a profession in itself, and it was only a minority who entered it with a sense of vocation.

At the same time as they were given the mission of bringing civilisation to the masses, the *instituteurs* were savagely humiliated to prevent them from demanding anything like

[1] Ida Berger, *Les Maternelles. Étude sociologique sur les institutrices des écoles maternelles de la Seine* (1959), 57.

proportionate rewards for their pains: the faith in education was surrounded by an elaborate hypocrisy. Guizot, the minister of public instruction, and a former university professor, who first organised training colleges on a uniform basis in 1832-4, gave firm orders that these colleges should avoid 'fomenting in the pupil-teachers that distate for their very modest situation, that excessive thirst for material well-being that today torments the destiny of so many men, and corrupts their character'. An enormous amount was demanded of them, but in the spirit of self-sacrifice. The discipline in the colleges should be 'severe' so that they would know how to instil the same obedience into children, because it was school discipline which determined whether 'people in later life had a proper respect for legitimate authority'. The pupil-teachers must not be taught anything beyond what was strictly necessary for the carrying-out of their duties: 'more general, vague and superficial subjects, unsuited to the modest functions of a village teacher' should be avoided. 'I expect a lot of you,' wrote Guizot. 'There will be, so to speak, no private life for you: the state asks not only for the tribute of your intelligence and know-ledge, but for the whole man.' But in return teachers 'must expect neither fame nor fortune, and must be content with the austere pleasure of having served their fellow men, obtaining nothing beyond their obscure and laborious condition'. The philosopher Jouffroy, in discussing the role of teachers at the Academy of Moral and Political Sciences in 1840, insisted that 'a critical spirit' was suitable only for the élite, who received secondary and higher education, and not for mere primary teachers. Victor Cousin said their job was noble but essentially humble, and the 'spirit of poverty' was essential to it. The *instituteurs* thus closely resembled the curés, who came from the same poor background, were also exempted from military service, and earned the same miserable pittance. The government was terrified, in the case of both of them, that they might win too much influence.

The republicans did a certain amount to raise their morale, by making them their chosen agents for the distribution of political propaganda. The historian Martin and the philosopher Renouvier wrote republican textbooks in the form of catechisms, which were sent out to the teachers. A journal,

L'Écho des instituteurs (1845–50), started up to defend their interests; and some of them played an active role in left-wing electioneering in 1848. This was enough for Thiers to accuse all 37,000 of them of being 'socialists and communists, veritable anti-*curés* . . . of consuming ambition', and to warn against the dangers of too much education for the masses. In 1851 some 3,000 *instituteurs* were dismissed as dangerous. The Second Empire at first shared these fears: it showered circulars upon them, forbidding them to play at politics, to visit cabarets or cafés, to frequent 'any society which was not in keeping with the gravity and dignity of their functions'. But it then saw them as valuable allies in its war against the Church; it invited them in 1860 to send in their views on education—an unprecedented piece of consultation: 5,940 of them sent in essays which showed a great sense of responsibility as well as of misery. A newspaper in 1863 commented: 'Constantly at the mercy of an inspector's report, or a denunciation, transferred frequently and on the least pretext, the *instituteurs* in the countryside had reached such a degree of moral wretchedness that every one among them who felt he had any good in him was emigrating to the civil service, the railways or private industry.' The government now began treating them with a little more respect: in 1867 it invited 700 of them to Paris to see the International Exhibition and Napoleon III himself entertained them. The Third Republic finally hailed them as the vanguard of progress, and the chosen instrument of the new enlightenment, and its school-building programme frequently gave the *instituteur* the most splendid house in the village from which to operate. A Pedagogical Museum was founded in 1879, and professorships of pedagogy established, to raise teaching to the status of a science. Leading politicians and philosophers took to writing textbooks to guide the *instituteurs*, so that they became participants in what was supposed to be a great national movement. But the republic was slow to raise their wages; in 1889, in the name of equality, their military exemption was ended; and it was by no means clear that they were the republic's favourites except in the rhetoric of politicians.

The *instituteurs* in due course became disabused and began to organise themselves against the government—but this was a slow process, because they were far from all being revolutionaries. At first they formed friendly societies (*amicales*) which by 1914 claimed 97,000 members; but these were largely controlled by the inspectors and headmasters, whose authoritarian methods some of the rank and file were beginning to resent. When, following the law on associations of 1884, some tried to form a trade union, the minister forbade it, for they were civil servants and 'to allow the regimentation of functionaries without the participation of their superiors, and even against their superiors, would be to consent in advance to the collapse of the whole civil service'. But revolutionary syndicalist ideas gained ground among some *instituteurs* after 1900, and in 1905 this small minority of extremists decided to form themselves into a union, affiliated to the Bourses du Travail and the C.G.T. They wanted better wages but, even more, self-government for the teachers, and liberation from the favouritism and arbitrariness of their superiors. Headmasters were still treating *instituteurs* like eighteenth-century ushers, forbidding them to visit cafés, insisting on their taking their meals as the headmaster's paying guests, at high rates: one example of a complaint was that the headmaster ate trout while the *instituteurs* were given herrings. In the 1904–5 elections for the consultative departmental councils, all the inspectors and headmasters were eliminated and replaced by ordinary *instituteurs*. In 1919 the *amicales*, following the lead of the syndicalists, turned themselves into a trade union (Syndicat National des Instituteurs), and at last in 1924–5 the government agreed to treat with it. Henceforth promotions and transfers had to be carried out in consultation with the union; but *instituteurs* were not able to gain any large wage increases, and the fact that an exceptionally large proportion of them became union members (about 80 per cent) meant that the older, more conservative elements directed their policy. They continued to repeat pre-war slogans, they continued to preach the pacifism of 1914 during the Spanish Civil War and even in the face of Hitler's violence. By 1939 they were strangely isolated within the nation, forming an idiosyncratic type, but not a model.[1]

One explanation is the training they received. The training colleges (*écoles normales*) were at first almost indistinguishable

---

[1] Max Ferré, *Histoire du mouvement syndicaliste révolutionnaire chez les instituteurs* (1955) unfortunately stops in 1922.

from ecclesiastical seminaries. The trainees were all boarders, sleeping in dormitories, with their lives regulated to the smallest detail from the moment they rose at 5 a.m. to their bedtime at 9. They were forbidden to go out without the director's special permission. Their drink allowance was fixed by ministerial decree at one-third of a litre of wine a day (mixed with twice as much water). The subjects taught were the very same things primary schoolboys learnt, and no more. Only in the Second Empire was the syllabus gradually increased to include music 'so that the *instituteurs* could contribute to the pomp of religious ceremonies and conduct tastefully and intelligently musical societies which are such a desirable form of competition to the cabarets'. The standard for admission was very low: the École Normale of the Rhône had fourteen new entrants in 1864, but eight of them could barely write. Many of these colleges were tiny, with just a couple of people on their staff. They were usually housed in old buildings, former nunneries or even wings of prisons. What held them together was a passionate dedication to hard work, a firm belief in slogging memorisation, a peasant determination to make good. They were dry, rigid, very institutional. It is true that in 1865 and again in the 1880s discipline was relaxed, the offence of 'insubordination' was abolished, seven weeks' holidays were allowed. Then the lecturers at the colleges got their emancipation, were no longer required to live in, or to attend to domestic arrangements. Two *écoles normales supérieures*, one for men and one for women, were established at St. Cloud and Fontenay-aux-Roses, which produced more sophisticated and dedicated lecturers, whose teaching methods were much more theoretical, and indeed often high-flown, 'marked by Parisian approval'. The syllabuses at the colleges were broadened, entry standards raised; in the 1880s they began teaching much the same syllabus as the lower forms of secondary schools; after 1905 the third year at training colleges was almost like the top forms or like the first year of the faculties, with a long essay which the trainees pompously called their 'thesis'; after 1920 the stimulation of 'intellectual curiosity' became an official purpose of the colleges. The colleges were thus gradually raised from primary to secondary status in fact, if not in name: in 1937 the minister Jean Zay proposed to send all the trainees to secondary schools and make the *écoles normales* provide simply short professional courses; and in 1940 the Vichy government did just this. The result, not unexpectedly, was catastrophic for teacher recruitment, because once the trainees were inserted into the secondary system, 80 per cent of them abandoned the idea of becoming *instituteurs* and moved on to better jobs. The expansion of the educational system meant that there were far more opportunities for promotion, and the best graduates of the training colleges preferred to become administrators or training-college lecturers, or to work for higher qualifications. But while they lasted, the *écoles normales* gave the *instituteurs* a sense of corporate identity; their old pupil associations were very vigorous; and an *instituteur*'s best friends were very often other *instituteurs*. From around the turn of the century, it became quite frequent for *instituteurs* to marry *institutrices*. Formerly, it had been considered scandalous for a woman teacher to marry and continue to work; but now the government decided that since it could not give them a living wage, the best solution was for the male and female teachers to combine in couples and earn two wages. The effect of this, however, was to accentuate the separation of the teachers from other professions.[1]

The *instituteurs* always had to contend with a great deal of hostility, both political and social, and it was almost inevitable that they should turn to their own unions and associations for strength. The peasants looked on them as wily children who had succeeded in avoiding the hard work that ordinary people had to accept; they resented their long holidays, short hours and the fixed wage they received regularly whatever the weather. The *instituteurs* were not quite bourgeois but neither were they peasants and they had difficulty in finding friends among either. The *instituteurs*, besides, sometimes had their pride: as one of them wrote, 'We had such a high view of our function that we considered ourselves bound to be extremely reserved and at least to have the appearance of distinction.' But as prosperity spread among the peasantry, they could less

[1] M. Gontard, *La Question des écoles normales primaires de la Révolution de 1789 à nos jours* (Toulouse, 2nd edition, 1964); M. Vallée, *L'École normale des instituteurs de Vesoul* (Vesoul, 1901); J. Ozouf, 'Les Instituteurs de la Manche et leur associations au début du xxᵉ siècle', *Revue d'histoire moderne et contemporaine* (Jan.-Mar. 1966), 95–114; J. P. David, *L'Établissement de l'enseignement primaire au 19ᵉ siècle dans le département de Maine-et-Loire 1816–79* (Angers, 1967).

and less be looked on as children who had made good. One cannot generalise too much about attitudes towards them, because these varied enormously according to local conditions, individual personalities and the roles they assumed. Thus in the department of the Manche, they were treated with deference on the coast but shunned by many peasants in the interior. In certain religious areas, the state's *instituteurs* might have classes of only half a dozen or even two children, because the majority attended the church school: here they were totally isolated. But when the balance of opinion was more even, the *instituteurs* could and often did enjoy enormous influence. They could become leaders of the left-wing party and be responsible for organising most of its social activities, which assumed a much greater importance because they were in constant competition with those of the church. One *instituteur* of the Deux-Sèvres (born in 1884) described how he worked in a village with 'two schools, two musical societies, two public libraries, two sporting clubs (gymnastics on the right, shooting on the left), two friendly societies, two public meeting halls, two electoral committees (the republican, and the Catholics of Poitou); two different annual festivals for the boys called up to the army, with only the republican one displaying the tricolour. Only the firemen formed a single subdivision, responsible to the Prefecture, or there would have been left wing and right wing fires.' All businesses likewise had their political label, except that when a trader wanted to keep the custom of both sides he sent his daughter to the church school and his son to the state one. Since the *instituteurs* were the main cause or symbol of this division, they became village notables. They won influence, however, not so much from their political opinions but from what they contributed to village life. More than half of them, at the end of the nineteenth century, were secretary to the mayor, in which capacity they were indispensable intermediaries for most dealings with the authorities. The *instituteurs* who also knew how to measure land, how to carry out calculations, and write letters for the peasants, on those subjects which concerned their daily lives, and who themselves cultivated a plot of land in their spare time, would be esteemed in a special way. It was often to their advantage if they were indistinguishable from peasants in physical appearance.

Nevertheless the peasants saw them as something apart, and in personal, as opposed to administrative, difficulties, shy peasants might well prefer to consult the *curé*. However, the stereotype of the *instituteur* at war with the *curé* was by no means universally true. For long the *instituteur* was his subordinate, and in some localities they lived in harmony. The stereotype indeed is proved inaccurate the more one studies the details of the lives of these men, who have left autobiographies and documents revealing an impressive independence of thought and much individual strength of will.

A Savoyard *instituteur*, born in 1844, has left some interesting memoirs which show the problems and the satisfactions of this first generation of popular *instituteurs*. He was the son of a peasant; by great sacrifices, he got into a training college; when his father died, it gave him a quarter scholarship—the rest of his fees to be a loan. 'Accustomed to the authority of my father, I accepted the discipline of the college willingly enough.' It was run by a priest and he was taught that his mission was to assist the priest of his village, to reinforce religion. At nineteen, he became an assistant *instituteur* with a hundred pupils, but on a wage of 400 francs which left him so hungry that he used to walk home, 33 kilometres each way, whenever he could, in order to get a square meal. But even his brothers and sisters thought he was not working properly, and profiting from the labours of others. The peasants envied the *instituteur* his ready cash, assuming that he must therefore be rich. On one occasion, a peasant asked him to lend him his salary of 400 francs, not realising that he had no other resources, no land, and that he had to live off his pay. His religious duties were almost as heavy as his teaching. He had to teach the choir to sing, to ring the church bells at five o'clock, to serve mass and to sing on Sunday both at mass and vespers, and generally to be at the beck and call of the *curé*. He had no holidays at Christmas or Easter because these were religious feasts. In addition he was secretary to the mayor. He also played the violin, so he was in demand at parties; and he could measure lands, so could be useful to the peasants. But when he offended the *curé* by marrying the *institutrice*, he was sacked; and he had to take another job on lower pay, and his wife could not get a teaching post there. He walked a hundred kilometres to the capital to see the inspector about this and get a transfer. Two of their children died of hunger; his wife got 'neurasthenia' from the worry, an illness that bore down on the rest of their lives. But he received a present of a dictionary of medicine from some grateful pupils, and his wife therefore took up advising women on their illnesses. Teaching was always only part of his life. He also took boarders; he learnt carpentry, and spent the vacations making rustic furniture. He quarrelled with one *curé*; but then the next *curé* treated him well, telling him to walk on his left while the mayor walked on his right; so he kept the cross in the schoolroom despite official orders. In his retirement, he was able to continue with his hobbies. Though his life had been very hard, there was an impressive stoicism about it. In 1870 he had voted *No* against Napoleon III, exclaiming, 'O magic power of universal suffrage, which gives the humblest man the right to affirm, for once, his personality, and to count as much as the most powerful.'[1]

This history may be compared with that of an *institutrice* two generations later. She entered the profession after 1945, but her memoirs reveal that abysmally primitive physical conditions could still survive, particularly in backward regions of France where time moved slowly. She started in the Lozère, in a school with fourteen pupils, aged five to fourteen. The school was so damp, she had two centimetres of water on the floor and lessons were taken wearing rubber boots. She had to live in a room upstairs, without running water or sanitation. André Maurois by chance learnt of this, protested to the authorities and within a few weeks the water arrived. It needed the intervention of a Parisian demigod to change things. The inspector answered complaints by saying nothing could be done; that he too had started in one of these depressed regions, in similarly bad conditions; promotion was the only way out.[2] These are just two stories: they are not typical, because there was always too much variety for that to be possible; but they show what could and did happen.

There were *instituteurs* who behaved like peasants, spoke rarely and slowly, did not hesitate to use the local dialect, and played boules with the villagers in the evening or cards in winter.

[1] C. Brun, *Trois plumes au chapeau, ou l'Instituteur d'autrefois* (Grenoble, 1950).
[2] Huguette Bastide, *Institutrice de Village* (1971).

But there were an extraordinarily large number who either could not or would not visit the café, and when they did, perhaps once a week, sat alone. The older ones, who had abandoned ideas of leaving their profession, who became trade union leaders, or who had lost their interest in sport, cultivated virtues of solidity. Some never read a book if they could help it—they were by no means all intellectuals—while others became experts in local history or geology. Many devoted the whole of their lives to teaching and were totally absorbed in their work. In general, they were serious people, having little in common with the dilettante iconoclasm of Paris: they accepted the need for order, they believed in what they were doing, they had faith in the power of knowledge. What distinguished them from the rest of the population more than anything else was perhaps their rejection of monetary and material ideals—a characteristic they shared only with the clergy, who were paradoxically seen as their enemies.

In the course of the twentieth century two new features altered the image and ambitions of the *instituteurs*. First, the men began leaving the profession. In 1891 for the first time more women than men were recuited; women could teach boys, but men could not teach in single sex girls' schools. The *institutrices* had less political dedication and less desire to be active outside the world of education. Secondly, the men took on educational work which was not just 'primary'—a word which no longer meant elementary, for the *écoles primaires supérieures* and the *écoles normales* could reach *baccalauréat* standard. The hierarchy in the primary sector became elaborate. In 1914 when an *instituteur*'s maximum salary was 2,450 francs, teachers at the *écoles primaires supérieures* earned between 2,100 and 4,100 francs, lecturers in training colleges 2,900 to 4,900, and directors of training colleges got an additional 1,000 to 1,600 francs. Primary inspectors earned 3,700 to 5,500; *inspecteurs d'académie* 7,166 to 8,666; inspectors-general 10,000 to 12,000 and rectors 13,000 to 18,000.[1] Innumerable grades and pay scales within these different jobs produced constant worries and grievances. The inspectors had a lot of power, so that their tours were dreaded: every *instituteur* got a mark when he was inspected, as though to impress upon him that by becoming a teacher he

[1] A. Lantenois, *Ce que l'instituteur doit savoir* (4th edition, 1928), 562–3.

had opted to remain at school. But the inspectors also had too many schools to inspect, so that they could not do their work properly and were often seen simply as arbitrary, bureaucratic obstacles. So the *instituteurs* had more and more internal battles to fight, which concerned only themselves.

An inquiry by two sociologists among the primary teachers of the Seine, published in 1964, showed just how far they had evolved. They were on the whole still left wing, but whereas 59 per cent of the men thought that 'present-day society is antagonistic to what I want from life', only 43 per cent of the women did, and there were even 7 per cent of men and 23 per cent of women who thought present-day society was good. 64 per cent of the men and 46 of the women were unbelievers, but 30 and 42 per cent were believers. This still implied that teachers were less religious than the population as a whole, but only 23 per cent of the men and 9 of the women were opposed to religion as such. All agreed that their prestige had sunk even though their paper qualifications had risen, but 65 per cent of the women (as opposed to 46 per cent of the men) declared themselves satisfied with their jobs. The repressed, aggressive male *instituteur* was thus being replaced by more contented women, who saw teaching as an emancipation in itself. These women were not blue-stockings—only 28 per cent of them were unmarried (as opposed to 15 per cent bachelors) and only 10 per cent thought it all right for a woman to have a better job than her husband (whereas 26 per cent of the men had no objection to this). Nearly three-quarters, of both men and women, said they belonged to the middle class, or the petite bourgeoisie. Their identification with the workers was gone (only 22 per cent of men and 9 per cent of women said they belonged to the working class). The primary school thus failed to identify itself with the proletariat, though it was designed for it; it remained the intermediary by which the proletariat—led by the *instituteurs* themselves—tried to escape.[1] This should not be seen as a failure or a betrayal. If the majority of the proletariat wanted to escape from that condition, then the *instituteurs* were in one sense clearing the path for them; but in the process they set up and were absorbed by a system which was too distant from the ordinary working world. The

[1] Ida Berger and Roger Benjamin, *L'Univers des instituteurs* (1964).

instituteurs were never really all that much more politically committed than the people at large. It was only a minority that took part in elections; only a tiny minority were freemasons; in most cases what they valued most was professional and intellectual independence—in exactly the same way as the peasant or the worker. But their weakness was that there were too many pressures on them, from the state, from politicians, from the church, from parents, from the children, from their superiors and their colleagues, not to mention the full share of family and personal worries that tormented them.[1] No other profession had to serve so many masters and it is not surprising that they fully satisfied nobody. They needed faith to survive in such conditions and they evolved one, which gave most of them a sense of satisfaction in having tried to advance the cause of progress. But they were judged in terms of the society that employed them.[2]

Teaching Methods and their Consequences

These different forces in French education led to the use of techniques which made the relation between school and the world outside it distinctly formal and uncompromising. The reactions of pupils to what they were taught, and the permanent results of their schooling, may be seen, first of all, in the way they were introduced to reading and writing. It is usual to isolate several methods, each claiming to be more modern than the previous one, and to say that, after vigorous battles between them, they gradually supplanted each other; but in fact the legacy of the past was seldom entirely lost, and one had rather an accumulation of methods superimposed. The continuity behind the revolutionary battles is as remarkable in education as in politics and government—even though there were many important changes in detail. Thus, to begin with, the method of teaching reading changed drastically around the middle of the century, with the adoption of the phonetic system. Formerly,

[1] Cf. Roger Crinier, *Caractérologie des instituteurs* (1963).
[2] J. Ozouf, *Nous, les maîtres d'école* (1967), the best study pending the completion of his thesis on the *instituteurs*; G. Duveau, *Les Instituteurs* (1957); André Ferré, *L'Instituteur* (1954); Serge Jeanneret, *La Vérité sur les instituteurs* (1941); Émile Glay and Henry Champeau, *L'Instituteur* (1928), by their trade union leaders; Henri Bibert, *Les Bourriques* (1911); C. Brun, op. cit.

reading lessons used to begin with memorising letters, then words, then sentences, as opposed to learning how each letter was pronounced and composing syllables from that. Though the second method, propagated by Hachette and especially Peigné after 1831, aroused much enthusiasm among its partisans, and though the Brothers of the Christian Schools adopted it in 1847, teachers were divided into two camps on the subject until at least 1870, and even in 1889 when the phonetic method had the support of the immense majority, there were still departments in the west, and some religious schools, which preferred the traditional one.[1] It used to be the practice to learn to read in Latin, partly because there were no unpronounced letters, and partly also because many parents and teachers considered they had done enough if they taught children to read their prayers and Sunday offices. Boys in larger schools were divided into 'latinists', the lowest grade, 'Frenchmen' when they moved on to read their own language, and they became 'writers' only after that, since it was a principle that the three Rs should be tackled in turn and not simultaneously. *Instituteurs*, besides, could not always teach all three, and a boy might thus learn to read but not to count or calculate. In 1880 the Inspector-General of Rennes reported that many *instituteurs* still believed this was a good thing, and children were not even given a pen or pencil till their second year at school. The fact that many schools at that time still did not have desks for their pupils to write on made any desire for change irrelevant. It was J. B. La Salle, the founder of the Brothers of the Christian Schools, who first broke with the Latin tradition, by producing his French spelling book, but he did not alter the religious character of the exercise: boys were taught to read out of his *Christian Duties* and *Christian Behaviour*, which consisted of lists of religious and moral principles.[2] Exactly the same kind of reading books were used in other schools in the mid-nineteenth century—for example, *Reading and Moral Exercises* by Émile Delapalme, a magistrate and brother-in-law

[1] I. Carré, *L'Enseignement de la lecture, de l'écriture et de la langue française dans les écoles primaires* (1889) (Mémoires et documents scolaires publiés par le Musée pédagogique, deuxième série, fasc. 27).

[2] H. C. Rudon and Ph. Friot, *Un Siècle de pédagogie dans les écoles primaires (1820–1940). Histoire des méthodes et des manuels utilisés dans l'Institut des Frères de l'instruction chrétienne de Ploërmel* (1962) is one of the few histories of teaching methods.

of Napoleon III's minister Baroche.[1] This book was reprinted thirty-eight times between 1843 and 1908, showing how long traditions survive. A great change occurred at the beginning of the Third Republic, with the wildfire success of *Francinet* and *Le Tour de France par deux enfants*, which were reading books with an interesting story and with a lot of factual information, but the content was still very moralising. After the decline of religion, great stress was laid on choosing only the very best prose, by the most admired writers. Reading, indeed education as a whole, continued to be seen as the conquest of values. Though the child was no longer regarded as sinful, he was now considered to be nothing in himself, infinitely malleable, and the aim was to raise him quickly to adult life and to participation in the achievements of humanity. This was the way the religious traditionalists and the new positivists met on common ground. 'To read', wrote the republican philosopher Alain, 'that is the true cult. That is why I am far from believing that the child must understand all that he reads and recites.' Alain's pupil, Jean Chateau (b. 1908) likewise insisted that no object was properly perceived until it was named: 'The word is the portmanteau to which the idea attaches itself. So vocabulary must at first be learnt by heart.'[2] Memorising, no longer of religious doctrines but now of admired prose and poetry, continued to occupy a major part of the children's efforts. There was an attack on this at the end of the nineteenth century, but it was only temporary and a reaction then set in once again. As a result, small children were made familiar with 'literature' in a very thorough way at an early age: even if they could not understand it, they could recite it, as they had once been able to recite their prayers.

Grammar likewise continued to be studied in great detail, if not in quite the same way as had been the practice when Latin was the language taught, at least in a similar spirit.

[1] E. Delapalme [1793–1868], *Exercices de lecture et de leçons de morale* (1843); id., *Premier Livre de l'enfance*, 43 editions 1849–1908; id., *Bibliothèque d'enseignement élémentaire à l'usage des instituteurs primaires* (1829–30), 25 vols. Compare the survival of the *Méthode de lecture* (1958) by Frères Théodorit and Job of the Christian Schools, the 57th edition of which appeared in 1923.

[2] Louis Legrand, *L'Enseignement du français à l'école élémentaire: problèmes et perspectives* (Neuchâtel, 1966), by a former *instituteur* and *inspecteur primaire* who obtained a doctorate and became chef du service de la recherche pédagogique—one of the most interesting analysts in this field.

The positivists loved grammar, because they saw in it a method of getting the child to pass from the 'intuitive' stage to a clear understanding of the rules and structure of language; they retained a belief in the value of abstract grammatical definitions, on the assumption that these would be spontaneously transferred to ordinary speech. So here again, after the temporary discrediting of grammar under the Second Empire, there was a revival of it. At the beginning of the nineteenth century, the standard grammar book was Lhomond's (1727–94), based on Latin models and containing simply a summary of the rules, without any exercises.[1] Then Noël and Chapsal produced their *New French Grammar* in 1823, which became extremely popular, reaching its eightieth edition in 1889, not counting pirated versions. Chapsal (1788–1858) was a teacher at Louis le Grand and Noël (1755–1841) was a renegade priest who sided with the Revolution, became a diplomat, prefect and Inspector-General of Education. They must be counted among the best-selling authors of the century: the titles of Noël's numerous textbooks and dictionaries occupy twenty-one pages in the Bibliothèque Nationale catalogue. They were not innovators, but they succeeded in giving the rules of grammar in a clear and orderly way, with simple formulae to explain them. They set a new fashion for the grammatical analysis of French, even if the result was not all that different from the old. Their greatest contribution was that they added exercises at the bottom of each page, in the form of a catechism. The book begins: 'French grammar is the art of speaking and writing correctly in French. To speak and write, one uses words. Words are composed of letters. There are two kinds of letters.' And the questions for the pupil at the bottom of the page were: 'What is grammar, what are words composed of?' Definitions of every part of speech were set out, complete with an enormous number of infinitely subtle distinctions, all to be memorised.[2] Napoleon III's ministers waged a war against this method, as encouraging parrot learning. Instead the principle was proclaimed that grammar should go from the concrete to the abstract, from example to rule; and in 1877 two other teachers, Fleury and

---

[1] C. F. Lhomond, *Éléments de grammaire française* (1780).
[2] F. J. M. Noël and C. P. Chapsal, *Nouvelle Grammaire française sur un plan très méthodique* (56th edition, 1875).

Larive, produced a new textbook which, claiming to carry this out, achieved even greater success, reaching its 229th edition in 1953.[1] In fact, it was not all that different in content to its predecessor, but had the advantage that it reorganised its facts between three different books, elementary, middle and senior, to suit the threefold division of primary schools just introduced.[2] With time, *instituteurs* varied the methods and made them increasingly flexible and inductive, but the stress on grammar survived. French children in the 1950s were learning analyses of verb and subject at the age of seven, when Swiss children did not attempt it till ten.

Accurate spelling continued to be valued very highly, and tests by Binet and others have shown that standards have risen since 1904, even in working-class districts of Paris (though Genevan children still spell better, as they did earlier).[3] The stress on accuracy in written French was associated with the continued use of dictation. This traditional practice was maintained with a whole new barrage of arguments about its virtues: it gave pupils practice in handling sentences; it directed their attention to grammatical constructions; it gave them models to follow in spelling, punctuation and capitalisation; it enlarged the vocabulary, and, not least, it prevented them from separating the spoken language from the written. An American professor who visited a French school in 1912 found, by tests, that French children of twelve could spell considerably better than American college freshmen. Good spelling, as the French Academy pointed out in 1694, was 'what distinguishes men of letters from the ignorant and from simple women'; the fondness for strict rules in this matter has increased very considerably with time, good spelling becoming a kind of social passport.[4] In 1889 an official commentator asserted that for long the study of French was above all the study of spelling, by reading, copying and taking down dictation, and that it was only in 1880

---

[1] J. F. B. Fleury and Larive, *La Première Année de grammaire* (1871, 201st edition 1917).

[2] Fleury was the father of Madame Durand, alias 'Henri Greville', author of the best-selling textbook on morals for primary schools. Fleury and Larive's textbook is said to have sold twelve million copies.

[3] Legrand, op. cit., 77, 109.

[4] Rollo W. Brown, *How the French Boy Learns to Write* (Cambridge, Mass., 1924), 60–1; Legrand, op. cit., 119.

that composition, which had hitherto been considered the preserve of the secondary system, was introduced. But in 1966 an equally authoritative expert complained that primary education had continued to be dominated by spelling and dictation: certainly a dictation every day remained normal; but it is true that dictation gradually came to be treated with less respect and a child would lose only a quarter or half a mark, instead of a whole one, for a spelling mistake. It was the same with handwriting. This used to be taught as an art in several varieties and one of the *instituteurs'* time-consuming functions had been to sharpen quills (until around 1870), but beautiful handwriting then came to be considered a sign of immaturity, and the smart *instituteurs* from the *écoles normales* liked to despise it as old fashioned. One of the causes of its downfall was that there was disagreement as to which style should be taught, while the civil service, which used to be one of the major patrons of calligraphy, increasingly cultivated illegibility, so that a new form of esoterism succeeded the old.

What struck American observers of the French system was the large place writing held in the schools and in their routine. 'The ideal of writing well has been held up before the schoolboy so long, and with such seriousness, that he attaches more importance to ability of this kind than the average American boy could at present be led to comprehend' (1915).[1] Composition was introduced into the system by Jules Ferry in association with *la leçon de choses*—one of the most popular slogans of the reformers—which was supposed to sharpen the child's powers of observation, in a properly scientific spirit. But though this produced far more interesting lessons, on subjects which would not ordinarily have been treated at school, it also involved spending a great deal of time in the study of words, in a far more thorough way than would be found in either England or America. Thus the pupil would be required to define a word, give examples of its various uses, learn its original meaning, compare it with synonyms and above all contrast it with its opposites. 'It is scarcely too much to say that the basis of all word-teaching is contrast rather than likeness.' The consequences of this should not be exaggerated, for they indicate only the mental attitudes the educators admired. But children

[1] R. W. Brown, op. cit., 47.

were trained to use words which did not come naturally to them. 'The feeling for words which the pupil develops', wrote the same American professor, 'becomes a permanent part of his life. The boy who has had training of this kind may still use slangy or worn speech, but he is at least aware of what he does. And he will often avoid the colorless word not because he simply knows that it should be avoided, but because his quickened nature instinctively revolts aganst it.'[1] It will be seen in due course how these tendencies were developed and pushed further in the secondary schools. But even the primary schoolchild, despite the warnings of ministers and inspectors who liked to insist that this level should remain essentially practical and working class, was given a training that had more than a hint of the literary in it. Each pupil was required to keep a notebook in which most of his written work was collected. The ideal was that nothing should be finally consigned to that notebook until it was absolutely correct. And the compositions collected for the International Exhibition of 1878 showed that the system could work very efficiently: even those sent in by children are incredibly mature, while those sent in by their teachers were very impressive, thoughtful and interesting.[2] However, just how responsibility for the fluency of these exercises should be shared between parents and teachers is not clear. Recent investigations have suggested that home background still plays a more decisive role in school success than any other factor (except perhaps in mathematics). This was always an important limitation upon the primary schools.

Moral Education

However, the heart of the new primary education developed by the Third Republic was moral and civic training. This was what the reformers considered to be their most original contribution;[3] this is what aroused most controversy among their opponents; and paradoxically, this was perhaps the part of the syllabus which had least practical effect. It represented, more than anything else, the intervention of theorists and professors

[1] Ibid. 57.

[2] *Devoirs d'écoliers français recueillis à l'exposition universelle de Paris, 1878*, edited by Bagnaux, Berger, Buisson *et al.* (1879).

[3] H. Marion, *Le Mouvement des idées pédagogiques en France depuis 1870* (1889), 31.

into primary education, of which they had little personal knowledge, imposing methods strangely out of touch with reality. They wanted to create a society whose members would be more than oppressed subjects, held to the observance of the laws simply by fear of punishment. Universal suffrage was a terrifying prospect when large sections of the population were considered 'savages' and 'barbarians' and the working classes were labelled 'the dangerous classes'.[1] For many, a common French language was the essential preliminary for national unity, but just as pressing was the need to gain acceptance for the moral values for which the new France stood. The first and second republics had both made a start; Hippolyte Carnot, as minister of education in 1848, had distributed little books (of roughly the same size as the *Thoughts of Chairman Mao*) which combined republican propaganda with exhortations to virtue and philosophical explanations of why one should be both virtuous and republican.[2] But it was Jules Ferry and Paul Bert who made this an integral part of the school syllabus. After 1881–2, the day's work had to be preceded by a little lesson on morals, in place of prayers. The ministerial instructions were drawn up by Henri Marion and the syllabus by Paul Janet, both professors at the Sorbonne. They declared that the lay teacher of morals should aim to complete what the priest and the father began, or failed to accomplish: he had to ensure that every child 'served an effectual moral apprenticeship'. Whereas the Church, by defining its dogmas, stressed what separated Catholics from others, the lay school, while avoiding religious controversy, would show children what they should have in common, above any disagreements—'those essential notions of human morality common to all doctrines and necessary to all civilised mankind'. These philosophers were of course no revolutionaries, and Ferry rightly summarised their ambition when he said that all they hoped to teach was 'the good old morality we learnt from our fathers and mothers'.

Because this seemed to infringe the rights of the clergy, because the approach of moral education was deist and rationalist as opposed to Catholic, and because it brought out into the open, before the children, political and religious disputes, moral

[1] L. Chevalier, *Classes laborieuses et classes dangereuses* (1958).
[2] Cf. Augustin Sicard, *L'Éducation morale et civique 1700–1808* (1884).

education became the object of a vast hostile campaign by the Church. A great attack was launched on the textbooks. It is necessary to see what this protest was about, but it will be shown that, from the educational point of view, the fuss was largely one about theory, not practice. The practical interest of moral education, it will be suggested, lies elsewhere. The textbooks which the republicans now produced, and which the Church immediately placed on the Index, were less important for what they achieved than interesting for what they revealed about their authors. Republican morality was distinctly conservative. Its great innovation was that it sought the rational assent of children to the generally agreed rules of society. It therefore reduced these to a level which was at once banal and immensely striking, because it dared say, in a few words, things which critical minds would want qualified and elaborated. Living together seemed a grim business when the rules were spelt out: the sight of the very skeleton on which all else rested was disconcerting. The exercise revealed just how unoriginal and old-fashioned the advocates of progress and science were— but they were terrifying none the less.

The trouble with the moral textbooks was that they were written for children, but almost none were produced to give guidance on how the subject should be taught. The teachers were left with the relatively brief instructions issued by the ministry; but these vacillated confusingly. In 1882 Ferry laid it down that the morals lesson should appeal above all to the emotions. A great deal depended on the way the teacher succeeded in arousing the feelings of his pupils. 'The teacher is not required to fill the child's memory, but to teach his heart, to make him feel, by an immediate experience, the majesty of the moral law.' But then in 1888 Octave Gréard (for several decades a powerful civil servant in the ministry of education) said the method should not be emotional, but intellectual. 'Coldness is preferable to declamation, lack of emotion to the pretence of emotion.' The nature of duty should be clarified and proved necessary by reason. Then again in 1923 the minister said that the approach should be to 'sensibility' and that the effectiveness of the teaching depended on its intensity and warmth of conviction. At this point, though the old regulations continued to be officially reissued, the ministry seems to have lost courage somewhat, and instead of demanding uniformity, declared that each teacher had better follow his own inclinations, and certainly prefer them to the textbooks.[1]

Moral education therefore reached the children in many different guises. Though from reading about the debates on the textbooks, one might imagine a revolution was being fomented in the classrooms in the 1880s, the programme took at least twenty years to get going. Many *instituteurs*, particularly in the west, just did nothing about it. They were not so much worried by exactly how God was discussed in the textbooks, as unaccustomed to, and uninterested in, dealing in these abstractions. An inspector reporting on the department of Morbihan in 1895–1900 said that the state schools were continuing to teach the Catholic catechism, just as though there had been no Ferry laws at all. Only a few *instituteurs* here had acquired the new moral textbooks; some at first simply refused to teach the new subject. But by 1900 the large majority had got into the habit of giving about three lessons a week on morals. They usually began by writing a moral maxim on the blackboard, reading it out and explaining it. Then the pupils copied it down and learnt it by heart. The 'practical' side consisted in putting up notices in the village saying: 'Alcohol is the Enemy', cutting out reports from the local papers of accidents and misfortunes caused by alcohol, and making 'respectful remonstrances' to parents when they were seen drinking. This naturally was not the kind of teaching parents wanted to encourage. So it might all end with just a Table of Honour listing virtuous deeds by moral pupils, for example X found a purse containing two francs: 'putting into practice the lesson he had learnt at school, he immediately brought it to his teacher'.[2] The inspector of Lons-le-Saulnier wrote (in 1889): 'The lessons are generally pale imitations of the country priest's sermons: they are either grotesque, declamatory and hollow, or banal, vague and embarrassed.' Another wrote: 'Morals are taught as formerly the catechism was, by question and answer, by yes and no.' The

[1] Brouard and Ch. Defodon, *Les Nouveaux Programmes des écoles primaires* (1914), 43–5; H. Gossot and F. Brunot, *L'Enseignement du premier degré: de la théorie à la pratique* (c. 1939).

[2] A. Aignan, Inspecteur d'Académie, *Notes et documents sur l'enseignement de la morale. Écoles laïques du Morbihan 1895–1900* (Vannes, 1900, copy in the Musée pédagogique).

inspector of Limoges found an *institutrice* 'disserting on the distinction between the body and the soul to little mites of seven or eight years', but that otherwise 'the teaching of morals does not exist in the schools of my district'. Some gave the lesson perfunctorily in five minutes; some turned it into 'a sort of public confession', getting their pupils to tell the class what good deeds they had done or seen. The subject was thus not popular with either parents, teachers or pupils. The textbooks which were preferred were not the philosophically disputatious ones, but those, like Lavisse's, which dealt with one virtue per lesson, with each precept numbered, so that teaching could be systematic.[1] Patriotism was probably the idea which was most widely propagated as a result, though one inspector, from Ribérac, claimed that his teachers were unanimously agreed their lessons had made lying less frequent.[2]

The hope that moral education would give young children a sort of elementary version of the *culture générale* that the secondary schools dispensed, or a condensed summary of accumulated human wisdom, was never fulfilled, despite numerous debates and constantly revised textbooks. Perhaps the nearest it got to success was at the École Normale at Fontenay-aux-Roses, the chief training college for *institutrices*, at the head of which Ferry placed Félix Pécaut, who exerted a profound influence on its graduates. He was a Protestant pastor who had in 1859 published a book, *Christ and Conscience*, which anticipated and even surpassed the audacity of Renan's *Life of Jesus*: in it he argued that Christ was not divine, his teaching was not perfect, but was capable of being improved with time. It was this attitude, of the extreme left of Protestantism, that Pécaut tried to give his pupils, in early-morning lectures, which were on the borderline of morals and religion, and which became so famous that they were printed in the *Revue pédagogique*. His pupils are said to have venerated him; spiritual life at the college was 'intense', with the accent on introspection, self-knowledge and moral rectitude.[3] But this was something that affected only an élite of *institutrices;* and it did not solve the problem of how to teach young children.

[1] E. Lavisse's moral books were published under the pseudonym of Pierre Laloi: *Les Récits de Pierre Laloi* (1888).
[2] F. Lichtenberger, *L'Éducation morale dans les écoles primaires* (1889) (Mémoires et documents scolaires publiés par le Musée pédagogique, deuxième série, fasc. 28).
[3] F. Pécaut, *Éducation publique et vie nationale* (1897).

In 1914 an inspector-general admitted that the methods for moral education 'in large part not only needed to be set out, but needed to be discovered'. The extent of his bewilderment may be judged from his suggestion that perhaps the lay theorists should look more closely at the methods of the Catholic Church, which used ceremonies, symbolism and group feelings, though he would not concede that it was necessarily more successful.[1] In 1953 a director of a teacher training college with long experience of this subject admitted that all those involved in it had been sadly disappointed with its results; he doubted whether it was worth teaching at all; with many people so sceptical, any advocate of it was likely to be laughed at.[2]

The experiment was essentially a product of a rationalist approach to education, and this is perhaps its main interest. It revealed how the approach survived despite the discoveries of psychology, which remained, as it were, locked up in a separate compartment. A sample lesson in moral education may perhaps show how this worked. It is taken from a pedagogic treatise by the inspector who specialised in the subject. The lesson was on gratitude. The teacher was told to begin with a definition of gratitude. He should explain gratitude to parents, teachers and benefactors, and he should contrast it with ingratitude. He would then show how gratitude was a duty, and how detestable ingratitude was. 'Speak of the satisfaction experienced in repaying a kindness received and of the loving and powerful bond formed between men by gratitude: give examples from school life.' The lesson should conclude with a summary: 'All benefits received lay upon us the duty of gratitude. Ingratitude is detestable; the fulfilment of the duty of gratitude gives the soul real joy.' The 'maxim' to be remembered was 'The heart also has its memory, its name is gratitude; ingratitude is a sort of treason'. The children should then memorise and recite two relevant fables from La Fontaine and a story from a reading book by Guyau, author of *Morals Without Religion*.[3]

The explanation of this kind of lesson is belief in the importance of the training of the will. Until around the 1880s, the

[1] R. Allier, G. Belot *et al.*, *Morale religieuse et morale laïque* (1914), 51.

[2] Robert Mériaux, *La Formation morale à l'école primaire. Du sentiment à la raison* (1953).

[3] I. Carré, *Traité de pédagogie scolaire* (1897), 397.

view upheld by most philosophers, under the influence of
Cousin, was that of Kant, that the will should train itself, by
self-imposed effort; and that the categorical imperative would
lead men to be good. A contradictory view, stemming from
Rousseau, that the child was basically good, and should simply
be allowed to develop naturally, away from corrupting influences, won, as will be seen, some support among infant
teachers, but never got far beyond this. Moral education in
primary education stood uncertainly between these two theories: the theories of the different levels of education were never
coherent.[1] The authors of the first syllabuses for the primary
schools were products of the Cousin–Kant school. Buisson,
however, stood halfway between them and the new psychologists. He favoured making school life more enjoyable but he
warned against turning it simply into an entertainment. Effort
and hard work were necessary at school, for otherwise they
would disappear from adult life too. Borrowing from Dr. F.
Lagrange's pedagogy of physical education and Ribot's theories on the psychology of the will, he argued that the education
of the will should be a prime purpose of the schools, but that
the child should be assisted towards a rational mastery of
himself by training, in the same way as muscles needed to be
exercised. Obedience of the will to its own law—moral autonomy—should still be the ultimate goal. Reason and conscience
must be the basis of education.[2] Gréard had insisted: 'Education
is the work of reason, addressing itself to reason and using
reason.' Jules Payot, Rector of Aix University, though critical
of these doctrines, produced a treatise on 'The Education of the
Will' which gave a preponderant role to 'meditation'.[3] By the
time Piaget showed, in his *Moral Judgements of Children* (1932),
how up to the age of about 8 children equated good with
obedience, how they gradually acquired notions of solidarity
and co-operation between the ages of 8 and 12, and how logic

---

[1] Cf. Debs, *Tableau de l'activité volontaire pour servir à la science de l'éducation* (Amiens,
1844).

[2] F. Buisson, *Education of the Will* (Washington, 1903); id., *Conférences et causeries
pédagogiques* (1888), especially on 'ensignement intuitif'; id., *La Religion, la morale
et la science: leur conflit dans l'éducation contemporaine* (1900), 178–80, and *passim*,
shows some of the contradictions. Cf. Zeldin, *Politics and Anger*, 353 and 366.

[3] Jules Payot, *L'Éducation de la volonté* (1907, 27th edition 1920).

and morals cannot be used to explain each other, the French system of moral education was already discredited in practice, but it survived in the syllabus. It was really only after 1945 that it was seen that this system, which claimed to develop the will, in fact did not require enough effort from the child, because it neglected his individual personality. As Hubert, another Rector wrote in 1948, 'Morals are not a lesson that one learns after having had them put into a formula; they are a discovery made at the price of personal efforts, an experience that one conquers.'[1]

Moral education was distinct from, but closely linked with, civic education. On this subject, again, there was disagreement. Jules Ferry wanted civic education to be purely factual and informative, instruction on the organisation of society and government. But more optimistic people hoped it would be something more, that it would 'bend children to the obedience that the laws required' and 'inspire in them respect for these'. The lessons were brief, adding up to only one hour a week. It was soon obvious that 'the results were almost nil'. The teachers' arguments that the laws should be obeyed because they represented justice and reason came up against the 'suspicious and defiant instinct of unenlightened children', as one expert put it in 1889, and the subject remained at 'a purely verbal level'.[2] The loss of faith in it can be seen by looking at Paul Bert's textbook of 1882 (a fascinating defence of patriotism and the French Revolution—with bitter denigration of the *ancien régime*—a paean in favour at once of progress and the *status quo*, arguing that inequality of wealth, which was 'natural', did not make France any the less a fraternal society, because equality of opportunity existed); this was 176 pages long; but by the 1920s the most widely used book, by Primaire, was a

[1] R. Hubert, *L'Éducation morale* (1948), 73–4. For a vigorous critique of French methods, see Gustav Spiller, *Moral Education in Eighteen Countries* (1899), published by the International Union of Ethical Societies, 206–31. For modern psychological views, Arlette Bourcier, *La Nouvelle Éducation morale* (1966). Cf. Arnould Clausse, *Pédagogie rationaliste* (1968); F. Alengry, *Psychologie et morale appliquées en éducation* (n.d., about 1907); Albin Liangminas, *L'Enseignement de la morale, essai sur sa nature et ses méthodes* (1938); Groupe des étudiants socialistes révolutionnaires internationalistes, *Comment l'État enseigne la morale* (1897).

[2] Léopold Mabilleau, *L'Instruction civique* (1889) (Mémoires . . . musée pédagogique, deuxième série, fasc. 29.) Cf. id., *Cours d'instruction civique* (1884, 6th edition 1909).

mere sixteen pages.[1] Some textbooks had been pretty controversial, urging the case for votes for women, regionalism,
pacifism and even listing the faults of Frenchmen side by side
with their supposed qualities. In 1920, instead of either civic
or moral education, teacher training colleges, in their second
year, taught 'sociology'. This caused something of a sensation,
but the minister responsible assured parliament that sociology
should frighten no one, because 'it produces not a sceptical
indifference, but the justification of our moral practices'.[2]
Another manifestation of civic education was the introduction
of military training and gymnastics into schools. This contributed to reinforcing the military atmosphere that flourished in
France till 1914, sustaining values which some claimed were
redolent of the *ancien régime*. In 1906, a vistor from Teachers
College, Columbia, reported that gymnastic apparatus was
almost unknown; practically all the swimming exercises referred
to in the official syllabus were performed on dry land; the
boxing was a series of formal movements against imaginary
opponents.[3] The teachers were much worried by their legal
liability for accidents that might occur.

There can be no doubt that some teachers, with powerful
personalities, did manage to make something of this moral
education. In particular, it was possible to have a practical
effect on children's behaviour by encouraging such things
as kindness towards animals. But there was always a basic
contradiction between the theories of equality and fraternity
the teacher preached, and the autocratic authoritarianism he
exercised in his class. It was rightly pointed out that though
he attacked the despotism of the *ancien régime*, he was often a
perfect example of despotism. The whole disciplinary system of
the schools, moreover, was inconsistent with its theories: effort
was demanded in return for prizes and marks. 'I have yet to
find a single class where the teacher ever rose to any ethical
basis above the idea of reward and punishment,' wrote an
American professor.[4]

[1] Paul Bert, *L'Instruction civique à l'école* (1882).
[2] Jean Beigbeder, *La Formation du futur citoyen à l'école primaire publique* (Paris
thesis, Alençon, 1923, reprinted Paris, 1924), 260.
[3] F. E. Farrington, *The Public Primary School System of France* (New York, 1906),
114.
[4] Ibid. 107.

Infant Schools

It was in infant education that most innovation was achieved, because this was a new branch with fewer traditions and vested interests to raise obstacles. *Salles d'asile* (rather than schools) had been started in some large towns to keep toddlers off the streets. They were the creation of private philanthropists; by 1837 there were only 800 of them, providing for 23,000 children. Though the intentions of these men were admirable, the results were grim. Many of the asylums were huge barrack-like structures, often with 200 or even 400 children in one room, with bitumen floors, and rows of benches on which they were tightly packed. A supervisor watched to make sure they sat still; a bell rang to get them to rise simultaneously, or blow their noses all at once. In 1840 an enterprising contractor offered to build *salles* capable of holding 6,000 children, so arranged that a single teacher on a high platform could see them all. In 1847 the minister of education himself believed that these establishments 'need no class equipment': the children indeed had no tables to write on, and they ate their meals from plates on their knees. Only in 1881 were tables prescribed, though most municipalities refused to buy them. It was in that year that Ferry abolished the *salles d'asiles* and renamed them *écoles maternelles*, with the mission, no longer of drilling infants in the parrot-like repetition of words they could not understand, but of giving them 'the *care* that their physical, moral and intellectual development required'. The emphasis was now to be on their general well-being, with an attempt to provide 'affectionate and indulgent gentleness', to bring enjoyment into their lives, habits of cleanliness, politeness, attention and obedience, which they were to acquire in organised games. The theorists behind this were a series of remarkable women: Madame Millet, who after visiting England introduced Buchanan's methods; Madame Pape-Carpentier, director of a training college for infant teachers in the rue des Ursulines, 1847–74, who was influenced by Fourierism, and attacked the punishment of children;[1] and above all Madame Pauline Kergomard (1838–1925). She was the daughter of a primary school inspector, the

[1] See her *Conseils sur la direction des salles d'asile* (1845).

niece of a Protestant pastor, and the cousin of the famous anarchist Reclus brothers. In 1879 Ferry appointed her inspector-general in charge of infant education. She tried to reduce classes to a maximum of 50—though in 1910 she herself reported that there were still classes of over 100: her intentions were never matched by the funds at her disposal. She attacked cramming, punishment, repression, the segregation of the sexes; she was an ardent feminist and wanted the equality of the sexes to start from childhood, but she also condemned single-sex schools because they 'killed children's sense of modesty (*pudeur*)' She was for great freedom, for a 'family atmosphere', but she wanted children to be given a 'social sense', rather than be left undisciplined. One of her first acts had been to get rid of any Froebel equipment she came across, saying it was too complicated; she opposed to 'the German method' 'the method of reason, common sense, personal independence, vivified by that fund of good humour, vivacity and natural wit which is peculiar to our national temperament'.[1] Later, there was no enthusiasm for the methods of Montessori either; these, it was claimed, did no more than what the French had already done in the *écoles maternelles*, and besides, Montessori owed her ideas partly to two French doctors, Itard and Séguin. But in 1900, the *maternelles* were attended by only one-quarter of children between 2 and 6; after that, they declined, following the closure of church schools, and between the wars only one-seventh of eligible children attended them. They appear to have been somewhat uneven in quality; but teachers had more independence, they broke the official rules, both in a liberal sense, to make them more practical, and also restrictively, when resources were inadequate for the grandiose projects the rules ordered. Some of the graduates of the new training college organised by Madame Kergomard were outward looking, and paid visits, for example, to the Decroly school in Belgium and the J.-J. Rousseau Institute in Geneva, but there were many more untrained teachers, barely aware of advances in the psychological or physiological sciences.[2]

[1] But a Froebel Society was established in 1880.
[2] Madame Pauline Kergomard, *Les Écoles maternelles de 1837 jusqu'en 1910* (1910); Ch. Charrier, *La Pédagogie vécue à l'école des petits* (1965 edition); Madame S. Herbinière-Lebert, 'Pédagogie de l'école maternelle' in R. Cousinet, *Leçons de pédagogie* (1950), 180–226.

Expansion

The *maternelles* had to wage a constant battle against many parents, who wanted their children to be taught the three Rs as early as possible, insisting on visible and rapid results. This pressure to extend the syllabus manifested itself throughout the primary system, so that the schools tried to do more and more. This led to a rather interesting result, in that primary education became almost autonomous, doing many of the things previously associated with secondary schools, but giving them a peculiar stamp, which was sometimes but by no means always 'practical'. The distinctive 'concentric' method introduced by Octave Gréard into the primary schools was that they should be divided into three classes, junior, middle and senior, all of which would have the same syllabus, but with different degrees of intensity. This applied the view that there was a basic body of knowledge which these schools should instil; a pupil who left early would thus have at least some smattering of it all. 'Since primary education is an education of principles,' wrote Gréard, 'and since principles cannot be too often represented if they are to penetrate, it is necessary that the child should pass constantly over the same ground.' The aim was also to end the old anarchy which left *instituteurs* alone to make as much progress as they could: henceforth the programme of the school was fixed in detail month by month, week by week. A child who moved from one town to another would thus miss nothing. Gréard, described by an admirer as a 'melancholy optimist', was descended from a long line of administrators, and he was a great believer in order, which he did his best to imprint on the schools. He was keen that they should not attempt to do too much: they must 'open access for everybody to careers where study is not necessary, they must give satisfaction to legitimate ambitions, but without over-exciting blind pretensions, which are as disappointing to individuals as they are fatal to society'. They must therefore be, first, practical and, secondly, moral. He wrote his thesis on 'Plutarch as a Moralist', whom he admired for preaching common virtues, in moderation and with no heroic element. Though serving the lay state, he was a Catholic, who regretted the decline in religious beliefs. He had been an efficient teacher of philosophy and 'he would have been a

perfect man if he had ever consented to amuse himself'. This
cultured, intelligent, methodical model of a civil servant told
the *instituteurs* that they must make the schools enjoyable, but
he had no fear that the systematic repetition he advocated might
also breed boredom.[1] Of course, the 'concentric method' could
barely be applied in small rural schools; and despite all ministerial injunctions, in 1906 it was estimated that at least 11 per
cent of primary pupils were still being taught by some form of
the Bell and Lancaster system, in which the older ones taught
the younger ones. This had been forbidden over fifty years
before, but died hard. Similarly, one should not imagine
Gréard's instructions were accurately implemented.

Geography and history were seen as part of moral and civic
education. The syllabus concentrated heavily on France; the
fostering of pride in the national heritage, both human and
physical, was the main purpose. There is no doubt that
patriotism was advanced by these lessons. Good pupils memorised a large number of dates, names and statistics about their
country; they could draw freehand a complete map of France,
divided into departments, and insert the names of all the sub-
prefectures. It was only in the junior form that world geography
was studied; in the upper two forms, three-quarters of the
lessons were on France. Reformers protested that the syllabus
tried to make children memorise the directories of the post
office, magistrature and army and the railway time-table;
reforms were decreed, but in general the primary schools did
not benefit from the brilliant development of French geography.
A different plan prevailed in history teaching. The first two
years were devoted to France, and the third to revision, plus
the addition of ancient history from Egypt to Rome. The
'concentric method' required that the whole of French history
be covered each year: in practice this meant that the French
middle ages were taught and retaught most thoroughly—a
strange result for the republic to achieve. The Merovingians
who started the course got a month, as much as the Revolution,
Consulate and Empire, which came last and was not always

[1] M. P. Bourgain, *Gréard, un moraliste éducateur* (1907) 64–5, 96, 113–14, 364;
O. Gréard, *Éducation et instruction*, vol. 1 ; *Enseignement primaire* (1887); Farrington,
op. cit., 101.

completed. There were demands from an early date that
Kulturgeschichte should replace anecdotal history, but it is
unlikely that any whisper of the *Annales* school ever reached
the primary classes.[1] Instructions were repeatedly issued by the
ministry, in history and in geography as also in the study of the
French language, that the teachers must relate their lessons to
the experience of their pupils, that Ferry's formula, *la leçon de
choses*, should replace the theoretical memorising. But, as the
ministry's instructions of 1945 themselves stated, these orders
were seldom carried out: 'Too often, *la leçon de choses* came down
to the study of a textbook or a summary: the pupils remember
only words which have no meaning for them. So exercises which
could make an important contribution to their intellectual
development are valueless and even harmful.'[2]

Another way by which the schools and the outside world were
supposed to be linked was manual education. This was inspired
partly by the thesis of Rousseau, Pestalozzi, Froebel and
Fourier, but even more it was seen as a practical answer to
France's industrial problems, to the decline of apprenticeship,
and to the fear that the best pupils of the primary schools would
increasingly try to become officials or clerks. The republican
worker-author Corbon, in his book *Professional Education* (1859),
criticised the traditional apprentice who simply knew his little
speciality and had no aspirations after improving his mind; he
demanded that the schools should combine education with
professional training, to produce a sort of workers' *culture
générale*.[3] These ideas were taken up by G. Salicis, a junior
teacher at the Polytechnic, who in 1873 got an official grant
to start manual education experimentally in one Paris school.
In 1882 Ferry made it a compulsory part of every primary
syllabus and appointed Salicis inspector-general in charge. The
teachers used were artisans, paid by the hour; the numbers of
hours devoted to the subject was gradually increased as the
children grew older. A model school of a new kind, with even
more emphasis on manual work (so that boys in their final year
spent nearly the whole of their time on it) was founded at

[1] H. Lemonnier, *L'Enseignement de l'histoire dans les écoles primaires* (1889);
P. Dupuy, *La Géographie dans l'enseignement primaire* (1889).
[2] Instructions of 1945, quoted by Prost, 279.
[3] A. Corbon, *De l'enseignement professionnelle* (1859).

Vierzon. Altogether, 12,000 schools tried it out (which shows once again how 'compulsory' subjects could be ignored by the majority). Only half of them had properly equipped workshops; the amateur teachers proved unsatisfactory; so an attempt was made to train ordinary *instituteurs* in manual work, which they resented, because it meant going on compulsory vacation courses. A special training college was founded but closed down two years later for lack of funds. Salicis argued that it was contradictory that the infant schools should develop manual dexterity and that the primary schools should then largely forget about it; but the tendency towards theory was too powerful for him. After his death in 1889, manual work became less and less manual. René Leblanc, editor of a journal, *L'Enseignement manuel*, began preaching that it should be regarded as part of science, as an intellectual training, and that once it became so, the *instituteurs* would drop their opposition to it. His ideas were adopted by the city of Paris, which abandoned the preparation for professional training and replaced it by simpler activities, like making objects out of paper; freed from any industrial purpose, it was made almost a part of geometry. But this does not seem to have had much effect outside Paris, where the whole idea languished. In rural areas, manual work became almost entirely agriculture, but this was kept theoretical: 'The child has in his head the names of grasses he has never seen, of fertilisers of whose composition and properties he is alike ignorant.' The most interesting work in manual education was probably done in a few private establishments, like that founded at Creil by the industrialist Somasco.[1]

Instead, the academic status of the primary system was strengthened by its extension beyond the education of young children by means of *écoles primaires supérieures*, which could keep pupils until the age of 17. These schools had two sections, general and professional, but the vast majority of pupils enrolled in the general courses, so that it was essentially an academic education that they received. The only difference between these schools and the *lycées* was that they claimed to adapt their syllabus to industry and commerce, and in fact they trained

---

[1] A. Panthier, *Enquête historique sur l'enseignement manuel dans les écoles non techniques* (1906); G. Salicis, *Enseignement du travail manuel* (1889); René Leblanc, *L'Enseignement professionnel en France au début du 20ᵉ siècle* (1905).

the growing body of clerks and junior supervisory ranks. They were accordingly very successful; they got the most ambitious pupils of the primary schools. In 1890 there were 296 of them; in 1937, 579. Some reached a very high standard and prepared, with excellent results, for the *baccalauréat*. The model was the Collège Chaptal, which attempted to copy the German *Realschulen*: founded in 1844, it expanded until by 1877 it had 1,300 pupils. In the early Third Republic several imitations of it were established in Paris and gradually the provinces followed suit. Some primary schools simply offered a 'cours complémentaire', which had the advantage that no fixed syllabus was officially laid down for it and this was one of the few areas in which local initiative had more or less free rein. But the teachers were the ordinary *instituteurs*. The *écoles primaires supérieures*, by contrast, developed into a self-contained system, with their own teachers trained to a higher level and earning more. Increasingly they performed much the same function as the 'modern' sections of the *lycées*. The aim of the inventors of these schools was thus foiled: these were schools for the people, but they did not provide technical training. Technical education had to be started as an independent system. Thus the number of parallel systems multiplied, each living its own life, not quite as though inhabiting different countries, but proud of its own approach and values. This was all the odder, because in fact they were moving closer in what they taught.[1]

New Methods

Not surprisingly, therefore, there were protests against these traditions and some interesting experiments were undertaken in order to correct their shortcomings; but if one is studying schoolchildren as a whole, one must at once admit that the experiments affected only a small minority of them, and a very small minority of teachers. For in these years France lost its leadership in educational ideas. It produced only a few of the major educational figures of the century, and much of its innovation consisted in borrowing from the more adventurous

---

[1] This is a sphere of education of which no history has been written. For the origins, see O. Gréard, op. cit. 139–72; statistics in A. de Mouzie and L. Febvre, *Encyclopédie française*, vol. 15 (1939), chapter 1.

experiments in the U.S.A., Switzerland, Germany and England. But there was considerable resistance to such borrowing, and when borrowings were made, for example, from Froebel, or from Baden-Powell, a lot of effort was spent pointing out that the French adaptation was specifically French, purged of nasty foreign elements. The xenophobia was by no means general: one is struck by the very considerable knowledge of foreign work which the leading educationists showed. Buisson was as well informed as anyone in the world about what was going on abroad, and he had visited many foreign countries. Education might well have been the subject in which knowledge of foreign developments was greatest: the reports on foreign educational systems, by official investigators, came out at regular intervals.[1] What is significant is that comparatively little resulted from all this interest.

The first move was to look at education more from the point of view of the child, to see what he wanted from it and to measure how far he was getting it. Progress in child psychology did not necessarily and immediately lead to changes in school methods, first because the new ideas were controversial, and secondly because they were studied for themselves, with little emphasis on practical application.[2] This is what Alfred Binet (1857–1911) tried to put right. He had studied in turn law, medicine, histology (his thesis was on the Nervous Intestinal System of Insects (1894)) and finally psychology. He was struck by the way discussion of educational questions was so often based on purely subjective polemic, without any effort to collect facts scientifically. He vigorously criticised in particular a debate held at the Academy of Medicine on overwork in schools, complaining that the statistical and medical observations were largely lacking. He wrote a book on *Intellectual Exhaustion* (1898) which concluded that no conclusion was possible until a great deal more research was done. He called for a *new pedagogy*, which would break away from the *old*, which he condemned as 'too generalising, too vague, too literary, too moralising, too verbalistic, too preaching . . . It solves the

[1] For example, see the work of C. Hippeau, *L'Instruction publique aux États-Unis* (1869), *L'Instruction publique en Angleterre* (1872), . . . *en Allemagne* (1873), . . . *en Italie* (1874), . . . *en Suède, Norvège et Danemark* (1876), etc.

[2] On child psychology see my *Ambition and Love*, ch. 12; *Anxiety and Hypocrisy*, chs. 1–3.

gravest problems by literary quotations from Quintilian and Bossuet; it replaces facts by exhortations and sermons; the word which characterises it best is *verbiage*'—an approach hardly conducive to winning him friends among the more or less conservative teachers. In 1899 Buisson and he founded the Société libre pour l'étude psychologique de l'enfant, renamed the Société Alfred Binet after his death, to inaugurate a new method, founded on observation and experiment. Here he first tried using questionnaires (borrowed from the American Stanley Hall) but since these often produced unconvincing results—they were rather inefficiently administered—he took to organising research by teams, each to solve a particular problem. These teams studied an enormous variety of subjects, such as methods of teaching writing, reading, spelling, and of preventing laziness etc. As a basis for all this, Binet, with his disciples Simon and Vanney, developed the intelligence test, which was to be his most celebrated achievement, as well as other scales for measuring educational attainment. People recognised that Binet's intentions were admirably scientific, but there was no denying that the immediate results of his investigations were not as helpful as his fine-sounding manifesto had led them to hope. Binet often had to admit that he had made mistakes which invalidated his work: it was one of his merits that he never hesitated to make these admissions publicly. Some complained that he used a great deal of effort to prove what was obvious: Binet held complicated experiments to prove that his intelligence tests were less arbitrary than the marks of teachers in examinations, but he aroused vigorous opposition. He had a long controversy in 1907 with Jules Payot, who was then editor of *Le Volume*, a weekly journal for *instituteurs*. Payot had launched an attack on dictation and spelling, arguing that children remembered whole words, rather than built them up from individual letters. Binet refused to accept as evidence simply the general impressions Payot adduced on the basis of his long experience as an inspector. He insisted on devising tests, and these proved that the teaching of spelling was useful. Vitriolic attacks were exchanged in the process. He also tried to prove that children who started to read at the age of six—as the kindergarten movement was urging—did no worse than those who began at five, as the primary school officials demanded.

He invaded a multitude of subjects sanctified by tradition and taught by highly experienced teachers, casting doubts on almost sacred principles like the examination system and even the religious neutrality of lay schools. He asked searching questions: he demanded an inquiry into whether neutrality was in fact achieved and, if so, what exact consequences it had on the mentality of children. Binet's importance came from an extraordinary capacity to detach himself from the accepted platitudes of his time, but he had never actually taught in a school, or indeed anywhere, so that he could be accused of being out of touch with reality. Nevertheless, his work encouraged a new way of approaching the problem of the abilities and aptitudes of children. It was to yield fruits also in more effective vocational guidance, and in the establishment of schools for subnormal children—a subject which particularly interested him. But the linking of the psychological investigations his disciples pursued, and actual educational reform, was a slow business.[1]

More immediately effective was the work of Roger Cousinet, who was able, as an inspector of primary schools, and therefore in close touch with the *instituteurs*, to start experiments in group methods, first in Sedan (1920) and then in thirty-seven schools in Paris. The schools were not completely reorganised, according to the principles advocated by the *École Nouvelle* movement, of which he was a leading light, and the pupils were given only a certain degree of participation in the running of their work. The idea behind this was that children should be encouraged to work in small teams, guided by their own interests and aptitudes, rather than sit passively in large classes. The initial experiment appears to have been a failure, both because the children found it difficult to adapt to this new demand on their initiative, and because the *instituteurs* complained that the new method increased instead of diminishing their hours of work. Cousinet had more success in applying group methods to play, as opposed to work.[2] At about the same time Profit, inspector of primary schools at Saint-Jean-d'Angély, introduced

[1] François Zuza, *Alfred Binet et la pédagogie expérimentale* (Louvain, 1948), contains a good bibliography. See especially A. Binet, *Les Idées modernes sur les enfants* (1909); F. L. Bertrand, *Alfred Binet et son œuvre* (1930).
[2] Roger Cousinet, 'Petite chronologie de l'éducation nouvelle', *L'École nouvelle française* (Mar. 1954); R. Cousinet and F. Chatelain, 'L'État présent de l'éducation nouvelle', ibid. (Oct. 1953); P. Foulquié, *Les Écoles nouvelles* (1948).

the co-operative idea into the schools of his district (1918), making the children themselves create school museums and organise scientific experiments on their own. This was designed to turn the school into the children's own institution. In 1939 some 9,000 such co-operatives were in existence, of varying effectiveness.[1]

The history of these efforts has still to be written, but just how much trouble an advocate of anti-authoritarian ideas could have was shown by the career of Freinet. Cousinet was an inspector who eventually won considerable administrative power, but even that was not enough to get his ideas adopted on more than a trial basis. Freinet was a humble *instituteur*, who worked on his own. Freinet never had any official pedagogical training, having followed a shortened course at an *école normale* after the 1914–18 war. He was the son of a peasant and a washerwoman; he suffered from tuberculosis; his weak health made traditional methods, with the teacher as orator, impractical for him. In 1920 he was appointed assistant *instituteur* at the little village of Bar-sur-Couz (Alpes-Maritimes). The headmaster was one of the old type of peasant-teachers, who knew, with no worries about technique, how to get his pupils through examinations and who spent half his time in the fields. Freinet read Pestalozzi, and Ferrière; he met Cousinet at the International Congress of the New Education; he was interested by Marx, Lenin, anarchism and the Geneva psychologists. But the theories he learnt about seemed too grandiose for his hovel of a school and he was not at home in the 'laboratory' atmosphere of the intellectual discussions of pedagogy. He wanted simply to do the best he could for the children in his school, to liberate them from the repressions forced on them by the traditional methods, with the ultimate goal of thereby renovating society as a whole. His first act was to abandon textbooks, which he denounced as contributing to 'the idolatry of the printed word, as a world apart, as something almost divine, whose assertions one always hesitates to dispute'; they killed the critical faculties, and enslaved the teachers, who used them to further the cult of examinations. With his meagre savings, he bought a printing press and made printing the centre of the

---

[1] Georges Prévot, *Pédagogie de la coopération scolaire* (1960); B. Profit, *La Coopération à l'école primaire* (1922); F. and L. Cattier, *Les Coopératives scolaires* (1937).

children's school activity: he used it to teach the child to distinguish between letters, to understand punctuation, and in discussion of the proofs, grammar and style could be studied with direct interest, because the children printed their own reading material, in the form of a school newspaper. In this way he hoped to salvage 'the treasures of good sense and originality' of humble people, to enable the child to educate himself, with the help of a teacher in the background.

He was an anarchist-communist, so he was not satisfied with the people like Ferrière who thought the ideal school could be established: Freinet insisted that a reorganisation of society was necessary first. He was keen to produce a unity between the school and life outside, to make the children accept that they would be workers, rather than try to become something else. Thus he complained that the teaching of mathematics was concerned with the problems of merchants, speculators and civil servants—with problems of profits and sales and interest— and that it needed fundamental reform. He began exchanging his school newspaper with other schools who took up the same idea: by 1939 there were several hundred of them. Freinet had to move from his village to a larger one, so as to get a double job with his wife, who was also a teacher and who assisted him with the increasing administrative labours involved in running what had become a sizeable movement. When he began, he had been unable to afford the paper for the printing, and only the friendship of the mayor's secretary enabled him to start on the back of voting ballots left over from an election. Now the production of printing presses, of newspapers, of a filing-card system which he started, to replace textbooks, showed how much unofficial action could achieve. But his political involvement aroused opposition in his new post. His inspector complained that his pupils knew none of the dates of ancient history, that they sat where they pleased, that the disorder in the classroom was anarchic. Quarrels with parents and local officials ended in riots, which led to his suspension. The administration had tolerated, even encouraged, him in his first post, but the limits of its tolerance were now revealed: it could not absorb an extreme left-wing movement. In 1940 Freinet was arrested. His was probably the most exciting achievement of an individual teacher in the interwar period. But it affected only a few.

Purged of its politics, so far as was possible, it was partially absorbed by the *Éducation Nouvelle* movement. After 1945 this became quasi-official, with headquarters in the Musée pédagogique: Freinet had become increasingly hostile to it, seeing in it a hideout of products of the bourgeois secondary system. The reformers were almost as bitterly divided amongst themselves as they were opposed to the traditional system.[1]

The history of France's education produces the same conclusion as the history of its politics, that the theories propagated do not provide an accurate guide to what actually happened. The educational world was full of bright ideas, of constant demand for reform, of innumerable projects; rival factions, speaking in the name of religion, morals, freedom, modernity and other causes, fought against each other in a whole array of specialist periodicals. But one needs to look beyond the legislators and inspectors in order to judge the effects of the schools. It certainly cannot be said that France lacked able men at the head of its educational system, but it may be questioned whether these were not, to a considerable degree, prisoners of the system they served. Because teachers and those interested in education vented their grievances in public, the paralysing effects of administrative hierarchy, centralisation and routine can be seen here with exceptional clarity. Thus for example, the inspectorate which controlled large parts of the system often succeeded in obstructing experiment and adaptation to local conditions, because its function was to ensure that the rules were obeyed; but its knowledge of what was going on was often superficial, and one is also amazed at the extent to which the rules were disobeyed. The inspectors appointed before 1880 seldom had direct experience of primary teaching; they were usually men who had escaped from secondary teaching into the quieter havens of administration; they were invariably ageing, if not old. The inspectors-general throughout this period had hardly ever worked in primary schools: they of course were never young and were so busy writing letters and reports that they had time only for rapid tours in the provinces. Their

[1] Élise Freinet, *Naissance d'une pédagogie populaire. Histoire de l'école moderne* (*Méthodes Freinet*) (1968), is a lively biography by his widow. Cf. Freinet, *L'École moderne française* (1945).

custom seems to have been to come in the fine weather of spring, summon all the local inspectors, get them to fill in long question-naires: every chief had to write a personal appreciation of his subordinate: every official had to report, in triplicate, that he still had the same name and birthday as at the last inspection; and when all this paper had been collected, the inspector-general selected one school in the whole academy to look at, which was regarded as typical and which was decisive for his assessment of the situation. That was how uniformity and blindness to the lack of it were simultaneously preserved; and the existence of this rigid hierarchy of course meant that everyone was able to disclaim responsibility for what happened.

It was not easy to make suggestions for really fundamental changes, because universal education and the republic became inextricably identified with each other, and few people there-fore dared say that the system was a source of confusion as well as of new opportunities.[1] But the administrators should not be blamed for its defects without it being added that they could not respond favourably to all the contradictory pressures upon them. If they were accused by the left of enforcing an excessively traditional or bourgeois syllabus, they could answer that the workers were very uncertain as to what they would put in its place. This was forcibly revealed when the Institut Supérieur Ouvrier was founded in the 1930s, to revive the old *universités populaires* (which had appeared and quickly died at the turn of the century) but this time with the aim of doing without bourgeois co-operation, going beyond the system of unconnected lectures, and establishing team-work, in the image of the society of the future. It turned out that even this militant minority of workers were not quite clear whether they did want a separate 'workers' culture' or not. In 1935 only about 2,000 people were induced to participate in their grand-sounding experiment, Zoretti, who was a leading theorist of mass education, spoke rather vaguely of group methods, but could think of nothing more original than football (as a means of 'concretising ideas of collective discipline and mastering the excess of indivi-dualism'), or scouting, rebaptised the Red Falcons, with its

[1] Cf. Ch. Drouard, *Les Écoles urbaines* (2nd edition, 1902), 72; T. Nandy, *L'Enseignement primaire et ce qu'il devrait être* (7e Cahiers de la quinzaine, 14e série, 1913).

leaders obligatorily members of the Confédération Générale du Travail or the socialist party.[1]

Similarly, parents did not know what they wanted. Liberal complaints about the schools' disciplinary methods were certainly justified. There was a flagrant contradiction between the schools' desire to develop fraternity and morality and their encouragement of competitiveness, which they took over uncritically from the past. Success in academic work was what had got the teachers where they were, and they praised it as the highest of goals. The award of marks in every exercise, the constant classification of pupils by order of merit, the obsession with examinations, introduced a new factor into popular culture. (The certificate of primary studies was introduced, unsuccessfully, in 1834, reactivated in 1866 and finally made a national, as opposed to a local, award in 1880; later, a variety of more senior certificates were added.) This was perhaps the key instrument that subordinated primary school children to values of those who were more privileged than themselves. Almost automatically it was designed to breed frustration or disappointment in children who did not come first: it pitilessly subjected whole generations of less-endowed children to repeated public humiliations. The theory of meritocracy did not concern itself overmuch with those who were unsuccessful, though they formed a high proportion of the pupils. The elaborate system of rewards and punishments reduced morals to a form of accountancy: good points or tickets were granted in every lesson, and others for general behaviour, punctuality and various virtues: each week these points could be exchanged for *billets de satisfactions;* they were used almost as current coin, to pay for points lost by inattentiveness or other faults, though serious offences were not redeemable in this way. All this compensated for an important achievement of Napoleon's, which more or less effectively abolished corporal punishment. But it does not appear that there was any serious opposition from parents to these methods. On the contrary, many parents, in their effort to keep recalcitrant children under control, pressed for even firmer and more authoritarian punishments by the schools. The educators felt therefore that they had to

[1] L. Zoretti, *Pour l'éducation des masses* (1935); Maurice Poussin, *L'Éducation populaire et le socialisme* (1933); Lucien Gachon, *Les Écoles du peuple* (1942).

educate parents. The École des Parents, founded in 1928 by Madame Vérine, sought to reconcile the old principles of paternal authority with new ideas about the autonomy and personality of the child: it held annual congresses and organised lectures, and in 1942–3 it obtained a state subsidy. But when in 1956 it carried out an inquiry among its 'correspondents', 60 per cent of these still said that they used 'authoritarian' methods with their children, including corporal punishment; 20 per cent said they had tried all methods, including liberal ones. Only 14 per cent said they had lost faith in authoritarian methods and only 21 per cent said they believed in liberal methods. The three great worries of parents regarding children were given as their *nervosité*, their poor academic results and indiscipline, though it is true that worry about school results was eight times more frequent with boys than with girls.[1] The teachers could thus be said to have contributed to the general atmosphere of anxiety. It should be added that most parents who expressed opinions were middle class, and the anxiety probably only gradually spread down the social scale.

Employers, for their part, clamoured for more practical teaching from the schools and less theory. They seemed to have little regard for the knowledge the primary schools provided. Michelin in 1911, advertising jobs in his factory, said that all he demanded from recruits was a good character, honesty and ambition: he would undertake to teach them what they needed to know to do their work. Private employers, often without formal educational qualifications themselves, were most ready to ignore school results; but increasingly the possession of paper qualifications was required, even though they were despised.[2]

The quarrel about church participation in education was part of this general ambivalence towards the schools. The republicans, like the Catholics, wanted everyone to have the same kind of education: both sides tried to force all children into the same mould; neither appears to have had public opinion behind it. In 1850 the situation was that boys went predominantly to state schools, but 50 per cent of girls went to

---

[1] André Isambert, *L'Éducation des parents* (1959, 2nd edition 1968), 62; C. Hippeau, *L'Éducation et l'instruction considérées dans leurs rapports avec le bien-être social et le perfectionnement de l'esprit humain* (1885), 181.

[2] Pierre Dufrenne, *La Réforme de l'école primaire* (1919), 71.

schools run by religious orders. In 1848 there were only 2,136 male church teachers (*frères*) but 10,371 female ones (*sœurs*) By 1863 these numbers trebled to 7,161 *frères* and 36,397 *sœurs*; and by 1875 roughly one-quarter of boys were being taught by the *frères* and two-thirds of the girls by *sœurs*. In the eight years 1852–60 alone, the nuns involved in girls' education received no less than 10 million francs in donations, and they were able to buy property worth 23 million francs. This was at a time when the state was spending only about 6 million francs a year, while parents contributed 18 million in fees (1862). One cannot conclude that these facts necessarily mean that the majority of parents wanted their children educated by nuns, because they were not always given a free choice, but despite the admitted incompetence and ignorance of many of the nuns, who were usually totally untrained, they enjoyed considerable popularity. The effect of the republic was to give most boys and girls the same education. By 1914 boys were almost entirely taught by laymen and only a quarter of girls remained in church schools. This was achieved very gradually, because the government, having proclaimed the principle, had to accept that local opinion often would not accept its policy. The laicisation of schools between 1879 and 1890 was carried out at a rate of only 600 schools a year, and at half that rate after then: not until 1897 did the last boys' school run by a religious order disappear. But there were then still over 5,000 girls' schools run by nuns, and in addition some 7,000 nuns were teaching in state schools, principally in Catholic regions. The second wave of anti-clericalism succeeded in closing down the remaining church schools, but about 60 per cent of them immediately reappeared with their teachers 'secularised', that is, nominally lay.[1] So the Church managed to retain about 20 per cent of primary school children. This meant, not that there was a small minority of dissidents dotted thinly around the country but rather that certain regions refused to accept the laicisation. In 1914 in the department of Morbihan, 48·9 per cent of pupils were in Catholic

---

[1] Maurice Gontard, *Les Écoles primaires de la France bourgeoise 1833–75* (Toulouse, 1964), 133; id., *L'Œuvre scolaire de la troisième république: l'enseignement primaire en France de 1876 à 1914* (Toulouse, 1967), 118. These works, as well as M. Gontard's *La Question des écoles normales primaires* (Toulouse, 1964) and his thesis, *L'Enseignement primaire en France 1789–1833* (1959), provide the fullest history of the subject, and are indispensable.

schools, while only 2 per cent in the Basses-Alpes were. In 1965 the eight westernmost departments of France had between 35 and 49 per cent of their children in Catholic schools, and certain regions of the north and centre had between 15 and 34 per cent.[1] The ideal of uniformity was thus only partially attained. Many people were still willing to pay for a religious education, even when a free public one was available, and this shows the failure of the republic to create a new morality which would effectively reconcile and sum up the basic belief of the nation. There was no such thing. The war against church education was also a war against patois, which was another reason why it was resented. 'The clergy', wrote Duruz in 1866, 'make it a matter of conscience to fight French as the language of impiety. [The Alsatian dialect], one of them has said, is a preservative against dangerous books and a safeguard against religious indifference.' A Breton priest declared: 'It is in French that evil books are published.' The victory of the republic was supposed to be a victory for a uniform Parisian culture.[2]

That is what it superficially seemed to be, and partly was, but one must not accept this without further investigation. It is usual to sum up the results of the spread of primary education by graphs showing the decline of illiteracy. Illiteracy, which was already diminishing very rapidly under the Second Empire, fell from 14·6 per cent in 1882 to 4·3 per cent in 1900 for men, and from 22·6 per cent to 6·3 per cent for women. But the tests of illiteracy were so simple that they meant little. Full attendance at school up to the age of 13 was not really achieved in this period: it needed the establishment of family allowances to prevent parents being forced to send their children out to work. In 1902 only one half of France's communes had carried out the provisions of the law of 1882 requiring them to establish *caisses d'écoles* to help poor children with the expenses of schooling.[3] So, though in 1914 the official method of classifying illiterates led the army to call only 1·92 of its conscripts illiterate, further

---

[1] See map in Prost, 479, and for a study of the obstacles to laicisation, Bernard Ménager, *La Laïcisation des écoles communales dans le département du Nord 1879–99* (Lille, 1971).
[2] Pierre Zind, *L'Enseignement religieux dans l'instruction primaire publique en France de 1850 à 1873* (Lyon, 1971), 249. But contrast M. Bréal, *Les Langues vivantes dans l'enseignement primaire* (1889), 2–3, which urges acceptance of patois by the schools.
[3] Farrington, op. cit. 48.

interrogation caused it to say that 35 per cent had an 'education which is nil or inadequate', in that they could barely do more than read and write in the most elementary fashion.[1] In 1920, the figure went up to 41 per cent. Marc Sangnier carried out some tests on conscripts in 1920 which showed how little of what the schools taught was remembered. History and geography in particular seem to have been totally forgotten: the most widely known fact was that Gambetta escaped by balloon from Paris, but many also believed that Napoleon had been burnt alive at St. Helena. This does not mean that the conscripts had no political or other opinions, and were not capable of expressing them forcefully and clearly, particularly in conversation.[2] It is important to discover just what these opinions were, what the school did not teach. Another chapter will suggest that the oral traditional culture of the nation survived more powerfully than is realised, and that what the schools attempted to inculcate was frequently shrugged off, or continued to live side by side, only half assimilated, with a totally different set of beliefs.[3]

One must weigh all this against the obvious fact that, in the course of this period, primary education came to be accepted, and demanded, as the essential basis of human dignity and equality, that it became the indispensable stepping-stone to advancement and social mobility, and that by joining forces with ambition, it emerged as one of the forces which affected society most powerfully.

[1] This compares with the 25 per cent of the men enlisted into the U.S. Army classified as being unable to read a newspaper or write a letter home. E. Ginsburg and D. W. Bray, *The Uneducated* (1953).

[2] See Zeldin, *Taste and Corruption*, ch. 2 on 'Conformity and Superstition'.

[3] See chapter 9.

5. Logic and Verbalism

IT may be that the mark by which one could recognise a Frenchman was often not so much his appearance—for that varied enormously—not necessarily even the fact that he spoke French—since not all did, and besides French had, to a certain extent, succeeded Latin as the universal language—but something much deeper and much subtler: the way he used language, the way he thought, the way he argued. This was by no means true of all Frenchmen and the traditional generalisation about their being logical or 'Cartesian' cannot be accepted at its face value, but it points to a genuine idiosyncrasy, which requires explanation. This was something of which the French were both very proud and mercilessly, if slightly ingenuously, critical. In 1871 Amiel wrote in his diary: 'The French always place a school of thought, a formula, convention, *a priori* arguments, abstraction, and artificiality above reality; they prefer clarity to truth, words to things, rhetoric to science . . . They understand nothing though they chop logic about everything. They are clever at distinguishing, classifying, perorating, but they stop at the threshold of philosophy . . . They emerge from description only to hurl themselves into precipitate generalisations. They imagine they understand man in his entirety, whereas they cannot break the hard shell of their personalities, and they do not understand a single nation apart from themselves.'[1]

The institution which specialised in developing, instilling and defending these qualities was the secondary school system. But one should not simplistically imagine that one can explain a national characteristic, or what passed for one, by showing that teachers professed it and pupils memorised it. The behaviour of certain groups was wrongly held up as being typical of the nation. The schools may have been maintained by the taxes, or the fees, of the rich, but they did not obediently serve their

[1] F. Amiel, Journal intime, 30 September 1871, quoted by A. Canivez, *J. Lagneau* (1965), 289.

interests. The theory that the rise of capitalist industrialisation caused education to serve capitalist ends, and no longer aristocratic or religious ones, does not fit the facts, if only because, as has been shown, capitalist power had not attained anything like supremacy in this period. The sociological platitude that every society's education reflects its values is equally impossible to use as a guiding explanation, because of the infinitely fragmented nature of French society, which allowed the teachers to develop their own independent values, peculiar to themselves. It has become common practice to write the history of French education in social terms, with the question of class bias as the dominating theme, the moral being that the principal function of the schools—rigidly divided into bourgeois and plebeian ones—was to maintain class divisions. There is much to be learnt from such a perspective, but it is also a misleading one, as misleading as the older perspective it has largely displaced, which saw education as a battle of enlightenment against obscurantism, with the fight about religious schools as central and decisive.

The history of education, perhaps more than any other form of history, has been captured by other disciplines and made subservient to politics, or sociology, or, not least, the hagiographical self-esteem of the teachers themselves. This book will argue, by contrast, that while industrialisation increased, parallel with it and largely independent of it, 'educationism' developed. This period was the age of education, and of educational illusions, as much as of industry and the transformations it produced. In France, in particular, the teachers, and politicians who followed them, made claims on behalf of education to challenge those of industry. At certain times, when the educational budget grew to unprecedented levels, when key positions in the state were held by schoolmasters, whose knowledge of philosophy or literature had somehow appeared to open all doors, it did indeed seem as though a new mandarinate had seized power. But the idea that they came to dominate the country was an illusion, a figment of their own imaginations, to which the loudness of their mutual praise and their near-monopoly of the written word gave a superficial plausibility. The extent of their influence reached only as far as they could see, and that was not far, for they lived in a closed world.

Their idealism, in any case, was rudely shattered by their head-on crash with reality in the two world wars of the twentieth century. After these, the self-proclaimed age of the mandarin vanished like a dream. The doctrine of the post-war era was productivity, and the new hero was the industrialist, the businessman, the materialist. These had been firmly entrenched in their own way of life all the while.

To understand the complex preoccupations which the secondary schools expressed, one must pull apart their different, and by no means mutually sustaining, activities, and look very closely at what they taught, and how they did it. A great deal is revealed, first of all, by philosophy, their crowning glory. French schools distinguished themselves from those of most of Europe by teaching philosophy to children; the senior forms in the secondary schools were the *classes de philosophie*. This was highly significant. To finish off their education, the élite of the nation were neither given responsibility as prefects, nor encouraged into athletic distractions, as were British children, but instead were offered a very peculiar intellectual training. It is easy to argue from this that the philosophy class was the means by which the influence of Descartes was perpetuated, and with official blessing, for the class was a state institution. It was there that Frenchmen learned their characteristic abstract and pompous vocabulary, their skill in classification and synthesis, in solving problems by rearranging them verbally, their rationalism and scepticism—paradoxically conformist—and their ability to argue elegantly and apparently endlessly. But this requires much more careful scrutiny.

The philosophy class was born by accident. Philosophy was a subject which originally was taught in the faculties of arts. In the fifteenth century, schools, attempting to make good the deficiencies of the decadent universities, began teaching it, so that it was no longer limited to clerics studying theology. But only the very best, most prosperous schools had the resources for this luxury: it was impossible for them to develop any really independent doctrines or methods of their own, so they remained in the medieval tradition. Philosophy, supposedly the instrument of rational liberation of the schoolboy, thus in fact kept him firmly tied to the past. Medieval philosophy was not a method of making discoveries or of advancing knowledge. All

that could be known was known and the philosopher confined
himself to exposing the truth, to inventing or tabulating
objections to it, and then to refuting these. It did not involve
research, but only disputation. It sought not to unshackle the
mind but to inculcate uncontested dogmas; it provided intellectual security and a ready way of handling all that threatened
this. It was for most people essentially a game, a sporting
activity for those who did not engage in real-life battles. It
certainly called for, and its practice developed, skills which were
valued in scholastic circles: philosophers had to have not only
knowledge, but also quickness of wit, vigour and aggressiveness
in disputation, self-possession, a certain showmanship, a love
of competition but also of communal life. Inevitably, superficial cleverness, the appearance of thoughtfulness combined
with a tireless verbosity, the ability to dispute about anything,
publicly and at all times, were the criteria of success. Arguments were therefore cultivated for their own sake, not from
an interest in truth; a complete lack of intellectual curiosity
was easily compatible with this verbal fencing; books existed
mainly as arsenals of arguments. This scholastic philosophy was
not dead in the nineteenth century. Both Cousin and Cournot
praised it, because, as will be seen, their view of philosophy was
not all that different. There can be no doubt, besides, that
scholasticism did teach people to express their thoughts, to
spread the conviction that conduct must be based on principles,
that principles could be discovered in all conduct, and that
the discussion of these was more important, or more interesting,
than action itself. The form in which arguments were presented
was given much attention. Some cultivated obscurity, jargon
and subtleties incomprehensible to outsiders. Others laid all
stress on beautiful presentation, turning philosophy into
rhetoric. This was a conflict which remained throughout the
centuries, for the scholastic tradition was by no means uniform.
The rhetorical strand in it was absorbed into the cult of the
humanities, which, after the Renaissance, became more
fashionable than philosophy. But in the eighteenth century,
though the mere professor of philosophy had sunk to the status
of a contemptible pedant, the *philosophe* emerged in a new guise,
as a man of the world who could discuss all subjects—a genera-
list rather than a specialist—who appealed to common sense

and to all classes, and who was at home equally in literature, science and art. It might appear that the greatest change of all was that the *philosophe* now revolted systematically against accepted ideas but though this was true, to a certain extent, as far as the leading lights were concerned, humbler imitators, following in their footsteps, adopted their poses in studiously conformist ways: they had discovered a new way of arguing. One is still dealing, however, with a very small number of people: philosophers were rare birds; in 1812 the subject was taught only in about sixty schools, and only eleven of these had enough pupils to warrant distributing prizes in the subject. It was only in the course of the nineteenth century that the French state took to creating a special class of civil servants who were professional philosophers in public pay, charged with multiplying their kind or at least giving schoolboys an outward philosophical veneer before they went out into the world. France was the only country in Europe to make philosophising a career, paying a good salary, and to have enough of these official philosophers, distributed over the whole country, for them to form a significant social and intellectual force.

This profession owed its growth first to the fact that it claimed the mission of defending the *status quo*, of reconciling the traditions of the past with the needs of the present, and of showing civilisation the dangers that menaced it. The man who set it up in this role was Victor Cousin, probably the most influential French philosopher of the nineteenth century, influential far beyond the boundaries of his specialisation, and the first of the species to become a minister.[1] He controlled the training and appointment of philosophy teachers during the July Monarchy and the Second Empire, long enough to imprint a lasting pattern on them, and he gave them a powerful protection which allowed their high pretensions to take root. Cousin developed a philosophical syllabus for schools which survived in its essentials for a hundred and thirty years. His own works remained as set books till 1880, and when they were dethroned, they were replaced by those of his faithful disciple Jouffroy, which survived till 1927—a typical piece of bogus modernisation. Cousin entrenched philosophy so firmly in the schools because he deliberately adapted it to the tastes of the

---

[1] For a fuller discussion of Victor Cousin, see Zeldin, *Taste and Corruption*, ch. 2.

middle classes, whom he recognised as being firmly conservative in moral attitudes; by making it the most important subject in the final examination of the *baccalauréat*, he gave it official status as the necessary hallmark of an educated man. But though the schools were told to teach little more than common sense, the distilled wisdom of the past and the slick skills of classification, there was the constant worry that they were undermining religion, for reason was regarded as a dangerous instrument. Philosophy was under heavy attack from the right wing up to the 1880s, and particularly during the Restoration and the Second Empire. Its teachers were spied on and denounced; their opinions were minutely studied by the authorities and the slightest suggestion of nonconformity could lead to their disgrace. Cousin warned his regiment that even a hint of irreligion would lead to instant dismissal. He has been much maligned for this, but if he had not protected the profession in this way, it would never have been given the chance to establish its roots. Moreover, Cousin's rule was never as complete as it appeared to be: the emissaries of reason were really quite few in number: he once claimed he had 200 of them, but a truer figure was 75. It was the distinction of many of them, the amount they talked about each other and got themselves talked about that gave the impression of a national force. The capacity to blow up their own importance was something they never lost.

Under Napoleon III, a terrified government for a time abolished philosophy altogether in schools, as too dangerous in a time of crisis. Cousin was attacked by some of his former pupils with a savagery that academic life was already developing. Amédée Jacques was sacked for atheism, which he admitted; Vacherot preached the very opposite of Cousin's eclecticism, that reason, faith and observation yielded different kinds of knowledge which could never be reconciled, and he was sacked too; Taine, and a number of lesser men, were penalised for challenging orthodoxy. But despite the flowering of all these dangerous doctrines, the philosophers persuaded the government that their subject was indispensable. In 1863, when philosophy was restored to the *baccalauréat*, it was Cousin's syllabus that was revived: his tradition was too firm to dislodge. As the profession grew, control over its uniformity became less and less possible. Lachelier (1832–1918) was perhaps the last man to attempt to hold the teachers within a mental framework that perpetuated the ideals of Cousin. Lachelier, the inspector-general in charge of the subject, ran the *agrégation* examinations on the principle that all that could be said in philosophy had been said, there was no more to discover or invent, and what teachers needed to do was simply to present the known facts in a lively way. He was determined to keep them from flirting with new subjects like anthropology or social science. Thus he twice failed Charles Andler, who took the *agrégation* in 1887 and 1888, largely because he disliked his excessive bias in favour of German philosophy. Andler therefore sat for the German literature *agrégation* in the following year, came first, and only under the auspices of modern languages was he able to write his important book on Nietzsche. However, the philosophers were with time left increasingly free; power in the subject became less concentrated; but that led to the rise of the *patron*, with his little clique of devotees, and the rebel counter-clique which challenged and replaced it, only to fall in turn.

It was under the Third Republic that the philosophy teachers' pretensions to social superiority reached their highest level. Under the July Monarchy they derived their standing from their role as emissaries of Parisian culture. Francisque Bouillier, who came first in the philosophy *agrégation* in 1837 and two years later was appointed professor at the faculty of Lyon, at the age of twenty-four, began his inaugural lecture with these words: 'I shall teach in the name of a school which has already caused some stir in the world, which has even, if I dare say it, already had a salutary influence in it and which I hope will lend some authority to my words.'[1] Jules Simon arrived in Caen at the age of twenty-one, the proud representative of the already proud École Normale Supérieure, and preached the pure doctrine of his master Cousin, with fluent charm and fashionable elegance. Bright men like him quickly left the provinces for Paris, while the humbler drudges who served out their time in obscure outposts benefited from their reflected glory.[2] Under the Second Empire, orthodoxy and

[1] C. Latreille, *Francisque Bouillier, le dernier des Cartésiens* (1907), 49.
[2] M. Chauvet, 'L'Enseignement philosophique à Caen depuis 1830. Souvenirs d'un vieux professeur', *Mémoires de l'Académie nationale des sciences, arts et belles-lettres de Caen* (Caen, 1891), 105–63.

adherence to the official truncated syllabus was more easily
enforced in the *lycées* of country towns; there were still plenty
of clergymen teaching philosophy who were happy to plod on
with the methods of the *ancien régime*, dictating old notes about
lifeless texts.[1] But even graduates of the École Normale, as an
eminent inspector-general, Cournot, said in 1860, often merely
'translated into catechistic formulae the brilliant utterances of
their teachers', and finding the teaching of philosophy of the
mind too difficult, they retreated to the construction of syllo-
gisms, to what was virtually the old scholasticism, rehashing
the old textbooks 'which they covered with a completely trans-
parent veneer of modernity'. At this stage, the teacher of
literature was more highly esteemed, as Renan rightly observed,
than the teacher of philosophy, because the latter was regarded,
and regarded himself, as simply one who put into more or
less fine phrases a doctrine which was supposed to be fixed once
and for all.

Two factors changed this. First, the philosophy teachers began
making friends with their pupils, building them up into
clienteles of admirers, who when they made their way in the
world raised up their former mentors to the status of important
thinkers, intellectual and moral guides. In the provinces, the
philosophy class was often quite small—half a dozen boys—and
the teacher was sometimes not much older than the pupils: together they could make the last year at school into an in-
toxicating experience, permanently memorable as the moment
at which intellectual adulthood and independence was achieved.
The teachers began dabbling in politics or the world of letters;
they published articles in journals they declared to be fashionable; they acquired a standing in the world outside the school.
The most famous of them obtained the teaching jobs in Paris,
where they might have as many as a hundred pupils in their
class: they were admired from afar, but they also won the
affection of the dozen or so favourites they would select for
special attention, inviting them to their own homes and helping
to launch them into literary circles. Secondly, the teachers
formed pressure groups which spread their influence beyond the
intellectual élite. In particular, they joined the socialist party

---

[1] Ch. Bénard, *L'Enseignement actuel de la philosophie dans les lycées et les collèges*
(1862), 25.

and played a leading role in it. Jaurès, a professor of philosophy, and seventeen *agrégés* founded *L'Humanité*: this was a great change from *La République française* founded by Gambetta and his group of barristers (though there was already one philosophy teacher in his set). In 1945 likewise Jean-Paul Sartre and three other *agrégés de philosophie* founded *Les Temps modernes*. The success of Marxist and other left-wing ideologies added greatly to the power of these teachers who knew how to manipulate dialectics and play with German metaphysics. It was no accident that they were attracted to this particular brand of political debate. Their skill was to give the impression that they were 'advanced', and leading a radically new crusade; they lost the mask of pedantry and even became fashionable, or at least there were sets which thought them so. But to appreciate more exactly the balance of innovation and tradition in their outlook one needs to look at them more carefully and individually.

The most celebrated philosophy teacher of the Third Republic was Émile Chartier (1868–1951), who, under the pseudonym of Alain, wrote, in his spare time, articles for the *Dépêche de Rouen* and *Les Libres Propos*. He produced several thousand of these; reprinted in book form they became best-sellers and they have been given the accolade of inclusion in the Bibliothèque de la Pléiade. By the time of his death, 785 books and articles had been published about him. Exhibitions have been held in Alain's honour, and there is a society to perpetuate his memory. His pupils included many authors who paid generous tribute to what they owed him, and helped him on to his pedestal of fame. Very little is in fact known about Alain as a personality, because he took care that he should appear to the world as a thinker, as a collection of ideas rather than of emotions. He refused to write an autobiography, and produced only a *History of my Thoughts*, in which he dismissed his childhood in a few pages as a period, like all childhoods, of foolishness. The purpose of wise living was to overcome and eliminate this foolishness. Significantly, however, he recalled that as a boy he used to spend long hours telling himself stories in which he was always the imperturbable and invincible hero: they were always military adventures; and all his life his reveries were of the same kind, in which he exterminated enemies. He interpreted this as revealing the basic pugnacity of humans, with their desire for honour and power; he admitted that these instincts of childhood remained throughout life; but he considered that 'virile resolution' and will-power could repress them and dispatch them into impotence. His whole life was indeed devoted to creating a personality, for himself and his pupils, which was the product of self-conscious and rational effort: that was what education meant. To achieve this, he made use of a carefully nurtured self-confidence, which led him to refuse all criticism of his writing, to the point that he made it a rule to refuse to allow a publisher to see his manuscript before agreeing to publish it. The literary world he entered was one where he could act more freely than in any other—writing exactly what he pleased, as much as he pleased—and where he could, without moving anything but his pen, 'pulverise' those who contradicted him. Literature and ideas were supreme in his eyes; and the school was therefore all-important as the vehicle of their transmission. He said he had nothing worth saying about his family, because he never thought much about it. This was one reason why 'family virtues' were seen as conflicting with the subversive criticism of the schools. This attitude, also, provides an explanation of why Alain could reject Freud, Einstein and other novelties with such firm assurance. The only man Alain fully admired, 'the only god he recognised', was his own philosophy teacher, Jules Lagneau, and he added that it was not insignificant that this man should also have had the best handwriting he had ever seen.[1]

Alain's idea of philosophy was based on the rejection of originality as either desirable or even possible. 'All has been said,' he wrote, 'but nothing has been finally understood. Plato thought for himself, not for me.' The philosopher therefore must rethink the thoughts of Plato. Invention was outside his scope: he could aim only at the discovery of what already existed. The great philosophers who deserved study advocated different systems, but they had in common an attitude towards human problems, and it was this attitude that was the essence

---

[1] Suzanne Dewit, *Alain, Essai de bibliographie* (Brussels, 1961); Alain, *Histoire de mes pensées* (1936), 19, 71, 90, 99; Henri Mondor, *Alain* (1953); Paul Foulquié, *Alain* (1965); 'Hommage à Alain', *Mercure de France* (1 Dec. 1951), 583–653; 'Hommage à Alain', *Nouvelle Revue française* (1952, special issue); Olivier Reboul, *L'Homme et ses passions d'après Alain* (1968).

of philosophy. 'Philosophy is not a system, it is a style.' Alain
was not really interested in ideas, but longed for commitment,
action, personal involvement. The fruit of philosophical study
must be the power of judgement, of making decisions. He denied
that objective certainty was possible: 'man is prejudice' he said.
He followed Plato (in Cousin's translation, of course) in thinking
that man was governed by reason, emotion and appetite, which
were in constant conflict, so that all he could aim for was
serenity and a sense of freedom of action, based on developed
powers of reflection. This was not all that different from
Christian salvation, except that for Alain salvation was something each individual settled with himself. Alain's masters were
Plato, Descartes, Kant and Comte: he was certain that meditation on the great works of the past was the way to wisdom.
The assertion of individuality concealed, therefore, a profound
traditionalism. Alain harboured a whole mass of prejudices
which his much-vaunted rationalism never questioned. He
accepted Comte's view that the black race was 'affective', the
yellow race 'active' and the white race 'intellectual'; he
remained a believer, like Comte, in phrenology and the
theory of four temperaments; he completely and vigorously
rejected Freud.[1] His teaching methods were therefore based on
a primitive psychology, which totally denied that children had
any special problems: the one thing he never wrote about was
childhood. Like so many other leading French educators, he
was himself childless; he was a bachelor until his retirement,
when he married his secretary. His influence on youth came
perhaps because he treated his pupils as adults. He argued that
children have no need for play: they do play only because they
are fed by adults and so have nothing more urgent to do. Things
should not be made easy for them, because what they enjoyed
above all in their games, and in all else too, was solving
problems, winning victories. 'The child is a little man: one must
respect his seriousness'; he lived in a magic world only because
he was unable to link his experiences, and because he could
not grasp the real world. The teacher should not therefore
try to understand the child and develop elaborate pedagogic
methods for him: he will get to know him by teaching him,
because the child's true nature is created in education: 'it is by

[1] Georges Pascal, *L'Idée de philosophie chez Alain* (1970).

teaching him to sing that I shall discover whether he is a musician'. So the teacher had no need to be a psychologist. But he could benefit from studying the sociology of the school. The school, thought Alain, was not like a family, and the teacher ought not to try and love his pupils like a father. On the contrary, a father was incapable of teaching his child precisely because he loved him; he could get obedience through emotional pressures, which a teacher could not. The school must have an impersonal, mechanical discipline, without anger and without pardon; it must be different from the outside world and indeed aim to keep the child protected from the outside world and from the realities of life. This was precisely the opposite of what the reformers of the primary school argued: it was in the tradition of the priest's seminary; and it was an ideal far more influential than the supposed bolstering of 'bourgeois' values.

Alain thought the child had to be prepared for the world on the model of Plato's myth of the cave: he had to be given ideas with which to master and understand the world, before he was let out into it. It is for this reason that he stressed intellectual education as vital: experience and apprenticeship were quite inadequate, because they failed to teach the art of reflection. Human society was based on the 'cult of the dead', and that is why education required a historical approach: the study of contemporary man was unsatisfactory because distance was needed to free the judgement from passion; and besides it was best to seek accord not just with a few of one's fellows in the present; one should aim at agreement with the greatest minds of all times. One needed the mediation of the finest examples of humanity of all ages in order to be fully human oneself, and to discover what was universally true. It did not matter if children did not understand all they were taught—it was best to start with the form and move to the content; obscurity had to precede clarity. Alain's syllabus placed the greatest emphasis on the education of the will: the school must teach children to work hard and to control themselves, for evil and bad judgement were the result of lack of will-power. He hated modern theories of education which tried to make things easy for the pupil. Not that he did not see the value of encouragement: he always folded up corrected exercises he returned, so that the mark he gave should remain secret. But he was hostile to the new primary school ideas about the value of teaching practical facts, and placing the child in concrete situations. His aim was to teach not facts, but how to think. This did not mean uniformity, for he had a modest view of the educator's powers: no one could make a crocodile anything but a crocodile, he said. But a teacher could help the child to develop his faculties in certain ways.[1]

Alain cannot be considered a typical philosophy teacher, but his ideas—expressed more fully than any other teacher attempted—reveal the complexities of the *classe de philosophie*, elitist, but attempting to make a doctrine out of common sense, rationalist but still bearing the imprint of scholasticism, at once other-worldly and partisan, individualist but also inspired by the past, historical, but picking out from history only what fitted in with its prejudices, encouraging cleverness and originality until they became routine. Philosophy could survive all revolutions, because it said that all doctrines were equally worthy of study and of criticism: what really mattered was the style with which this was done.

What was supposed to distinguish French philosophy from that of other countries was that it tried to be not a technical speciality, but a general survey of the whole of life, bringing together all the disparate information the child had accumulated into a meaningful and coherent synthesis. It sought not to inculcate knowledge but to stimulate reflection. More particularly, it tried to encourage reflection about general and universal problems. The teacher set an example because the method especially favoured was the 'personal lecture', in which he expressed his own opinions, while giving due consideration to those of others. The pupils were taught to think for themselves by regularly having to write *dissertations* (short essays) in which rigorous reasoning and accurate use of language were demanded. Though there was a syllabus, the teacher was not bound to follow it, and the most famous of them followed it least. But the basis of all their teaching was the interpretation and criticism of texts. Personal experience and converse with great minds were thus used to enable the young to meditate on the difficulties of the human condition, to be aware of a wide range of problems and to learn how to discuss them. The

[1] G. Pascal, *Alain éducateur* (1969).

purpose of the philosophy class was frequently debated, because it was so uncertain what it achieved, but there was a remarkable coincidence of views as to what it ought to be. A circular by the minister of education, Monzie, in 1925 summarised the generally accepted doctrine when it said that the function of the class was to 'allow young people to understand better, by this new kind of intellectual effort, the significance and value of those very studies, scientific or literary, that they had pursued till then, and to produce some sort of synthesis out of them'. Before going on to specialise for their individual careers, they were armed by it 'with a method of reflection and some general principles of intellectual and moral life to sustain them in their new lives, so that they should be men with a trade, but capable of seeing beyond their trade, citizens capable of exercising that enlightened and independent judgement that our democratic society needs'. But it was significant that the circular then warned against a host of abuses to which the class was liable, and it was clear that these abuses existed: abstraction, memorising, scholasticism, dictation, cramming. The *baccalauréat* made philosophy into a subject of widespread study but it also very nearly killed it by imposing on it all the restraints and compromises that examinations inevitably involve.[1]

As rival disciplines developed in the secondary syllabus, so the protests against this claim to supremacy were increasingly challenged. Gustave Monod, founder of the *Revue historique* (1876), demanded that philosophy should be altogether abolished in schools: it was justified only when the faculties were not functioning properly: but now that higher education was being revived, it should return where it belonged. As it was, boys were being accustomed 'to talk and write about things they did not understand'. Either they did not take philosophy seriously, or else it led them to 'contract a dangerous over-excitation of the brain'. The army of philosophers the system created had not made France any better at philosophy, for its prestige abroad in the subject was not high: French philosophy was 'distinguished by its obscurity and its subtlety'. It did not

---

[1] *Pour et contre l'enseignement philosophique* (1894), articles reprinted from *La Revue bleue* (1894) by F. Vandérem, T. Ribot, E. Boutroux *et al.*; U.N.E.S.C.O., *The Teaching of Philosophy: An International Enquiry* (1953), contribution by Georges Canguilhem, inspector-general in charge of philosophy teaching in France.

dare tell boys of sixteen all its doubts, so it got out of it by
enveloping itself in clouds. 'Philosophic loquacity and gibberish
are, in my view, among the most certain causes of the intellectual decadence from which we suffer.' The psychologist
Ribot, though a philosopher by training, agreed that philosophy
was above most pupils' heads: it bored the majority of them,
and intoxicated the rest with generalisations and formulae they
could not really use, because it needed years to be able to
make sense of them. A journalist claimed that perhaps only 15
per cent of pupils understood what it was about.[1] This was in
the 1890s. In 1968 the philosophy class was attacked in exactly
the same way, and not least because it had been incapable of
moving with the times. Seminars were held at the University of
Vincennes and elsewhere to uncover its reactionary implications. It was pointed out that though it claimed to avoid
dogmatism, it took as its starting-point individual consciousness;
its basic doctrine was subjectivity; it was inescapably the
vehicle of an ideology. It was consistently hostile to materialism,
from the time when, under Napoleon III, Fortoul ordered it to
'show the invisible and immutable plan of the Divine Wisdom'
at work in the world, and Duruy justified it as 'the best remedy
against materialism', to Monzie in 1925 warning against
'extreme ideas' and 'doctrines which attract by their novelty or
trenchant character'. It continued to equate truth with beauty,
from Cousin to Simone Weil; Marx entered the syllabus only
in 1960. It was sustained by a deep conceit, from the traditional
first lesson devoted to self-praise at the expense of science, art,
religion and 'vulgar ideas'. It taught self-knowledge 'as a
thinking being': it played down emotion and the unconscious.
(There was a curious reason why 'the passions' were excluded
from its syllabus: they used to be studied in rhetoric: they
belonged to another syllabus, and when rhetoric was abolished,
so were the passions.) It perpetuated not only Cousin's spiritualism, but also his eclecticism, for the method was always
synthetic, aiming to reconcile as many authors as possible, to give
at least partial satisfaction to different traditions. It perpetuated
his historical approach also, for it always went back to past
texts. Originality did not go beyond quoting a philosopher

---

[1] F. Vandérem, 'L'Enseignement de la philosophie', *Revue politique et littéraire*
(*Revue bleue*), Jan. 1894, 1. 125.

whom everyone else had forgotten. Its criticism was superficial, because as soon as a new author like Hegel, Marx or Freud, was forced upon the philosophers, they did their best to integrate him into the system. They would cut down a little on Malebranche or Lucretius to find room for Lévi-Strauss or Sartre. Philosophy half-heartedly tried to find room for more and more as the natural and social sciences grew, so that it became increasingly superficial.[1]

There can be no denying the stultification of the examination questions. Thus though some teachers were doubtless brilliant and independent, the manufacture of textbooks and, even worse, model answers was a flourishing industry. One such book, for example, was published in 1897 by an Academy Inspector, *professeur agrégé de philosophie*: it listed 770 questions asked during the period 1867–1891, rearranged them under a smaller number of headings and provided fully written-out essays as model answers. The thirteenth edition of this book was published in 1939, without any modifications: the questions of 1867 were still considered relevant.[2] The reports of examiners in the *baccalauréat* show that candidates had difficulty in absorbing even these potted formulae. One report analysed in detail sixty-seven answers to a question about the will. Twenty-five candidates seemed to know nothing of any philosophical theory on this subject; and nearly all the others were aware of only one.[3] A question on Aristotle's dictum, 'Man is a political animal' could get an answer that 'There are nevertheless men who are not interested in politics'. In 1948 a question on the contrast between the thinker and the man of action produced the notary and the clerk as examples of the former and the cook and the merchant as examples of the latter. In 1957 a question on behaviourism revealed that there were those who attributed this theory to Monsieur Behavior.[4] The cramming books—of which there were extraordinarily large numbers—divided

[1] François Châtelet, *La Philosophie des professeurs* (1970); Lucien Sève, *La Philosophie française contemporaine* (1962); Roboald Marcas, *Précis de philosophie moderne* (1968)—a parody of a philosophy textbook.

[2] E. Rayot, *La Composition de philosophie* (13th edition, 1939).

[3] G. Texier, 'Que savent les candidats?', *Revue de l'enseignement philosophique* (Oct.–Nov. 1953), 33–5.

[4] René Manblanc, 'La Classe de philosophie: son présent et son avenir' *Cahiers rationalistes*, no. 179 (Apr.–May 1959), 102–31.

philosophy into a number of -isms and showed how standard questions could be answered by standard replies. What they said was often quite sensible, but capable of being misused to result in parrot-like sophistry.[1]

One witty teacher sarcastically produced a 'perpetual answer' or 'master key' which could be applied to any question, on the basis, as he said, of long experience of marking *baccalauréat* scripts, where he had found the same introductions, arguments and conclusions being endlessly repeated. The typical essay would read as follows: 'The problem of (copy the question) is one of the most important in philosophy and since earliest antiquity, men have not ceased to produce solutions as numerous as they have been varied. Some have tried to solve it in one way (do not say how), others in other ways. It is at once obvious, however, that both positions (no details) are much exaggerated and that a solution can only be found in a harmonious synthesis of the two points of view, for as the Sage (do not say who) said, *in medio stat virtus.*' This is the introduction. The 'development' must concentrate on not revealing ignorance: 'Man has an innate curiosity, a need to know the cause of things (no details). Already the young child (girls should say "the little baby") demands to know . . .' There are endless variations of these platitudes, like 'Science advances with giant footsteps' or 'Man cannot live alone'. Quotations should be added, but they need to be attributed only to a 'great French writer' or a 'celebrated thinker'. (Many teachers used to dictate quotations of all sorts for their pupils to memorise.) These platitudes should then be submitted, for a paragraph, to 'criticism': 'A totally new light is cast on the problem by this definition . . . However, this affirmation seems to us to be open to criticism'; and when the pupil is quite lost, he should end the paragraph, 'Consequently, what we have argued follows clearly from this'. The conclusion should either copy the introduction, beginning: 'That is why we can say . . .', or, more elegantly: 'What ought one to think of such a problem? Philosophers are still debating it.' The 'national ending' should round it off: 'And so we can say that X is truly French.' This was not too wild a caricature of what many pupils churned out.[2]

---

[1] e.g. Robert Lenoble, *Conseils pratiques aux jeunes philosophes* (1939).

[2] Jean Brun, 'Modeste projet en faveur d'un corrigé perpétuel de dissertation

With time, the distance separating the best from the worst may well have increased. Some able teachers encouraged their clever pupils to read widely, and the subjects covered by them ranged over increasingly varied topics, though politics, psychology and ethics were the most popular. Many writers have recorded the exhilaration they experienced as new intellectual horizons were opened to them in this class. The teachers encouraged the taste for obscure and original studies because they aimed above all at winning successes for their pupils in the *concours général* and the entrance examination for the École Normale Supérieure. The bright pupils benefited from the freedom and the guidance they received. But as science became more popular, philosophy was taken increasingly as a soft option by those least suited to academic work of any kind. Between the wars the proportion taking philosophy diminished, though the total numbers rose because of the large influx of girls into the subject. Whereas in the 1920s only about 10 per cent of candidates were girls, in 1950 77 per cent (in the Paris Academy) were girls. Though philosophy was supposed to be a general subject, surveying all the others in the syllabus, and above them, it had by then lost its supremacy, and become a speciality like any other, locked in its obscure jargon, contemptuous of the sciences and in rivalry with them.[1]

The generalisations about France's philosophical spirit, and the philosophy class as the instrument propagating it, must be interpreted with due allowance for the vagueness of the notions and the imprecision of the instrument. There can be no doubt that France did develop, in this period, an official philosophical army, led by the *agrégés*, and with soldiers in every *lycée*. Cousin declared in 1850 that 'a philosophy teacher is a functionary in the service of moral order, appointed by the state to cultivate minds and souls', but Renan laughed at the idea of a government having an official philosophy, saying it was as absurd as having a governmental doctrine on chemistry or geology. Though paid by the state, the philosophy teachers

philosophique', *Revue de l'enseignement philosophique* (July–Aug. 1951), 35–8. This review also reproduces the winning essays of the *concours général*.

[1] D. Dreyfus, 'La Philosophie peut-elle s'enseigner?', *Revue de l'enseignement philosophique* (July–Sept. 1952), 3–6, and debate on the function of the philosophy class, ibid. 55–68. On girls, see Françoise Mayeur's thesis.

were not tame propagandists preaching an authorised doctrine: they valued their security as civil servants but they reacted against the implication of subservience by increasingly assuming independent attitudes. During the Second Empire, they had to be obedient, because they were brutally sacked if they were not, but under the Third Republic teaching was orthodox because of an absolutely self-imposed tyranny: they had been the victors of the examinations in their youth, and they then taught their pupils to play the same game. But this was a game played at school; only a small proportion of the school population stayed on long enough to participate; even fewer learnt to do so with any skill; so the number of those actually permanently marked by the philosophy class was very small. It is true that they included many highly intelligent and articulate people who made a stir in the world. Certain branches of literature, some serious newspapers and periodicals echoed their language, in so far as they were run by them, or by writers who admired them; and this no doubt widened the circle of those who cultivated the philosophical style in speech and writing—in all its variations from clarity to verbosity. Because they were at the top of the educational hierarchy, those who wished to appear educated might ape them; and in this period, when education was new to most people, their influence had the attraction of novelty. The examination system sustained it. But the philosophical style was very far from being universal in France. It did however help to produce a certain kind of Frenchman, with high pretensions. These pretensions should not be taken at their face value, but in certain groups they were.

The statement that the French nation was 'Cartesian' is untenable, and it is doubly so, because Cartesianism in fact had a very chequered history. The identification with Descartes was certainly made frequently: thus even a respectable philosopher, in a study of Descartes written between the wars, concluded that Marshal Foch was the last contemporary incarnation of the Cartesian spirit and it was this that had won the war. A German critic writing at the same time explained extraordinary claims of this kind by saying that Descartes's ideas had been so simplified that they had come to represent simply the common sense that every French peasant was supposed to possess; that the French were not really interested in philosophy for its own sake, as the Germans were or the ancient Greeks had been; their culture was literary; philosophy had accepted this tutelage and Descartes was the greatest of French philosophers because he had identified himself at once with clarity and good French prose.

Descartes has had many different incarnations over the last three hundred years. He has by no means always been praised by the French; he has had violent opponents; his significance can (like Rousseau's) be interpreted in many ways and Paul Valéry rightly talked of 'a plurality of plausible Descartes'. If he does epitomise something permanent in French attitudes, then people were a long time in recognising it. He was paradoxically first raised into a symbol and a hero by various religious groups, the Oratorians and Jansenists, who used him against the Jesuits. The Jesuits put him on the Index and set the Sorbonne to condemn him; but then they found him a useful instrument in other battles and produced an anodyne version of him. Cartesianism is loosely supposed to mean the triumph of individual reason, the proclamation of reason's ability to understand and solve all problems, the rejection of authority, the questioning of all dogmas, the universal doubt, the assertion that man is above all a thinking being, who is not dependent on sensations and experience for his ideas or for the discovery of truth. All this has not found equal acceptance. Thus the French Academy in 1765 crowned A. L. Thomas's oration in praise of Descartes as the greatest of all thinkers since Aristotle, but Voltaire at around the same time declared that Descartes's influence had vanished after 1730. Some contributors to the eighteenth-century Encyclopedia identified themselves with Descartes, developing what they considered to be his materialist and mechanistic message, but in the nineteenth century Cousin used him precisely to destroy the influence of the Encyclopedists, declaring him to be the father of spiritualism. In the 1860s, it was said that 'the teaching of the state is founded entirely on Cartesian ideas'.[1] The philosopher Fouillée in 1893 praised Descartes as 'perhaps the greatest of all Frenchmen', who was responsible for a revolution as important as that of 1789.[2] But in 1896, the rising star of the world of literary

---

[1] *Larousse du dix-neuvième siècle* (1864–76), 'Descartes'.
[2] A. Fouillée, *Descartes* (1893), 6.

criticism, Gustave Lanson, denied that Cartesianism had exerted any such profound influence, and asserted that the method of arguing from simple principles was 'a profound and permanent disposition of the French mind'. Cartesianism was mathematical and incapable of generating an aesthetic; it had even destroyed respect for classical antiquity and so for poetry and art; though it was true that it had set a fashion for writing on specialised topics in language which all could understand.[1]

Opposing schools have continued to interpret Descartes in opposing ways. There are of course many types of rationalism; and it is possible to argue that Descartes's was not a sceptical variety, not essentially critical at all, that it used doubt only to build a new dogmatism more soundly, in which reason could know the world adequately because it was reason which participated in the reason of God. There were certainly profound variations in the nature of rationalism in each of the centuries since Descartes's time. The Cartesian rationalism of the Cousin school was thus definitely not individualistic; and the rationalism of Comte was not Cartesian, since it tried to separate science and metaphysics.[2] Descartes has obviously been a flag flown to indicate support for a number of different causes. But the uncertainty about his precise significance is the key to understanding his influence, or, more precisely, the place of Cartesianism in French life. If that means rationalism, then rationalism had several faces to it, worn at one extreme by the Jesuits and at the other by the sceptics and the materialists. The French could identify with this doctrine because it could be interpreted so variously. Cartesianism, like *la France bourgeoise*,

[1] G. Lanson, 'L'influence de la philosophie cartésienne sur la littérature française', *Revue de métaphysique* (1896), reprinted in his *Études d'histoire littéraire* (1929), 58–96.

[2] A. L. Thomas, *Éloge de Descartes* (1765); Francisque Bouillier, *Histoire et critique de la révolution cartésienne* (Lyon, 1842); Robert Aron, *Les Frontaliers du Néant* (1949); Roger Lefèvre, *Le Criticisme de Descartes* (1958), id., *La Pensée existentielle de Descartes* (1965); Roger Verneaux, *Les Sources cartésiennes et kantiennes de l'idéalisme français* (1936); Jean Laporte, *Le Rationalisme de Descartes* (1945); C. Latreille, *Francisque Bouillier, le dernier des cartésiens* (1907); Henri Mongin, 'L'esprit encyclopédique et la tradition philosophique française', *La Pensée* (1945) 5. 8–18 and (1946) 6. 25–38; C. J. Beyer, 'Du cartésianisme à la philosophie des lumières', *Romanic Review* (New York, Feb. 1943), 18–39; G. Sortais, 'Le cartésianisme chez les Jésuites français', *Archives de philosophie* (1929), vol. 6, cahier 3.

is a very woolly notion and that is its strength. Most people could in some degree accept something in it. In that sense, it was a characteristic Frenchmen shared.

The philosophy class has been both praised and attacked by various writers. It could make a powerful impression on clever children. It could alter the whole course of a life as it did for Maurice Barrès, who in *Les Déracinés* made the philosophy teacher a dangerous maniac specialising in cutting boys away from all traditional values, so as to get them to worship abstract gods. André Maurois, looking back on his own adolescence more benignly, thought the philosophy class filled him with self-confidence. He could henceforth spout quotations to prove he was always right. 'I gave the impression of being a pedant, a prig, a scoffer. With women I affected a high-handed manner; I behaved as though I were in a play by Marivaux or Musset, by Dumas fils or Becque.' In his courtships, instead of making pretty speeches, he talked about Spinoza. This kind of pretentiousness was superficial. With some it may have lasted all their lives. With others, it was a veneer which could conceal timidity and even compassion. But there were some who reacted vigorously against philosophy. Lévi-Strauss claimed he became an ethnologist because he realised, in his first year as a philosophy teacher, that there was no more to be learnt once he had mastered the tricks of this game: he would repeat his lessons for the rest of his career. It was a game by which every problem, serious or futile, could be given the appearance of being solved simply by applying a method, which was always identical: show that the common-sense view of it was liable to criticism, but then how this critical theory was in turn false, and conclude, by an analysis of vocabulary or a play on words, that the truth had two sides to it and all these arguments could be accommodated within it. 'These exercises', said Lévi-Strauss, 'quickly become verbal, based on skill at making puns, which becomes a substitute for reflection, on assonances between terms, on homophony and ambiguity, which combine to provide the raw material for these speculative *coups de théâtre*: ingenuity in them is the mark of good philosophical work.' Not only did this reduce the subject to a boring uniformity, with a unique method which provided a passkey to everything in it, but it removed any possibility of scientific exploration, and deflated it with the aesthetic contemplation of consciousness by itself.[1]

But it may well be asked whether Lévi-Strauss ever escaped completely from this tradition. He condemns philosophy's games with illusion and being, the continuous and the discontinuous, essence and existence, but his own work was centred around similar oppositions, like the raw and the cooked. He is an author whose reputation was won also because he wrote so beautifully. The distinction between philosophical writing and beautiful writing needs to be explained further. The relationship between the two will provide the key to one of the most important sources of unity among the educated classes.

Rhetoric

French philosophy, in this period, was with few exceptions not original and it aroused little interest in other countries. This may partly have been due to the fact that it was, at least in the way it was taught, to a great extent a literary exercise, in which the studied expression of obvious ideas in impressive language took precedence over the solution of problems. Originality that might have been philosophical was channelled into political and social theory, which was outside the scope of the schools and not subject to its rules. Philosophy was not an autonomous study. Even though it was taught at the conclusion of the school course, it was much influenced by the literary preoccupations which predominated over the syllabus as a whole; and to understand therefore why philosophers expressed themselves in the way they did, one must examine not only the traditionalism of their subject-matter, but also their style, which they picked up partly from the teachers of rhetoric and belles-lettres, who had pretensions as high as theirs.

All languages have some differences between their spoken and their written forms, and the differences have important social and psychological connotations. Democracy and widespread literacy reduce the differences to a minimum, as in America, while societies where learning is confided to a small élite can have a written language almost unintelligible to the uneducated, as in Arabic. In France, the schools remained the

[1] C. Lévi-Strauss, *Tristes tropiques* (1955), 54-5.

heirs of classical traditions, admirers and guardians of what they considered polite language, as enshrined in the great works of literature of the past. They were, however, revolutionary as well as conservative, for they saw their mission as the spread of this polite language, conquering dialect, accent and vulgarity, so that ideally people would talk as they wrote. The implication was that they would also learn to think as they were supposed to write, in an orderly and logical way. The mechanisms they employed were not always the same ones. Until the mid-nineteenth century, the way an educated Frenchman learnt to write good French was first to learn to write Latin, and secondly to read French authors whose style had been approved by universal consensus, usually after the lapse of a century or more. Imitation of ancient models was therefore what schoolmasters sought to inculcate. This was the basis of the *classe de rhétorique*, the final class but one, but the point at which many pupils left school; philosophy was often considered superfluous, while rhetoric was at times so popular that some pupils, with no academic ambitions, stayed on in the class for two years.

The rhetoric class taught the *discours*, the art of making speeches, writing letters and expressing oneself in a way that would show one's taste, education and dignity. The models the pupils had to follow were those of ancient Greece and Rome, partly because this raised them above vulgar dialects, partly because it presented them with noble and moral heroes and partly because it removed them from contact with the con-taminating controversies of contemporary life. Artificiality was the essence of this ideal: since man was not only sinful but disgusting, the way to make him pleasing was to dress him up in clothes which, it was hoped, would make him have elevated thoughts, and gravity and nobility in expressing them. The writing of speeches as though one were a Roman Emperor was designed to encourage not sincerity but conformity. It helped powerfully to produce what Michel Bréal called that 'intellec-tual illness which consists in paying each other with words, shutting oneself up in a role and drawing out of one's head passions one does not feel'. To call this an illness, to label it all as typical and institutionalised bourgeois hypocrisy, is, how-ever, to do it an injustice. All education, almost by definition, involves the encouragement of artificiality and the holding-up of values of one sort or another. The passion for words as fascinating in themselves was not surprising in people whom words introduced to new experiences. Jean-Paul Sartre recalled that as a boy the sight of a plane-tree in the Luxembourg gardens encouraged him not to observe it carefully but rather to find adjectives or phrases to describe it: in this way, he said, 'I enriched the universe with a mass of shimmering leaves'. He could 'raise up cathedrals of words' from simple sights.[1] In such a situation, literature could almost be confused with prayer. Pushing the claims of literature still further, the professional handlers of words could think that the preservation of these constructions was their principal duty. This has remained a powerful element in the attitude of the schools towards the teaching of language; and it is in keeping with it that the new science of linguistics has been welcomed as the key to universal understanding. It is not surprising that many teachers of literature took a long time to accept the opening-up of the secondary schools to all and sundry. Sincerely republican and democratic though they were, they considered that mastery of the language required such delicacy of taste, that it could not be picked up by anybody. In the early twentieth century, Lanson, a leading professor of literature, insisted that the increasing hordes of schoolchildren were too 'practical and scientific' in their attitude to be able to appreciate literature; the majority came from uncultured homes, where respect for books had either never been acquired, or had vanished before the invasion of the newspaper. He saw the 'primary school spirit' as a danger that threatened the secondary schools; elitism was a literary creed for him.[2]

The teaching of French came late to the secondary schools. In 1803 a selection of French classics were recommended for study, mainly in the *classe de belles lettres*, which was then the name for the second year of the rhetoric class, but French was regarded as subsidiary to the main subject of study, which was the Greek and Latin classics. Bossuet was designed to act as a counterpart to Livy, for example, but far less attention was paid to him, or indeed to any French author. In 1840 Cousin instituted an oral examination on a French text in the

---

[1] J.-P. Sartre, *Words* (Penguin translation, 1967), 89, 113–15.
[2] G. Lanson, *L'Enseignement du Français. Conférences du musée pédagogique* (1909), 9.

baccalauréat and enjoined that it should be studied with as much care as ancient texts, but in 1850 French was still generally being given only ten minutes a day, usually at the end of the classics lesson. It was only in 1880 that a larger selection of French set books was prescribed—Bossuet, Pascal, Voltaire. Only in 1885 was the study of nineteenth-century authors permitted, but 'with prudence'; only in 1890 was the injunction to prudence dropped. Thus the ancient classics surrendered their dominance of the syllabus to French literature only in the second decade of the Third Republic. But there was much disagreement as to what this new subject should involve.

When the study of French was still part of the study of rhetoric, it was on form and presentation that the teachers concentrated. They followed the methods perfected by a whole host of distinguished predecessors, over many centuries, among whom Aristotle, Cicero and Quintilian, however, still held pride of place. Though rhetoric, in the early twentieth century, came to have a pejorative meaning, it survived so long because it provided an exceptionally comprehensive and orderly analysis of human speech. It studied what to say, how to order it and how to express it (*inventio, dispositio, elocutio*); it distinguished between the different aims a speaker could set himself, and showed how he could best attain what he was setting out to do; it showed the different methods to be used in judiciary, deliberative and demonstrative rhetoric, how to persuade, how to move and how to please; and it went into great detail to place this advice on such a systematic basis, that eloquence was almost reduced to a mechanical operation: almost, but not quite, for it did not claim that simply following its rules would make one automatically eloquent. Intellectual, social and physical gifts were needed to excel, but the rhetorician could put these to their best use, and could warn of the dangers to be avoided—in logic, in gesture, in tactics. Just how interesting this kind of study could be may be seen from the *Course in Literature, Rhetoric, Poetics and Literary History* by E. Geruzez, professor at the Sorbonne, published in 1841 and reprinted over fifty times in the next fifty years. This was the standard textbook used in schools during this period. It presented rhetoric as 'a science of observation based on the study of the human mind and on the masterpieces of eloquence'. It defended rhetoric as

being to eloquence what poetics is to poetry, what logic is to
reasoning, because it facilitated the operations of the mind and
analysed what would now be called the psychology of inter-
personal relations. It argued that by teaching people to express
themselves well it was forging 'the best possible instrument man
could have for the advancement of letters and of science, and
for the commerce of life.' The weakness of schoolboys following
this course, however, had traditionally been their almost total
ignorance of literary history, so that they studied the 'extracts'
presented to them divorced from the context in which they
were written. Geruzez attempted to remedy this, saying that
'the history of literature has become in our time a veritable
science', which showed the links between ideas and events, and
'revealed in a new light the revolution of empires'. At the same
time, rhetoric was, as it had always aimed to be, a course in
morals, seeking to inspire good conduct by the contemplation
of literary beauty. 'The domain of literature embraces the
whole expanse of human thought'; even if it avoided going into
the details of science or erudition, it surveyed their general
results.[1]

These were large claims, and Geruzez was himself aware that
the aims of rhetoric would be attained only by gifted people.
It was a dangerous subject, because it could so easily degen-
erate into trivial classification and tiresome pedantry. One of
the principal activities of the schools was indeed to reduce it,
for the majority of their pupils, to the level of banality, imitation and interminable repetitiveness. That is why under the
Second Empire there was a revolt against rhetoric. Dionysus
Ordinaire, one of Gambetta's lieutenants, led the protest with
what seemed a radical challenge: rhetoric, he declared, could
not be taught, and fashions, besides, were changing: the epic
was dead, antique tragedy had been replaced by popular drama,
the novel had arrived, the very idea of eloquence with its
measured gestures had become bourgeois, usable only in the
boring circles of respectable worthies. Eloquence was a natural
gift, and the best way to develop it was to avoid getting embog-
ged in the rules of the rhetoricians. Instead of studying them, it
would be more sensible to see what the great masters of literature

[1] E. Geruzez, *Cours de littérature, rhétorique, poétique, histoire littéraire* (26th edition
1887), v–vi, 137.

had done, and to concentrate on modern and contemporary masters. The motto he held up was: 'Be yourself, imitate no one'. Demosthenes was popular not because he followed the rules but because he loved his country. Conviction was the most irresistible of charms. One can see the links here between political developments, the new democracy and the educational syllabus. But one should not exaggerate the practical significance of this challenge. Having made his protest, Ordinaire nevertheless went on to describe all the old rules; he insisted that the proof of their value was that they had continued to be repeated without change since Aristotle; and he ended with a long commentary on Cicero's *Rhetorical Art*.[1]

In the 1880s, there were still questions being set in the *baccalauréat* about the rules of rhetoric.[2] In the French composition practised at school at this time, the great virtue encouraged in pupils was docility, respect for accepted ideals. Teachers tended to do most of the thinking for their pupils, to give them headings for each paragraph, to confine contributions to strict limits, four paragraphs being generally demanded, as though an essay was an architectural edifice, to be constructed in the same way irrespective of the ideas it contained. A certain kind of harmony was thus required between the paragraphs, which had to be of predetermined length. The subject-matter had preferably to be turned to a moral purpose, so that a 'speech by Henri IV on the Edict of Nantes' would turn into a eulogy of liberty of conscience. This was encouraged as a means of teaching pupils to see general ideas behind details, but it inevitably produced a lot of empty phraseology, and all the more so since the most esteemed approach was to argue by allusion, to suggest one knew more than one said. The detailed attention to style certainly taught people to express themselves methodically and in an orderly fashion, even if it did impose a pattern of formalism and pretentiousness. It taught them to know the works of a few authors very thoroughly, in that it was customary to limit the study of French literature to a few books. But French composition was more than just style, because the

[1] D. Ordinaire, *Rhétorique nouvelle* (1867); cf. E. Laboulaye, *Rhétorique populaire* (1869).

[2] James Condamin, *La Composition française: conseils et plans synoptiques pour traiter 850 sujets proposés aux candidats au baccalauréat* (Lyon, 9th edition 1886), 1–8.

subject-matter on which pupils wrote gradually expanded: though the content was mainly classical, French literature, history, morals and aesthetics were also written about. In the 1890s developments in these subjects, and the rise of new social sciences, led to French composition becoming increasingly abstract. The details of literary texts were skimmed over, and instead pupils were asked to draw out of them the 'immutable general laws' which ruled them. Poems and plays were used as a basis for comparison and generalisation designed to produce complex classifications and universal formulae. The bright teachers of these years would ask their pupils what they were really interested in: they often got the answer that it was geography or literary history (it was the age of Vidal de La Blache and Brunetière) and they would accordingly ask their pupils to write their compositions about these. This 'philosophic method' appeared to be exciting and broadening, but it was based on superficiality if not total ignorance, and it gave rise to even more angry accusations that these so-called literary studies taught people simply hollow verbiage of a high-sounding kind. Examination questions were now so general that there was no chance that the candidates could possibly have the information necessary to answer them. No concession was made to their youth and the questions at the *baccalauréat* were not significantly different from those at the *agrégation*.[1] The result was that the spirit of the old rhetoric lived on: pupils simply could not avoid padding their essays with empty declamation.

The enemies of rhetoric triumphed in 1902, when the subject was removed from the syllabus. The principle behind the republic's education since Ferry's time was that it should be factual, based on observation and not memory. This had been difficult to apply. But gradually the literature specialists developed it into the *explication des textes*, which now became the basis of the teaching of French. At its best, when properly executed, this could be a quite extraordinarily thorough analysis of language and ideas, drawn from a short piece of prose or verse. Imitation was now replaced by analysis; the aim was the cultivation not of style but of understanding. The pupil was asked not to express his personal feelings on reading the

[1] F. Lhomme and E. Petit, *La Composition française aux examens et aux concours* (6th edition, 1917), covering the years 1882–1916, preface.

text, but to produce a methodical and careful explanation of it, trying as far as possible to put himself into the author's skin, to understand him as fully as possible. He had to show what the general sense of the text was, how the dominant idea was developed; what the text's aesthetic or moral character was, what kind of intention or spirit it conveyed, how it came to be written, how it fitted in the rest of the author's work, how valid were its arguments, how it was received and how influential it had been. He had to dissect the language used, examine the words and sentences, their origins, their musical and picturesque qualities, and compare the style to that of contemporaries. Finally he had to show what general questions the text posed, say whether it solved some general problems of composition or style, whether it threw light on the working of the literary imagination, or on the forms of expression. An example of *explication de textes* by a teacher, published as a model, ran to twenty-six pages in a commentary on as many lines of verse by Victor Hugo. In its thoroughness and comprehensiveness, it set new standards.[1] This method has remained the basis of French literary studies ever since; it has provided the framework for a great deal of penetrating and ingenious research, and it has been the model influencing many other forms of writing.

However, the teachers undermined the value of what was one of their most important contributions to society by two developments of it, in opposing directions: they were too ambitious in the range of subjects they tried to apply it to, and they bastardised it by producing all sorts of ruinous short cuts to help their pupils pass their examinations. Pretentiousness was often their answer to the contempt they saw around them, while the *baccalauréat* brought out what was worst in them. The study of grammar was increasingly considered too pedestrian. It used to be a major preoccupation in the study of Latin, and French grammar used to be modelled on that; but as Latin was replaced by modern languages, the interest in the rules diminished. The result was that examiners regularly complained that candidates could not write grammatical French, could not spell, and even could not understand it— though it is fair to add they had been complaining about the

[1] G. Rudler, *L'Explication française. Principes et applications* (1902).

inability to understand throughout the nineteenth century. There was considerable evidence to support those who claimed that schoolboys played with words they could not comprehend. At the same time, however, as a reaction against grammatical study set in, teachers tried to make their subject more intellectualist, more concerned with ideas, making even greater demands of their pupils. The tradition lived on that study of great authors should be a moral experience, teaching artistic and literary ideals. This had been easier to do in the eighteenth century, when there was a precise code of taste and fixed rules, so that pupils could recognise the application and violation of these; they knew what to look for; but now individual sensibility and appreciation entered the scene and vastly complicated the activity. Some teachers thought it was enough to get the pupils to understand the spirit of an author and the meaning of his text, so that being able to read him out aloud with full expressiveness should be the ultimate aim. This was the tradition of *elocutio*, which also survived, and skill in reading aloud continues to be cultivated with impressive success. Some teachers were willing to leave it to the pupils to take the initiative in asking questions about the texts. But the most ambitious teachers of French aspired to making their subject the vehicle for the moulding of their pupils' minds. They said that whereas previously somebody like Bossuet might be studied as a work of art, now he ought to be read also for the theology, the history and the ideas he contained. From this they moved on to using the authors as commentators on 'the principal human questions', which became the central object of the lesson. 'What is Science?' might be one such question; 'How did reason progress in the eighteenth century?' or 'What were the political ideas of Montesquieu?'. As one distinguished teacher said, literature was the 'popularisation of philosophy'. Pupils were thus introduced to the deepest problems at a remarkably early age, and expected to write about them with maturity.

But, of course, since they also had to pass examinations, they were helped along by a whole variety of cribs and textbooks. The informal, often highly personal lecture by the teacher, which could make these French lessons so inspiring, was supplemented by the dictation of model answers, potted definitions and summaries, which were laboriously copied into different exercise books and mercilessly memorised. While on the one hand the pupil was encouraged to use his own judgement, he was on the other hand told what the right answers were, even if they were well above his head. So in examinations, his intelligence had to be displayed by the ingenuity with which he presented the facts and attitudes expected of him. The writing of essays became above all a matter of *dispositio*. The plan of the essay was all-important. Much effort was devoted to practising its construction. Those who sought simply to pass their examination would be content with a symmetrical construction, divided into parts, as the old rhetoricians had taught. It was more ambitious to add movement and progression to these different parts and to lead up to a climax in the argument. But then the ideal became to have a dialectical progression. An ordinary progression would simply, for example, describe a man first physically, then intellectually, then morally. If one wanted to 'dialecticise', one would make these into thesis, antithesis and synthesis, which was increasingly recommended. A leading guide on how to write essays, published in 1955, said 'The essay is like a universe where nothing is free, an enslaved universe, a world from which everthing which does not serve the discussion of a fundamental problem must be excluded, and where autonomous development is the gravest fault one can imagine'. The key to success was to spot the most general problem into which the subject fitted; and no one trained properly should ever be 'really surprised by any general subject'.[1] But it was naïve to imagine that the essay should be simply about the general problem. Rather it had to be about what people thought of the problem. Ultimately, therefore, at this level, a beautiful style was no longer as useful as brilliance in producing formulae; the proliferation of memorised quotations was now replaced by skill in producing analyses and paraphrases. The passionate interest in how ideas should be expressed was cultivated from an early age; and it spread beyond the school. The civil service, which in the eighteenth century had prided itself on writing beautiful prose, indistinguishable from that of men of letters, always gave great weight to the way reports were written; in the nineteenth it paraded pomposity and verbiage, no doubt from misplaced notions of

[1] A. Chassang and Ch. Senninger, *La Dissertation littéraire générale* (1955), 6, 8.

traditionalism; more recently, it too has stressed the importance of the plan, of precision and analysis.[1]

At the same time, however, another trend was increasing the scientific character of the study of French, stressing erudition and objectivity. This involved transforming it, to a great extent, into literary history. The key figure in this movement was Gustave Lanson (1857–1934), author of the history of French literature which reigned supreme in the first half of the twentieth century. One must beware of making him into too much of a symbol, or of attributing too much success to his methods. His textbook is regarded as having ousted that of René Doumic (1860–1937), but the two men were exact contemporaries. Doumic was both perpetual secretary of the French Academy and editor of the *Revue des Deux Mondes*, where he maintained the cult of classical taste and animosity against any new ideas. The Academy and the schools were not necessarily on the same side.[2] But Lanson wanted the study of French literature to have all the vigour, exactitude and gravity of a science. He thought that commentaries on authors were not justified unless they were based on 'exhaustive' study, that nothing should be left out of their bibliographies, that all available texts should be scrutinised and compared, that influences and sources should be chased to the farthest limits. He aimed to turn the study of French literature into a rigorous discipline: he gave lectures which could sometimes be nothing but an enormous bibliography, catalogued inexorably, which, however, his audience would copy down with religious respect, for this, at last, seemed true scholarship. There were complaints that all this was too Germanic, and that his critical editions, with their mysterious symbols, looked like works of geometry. This was indeed how some people interpreted and applied what they thought was his method: the study of texts could thus be reduced to a laborious palaeography, from which capricious taste could be banished and hard work assured of its reward.

Lanson, however, was in real life a many-sided man and a remarkably gifted teacher. It is true he appeared cold, radiating

[1] Jean Datain, *L'Art d'écrire et le style des administrations* (1953, 15ᵉ mille 1970), 12; G. Genette, 'Enseignement et rhétorique au 20ᵉ siècle', *Annales*, vol. 21 (Jan.–June 1966), 292–305.

[2] R. Doumic, *Histoire de la littérature française* (1900) reached its 25th printing in 1908, and a new edition was published in 1947.

intelligence rather than warmth, but this was a superficial impression. He was the son of a glove manufacturer, his mother was the daughter of a mirror merchant; he came from an unfrivolous and determined background, where people were bent on improving themselves. He was contemptuous of those who thought they could acquire good taste without effort. He graduated, top of his year, from the École Normale in 1879, defended his thesis in 1887, where he first revealed his extraordinary powers of argumentation, vigour, obstinacy, imperturbable calm and self-control, which were to make him the dominant figure in every conference and meeting he attended. He was appointed to a post at the Sorbonne at an exceptionally young age, and rose to be Director of the École Normale.[1] But he was most at ease, perhaps, lecturing to girl teacher trainees at Sèvres, where there was less wildness and independence than in the rue d'Ulm; and *The Principles of Composition and of Style*, which he published in 1887 when he was still a schoolmaster at the Lycée Charlemagne, give a fairer picture of what his methods were at the level of secondary education. They show that he was not the advocate of an exclusive or narrow doctrine: all attempts to analyse teaching methods inevitably oversimplify, and neglect the large middle ground on which contending parties were agreed. Lanson was aware of all the faults conscientious teaching could lead to. He declared himself, at the beginning of this book of precepts, to be against precepts and against formulae which would simply be memorised: he castigated vagueness and verbosity. He said that in teaching literary style he was aiming to teach how to think well, and how to judge books. Sterile criticism was the result of failing to see how much effort was needed to do it properly. He advocated intellectual effort, not at the expense of sincerity of sentiment, but because only an exercised mind could express exactly what a person felt. He urged his pupils to read a lot, but also to argue with the authors they read, so as to benefit their intelligence as well as their memory. Conversation used to be the main source of instruction: it was now a dead art, but it could be fruitful if it was an instrument to clarify ideas and if it was treated as more than a distraction. Introspection was necessary too, to educate one's sensibility by asking oneself

[1] For his work there, see chapter 7.

what one was feeling—dissipating the confusion of one's emotions into clear ideas, distinguishing, for example, between one's
love for one's mother, one's dog, one's clothes and one's
favourite poet. He had an ideal, which he thought existed in the
eighteenth-century *salons*, of a general education, produced by
the assiduous cultivation of clarity; and it was this that produced
a good style of writing. He repeated the injunctions to seek out
the general idea, to study the *lieux communs* which were at the
basis of all thought, to free principles from all personal and
local circumstances so that they could be clearly understood,
and indeed he divided his book in the traditional way of
rhetoric, into Invention, Disposition and Elocution. It is true
he added a chapter on the relationship of words and things,
warning against mistaking abstract names for concrete realities,
which he claimed was a vice women were particularly liable to.
(He complained that foreigners had too stereotyped an idea of
Frenchmen, but he had a similar, contemptuous view of
women.)[1]

With time, he became pessimistic about the possibility of
spreading taste and refinement to the mass of pupils. He
looked back nostalgically to the days when the teacher was
allowed to concentrate on a handful of bright pupils while the
others 'were content to have sat on the same benches as this
élite'. The fathers of those who were ignored did not complain,
but were proud of the few successes the *lycée* won in the national
examinations. The pressure of examinations had indeed turned
French into a mere speciality, and morals and history had won
their independence. So pupils were now simply being exercised
in mental games, taught to write paradoxical and over-clever
answers, which 'they deformed into gross and pretentious
affirmations from which the fine grain of justice had disappeared'. There was little point in getting them to regurgitate
'strange pot-pourris' of the leading critics and textbooks. The
danger now was that French literature might be regarded as
'the realm of vagueness, arbitrariness and whim'. Its sights, in
the new schools for the masses, should therefore be lowered. It
should cease to appeal to the imagination which was only 'an
apprenticeship in pretentiousness and false elegance'. It could

[1] G. Lanson, *Principes de composition et de style* (1887, 5th edition 1912); cf. his
Conseils sur l'art d'écrire (1890, 10th edition 1918).

not hope to make the majority of its pupils into artists. It should be content to teach them 'to produce a good report, a straightforward statement, in a precise, clear and orderly style, without literary qualities but with method and exactness'. The primary schools were supposed to teach this; the secondary schools could not be doing badly if they succeeded in achieving it.[1] This does not mean that Lanson wished to abolish the role of sensibility in the study of French. It is true that he insisted that 'reason was the most perfect and noble of human faculties' and that it was the intellectual element in prose that, above all else, gave value to it; but he valued the pleasures to be obtained from artistic form. He argued, however, that spontaneous taste was inadequate: only when it was based on reflection, and on historical study, could it yield worthwhile fruits. One should value one's personal impressions, but one should also try to understand why one felt as one did. He tried to be even more scientific than Taine, which is why he was suspicious of theories of literary evolution: ultimately it was the creative genius of the individual writer that interested him.[2]

These controversies among the teachers of French are significant in several ways. First, they show that beneath the various arguments there was a considerable amount of consensus. Learning the language was to Frenchmen more than the acquisition of a practical tool. It involved the training of the mind also, and the development of certain ways of thinking which they valued. This meant, secondly, that they tried to encourage an intellectualist approach to all the problems that language could express; they tried to get their pupils to see general principles behind details, and to place their arguments under the protection of universal laws. So, thirdly, they insisted on a great deal of attention being paid to the presentation of arguments, to ordering them in a way that appeared logical, clear, well planned and divided, as far as possible, into three parts. But, finally, they were not innovating as much as they imagined; their new pedagogical methods were not all as new as they thought. They were in many ways still imprisoned in the

[1] G. Lanson, *L'Enseignement du Français* (1909), 1–24.
[2] *Gustave Lanson 1857–1934*, published by the Société des Amis de l'École Normale Supérieure (1958).

old laws of rhetoric, though they might have varied their emphasis. The teachers did not therefore transform the character of social relationships by imposing a new usage of language. But it is certain that they popularised among a far larger audience ways of expression which had once been confined to an élite or to pedants, and to this extent their efforts were rewarded by many Frenchmen sounding different, arguing differently. The question, however, which they did not ask themselves, was whether this form of discourse was suited to the non-literary world, where what one said, and how one said it, could have practical and serious consequences. The prestige of their academic certificates, guaranteed by the state, led many people to adopt their way of talking, and so to imagine that a problem was solved once it had been clarified. A veneer of principle became almost necessary to anyone who wished to appear educated. But it is not certain that they therefore made the articulate section of the country into a class that was genuinely united in its mental mechanisms. A professor who has studied the oratory of politicians has shown how each party has its own particular style—the left makes longer speeches than the right, uses more metaphors, more adjectives and adverbs, while General de Gaulle employed twice as many subordinate clauses as his rivals.[1]

No doubt one could take this kind of analysis further to show the differences in the style of different professions and different social groups. Until more research is done, therefore, it is not possible to conclude firmly about the results of the schools' cult of rhetoric, but any exposition of its influence must be qualified in two ways. What the schools taught was assimilated with varying degrees of comprehension, and much speech and writing attempting to conform to their noble ideals was only a parody of it: they could never fully approve of the mediocrity they engendered. Their claim, that they contributed to increasing clarity, must be judged by studying how Frenchmen behaved in practice. If the resolution of daily problems into abstract terms was one consequence, then it may be that this not infrequently also complicated people's lives and created more disagreements than might otherwise have been noticed. But that was perhaps the way they came to like it.

[1] Jean Roche, *Le Style des candidats à la présidence de la république 1965-9. Étude quantitative de stylistique* (Toulouse, 1971).

Whatever their direct results, the prestige of rhetoric and philosophy also led to some paradoxical and unexpected consequences. Precisely because their methods could be dogmatic, they stimulated fecund rebellion: they produced not just conformity but also innovation, and sociology, for example, was one of the children of the rebellion against philosophy. Philosophy's ambition to be universal in its interests could mean superficiality, but it was also one of the most important stimuli for the introduction of foreign ideas into France, and in particular it was constantly building new bridges to Germany. By itself, philosophy often seemed to be sterile, but it was like a celibate having constant affairs, and in combination it could be highly fruitful. Rhetoric, for its part, might be hollow, but it could also create enthusiasm. French ideas were often presented in a way that gave the impression that new continents were being discovered, or rather were about to be discovered. The excitement generated made intellectual life probably more exhilarating than anywhere else in the world, even if the excitement had to be paid for with the subsequent gloom of disappointment.

6. Privilege and Culture

'IT is not with fine words that one manufactures beet sugar; it is not with Alexandrine verses that one extracts sodium from sea salt.' So said the scientist Arago in parliament in 1837, in a debate in which the preoccupation of the schools with the classics and with useless knowledge was challenged. But the poet Lamartine, soon to be made head of the Republic, replied that, 'If the human race were condemned to lose entirely one of these two sets of truths—either all mathematical truths or all moral truths—I say that it ought not to hesitate to sacrifice mathematics. For if all mathematical truths are lost, the industrial world and the material world would no doubt suffer great harm and immense detriment, but if man were to lose a single one of those moral truths, of which literary studies are the vehicle, it would be man himself, it would be the whole of humanity which would perish.' The attitudes of France towards material and literary values were mirrored in the controversies about the school syllabus, in the struggle of the arts against the sciences.

A superficial view of the educational system might lead one to suppose that this was a country in which literature was held in quite exceptional esteem; and it seems consistent with this that it should also be a country which long resisted industrialisation. There is truth in this view, but it is not the whole truth. It was indeed the case that the schools had their attention turned above all to the study of the past, and in particular of past literature—a preoccupation justified in the interests of perpetuating 'the humanities'. It was also the case that the schools fought endless battles to preserve Latin as the basis of their syllabus and opposed the introduction of scientific subjects into it. But, as so often happened in France, the dust generated by these controversies obscured the fact that quite a significant number of pupils did specialise as scientists and that a lot of modernisation of the syllabus did take place. The *lycée*, concentrating on rhetoric and philosophy, was the most esteemed of educational institutions, particularly among those who had been to it, but it coexisted with other types of schools which many people preferred. Moreover, even within the *lycée*, there were mathematicians who avoided the rule of the classics almost completely. A picture of the educational system which suggested that it was all of one type, or that it was exclusively retrograde would be inaccurate. The way it undertook its modernisation, and the place it accorded to science are, indeed, highly revealing about the organisation of society as a whole.

The *lycées* represented the preservation of the secondary schools of the *ancien régime*. In the 1790s, an attempt had been made to break away from this tradition, by setting up a radically different system, known as the *écoles centrales*. These did not have classes of boys of the same age, placed under one master and subject to strict discipline, but instead offered courses given by specialised teachers, which the pupils could take according to their inclinations. Their syllabus had as its basis not Latin, but drawing, designed to teach decoration and to serve as the basis both for scientific and artistic training—and over ten times more pupils enrolled for this than for the course in belles-lettres. It included modern as well as ancient languages (each province choosing the language of its nearest foreign neighbour); it transformed the old grammar into general, philosophical grammar, seeking to penetrate the ideas and logic of language; it abandoned ancient for contemporary history and added a course in contemporary politics and legislation; it made belles-lettres into a study of the psychology behind literature; it introduced courses in experimental physics and chemistry, as well as mathematics, requiring each school to have a laboratory, a library and a garden. The teachers were given security of tenure, independence and self-government. The pupils were liberated from disciplinary controls; boarding was abolished; hours of work were gradually reduced as pupils got older, so that they could read on their own. This was supposed to be an education directed at instilling not worship of the past but a spirit of inquiry into the present and into the facts of real life. The school was no longer to be a retreat from the world. But these *écoles centrales* were the pipe dream of the Ideologues, who themselves had an inadequate appreciation of what the world was like. The schools were too peculiar to appeal to the middle classes; few pupils were sent to them; and there were not enough teachers qualified to offer the courses, most of which were never in fact given. The whole idea was soon condemned as dangerously revolutionary and it vanished as all but a utopia, which, moreover, never had more than a tiny group of believers in it.[1] Henceforth, those who were keen on practical education diverted their endeavours towards the primary schools, and those interested in more science put their hopes in the faculties. The secondary schools remained the bastion of literary studies.

The heritage of the Jesuits was that only one side of the Renaissance tradition was preserved—the study of antiquity, but not that of science; their aim to produce polished and fluent conversationalists overrode the interest, which some people, like Cardinal Richelieu and Abbé Fleury, had expressed in the seventeenth century, that the schools should train different types of pupils, and not simply for the world of fashion, of letters and of the liberal professions.[2] So the compromise between mathematics and the classics, briefly attempted by the Consulate, was abandoned under the Empire. Science was postponed till after the child had acquired a literary training. The *classe de mathématiques* was relegated to the final year, as an alternative to the *classe de philosophie*, and virtually limited to those seeking admission to the Polytechnic and other advanced scientific schools. Mathematics was taught in an abstract way, with no applications. In 1846 no natural science was taught in *lycées* in the first three years, and it was offered only as an optional subject, for one hour a week, to be taken on the Thursday holiday. An inquiry held in that year brought to the fore the demands of the scientists, led by the chemist J. B. Dumas, for a change in this state of affairs, but the Revolution prevented any actual reform being brought about, and, as will be seen, change was diverted from the general programme of the *lycées*, to the idea of creating special schools for scientists. The literary vested interests remained impregnable. Too many other battles were being fought

[1] But one of these was Francisque Vial, Director of Secondary Education: see his *Trois Siècles d'histoire de l'enseignement secondaire* (1936), 71–153, for an adulatory account of the *écoles centrales*.

[2] C. Falcucci, *L'Humanisme dans l'enseignement secondaire en France au dix-neuvième siècle* (Toulouse, 1939) is an erudite thesis recounting the history of the controversy.

at the same time for scientific education to be capable of becoming a major issue. It is quite wrong to suppose that republicans were in favour of it. They were absorbed by the struggle with the Church; they placed their faith in moral education, and there were many of them who were firm believers in the classics. They put their efforts into upholding the educational value of pagan antiquity, against those clergymen who, while defending the study of Latin, wanted to make it the study of Christian Latinity.[1]

The Second Empire changed the situation in two ways. First, it introduced *bifurcation*, which meant that pupils were able to opt between science and letters after their third year. It did not separate the two specialisations completely, for the scientists had to do some literary studies and the classicists got a smattering of science. The idea behind this was to make it possible for preparation for the scientific *grandes écoles* to start earlier, rather than be concentrated into intensive cramming after the *baccalauréat*; and it was also an attempt to make the *lycée* more competitive against the church schools, offering a distinctive syllabus, directed once again towards state service. Enormous howls of protest greeted this reform and most historians have continued to malign Fortoul, the minister responsible for it. The trouble with it was that it was bound up with other, clearly repressive moves, based on fear of the small minority of revolutionary teachers. The classicists were indignant that their age-old supremacy was being challenged; the philosophers cried loudest because their subject was abolished altogether, and turned into logic (alias scientific methodology). *Bifurcation*, however, was not all that much of an innovation; it simply reorganised the methods by which pupils could specialise in science from about the age of 14, which a few already used to do in any case, but it tried to turn this specialisation into a coherent education. The study of letters remained the basis of the new scientific syllabus: 'The Emperor', declared Fortoul, 'does not wish there to be two nations in the *lycées*'; his aim is to divert some of the growing mass of unemployable arts graduates into training that would fit them for industry. The classicists replied that this watering-down of their syllabus destroyed all its moral value,

---

[1] Abbé J. Gaume, *Le Ver rongeur des sociétés modernes, ou le paganisme dans l'éducation* (1851).

and that scientific education could have none. Many scientists, paradoxically, shared their prejudice. This was an important reason why science never sought pride of place at school: the science teachers often accepted the claims of the classicists, and they liked *bifurcation* because, by keeping some literature in the scientific syllabus, it gave it a more respectable status. Other scientists, however, regretted *bifurcation*, because they were intent on developing their own purely scientific schools, and knew that this would damage their separatist cause. Nevertheless, despite the enormous amount of disagreement in political and teaching circles, the new system was popular among parents. Within a year of the new system being started, the pupils opting for science outnumbered those who stayed on with the classics in forty-five out of sixty *lycées*. Some Paris *lycées* were divided equally, and some in small towns, which catered for a traditionalist clientele, but the large provincial *lycées* on the whole favoured the new system and some went on to establish strong and lasting scientific traditions. Those in the ports and on the eastern frontier, which prepared for the naval and military schools, found it suited them well. But it was never given a proper chance. As Pasteur said, there were just not enough science teachers to allow a sudden expansion. In practice, some continued to teach what they had always taught. The industrialists, moreover, were at this very time abandoning their support for science in the schools. This can be seen in a particularly striking way at Mulhouse, where, early in the nineteenth century, they had established a school for their children, to give them a scientific education. But during the Second Empire they gradually increased the literary content and henceforth they preferred to obtain the literary *baccalauréat*, as a surer mark of respectability.[1] Some declared that it was important to cultivate 'French taste' because that was what made French products distinctive and saleable. The doctors dealt *bifurcation* its final blow: it had allowed admission to medical schools simply with a *baccalauréat ès sciences*: they protested that this would introduce uncultured ignoramuses into the profession and in 1858 got the *baccalauréat ès lettres* restored as a compulsory qualification for medical studies. In the early 1860s between a third and a quarter of headmasters were still in favour of *bifurcation*, but it

[1] R. Oberlé, *L'Enseignement à Mulhouse de 1789 à 1870* (1961).

was, for practical reasons, doomed. The isolation of the scientists in *math préparatoire* was restored: this was limited *bifurcation* for a few but without the common literary education which was the real essence of *bifurcation*.[1]

The historian Victor Duruy, Napoleon III's most famous minister of public instruction, had been horrified, when he had had to tour the country as an inspector-general, by the obvious uselessness of the classical syllabus for so many people. He had watched the sons of well-to-do farmers stuttering with pain and incomprehension through their Latin translation, simply because that was the only respectable education which someone who was making his way up in the world could buy. Duruy protested that 'we are stealing these people's money'. The boys would become farmers in their turn; their smattering of Latin was wasted and soon forgotten. So when he became minister, he started up a new branch of 'special secondary education' designed for the agricultural, commercial and industrial classes. This, again, was not a totally new thing, for the *lycées* had long had 'special courses', which were supplementary, practical classes given in *lycées*, usually by less qualified teachers, for the benefit of pupils who left school early and had no ambition to enter the liberal professions. Duruy developed these into an autonomous system, making them less technical, including in their syllabus history and literary history, modern languages (but not Latin) and morals (but not philosophy). Special education was not industrial training, and indeed only partly secondary. It was aimed at a lower social class than the classical *lycée*: Duruy said it would provide the non-commissioned officers of the industrial army. His often-praised liberalism had its limits: he believed in education corresponding to people's social status, even though he also talked about the rule of merit, and the people who sent their children to these new forms were indeed of the lower middle classes. Duruy tried, however, to modify the traditional approach by making them less theoretical and involving more 'applications': 'no metaphysics, no abstraction:

---

[1] R. D. Anderson, 'Some Developments in French Secondary Education during the Second Empire' (unpublished Oxford D.Phil. thesis 1967), particularly chapters 4, 5 and 8, using the Fortoul papers. Maurice Gontard has since written a biography of Fortoul. For an excellent general survey of all levels of education under the Second Empire see R. D. Anderson, *Education in France 1848–70* (Oxford, 1975).

let the word concrete be held in honour', he said. He established an *agrégation spéciale* to give the teachers a respectability equal to that of the classical teachers, which they sorely needed, for most were former primary teachers. A special teacher training college was established at Cluny, in three sections—applied science, modern languages, and literature and economics. This survived till 1891, when special education was fully absorbed into the secondary system and became 'modern education'.[1]

Neither special nor modern education gave a scientific training. These were not revivals of the *écoles centrales*. The dominance of literature was seen in the study of the ancient world being replaced largely by that of modern languages. Special education was an education for clerks and shopkeepers, more than for factory managers, useful though it might be. There was not all that much to distinguish it from the *écoles primaires supérieures*, apart from the quite significant fact that it was more expensive, in that it charged the same fees as the *lycées*. Between 1866 and 1880 only 5 per cent of its pupils completed the whole course; and 45 per cent left in the first two years of their schooling. But in 1886 the course was lengthened from four to six years. It ceased therefore to be limited mainly to those who had not the time to do a full *lycée* course and it graduated into a comparable alternative to classical education. It still lacked prestige, in the eyes of those who had received a classical education, but it was popular all the same. Side by side with the traditional classical course, which tended to absorb the attention of historians and indeed most writers, there was that of 'modern humanities', as it was called, which had rather different pretensions. By the turn of the century, half the secondary school population was opting for it. Between 1865 and 1880, 68 per cent of secondary pupils were 'classical' and 32 per cent were modern. In 1894, however, after the incorporation of special education into the secondary system, the classics fell to 53 per cent and the moderns rose to 47 per cent. In 1899 the classics and the moderns were exactly equal. In 1900 the moderns were in the majority, with 52 per cent. But this was not the triumph of science. For a time during the Second Empire, almost the same number of *baccalauréats* were awarded in science as in letters: in 1854 and 1855, indeed, there were even a few more scientists than classicists:

[1] The best account is in Anderson, op. cit.

but in the years 1870–90, there were roughly four classical *bacheliers* to every three scientific ones. The establishment of a modern *baccalauréat* (in 1881) made little difference to this: it was not taken by many people at first: pupils who opted for modern education were not interested in certificates, and it was not science that they studied in any case. The ministry of commerce, indeed, even granted holders of the modern *baccalauréat* various privileges, in its competition, over holders of the science *baccalauréat*. But modern education increasingly became a caricature of classical education, more and more literary, with only the ancient languages left out: the teachers lost the opportunity to make something really positive out of it and it fell into the status of a poor relation. In the period between the two world wars, by which time the modern *baccalauréat* had been abolished and incorporated into a general examination, there were regularly twice as many pupils obtaining the *baccalauréat* in letters as obtained that in science—and sometimes more than that. So whereas in 1891 nearly 3,000 obtained the science *baccalauréat*, in 1935 there were still only 3,365. At the same time the *bacheliers* in letters rose from 4,142 to 8,574.[1] This is explained not only by the failure of 'modern' pupils to finish their courses, but also by the amount of time given to science in schools, as shown in the accompanying table.

Percentage of time spent by pupils in the course of their seven years at secondary school

I: If they chose the most classical options:

	Philosophy	Letters	Modern Languages	History & Geography	Science
1852	2	67	5	13	13
1864	5·5	60	6·5	12·5	15·5
1880	5	52	11·5	15	16
1890	5	58·3	7·3	13·8	15·4
1902	6	49	14	17	16
1925	5	48	13	15	25
1938	5·4	43·5	11·7	14·5	25·2
1952	5·8	44	14·2	15·9	20
1962	6	42	14·3	15·1	22·7

[1] Statistics in J. B. Piobetta, *Le Baccalauréat* (1937), 304–8.

II: If they chose the most modern options:

	Philosophy	Letters	Modern Languages	History & Geography	Science
1852	2	47	5	13	32
1865	0	15·5	17·5	13	54
1882	8	20	16	12	43
1891	6	20	27	13	31
1904	2	16	23	13	36
1925	2	24	27	16	31
1938	1·9	24	27·8	14·4	31·7
1952	2	21·4	27·8	15·1	35
1962	2	21·2	26·7	14·9	36·1

Based on V. Isambert-Jamati, *Crises de la société* (1970), appendix II.

Except for a brief period during and a little after the Second Empire, science, even in the most 'modern' option, was never given more than one-third of the pupils' time; and mathematics was always given at least half of this time, so that the bulk of scientific teaching was theoretical. Until 1902 (and in some schools long after that) the standard textbook in geometry, for example, was that of Legendre, first published in 1794, the main effect of which was to require pupils simply to memorise definitions and proofs.[1]

It was not for lack of trying that the state failed to provide the types of education people wanted, or needed. The secondary syllabus was altered no less than fifteen times in the course of the nineteenth century and between 1802 and 1887 no less than seventy-five decrees of various kinds modified the organisation of the schools. In 1899–1902, a major effort was made to consult all sections of opinion, in a parliamentary inquiry whose findings filled seven large volumes. As a result of this, a law of 1902 attempted to diversify the options open to pupils, by setting up four different combinations of study—from the old Greek and Latin specialisation at one extreme to sciences and modern languages at the other, with Latin, science and one modern language as a third option, and Latin and two modern languages

[1] A.-M. Legendre [1752–1834], *Éléments de géométrie* (1794, 14th edition 1839, 11th revised edition 1868; translated into Spanish 1826, into Turkish 1841, Argentinian edition 1886). For the reform of teaching in geometry, see Charles Meray, *L'Enseignement des mathématiques* (1901) and *Nouveaux Éléments de géométrie* (1874, new edition 1903).

as a fourth. The partisans of the classics got better terms than they had a right to expect, for over the previous fifteen years the number of pupils specialising in the classics had fallen by over a third. Latin and, even more, Greek were already, and noticeably, losing their popularity after 1885, but the generation educated on the classics were in power and loath to condemn knowledge which they thought had made them what they were. So much so, indeed, that in 1923 a conservative government even tried to reintroduce compulsory classics for everybody during the first three years of secondary schooling. But at the same time this government also saw the need for more science, and invented the formula of 'scientific equality', proposing that all options should also have a common scientific basis. This is what the radicals established in 1925, but only by increasing the length of the school day. In 1941 the Vichy regime yielded to the protests about overwork and returned to the four options, with science as a specialisation. It was clearly impossible to conciliate all interests and it is unjust to condemn these different systems, since no one had a generally acceptable alternative. The triumph of science would have destroyed too many traditions. Paul Appell, dean of the Faculty of Sciences of Paris and rector of the Academy of the capital, considered that the *lycées* had made certain characteristics—'imported by the Jesuits from China' as he liked to say—so specifically their own, that they left no room for a genuine acceptance of the scientific approach. The *baccalauréat*, towards which everything in the *lycée* was directed, meant that the memorising of correct answers, rather than the spirit of inquiry and research, was supreme: 'everywhere it is the book that rules'. Theory was preferred to experiment; and even the pupils best endowed for science were forced to go through the same syllabus two or three times in order to gain admission to the Polytechnic: stamina in repetition, not independent thought, was the quality encouraged. He placed his hopes therefore on the universities, lamenting that the products of the *lycées*, devoted to literary studies, could not be got to change their ways.[1]

These educational controversies revealed the existence of several different types of ambition, which sought gratification through the schools in different ways; and that is why, in prac-

[1] Paul Appell, *Éducation et enseignement* (1922), 90–7, 113–24.

tice, so many varieties of schools developed, despite the passion
for uniformity and monopoly that tormented the politicians. At
the inquiry of 1899 it was pointed out by several witnesses that
the syllabus was only one out of many factors that mattered to
parents. Those who were involved in state service and the liberal
professions were interested in the *baccalauréat*, which raised their
children into membership of what people did not hesitate to call
the ruling caste. There were parents who believed that the
classics were a necessary foundation for a truly educated man,
but, apart from some whose literary attainments qualified them
to make such a judgement, the majority saw in Latin simply a
way of entering certain jobs, or of distinguishing themselves
from the lower orders, because they could afford to cultivate the
superfluous. But Édouard Aynard, a banker from Lyon, noted
that the idle rich were now under attack and the ideal of being
a man of leisure and pleasure was becoming discredited. Previously, dandy young men used to refuse to enter the family
business and so allowed the graduates of the *lycées* and the
universities, often of humble origin, to make their way into
important positions in industry and commerce. But now the rich
were agreeing to follow in their fathers' footsteps and the best
jobs were thus being kept within the family. The only way for
one without fortune to make his way (unless he was exceptionally brilliant) was to start at the bottom. The holders of *baccalauréats* had to resign themselves to this. But employers saw that
they were resigned, discontented, feeling that society owed them
something better; and so they might often prefer to take on a
boy of fifteen without any certificate or pretensions, who would
do as he was told. The constant confusion in secondary education was due to its overproduction of boys with diplomas which
were useful only in certain limited professions, and to its direct-
ing its efforts above all to preparing its pupils for admission to
the universities, which most, in this period, did not want to
enter. The teachers inevitably thought that the best pupils
should become teachers. But the lower middle classes, which
were faithful clients of the *lycées*, had other horizons than the
civil service. A teacher of a 'modern' course told the inquiry that
the parents of his pupils did not care much what their boys
learnt: 'the essential thing was to have their children brought
up in a bourgeois institution . . . The *petit bourgeois* puts his son

into a *lycée*, not to make a learned man out of him, but so as not to put him in the same school as that to which the sons of his servant and his concierge go.'[1] An investigation carried out in the 1880s in Paris showed clearly that 'modern' education appealed to a distinct class—the foremen, clerks, small business men.[2] The aspirations of these people did not press the state to increase scientific education. 'Modern' education was therefore also largely useless, for the literary methods of the classics were simply transferred to modern languages.

If they wanted more practical advantages from their schooling, it was to the Church more than the state that these people turned. The Church was not restricted by the all-important distinction between primary and secondary, and it was infinitely more flexible. Despite the increase in population, the state had established only one new *lycée* in Paris between Napoleon's day and Ferry's. In 1880, indeed, Berlin had five times as many gymnasia as Paris had *lycées*. The number of pupils at the ten *collèges* of Paris in 1789 was 5,000; in 1880 the *lycées* that succeeded them had only 6,792. The state thus provided for a small circle of people that had dealings with it. Other people looked elsewhere and the Church created schools of all kinds to meet their diverse needs. Its flexibility was even more notable in the provinces, where uniform *lycées* were distributed without regard for the demand. Thus one of the first results of the invention of special secondary education was that the Church transformed about fifty of its *écoles primaires supérieures* into 'special' colleges, giving them a new social status, but also keeping the practical primary bent. At the same time, it continued to establish and develop its aristocratic schools, which emphasised character training rather than examinations. It provided a whole range of schools—contrasting with the more fixed pattern of the *lycées* —catering for every degree of snobbishness, and at every price. But, of course, science was not the Church's strong point. The modernisation of the syllabus thus, to a certain extent, used up its impetus in the creation of numerous new gradations of social differentiation, rather than in introducing new teaching methods.

[1] *Enquête sur l'enseignement secondaire* (1899), 2.108, and Annexe (rapport général), 34.
[2] O. Gréard, *Éducation et instruction* (1887), 2. 55.

Keeping up with the times was no easy matter when so many forces were pushing the schools in different directions. Thus on the one hand the *lycées* had to perform what they considered their traditional function, of training the élite of the literary and civil service worlds, but their traditional methods were breaking down before the increase in pupil numbers: these doubled between 1850 and 1920, and doubled again between 1930 and 1938. The attractions of the civil service were, moreover, diminishing; new opportunities were being offered in commerce—previously despised; new ambitions were developing and new ideals were being invented. The school-teachers were faced not only with the problem of how to react to these changes and how to reassess their work in relation to them, but also with the need to defend and improve their own status when traditional values were everywhere being undermined. They had the alternative of trying to forecast which trends would be victorious, or of making the schools guardians of the truths they had grown up with and on the whole continued to cherish. That is why one cannot see the schools as simply 'reflecting society' and propagating its ideals, quite apart from the fact that the schools had a long history of providing a retreat from the world. A sociologist, Madame Isambert-Jamati, has attempted to study the attitudes of the schools towards society on a quantitative basis, taking as her source 2,000 speeches made at school prize-givings between 1860 and 1965. The exhortations and platitudes uttered at these ceremonies are taken as evidence of what head-masters, senior teachers and local dignitaries thought they were doing. The results of this computerised study are highly instructive in that they do show marked and interesting adaptations. The dating of the changing attitudes cannot be too precise, because the people who make speeches on these occasions are nearly always old men; they could easily be expressing ideas picked up thirty or even fifty years earlier. The processing of this mass of banality through computers is designed to produce averages, which are inevitably simplifications.

Nevertheless, it is the case that under the Second Empire, many of these speakers praised the *lycées* as a training ground for the country's élite 'whom the favour of Providence', as one speaker put it, 'has placed on the best rung of the social scale: you are destined to rule'. But different types of speakers looked for different results from this training: the arts masters stressed the development of taste, the science masters and administrators, following the current governmental policy, thought the schools were providing intellectual exercises to equip people to cope better with problems; while the 'notables' were not very interested by the syllabus but saw in the schools institutions which were preparing boys to enter their own class and become like themselves. Much was made of the need to obey authority, to maintain discipline. But averaging out all the points made, this was the period when most stress was placed on the school as a retreat from the dangers of the world, as protecting children; and also on its helping to inculcate the values society cherished —the true, the good and the beautiful, as defined by Victor Cousin.

In the founding years of the Third Republic, 1876–85, numerous changes were made to the syllabus, introducing more French, history and geography; more stress was laid on developing the individual judgement of pupils; and much was made of the republic as the regime of the rule of merit. But only 20 per cent of prize-givings mentioned this ideal of education being open to all. Thirty-two per cent still talked of the *lycée* as training an élite (a proportion even higher than under Napoleon III); and the liberal professions were still regarded as the natural outlet for pupils (87 per cent of speeches, as against 57 per cent mentioning technical jobs). Those who favoured 'discipline' were now balanced almost exactly by those who spoke in favour of individual initiative, just as those who continued to believe in the school as a retreat from the world were now balanced equally by those who were discarding this idea. The most popular theme was now patriotism (75 per cent), followed by the need to improve the world, the need for action, rather than just preserving old values. This new attitude was common ground between the notables and the history teachers, but the literature masters were still interested in styles of life and the importance of knowing languages. These divergences give one a hint of the sort of things teachers said to their pupils, as asides, as they glossed the same old set books: they obviously did not all say the same thing, and apart from a general agreement on flag-waving, a good half of them probably rejected the ideals of Ferry, with which the period is usually associated.

With time, as more and more reforms rained on them, many teachers retreated into attitudes of self-defence. By the turn of the century, the notables were being threatened also in their privileges. So in the years 1906–1930 the most frequent topic at prize-givings became the importance of disinterested knowledge and the preservation of taste. The teachers had once included many advocates of modernity, but when modernity actually arrived, and they saw their pupils abandoning the classics, and actually preferring action to education, they were horrified. Now they stressed instead the value of education for its own sake; there were references to science in only 9 per cent of the speeches. In the 1930s this attitude was altered slightly, in that education was now praised as developing the critical faculties and mental qualities such as clarity and precision, which could serve society better. There was no more preaching of adherence to social values, but this implied that the schools were now confident in values of their own. Children were seen less as adults in the making, than as having problems of their own, which the schools catered for, and this to a certain extent was a modification of the old idea of the school as a refuge. The study of the past was no longer mentioned as the main concern of schools, but it was not contemporary politics or economics that attracted comment: instead it was 'human nature' in the abstract that was now held up as what pupils should be taught to understand, and it is significant that, for this, it was to the literature of the seventeenth and eighteenth centuries that speakers turned most for their illustrations. The schools were thus redeveloping as small societies, seeking out roles for themselves which were not modelled on what the politicians were preaching in this highly agitated period: agitation outside could produce a search for the opposite inside the schools.

One explanation of this independence is that the relations of teachers and pupils were changing. The old authoritarianism was discredited. One teacher told his pupils: 'Be our friends, be our teachers.' This was the period when adolescence won a new respect, so that the whole idea of teaching was in danger of being challenged. By the 1950s, teachers could no longer easily think of themselves as superior to their pupils, and their function in society became very difficult to define. While the world outside absorbed itself in economic reconstruction and profiteering, the literature teachers condemned efficiency as vulgar, and proclaimed the grandeur of disinterested effort, of taste. References to science were now made in only 10 per cent of prize-givings—no more than references to philosophy, which was mentioned ten times more than in the 1930s, because it was now emerging as a provider of a common cultural language for those who were above the fray and claimed to judge it. Philosophy had the advantage that it was more esoteric than literature—still the most widely respected subject for developing taste—and it went beyond taste. The philosophers were the new élite who spoke Latin when few people did, or better still Greek or Hebrew. Only in the 1960s did the study of contemporary man and society become the goal most frequently urged. Even after due allowance is made for the limited value of these prize-giving speeches as indications of general trends, they do at least suggest that the schools were often as concerned to defend themselves as to serve society and play up to its latest obsession.[1] That is an important reason why one cannot look to the schools for simple explanations of changing attitudes in the country as a whole, or talk of the influence of teachers in general terms. Some teachers were articulate out of all proportion to their numbers, and created the illusion that society as a whole was worried by their problems; while, on the other hand, the teachers in the 'modern' schools were not given to proclaiming grand principles or to rationalising their activities, and their work—which affected half the pupils in the secondary schools—has gone largely unrecorded.

Rebellion, Discipline and Competitiveness

If the question of the influence of schools is to be understood, the relations between teachers and pupils must first be examined more closely.

'Merchants of Greek! Merchants of Latin! Hacks! Bulldogs! Philistines! Magisters! I hate you, pedagogues! Because, with your grave self-assurance, infallibility, stupidity, You deny ideals, grace and beauty!

[1] V. Isambert-Jamati, *Crises de la société, crises de l'enseignement. Sociologie de l'enseignement secondaire français* (1970).

Because your texts, your laws, your rules are fossils!
Because, with your profound airs, you are imbeciles!
Because you teach everything and know nothing!...'[1]

This translation of a verse by Victor Hugo presents the other side of the school, the resistance it generated to so much that was taught, simply because it was taught. There were an extraordinarily large number of Frenchmen who recalled their schooldays in these years with horror and pain: even if life later brought them more serious misfortunes, schooling was probably a disagreeable experience for the majority who went through it. With time, more and more children had to undergo it: the proportion of those whose temperaments and interests it did not suit may well have increased. Until scholars dig up and scrutinise a vast mass of end-of-term reports, it will be impossible to say how the reactions of children varied at different periods and whether, when schooling was made compulsory for everybody, it was accepted more or less willingly. But schoolchildren certainly had grievances of a very positive nature. Following the new situation created by the events of 1968, their opinions and protests have been collected and analysed in great detail by sociologists. It is striking that these do not differ very much from those of the previous century—though knowledge of their discontents in the past is of course far more fragmentary. Just as the teachers' refusal to allow their pupils to wear long hair or mini-skirts was a source of bitter resentment in 1968, so in the 1840s there is a record of a *lycée* going on strike because its headmaster forbade the senior pupils to wear beards and expelled one who protested insolently to him.[2] During the Second Empire, the irate pupils of the *lycée* at Poitiers barricaded themselves in their dormitories and were expelled only when the troops forced their way in, under the command of the garrison general himself. In 1870 no less than twenty-one pupil revolts were recorded. But the real crisis of pupil–teacher relations occurred in 1882–3. It began with a mutiny at Toulouse, in protest against excessively strict discipline and as a result also of grievances against individual teachers. The headmaster, backed by the Inspector and the Rector, dealt with it firmly by

[1] V. Hugo, *Les Contemplations* (1856).
[2] *Lycée Henri Poincaré: le livre des centenaires* (Nancy, 1954), 56.

mass expulsions, sending telegrams to the parents to remove their boys at once and escorting these to the station without delay. The pupils were defeated by their lack of unity. Soon afterwards the *lycéens* of Montpellier therefore called a congress, which was attended by representatives of a dozen *lycées*, mainly from the south, but from as far as Lyon, Nantes and Nevers too —though the congress had to change its venue secretly to Albi, to avoid repression. It produced a petition demanding the establishment of committees of pupils to act as intermediaries between the boys and the administration, a five-day week, the taxation of concierges who exploited boarders, an amnesty for boys involved in the mutinies and—on the academic plane— that Greek and Latin should be made optional, but that two modern languages should be compulsory. A newspaper entitled *The Rights of Youth* appeared. The boys of the Lycée Condorcet demanded that headmasters should be elected. It was, however, at Louis-le-Grand, the largest of the Paris *lycées*, that the most serious agitation occurred, to be reported extensively by the national press. Following a protest against the punishment of a boy, considered too severe, the headmaster had expelled five leaders of the protest. Violent demonstrations followed: the pupils smashed the furniture and resisted with iron rods the police who were summoned to quell them. The headmaster got permission from the Under-Secretary of State to expel the whole of the top form if necessary. He sent telegrams to their parents to remove them. Ninety-three pupils were expelled from Louis-le-Grand and twelve others were forbidden to attend any other state school.[1] These disturbances led to the whole question of discipline and authority being re-examined and new regulations were introduced in 1890, which considerably diminished the rigour of school life. To some extent, therefore, there were two periods in the history of school discipline, before and after these events. But many underlying features survived into the Fifth Republic, even if punishments could no longer be doled out as they once had been. However, the repetitive way in which, at intervals, leading authorities in the educational world proclaimed that there was a 'crisis of authority and of discipline'

[1] R. H. Guerrand, *Lycéens révoltés: étudiants révolutionnaires au 19ᵉ siècle* (1969), 66. O. Gréard, 'L'Esprit de discipline dans l'éducation', in his *Éducation et instruction: Enseignement secondaire* (1887), 2. 163, gives the figure 89, not 93.

shows that there were constant and fundamental problems, to which solutions were not found.

The French were proud that they had been the first people to abolish corporal punishment. Already in 1769 when new regulations were drawn up for Louis-le-Grand, there was no mention of beating, but instead 240 articles spelling out an elaborate variety of non-violent methods of control. In 1809 Napoleon simply generalised these. In 1854 Napoleon III made them somewhat less severe, by abolishing three of the sanctions still in use: imprisonment, relegation to a 'table of penitence' and 'deprivation of uniform'. The pupils were thus controlled by black marks, detentions of varying types, and expulsion. The law did not interfere with the *lycées*' brutal initiation rites and 'sending to Coventry' but there was nothing like the English fagging system, which was judged highly offensive to the doctrine of social equality. The physical conditions to which the boys were subjected were, however, often grim in the extreme. Most *lycées* were started in old church buildings confiscated at the Revolution, old hospitals, barracks and convents. In 1887 only one-fifth of them were purpose-built. An inspector visiting the college of Pertuis in 1877 wrote: 'Is this a school, a farm, or an inn, this vast ramshackle hut with rotting shutters and a bare courtyard?' At Grasse the college was a former perfume-distillery in ruins 'sordidly poor and completely neglected. Nothing has been mended, nothing cleaned: there is no desire to live.' At the *lycée* of Nancy, academically one of the best in the provinces, pupils complained, during the July Monarchy, that the mattresses they slept on—stuffed with straw or maize leaves—were so infested with lice as to make sleep difficult: the modernisation which followed involved the introduction of iron beds, and the provision of a bedside table for each one, instead of the single shelf which was all they had had to keep their property on. But in 1842 visiting inspectors were 'suffocated' by the smell of the latrines. In the 1860s a new bathroom was installed for the washing of feet, which was made obligatory once a fortnight. But in 1969 schoolchildren were still complaining about dormitories with seventy beds in long rows, saying that their buildings were like prisons—complete with grilles—but also dirty, ramshackle, uncomfortable, and noisy; they were still protesting, as they put it, against 'Napoleonic discipline' and furious punishments—like 700 lines.[1] Food—though a major preoccupation and provided with varying skill by bursars intent on economy—does not appear to have aroused anything like the dissatisfaction common in English schools. Boys, however, had a constant war directed at them to repress their sexuality—hard beds and coarse sheets were provided as anti-aphrodisiacs—and in 1969 they were still saying that homosexuality was one of the greatest problems of the schoolboy's life. Futile rules were made to control their leisure reading: in 1920 a pupil was expelled from the Lycée Buffon after a pornographic work, which the headmaster euphemistically called 'a particularly ignoble paper' was found in his possession: it was in vain that the boy protested he had picked it up at a religious club. In 1928 a ministerial order was issued forbidding pupils 'to form associations which elect a president and officials, sport insignia and claim to impose rules of any kind on members. In establishments of public education there is only one authority, that of the staff charged with administration, teaching and surveillance. Pupils, of whatever seniority, may not have relations with their teachers except individual ones, and collective representations may be allowed only in exceptional circumstances, and when they directly and exclusively concern academic work.' The government of the Liberation repealed this regulation in 1945.[2]

In the academic subjects they taught, the schools were confident that they were giving their pupils not only knowledge, but also the intellectual qualities needed to cope with life, to see its meaning and to judge the value of competing claims made upon them. But these mental powers—even if they were developed—were undermined by several contradictions in the emotional education which was offered. In the first place, though the schools preached respect for parents, they also saw themselves as rivals of the family. Boarding, the *internat*, was the expression of this ambivalence. In 1809, 63 per cent of all pupils in the *lycées* were boarders. This was seen as an indispensable part of the idea of the school as a closed world of its own, reinforced by the use of the *lycée* as a training ground for state servants, and by the desire to open it to merit, irrespective of where the parents resided. These various aims did not mix too

---

[1] Gérard Vincent, *Les Lycéens* (1971), based on 5,000 essays by schoolchildren, 66, 75.   [2] Guerrand, op. cit. 36.

well, for dissatisfaction with the way the *internat* worked in the *lycées* increased steadily. Part of the trouble was that the state delegated the duties of looking after the material side of the boys' lives to a separate class of despised and underpaid *surveillants*, known colloquially as *pions*. These were of two kinds. Some were youths who aspired to become teachers but, having no qualifications, took on the task of waking the boys up in the morning, keeping them in order during their meals, recreations and homework periods and supervising their discipline in general. They were supposed to study in their spare time, but they were on duty from when the boys rose to when they went to bed; they were paid a derisory pittance; they were lodged in attics and boxrooms without any comforts: it was the lowest possible job a youth could get: 'not even the most junior clerk, not even the convict was less happy than he'.[1] Most of them tried to move to something better as soon as they could; but some despaired of escaping and lived on, resigned, despised. The boys had no reason to respect them, so that a war waged between them, with vicious discipline being counteracted by merciless teasing and practical joking on the part of the pupils.[2] These ushers were employed by the headmaster on the same terms as servants, dismissible without notice. In the 1880s they formed themselves into an association and gradually won better conditions; but in 1900 only 3 per cent of them managed to get teaching jobs.[3] In 1923 they won guarantees against arbitrary dismissal; in 1937 they had a law requiring them to hold a *baccalauréat* and to have six hours a day free for study; they were dignified with the title of *maître d'internat*. Though their status improved in time, they continued to bear resentments. They opposed the relaxation of discipline, which they said would make them victims of the pupils' whims instead of those of the headmaster: liberty should not be given to the children until it was given to them.[4] The system by which the teacher just gave his

---

[1] Édouard Ourliac, *Physiologie de l'écolier* (1850), 107.

[2] For a description of the *pion's* life, see Alphonse Daudet, *Le Petit Chose* (1868).

[3] Paul Verdun, *Un Lycée sous la troisième république* (1888); Louis Durien, *Le Pion* (1880); Roger Rabaté, *De la situation économique et morale du personnel inférieur des lycées* (Paris law thesis, 1909); *L'Enquête sur l'enseignement secondaire* (1899), rapport, chapter 3.

[4] Maurice Loi, *Guide du surveillant* (1949) by the secretary-general of *L'Union du personnel de surveillance*.

classes and then went away, like a university professor, meant that sending one's boy to a *lycée* involved having him brought up by men who were regarded as little better than failures. This was very different from church schools, where at least the ushers were priests. The result was that the number of boarders in the *lycées* fell drastically under the Third Republic, to only 29 per cent in 1908. Parents who were compelled to send their children away from home increasingly preferred the church schools, which had over half of their pupils as boarders.[1] It was not irrelevant that boarding cost substantially more in state, as opposed to church schools, because the state tried to make a profit out of it, to subsidise the salaries of its teachers. During the July Monarchy and the Second Empire, a frequent compromise was to live in a private *pensionnat* and attend the *lycée* as a day boy; even pupils of church schools used to attend lectures at the *lycée*; and teachers used to move between the public and private sector. But this virtually disappeared during the Third Republic as the *lycée* hardened in its hostility to its rivals.[2]

As Alain defined it, the role of the *lycée* was to be a forcing house, to lead its pupils to the highest intellectual attainments, but in doing so, to compel them to become adults as soon as possible. In the name of Kant's categorical imperative, it saw its mission as liberating the child from his animality by imposing self-discipline on him, for the child who was indulged would remain savage all his life. The *lycée*'s disciplinary system had once been military. Under the republic it was reconstituted on a liberal basis, with much pedagogical and philosophical justification, but in practice it turned out to be highly authoritarian still. Thus Jules Payot, one of the new theorists, hoped that there would be voluntary submission to the teacher who showed calm, firmness and tact, but he still saw the teacher as a figure in authority.[3] Bergson opposed to the old system of breaking children in like horses, the authority based on charisma and the influence of the teacher seen as a model and hero. The experts were fully aware that severity produced 'rebellion, maladjustment, bitter or mistrustful pride', and that the teacher's

[1] 55% boarders in *petits séminaires*, 50% in diocesan schools, 47% in schools run by secular priests, 43% in independent lay schools, 30% in state *collèges* and 26% in *lycées*. Figures given in *L'Enquête*, rapport général (1899), 55.

[2] Jacques Rocafort, *L'Éducation morale au lycée* (1899).

[3] Albert Autin, *Autorité et discipline en matière d'éducation* (1920).

power could be an instrument of 'institutionalised sadism'. But routine was one of the strongest elements in the schools, and not least because many teachers self-confessedly became teachers in order to get their own back for the humiliations they had suffered as pupils. In 1968, a survey showed that 89 per cent of *lycée* pupils thought their teachers humiliated them, at least sometimes: they did not mean by that that teachers exercised authority over them, for they agreed overwhelmingly with the teachers that 'authority' was the most important quality a teacher had to have. But, next to that, the pupils valued love of children in teachers, while the teachers thought knowledge was more important; the majority of pupils complained against favouritism, which almost invariably went to those who were academically most successful; they wanted affection independently of their performance and that is what they did not get. The teachers replied that their classes were too large for them to take an interest in everybody.[1]

The result was that the pupils devised methods of protecting themselves, which considerably reduced the influence of their teachers. In memories of their schooldays, what they remembered most frequently was the ragging of teachers, which incidentally enabled them to forget the sufferings they underwent at their teachers' hands. Ragging was the reverse side of discipline, and between them they reveal how great the resistance of the pupils could be. During the July Monarchy Edmond Saissct thought he was performing his duties as a *lycée* teacher adequately simply by having a conversation with the best boys in the class, who sat in the front rows; he left the rest to their own devices; when the noise in the room became too great, he came down from his rostrum to hear what his 'dear disciples' were saying. This was quite common; to ignore a 'half-silence' was considered an achievement; which shows how, paradoxically, the teachers succeeded gradually in imposing their dominance over their pupils, despite their protestations of liberalism. The pupils replied to the favouritism shown to the successful by giving their admiration to the brave, who defied the teacher and could go furthest in flouting the rules of discipline. This attitude was organised into a formidable institution by the formation of cliques and gangs. Marcel Pagnol recounts that when he entered

[1] Vincent, op. cit. 61.

the Lycée Thiers at Marseille, he at once became part of a self-sufficient group of friends: as a *demi-pensionnaire* he spent eleven hours a day at school, so he knew nothing of the family of even his best friends. In these cliques, the pupils developed rules of their own, which neither parents nor teachers could influence much. One of these was exclusiveness: the claim to superiority, hostility to the *externes*, the day-boys (who however were used as emissaries, agents and pimps, to bring forbidden food and books into the school, and who could introduce fashions from the outside world).[1] Often these groups would choose leaders who would have precisely the opposite characteristics of the teachers—brutal ones if the teacher was weak, or cordial ones if he was severe; and with effective leaders, they could wage veritable wars of attrition against selected victims. The friendships formed here might last throughout their schooldays and sometimes throughout their lives: that was their positive side; but lying, cheating against teachers, bullying against the weak, group loyalty before all else were also developed. The school was partly responsible for allowing this, because it based its teaching methods on the encouragement of emulation and rivalry between the pupils. The sociability the politicians talked about was demanded only on a certain level. One of the major weaknesses of the school was that it did not appreciate how its pupils developed two different personalities, indeed two languages—an official one used in relations with teachers, and a slangy one, used among themselves. The influence of the teachers could not penetrate into this second world of the cliques. It has been suggested, in the chapter on primary education, that the *instituteur* failed to dislodge the primitive or superstitious mentality that his pupils inherited from their traditional backgrounds. Primary pupils seldom formed cliques, or threw up leaders, to resist their teachers. Unity was developed only in the secondary schools, and it was there that an additional way of life was developed, with moral attitudes different in many ways from that advocated by the schools. At the secondary level, there were thus three superimposed but independent cultures to which the pupils belonged: the academic, the adolescent and the family. The teachers, and the successful, academically

---

[1] J. Fontanel, *Psychologie de l'adolescence — Nos lycéens* (1913); Roger Ikor, *Les Cas de conscience du professeur* (1966), 212–19.

inclined children, were perhaps the only ones who reconciled these—by subordinating them to a single ambition. But for the majority, the tensions between them were both a source of conflict and a method by which the pressures of any one of them could be limited.[1]

Another of the contradictions between the intellectual and emotional work of the schools emanated from their attitude towards competitiveness. The problem had quickly been spotted during the first Revolution: in 1801 the Institut offered a prize for an essay on the question 'Is emulation a good means of education?'. The Jesuits (as will be seen) had made it the very basis of their school system, urging on their pupils to excel by stimulating rivalry between them and by an elaborate variety of honours and rewards. The winner of the prize concluded that some change was needed, that emulation under the *ancien régime* had been 'monarchical' but a democratic republic ought to find some alternative. There had been philosophers in the eighteenth century such as Bernardin de Saint-Pierre, who had thought that emulation ought to be eradicated; Rousseau had wanted to limit it to emulation against oneself; and some opponents of the Jesuits had protested that it was contrary to Christian humility. But the revolutionary doctrine of both fraternity and equality was in practice somehow reconciled with the maintenance of competitiveness. The nineteenth century, indeed, not only generalised it but sharpened and institutionalised it, and most notably of all, in the secondary schools, through the examination system. There was ample theoretical justification produced for it. Prévost-Paradol, the liberal moralist, declared that the desire for glory was one of the purest of emotions, that ambition was commendable provided it was directed at winning a reputation and men. Those who wanted money or pleasure were not ambitious but simply greedy or voluptuous. The ambition 'to make others adopt one's will and so . . . to will through them and act through them . . . gave one something like the Divine power': it extended one's strength, it elevated and indeed transformed human nature. Henri Marion, the republican philosopher of education, despite some reservations, thought emulation ought to be maintained, because it was the best way

[1] R. M. Mossé-Bastide, *L'Autorité du maître* (Neuchâtel, 1966); and Zeldin, *Ambition and Love*, ch. 12.

of getting pupils to stretch themselves to the limit. An inspector-general, who gave a lecture in 1913 'On the utility of rewards and particularly of school prizes', defended the honours, medals, honourable mentions and constant classification by merit, which were studiously maintained by the teachers (who had of course themselves been the victors of this system): he insisted that these were not the product of French vanity. Prizes were necessary because children were not perfect and would not work well simply to obey the categorical imperative. The struggle they involved was a useful preparation for the struggles of life. Some-how, the jealousies and disappointments they engendered must be mitigated; but no better method was proposed than the award of yet more prizes, for 'good conduct', which everybody, however stupid, had a chance of winning.[1]

Constant comparison of pupils against each other was a basic element in the schools. Marks were awarded for every exercise. One zealous teacher is even reported to have given three marks for every exercise: one which judged the work itself, a second which graded it by comparison with previous work and a third by comparison with the standard reached by other pupils. The state greatly increased the competitiveness by making pupils of the whole country compete against each other in national *concours généraux*. These were previously limited to the Paris *lycées*: in 1865 Duruy, in a spirit of democracy, drew the provincial schools in. Complaints about the ill-effects led to the abolition of the *concours* in 1903, but, by public demand, they were restored in 1922—the habit was too ingrained for it to be exorcised, any more than alcoholism could be. An inspector-general wrote in 1879 of his youth that these *concours généraux*, by which every child in the country could hope to be marked out as the best of his generation, were 'the sole preoccupation of everybody—headmasters, teachers and pupils. We were ceaselessly reminded of the great day, when we would have to bear the school's flag: it was to this goal that all our exercises, all our efforts were directed.' Parents were willing to play the game, even if their children were bound, except in very rare cases, to lose. The newspapers reported the details—as they still

[1] E. Jacoulet, 'Émulation', in F. Buisson, *Nouveau Dictionnaire pédagogique* (1911), 1. 544–8; Frédéric Queyrat, *L'Émulation et son rôle dans l'éducation. Étude de psychologie appliquée* (1919); Henri Marion, *L'Éducation dans l'université* (1890), 280–9.

do—even publishing the winning essays. It was acceptable, perhaps, because it was an alternative to the national lottery.

The *baccalauréat* was established by Napoleon as a method by which the state could test the abilities of those whom it recruited to serve it. At first, it involved only an oral examination, lasting half or three-quarters of an hour, during which the candidate was given a passage from a book he had previously studied and questioned on it. Eight candidates could be examined simultaneously by the 'jury', who would often correct and comment on the answers: 'I have never had a better Latin lesson', said Gréard, 'than the day I presented myself for the *baccalauréat*.'[1] Pupils of seminaries could get the certificate without any examination at all, simply on the presentation of a certificate from their teacher and their bishop; and the pupils of the *lycées* generally found that their examiners were their own teachers, acting as members of the faculty. Under Napoleon, it concerned very few people: in 1810–14, the Paris faculty of letters awarded between 67 and 164 *baccalauréats* annually, plus about 10 *baccalauréats* in science. No one worried about it then. Only those who needed the certificate, to enter the faculties of theology, law and medicine, bothered to obtain it. But under the Restoration, it became necessary for admission to the civil service and the liberal professions; in 1830 the written examination was introduced; in 1841 Cousin tried to increase uniformity of standards, for some faculties were notoriously lenient; in 1847 schoolteachers were no longer allowed to examine, and the faculties were developed as examination bodies. In this period, there were definite questions the candidates could prepare for—2,500 of them in all—and one was chosen out of a box. This resulted in textbooks being published to provide the right answers and crammers known as *boîtes à bachot* or *fours à bachot* sprouting, often on the basis of no fees being demanded unless the candidate passed, and some guaranteeing a pass within two months —a reasonable enough proposal, since it was simply a matter of memorising certain facts. The satirical magazine *Le Charivari* in 1849 carried seventy-eight advertisements of this sort, placed between a cure for venereal diseases and the announcement of a public ball. The historian Lavisse complained that the result of this was that the *baccalauréat* ceased to be proof of ten years of

[1] J. B. Piobetta, *Examens et concours* (1943), 11.

classical education and became something one could cram for in a few weeks: he was of course looking back to a golden age that never existed. Protests against it multiplied: the anticlerical prime minister Combes inveighed against it as an obstacle to true learning, which ought to be replaced by a straightforward school-leaving certificate. But when the parliamentary inquiry of 1899 collected public opinion on the subject, it discovered that the spokesmen of local government—the *conseils généraux*—were generally in favour of it: that of the department of the Rhône said firmly: 'Secondary education is very well organised.' The president of the inquiry castigated the *baccalauréat* as a social institution which divided France into two castes, one of which claimed the right to monopolise all public offices. But it had by now also become a vested interest and a goal for ambition among too many people. It easily survived all attacks.[1]

A new science arose to study examinations—'docimology'. In the 1920s, there were protests that it was time to clarify exactly what the *baccalauréat* was testing, whether intelligence, culture, memory, writing skills, rapid reflexes or efficient teaching. Psychologists carried out experiments which showed that different examiners could mark the same answers in wildly different ways: in French composition the maximum divergence between them could be as much as 13 out of 20 (i.e. when answers were marked on a scale from 0 to 20, the same script could get a mark of say 3 from one examiner and 16 from another); in philosophy it could be as much as 12, and even 8 in physics. The average variation in philosophy was 3.36 out of 20; and 23 per cent of philosophy scripts, when marked by more than one examiner, received marks which diverged by five or more points. These differences were due partly to some examiners giving most of their marks around the middle range, while others, reacting with more emotion, frequently touched the extremes; some examiners marked down heavily when they encountered one important mistake, while others ignored it; but apart from these different techniques, there were also straightforward disagreements about quality which could not be reconciled. Relevance was very important to some in French composition, and its lack taken as a sign of an inability to concentrate; a logical presentation, with a preamble, paragraphs and a conclusion, seemed

[1] J. B. Piobetta, *Le Baccalauréat* (1937).

indispensable to others; while originality appealed to still others.[1] Officialdom replied that these were faults it was aware of and was trying to remedy; more skilful and experienced examiners could avoid these pitfalls; and besides, since 1890, it was permissible for pupils to produce the record of their school performance at the *baccalauréat*, so that it could be taken into consideration in deciding the result. The examination system was defended not simply as an unfortunate necessity but as having positive virtues. Piobetta, the university official in charge of the *baccalauréat* between the world wars, declared that 'examinations and competitions are part of our way of life. Some of them are an integral part of our oldest institutions. All of them have become the pivot of our social hierarchy. Careers, public or private, that do not require the possession of a diploma are becoming increasingly rare. Titles and grades, with the official stamp on them, constitute veritable letters of nobility to which rights and prerogatives are attached.' This was as it should be, for merit had thus triumphed over favouritism and intrigue. Examinations were not just a test of knowledge, but also of will, temperament and personality. They showed people that one had to work and fight in order to succeed, and so they prepared children for the struggles of life. Examinations, he concluded, were 'beautiful and good'. He agreed they had their limitations: if in 1942 for example, all candidates who mis-spelt the word session in their application forms had been failed, then 10 per cent, i.e. 3,000 pupils, would have been eliminated. It was true that 'standards were falling', that cramming was dangerous, and the mandarinate of China was a terrible warning. But that was reason only to improve the system, not to abolish it.[2]

Strangely, Piobetta had public opinion behind him. Children may have hated the *baccalauréat*, but parents valued the status it accorded, and the prizes in this loaded lottery were enough to make people forget the disappointments it caused. Even in 1968, when traditional educational institutions were attacked as they never had been before, the *baccalauréat* still had its defenders. Significantly, the most prominent of these was the president of

---

[1] International Institute Examinations Inquiry. Commission française pour l'enquête Carnegie sur les examens et concours en France, *La Correction des épreuves écrites dans les examens. Enquête expérimentale sur le baccalauréat* (1936), 129, 198.

[2] J. B. Piobetta, *Examens et concours* (1943), 86–101.

the Federation of Parents' Associations, who, while conscious of its faults, complained only that not enough children were able to obtain it: he did not want to abolish it, but to alter it so that as many children as possible could obtain it; and he wanted it to give automatic right of admission into universities. By then, many university teachers, overwhelmed by the enormous increase in the numbers of students, were demanding the right to select only the ones they judged suitable, arguing that a *baccalauréat* was no proof of the qualities higher education valued. Those who breached the *baccalauréat* barrier found that new ones were being raised beyond it.[1]

If the *baccalauréat* was indeed the crowning glory of the secondary education system, then that system must inevitably be judged to have been a failure, because only a small minority of those who entered it succeeded in obtaining the certificate. Its failure rate, as its critics put it, was such that it would have gone out of business long ago, were it not bolstered by these social prejudices. The year 1846 was the first in which more than 4,000 pupils obtained the *baccalauréat*, 1869 the first year the figure reached 6,000, 1891 7,000, 1904 8,000, 1919 10,000. Between 1885 and 1918 altogether only 200,000 people obtained the ambiguous honour of belonging to the 'prolétariat des bacheliers'. This was at a time when the secondary school population was growing as follows:

		Pupils in secondary *lycées* and *collèges*	
1850	30,000	1930	66,870
1860	35,000	1935	99,250
1871	39,000	1938	119,870
1881	53,000	1942	147,560
1890	56,000	1946	166,740
1900	58,800	1955	217,750
1910	62,000	1960	342,840
1920	62,000	1964	564,210

The pass rate of those who took the examination was on average

[1] Jean Cornec, *Pour le baccalauréat* (1968). For the qualities required in the *baccalauréat*, see the advice of André Piot, *L'Art de concourir enseigné aux étudiants* (Avignon, 1944), and J. B. Piobetta, *Le Succès aux examens* (1954).

only about 50 per cent. (In 1932, to take a year at random, it was 42·45 per cent; in the 1960s it was about 60 per cent.) But most secondary pupils did not even try to obtain it: they left school early. In 1900, 40 per cent of pupils had left by the end of their third year, and naturally it was the poorer children who dropped out most. In 1967, it was still the case that 76 per cent of pupils admitted into the *lycées* did not obtain the *baccalauréat*, and of those who did sit for it, one-third failed to obtain it, even after three successive tries. The success record of the *lycées* thus did not rise above 24 per cent. One failure, as the president of the parents' association said, was a 'family drama', but 100,000 failures a year was a 'national disaster'.

It is not surprising that there were complaints that the examination system was creating a whole mass of people whose 'energy was often irreparably destroyed, and who became melancholic, enervated, agitated and *abouliques*'.[1] Already in 1848 a commission was appointed to 'examine the effects produced on the health of pupils by the relationship between hours devoted to study and those given to sleep, recreation, gymnastics and promenade'. The overburdening of the syllabus became a constant theme of debate, but with little practical result since the virtues of hard work, approval of the desire to succeed, and the ambition to provide a complete general education all contributed to maintaining the maximum pressure on children. The advance of knowledge inevitably increased the amount that had to be learnt, at an accelerating rate: and in the 1960s candidates for the *baccalauréat* were expected to read twice as much as those of 1930. In 1963 an inquiry revealed that the minimum preparation required to pass that examination was sixty-one hours a week for the mathematicians, fifty hours for the experimental scientists and forty-nine and a half for the philosophers, though if optional subjects were added the totals were raised to sixty-six, fifty-seven and fifty-two hours.[2] The *baccalauréat* produced a distinctive physical type. In 1906, 33 per cent of the boarders of a *lycée* in Lyon were found to be short-sighted and 18 per cent of the day boys, and as they progressed into the senior classes, the percentage increased. In the Collège Rollin, 10 per cent of pupils in the bottom class were short-sighted and 55 per cent

[1] Jules Payot, *La Faillite de l'enseignement* (1937), 79.
[2] Jean Capelle, *Contre le baccalauréat* (1968), 62.

of those in the *classe de philosophie*.[1] But little research was attempted on how children reacted to the failure which the majority were bound to encounter. The problem of how far this failure was due to difficulties in adapting themselves to school life, to temperament and background, quite apart from the question of intelligence, was seen to be important by some, but it was only in the 1930s that vocational guidance began to be practised even on a small scale.[2] No one has yet calculated how much the schools, with their competitiveness and their dedication to examinations, contributed to the creation of all that depression, nervousness, neurasthenia and melancholy, which is studied in another chapter.

State and Private Education

The schools might once have been expected to study the same Latin passage at the same time, in every classroom throughout the country, but in practice there was infinite variation created by the eccentricities of the teachers and the pressures of local conditions. Centralisation gave them status, but human weakness made them what they were. No ministerial order could be enforced until it had travelled through the hierarchy; but officials, headmasters and teachers often hated, despised or feared each other, and these animosities stirred up resistance which could completely transform the spirit in which the orders were applied. Francisque Sarcey, a successful journalist, began his life as a secondary teacher under Napoleon III. His experiences show how the struggles of the political world were reproduced in microcosm: just as the elector resented the power of the government and was constantly ridiculing it and getting round its laws, while trying to derive all possible benefits from it, so the teachers hated the headmasters and inspectors, whom they condemned as failed teachers. They ganged up against the administrators in almost childish ways. Sarcey's headmaster passed on to him a ministerial order that every teacher should keep a notebook with a full record of the lessons he gave and the

---

[1] Union des Associations d'anciens élèves des lycées et collèges français, *Bulletin trimestriel* (Oct. 1906), 22.

[2] André Le Gall, *Les Insuccès scolaires* (1954); Dr. Jean Philippe et Dr. G. Paul-Boncour, *Les Anomalies mentales chez les écoliers. Étude médico-pédagogique* (1905); Dr. Jean Philippe, *La Psychologie des écoliers* (1906).

marks he awarded, and the progress made by each pupil daily. Sarcey protested that it was impossible to assess progress daily, but was forced to obey orders. So he invented a different adjective for each day: incessant, extraordinary, unheard-of, incredible, stupefying progress. He was summoned by the furious headmaster, but he replied that he had been appointed by the minister to assess the pupils' progress and only he could do it: if he was stupefied by it, then it was his duty to say that the progress was stupefying. This kind of sniping was a permanent feature. But on the other hand most teachers had a profound faith in the values of what they were doing, and despite the limitations of their own knowledge, they taught with a conviction which sustained the system much more than the regulations. Sarcey recalled how in the *lycée* at Chaumont in 1851—a third-rate school at which he, who had failed the *agrégation*, was among the most distinguished members of the staff—it was precisely those teachers who were academically weakest who exercised most influence on the boys. The professor of philosophy had dictated the same lessons for twenty years, rearranging the same materials only very slightly to accommodate them within the different syllabuses which were introduced from time to time, and continuing to teach the lectures of Larouviguière, from whom in his youth he had picked up all he knew of philosophy. But he was more respected than the fashionable youngsters with the latest theories; and his influence must be measured not in terms of what he taught but of the way he did it, and of the relationship he established with each pupil. The generalisations about the schools need to make allowance for the infinite variations of individual personality. The teacher of literature in this school taught the classics mainly by reading them out to the accompaniment of dithyrambic praise after each phrase— a method which was once fashionable and had by then ceased to be so, but some pupils were deeply moved and roused to a similar admiration; others looked back on it as proof of the puerility of teachers.[1]

The atmosphere of each institution, moreover, was special to it and schools built up traditions which became more tenacious than the vagaries of governments or staff. Thus the *lycée* of Nancy, founded in 1803 to replace a Jesuit school, was highly

[1] Francisque Sarcey, *Souvenirs de jeunesse* (1885), 183-94.

responsive to local demand. Though it resembled a barracks under Napoleon and a monastery under the Restoration, the headmaster, conscious of parental anxieties, promised his pupils 'the love of a father, the benevolence of a protector and the zeal of a friend': in 1840 an inspector complained that the boarders were left very much to their own devices: 'the discipline was completely negative and there was total lack of moral direction'. In 1831 the school started 'industrial classes' to prepare for professions which did not need Latin; in 1836 it had a 'modern laboratory', in 1838 an 'electromagnetic apparatus', in 1851 a commercial course and in 1854 a gymnastics teacher. Under the Second Empire the school developed its scientific specialisation, thanks to a headmaster, V. A. Davau, who was an *agrégé des mathématiques* from the École Normale Supérieure. It had four mathematics teachers, and all was organised with a view to winning admission to the *grandes écoles*. In 1860, 200 out of the 261 boys in the top forms were scientists. Between 1856 and 1870 no less than seventy-four pupils went on to the Polytechnic; in the early years of the Third Republic as many as fifteen used to get into it each year, though the numbers fell to between five and ten after 1900 and only one or two by 1939, as it became the fashion to go to the Paris *lycées* for a final year, from which the chances of success were considered (not altogether justifiably) better. The pupils were taught intensively, not only by their very able teachers, who received extra pay to give extra discussion and revision classes and mock examinations, but also by successful former pupils, who had been through the *écoles speciales* and came back to give occasional lessons. Weekly tests were a regular feature. Literature was not neglected in the school as a whole; the philosophy and mathematics classes were indeed roughly equal in numbers; but Latin was dropped by more than half the boys, and there was not the same competitiveness among the classicists. The number of classicists from the whole of France who could hope to get into the École Normale Supérieure was small (about thirty a year), compared to the 200 scientists admitted annually to the Polytechnic. This was the main reason why preparation for the former was quickly concentrated at a few Paris *lycées*, mainly Henri IV and Louis-le-Grand, and why the victors in this struggle were such a clearly defined clique. Nancy thus did not have an autonomous *Khagne* (classical top class, preparing for the École Normale Supérieure) and Lucien Febvre, one of its pupils, went to Paris to finish his schooling. By contrast, Nancy had a very strong *Corniche* (scientific top class, preparing for the military school of Saint-Cyr), which in the years 1880–1914 had on average fifty-one pupils, with a success rate of between 27 and 48 per cent, so that no less than 1,310 pupils of Nancy went on to Saint-Cyr between 1806 and 1953. Saint-Cyr was easier to get into than the Polytechnic; it did not require ceaseless hard work; and the *Corniche* had a slightly less intellectual and more social atmosphere than the other top forms, with a solemn annual dinner to celebrate the battle of Austerlitz, ghastly initiation rites, fines on freshmen for breaking the rules, and a special badge to differentiate them. A *classe d'Agro* catered for the sons of the local landowners; others prepared for the Haute École Commerciale, the École Centrale, the École Vétérinaire, etc.; in 1945 Nancy and Bordeaux were the two provincial *lycées* which also established a *Colo* (preparing for admission to the École Coloniale). The *lycée* of Nancy was the school that produced Maurice Barrès—who was desperately lonely, crying every night in his dormitory— Marshal Lyautey, President Albert Lebrun, the mathematician Poincaré, and above all the civil servants, lawyers and engineers of the region. It owed its unusual success to the fact that it performed a service better than any rival. It was conscious of the competition of the local church schools, and it could not meet it on the social level. By 1938 its boarding pupils were down to 236 out of 1,140, partly because the boarding fees were twice as high as those of the cheapest *internat* in the region. It introduced sports, excursions, hobbies like beekeeping and aero-modelling, but its function was above all intellectual, oriented towards examinations. This meant that it appealed only to certain types of families, and different specialisations, such as *Khagne* and *Corniche*, attracted boys from noticeably different backgrounds. In 1950 an analysis of its 1,600 pupils showed that only 8 per cent had well-to-do parents and 36 per cent poor ones; nearly 10 per cent were orphans. Attempts had been made before the war to take in more pupils from primary schools, but without much success, because these preferred to go to the *école primaire supérieure*, which had a shorter course. The *lycée* had a character of its own, though when one places it—and schools like it—under a microscope, one sees still more minute societies within it.[1]

However, the measure of the failure of the state *lycées* to provide, even in all their varied forms, the kind of education parents wanted is the rapid revival of church schools. Once freedom was given to the Church, it recruited very nearly one-half of all secondary pupils, even though the state replied by making its own *lycées* partly free. In the first half of the nineteenth century, there was a lot of private enterprise in providing secondary education, and up to one-third of pupils were taught in lay private schools, but these, mainly second-rate crammers, virtually vanished in the second half of the century, to be replaced by church schools.[2] These statistics are not entirely comparable, since not all schools provided teaching right up to the *baccalauréat*. In 1842 the private schools entered only 6 per cent of the 5,000 candidates for the *baccalauréat*, but by 1932 they entered 55 per cent of the 14,640 candidates.

Proportion of Pupils in Public and Private Secondary Schools (%)

	State *lycées* and *collèges*	Lay Private Schools	Church Private Schools
1855	42	36	22
1867	47	28	25
1887	56	13	31
1899	51	6	43
1920	59	41	
1930	56	44	
1937	51	49	
1951	57	43	
1965–6	79	21	

'If I had a son, I would rather send him out as a cabin boy on a fishing boat than have him exposed to the dangers which I myself ran in the schools of the university.'[3] So wrote Montalembert, one of the most active opponents of the state's monopoly of education, and a lot of people agreed with him, for the rise of the church schools was the result not of the efforts of a

[1] Lycée Henri Poincaré, *Le Livre des centenaires* (Nancy, 1954).

[2] For a history of a lay private school, see G. Ruhlmann, *Cinq siècles au collège Sainte-Barbe* (1960). This school, whose pupils included Eiffel, Péguy, Herriot, Louis Blériot and Léon Gaumont, went bankrupt in 1900 but was saved by the state's generosity.

[3] A. Trannoy, *Le Romantisme politique de Montalembert avant 1843* (1942), 64.

centralised government, but of the totally uncoordinated initiative of many individuals and small societies. Their competition was exacerbated by political disputes, but they also represented quite widespread feelings about how children ought to be brought up. It was the Jesuits who had set the pattern which these schools were more or less to follow. By the middle of the eighteenth century, the Society of Jesus had no less than 699 schools all over the world, ninety-one of them in France. These last had been closed following the expulsion of the order, but in 1849 the first Jesuit school of the nineteenth century was founded in Avignon and by 1880, when they were again expelled, they had established twenty-seven, with over 10,000 pupils. Their popularity was such that at Vannes, for example, their school, opened in 1850, had 400 pupils within four years; in Paris, their Collège de l'Immaculée-Conception, started in 1852, had 600 pupils in 1867 and 800 in 1875, and the Collège Vaugirard rejected as many applicants as it admitted. Originally the Jesuit schools had been entirely free, and they had only day-boys, but the pressure from parents was now such that in the nineteenth century they were predominantly for boarders. Church schools had the advantage that, because they employed mainly priests, they had far lower expenses on salaries, and their fees were usually lower; but it was not just cheapness that made them popular. In 1865, the average annual fees in the different types of school were as follows (in francs):

	Boarders	Day-boys
Lycées	739	110
Municipal collèges	649	72
Catholic schools	630	97
Jesuit schools	764	70

Some of the most expensive schools were Catholic as well as some of the cheapest; the Catholics awarded scholarships, in the same way as the state did. They were thus able to cater for an even wider range of social groups than the state's secondary schools. The Jesuits attracted the sons of the aristocracy and of the high bourgeoisie; by the late 1870s their fees for boarders in Paris were 1,400 francs. At the other end of the scale were the *petits séminaires*, designed for the poor and frequented mainly by peasants. They always included poor boys, picked out by the *curé* as the brightest in the village and destined for the priesthood, but the majority of pupils in the *petits séminaires* never became priests. In Savoy, these schools collected their fees in kind—corn or wine—to put themselves within reach of even the humblest. It was customary for the church schools, in any case, to charge fees according to the ability of the parents to pay. Between these two extremes there grew up a multitude of schools, started by individuals or by different orders, and responding to local conditions and the demands of different classes in a far more flexible way than the more uniform state system. In particularly religious regions, the state schools were often largely staffed by priests, at least during the Second Empire and the early years of the Third Republic, so the contrast between public and private education was not always obvious.[1]

The church schools sought to distinguish themselves in the way they looked after the moral and physical welfare of the boys. Taine, touring the provinces as a state inspector of education and therefore not predisposed in favour of its rivals, reported in the 1860s that the Jesuits were popular because they were fashionable, 'because the food and the personal care are reputed to be better, because good contacts are made there . . . The Fathers make themselves comrades of the students, while [in the *lycée*] the teacher is cold and the usher (*surveillant*) is an enemy . . . Very great attention to the food, the dress, the manners of the students.'[2] The Jesuits conceived of the schools as partly religious communities, organised as families, and partly a reaction against the Napoleonic idea of the school as a barracks. They addressed their pupils not as *élèves*, nor *messieurs* (as in the *lycée*), but as *mes enfants*. They gave each class a single principal teacher who, as far as possible, progressed with the pupils from year to year, and who was expected to get to know each pupil individually and intimately. These were priests and so too were the *surveillants*, who were not considered inferior, but just as essential a part of the school. Their task was 'to help their

[1] Robert Anderson, 'Catholic Secondary Schools (1850–70): A Reappraisal', in Theodore Zeldin, *Conflicts in French Society* (1971), 51–93; J. W. Padberg, S.J., *Colleges in Controversy: The Jesuit Schools in France from Revival to Suppression 1815–80* (Cambridge, Mass., 1969).

[2] H. Taine, *Carnets de voyage: notes sur la province 1863–5* (1897), 225–8.

pupils' work, to put the finishing touches to their education, to form their character and to enlighten and develop their religious feelings, in order to make them faithful to God and useful to their country'. The *surveillant* was also in charge of games, which were much encouraged, and in extraordinary variety.[1] Since many of the schools were rural, often splendid country mansions, long walks were a frequent relaxation, as well as gymnastics.[2] Lay teachers were brought in on a part-time basis for drawing, fencing, music and foreign languages: César Franck, for example, taught at the Jesuits' Vaugirard school for a number of years. The boys were given 'offices of trust' to develop their sense of responsibility, as bell-ringers, librarians, sacristans, 'quaestors' (to deal with lost property), 'aediles' (to report necessary repairs) and treasurers of the poor (to collect alms). The ushers were instructed to 'command with extreme gentleness', as a much quoted book of advice on discipline put it.[3] 'How can you expect the yoke of authority to be bearable without gentleness?' The boys should be treated with respect, 'because they are deserving of respect', 'because they are stronger than we think' and 'because it is the only way to persuade them'. They must be got to behave well but freely, since force will only make them hypocrites. They must be persuaded that happiness was not to be found in the enjoyment of sensual pleasures and external advantages, but in moral satisfactions. Their evil inclinations must be opposed by showing them the evil consequences they bring about. But all children were different and the character of each one should be carefully studied, his fears, his sorrows and his faults. Children cannot be made to work hard 'as are battalions of soldiers': great care must be taken not to anger them. Punishment should be used only 'with extreme discretion', and teachers should 'wait patiently for the results of the child's efforts'.[4] The state's experts on pedagogy were well aware of much of this, and men like Henri Marion, for example, had his

---

[1] C. de Nadaillac, S.J., *Les Jeux de collège* (1875).

[2] For photographs of church schools, see the *Annuaire de l'enseignement libre français* (e.g. 1927).

[3] Amédée de Damas, S.J., *Le Surveillant dans un collège catholique* (1857), 156.

[4] On Amédée de Damas (1821–1903), author of about 44 educational and religious pamphlets, see the biography by J. Burnichon (1908). Cf. Abbé Simon, *De la direction des enfants dans un internat des garçons* (1904); and Emmanuel Barbier, S.J., *La Discipline dans les écoles secondaires libres. Manuel pratique du surveillant* (1888, 3rd edition, 1897).

book *Education in the University* recommended to priests training as teachers. The deeply humane attitudes of some religious teachers were, however, counterbalanced by a terror of homosexuality and indeed of all sexuality. Friendships between just two boys, or between a teacher and any one boy, were to be avoided at all costs, as every manual repeated. One, for example, insisted that 'in bathing, pupils must be forbidden to touch each other under any pretext, even under the pretext of helping others to swim'.[1] The rapid expansion of the church schools meant that standards were, in some orders, lower even than those to be found in the obscure municipal colleges; animosities could flourish despite the religious atmosphere, with teachers and pupils denouncing each other in the name of virtue.[2] But there does seem to have been a greater confidence in these schools on the part of parents, who probably went to see the teachers more frequently than in the *lycées*; and the teachers felt they owed more to the parents, who paid them.[3] The headmasters of church schools—unlike the *proviseurs* of *lycées*—were not simply administrators, but played an important educational and moral role; and they were able to attract parents by the personal stamp they could imprint on their schools.

It was the Jesuits who had originally developed emulation into a fundamental educational method. Contests of all kinds were constantly being organised, with prizes, rank listings, fanciful Roman titles, and an 'Academy' to which the best pupils were elected. The lengths to which this could go are illustrated by the (rather unusual) habit of one teacher at Saint-Acheul School, Amiens, to offer a pinch of snuff at the end of each day to the best pupil of the day; and the best pupil of the week was given the privilege not only of satisfying his own appetite but also of offering a pinch from the teacher's snuffbox to his classmates who had received high marks. The pupils were also divided into two camps, Romans and Carthaginians, with an *imperator* or consul at the head of each, assisted by tribunes, praetors and senators, and subdivided into decuries, all arranged hierarchically, and every individual pupil was allocated a definite

---

[1] Abbé Charles Guillemant, supérieur du petit séminaire d'Arras, *Précis de pédagogie à l'usage des jeunes professeurs de l'enseignement secondaire* (Arras, 1905), 62.

[2] Firmin Counort, *A travers les pensionnats des Frères* (1902).

[3] Gérard Avelane, *Carnet d'un professeur de troisième* (1969).

rival in another decury.[1] How far these methods gave better academic results than were obtained at state schools is difficult to say: by the nineteenth century there was probably not much to choose between the two systems from the point of view of the amount of emulation they encouraged. Both systems recruited from so wide a spectrum of society that one cannot say that the pupils of either came from more ambitious backgrounds. The quality of the teaching varied considerably. The Church's teachers probably always had inferior academic qualifications but that sometimes meant only that they had not been through the official university channels. The Jesuits in the nineteenth century did not have that reputation for erudition they later acquired: it was only after their expulsion in 1882, when they were more or less forced out of secondary education, that they decided to specialise in research and high intellectual standards. In the twentieth century, an increasing number of priests obtained high university honours: but on the whole the teachers of the church schools were less brilliant than those in the *lycées*. Still, they used the universal cramming techniques and prepared for the same examinations. They were as attached to the classics as their lay rivals. In 1852 the Jesuits even decided that Alvarez's *De Institutione Grammatica*, first published in 1572 and one of the most widely used of all Latin grammar books, should be restored as their standard textbook—a reactionary move which was not typical of them. Though the church schools were always more literary than the state ones, partly because they wished to avoid the expense of laboratories, they did not all neglect science. The Jesuit school in the rue des Postes specialised in preparing pupils for the *grandes écoles* and won remarkable successes. The church schools produced their own textbooks, so their teaching had a distinctive flavour, and this meant that they were able to do better for their pupils than the state in certain subjects.

Thus in 1932, a comparative study was made of the *baccalauréat* results of public and private pupils and it showed that, in over-all totals, the state schools got better results: 53 per cent of the state's candidates passed, as opposed to only 33 per cent of candidates from private schools; but the highest pass rates in the philosophy papers were obtained by the church's pupils

[1] E. Durkheim, *L'Évolution pédagogique en France* (1938), 2. 112.

(74 per cent). The interest shown in theological and moral questions throughout their school careers made philosophy easier for them to master. By contrast, in the mathematics papers, the pass rate for the church's candidates was a very feeble 28 per cent.[1] No doubt those who wished to specialise in science changed to a Paris *lycée* in their final year; but generally speaking, the church's pupils were less interested in obtaining the *baccalauréat*, because increasingly more of them came from the business, industrial and agricultural world, where it was by no means indispensable. In 1900 a Jesuit author claimed that less than one-third of the pupils of church schools stayed on to the end of the course (at least in the same school). The church schools produced, according to his estimate, only one-third of the entrants into the Polytechnic, and even only one-quarter or one-fifth of entrants to Saint-Cyr. On the other hand they turned out a fair number of industrialists (particularly in the north of France, for in the south their pupils went more for the liberal professions). Thus between 1850 and 1870 Saint Clement School at Metz turned out 68 priests, 219 army officers, 70 magistrates, 68 engineers and industrialists, 84 businessmen and financiers, 35 lawyers, 5 ambassadors and consuls, 2 prefects, 2 deputies, 2 university professors and 6 journalists.[2] So it may well be that the church schools paradoxically made more of a contribution to the industrial revival of France after 1950 than may appear at first sight, not so much because they discouraged the obsession with civil service careers—which was more influenced by family traditions—nor simply because they served a clientele that produced more children, but because they tried to turn their pupils away from philosophic doubt. Their pupils, as one of them said, had read neither Sartre nor Heidegger.[3] But no one has yet attempted to apportion statistically the responsibility for this new phase in French history as between the two rival educational systems.

There can be no doubt, however, that in the period between the two world wars the church schools experienced a revival of remarkable proportions. There had always been room for

[1] C. Bouglé, *Enquêtes sur le baccalauréat* (1935), 117.

[2] W. Tampé, S.J., *Nos anciens élèves* (1900).

[3] Compte Rendu des Journées nationales d'Études, 1953, Union des Frères Enseignants, *La Vocation du Frère Enseignant* (1953), 3.

Catholics in the state system, not only in the mid-nineteenth century when the state schools were Catholic and taught religion, but even later when, in many parts of the country, teachers who did not share the rabid anticlericalism of the politicians continued to behave in the traditional way. It is true that a Catholic boy attending a *lycée* might find himself subjected to ridicule, as happened to Jacques Valdour, whose memoirs of his childhood show that teachers could sometimes be maliciously intolerant. His first impressions of his *lycée*, which he joined at the age of 9, was that the pupils did not seem to like each other and that they detested the teachers. 'Reciprocal hostility seemed to be the law.' The teachers seemed to dislike their work, and disappeared after it; God and religion were never mentioned, except occasionally to be ridiculed. The mathematics teacher would say ironically when someone could not do a sum, 'But even the Ignorantine Friars would be capable of it.' When Valdour misbehaved, he would snap at him, 'This boy is trying to play the fool with me, in his little, hypocritical way. One can see clearly that he has been brought up by the *curés*.' And when a boy made a mistake, saying, 'But sir, I believed . . .': 'I believed,' replied the teacher. 'What does that mean, to believe? Belief is a neurosis. I believe in nothing. To believe is absurd.' The history lessons were a defence of 1789 and a condemnation above all of Napoleon III: 'Never forget his perjury to the republic': his claim to have won seven million votes was a sham: he used voting urns with false bottoms. Valdour says the painful result of his going to a *lycée* was that he found a terrible conflict between what he was taught at school and at home. He had thirty comrades in his class; when they left the *lycée* only one remained a Catholic.[1]

This is an extreme testimony by a Catholic militant, and there were doubtless other reasons why boys lost their faith. The important point is that parents did feel that they were losing control of their offspring when they sent them to state schools. They very seldom conceded that children had traditions and a way of life of their own making, and that their changing fashions could be, at different times, atheist or religious. There was little discussion of just how much difference a Catholic school meant to the future beliefs of its pupils. The Jesuits, for example, gave

[1] Nic [Jacques Valdour], *Le Lycée corrupteur* (1905), 41–54.

very little formal religious instruction—only two periods a week, while there were other Catholic schools in which piety was intense. Even at a *petit séminaire* the general education could be so formal, basing itself on such old-fashioned textbooks, that plenty of scope was left for individual children to develop in their own way. Jean Calvet, who later became dean and rector of the Catholic Institute in Paris, was tormented at his primary school, though it was run by friars, by the humiliation of being the son of a poor peasant, who had to eat sandwiches at midday with the other poor ones, while the sons of the grocer, the hairdresser and the notary, who wore high collars and short breeches, went home: there was bitter division between the boys of the *bourg* and those of the farms, and they were always fighting. The lesson Calvet learnt from this Catholic school was the importance of force, because only force saved him and his friends from persecution: 'I have never been able to forget the contempt of which the little peasant comrades of my youth were the victims.' At his *petit séminaire* 'there were no more castes: we were all more or less sons of peasants'. The only aristocracy was that of intelligence: the clever boys were admired and no one was allowed to tease them. The school, however, had very few books, so Calvet was reduced to reading dictionaries for his entertainment. There was a great respect for memorising: whole plays of Racine, whole books of the *Aeneid* were learnt off by heart; and prizes were awarded to boys who could recite without mistakes. They were forbidden to buy any books except an almanac once a year, and the boys learnt that off by heart too, holding a competition amongst themselves as to who could be most accurate. The winner was called the *Bachelier en Almanach*; but one boy outdid the rest by reciting his almanac backwards. In old age Calvet used still to quote bits from it, even advertisements in it: 'Henri Chevaly, prize-winning pharmacist, first class, at Carpentras (Vaucluse), manufactures an embrocation of incomparable virtue.' The boys were taught Catholic doctrine, but left to be pious in their own way.[1] The history of the anticlerical Émile Combes, among many others, showed that this kind of education was no guarantee of orthodoxy in adult life.[2]

---

[1] Mgr. Jean Calvet, *Mémoires* (1967), 28–43.
[2] For Combes's rebellion against his religious background, see Zeldin, *Politics and Anger*, 319–20.

At the other extreme Jaurès's assassin, Raoul Villain, who was a *surveillant* at the Collège Stanislas (one of the best Catholic secondary schools in Paris), illustrates the extreme mysticism into which a boy with an unhappy home background could be led. His father had remarried after his mother's death and neglected him; Villain was too unmethodical to be able to pass the *baccalauréat* and just before the war broke out had abandoned hope of ever getting it; he believed that he had a mission like Joan of Arc to kill Jaurès and that the success of this was dependent on his chastity, which he had scrupulously preserved in order to keep himself fit for his patriotic duty.

The expansion of Catholic education between the two world wars therefore represented, to a certain extent, a desperate and not altogether clearly thought-out attempt by parents to keep control of their children, and it is significant that it occurred when it did. It was above all else the work of parents. The old boys of the Catholic schools began forming associations which did a great deal both to finance expansion and to find jobs for pupils from them. In 1930 the A.P.E.L. (Association des parents d'élèves de l'enseignement libre) began spreading throughout the country, with a journal *École et liberté*, renamed *La Famille éducatrice* in 1947; by 1953 it had 450,000 members.[1] While the number of state secondary schools even fell from 561 to 552, Catholic ones increased from 632 in 1920 to 1,420 in 1936. This was not due to any large benefactions on the Anglo-Saxon model, and the Catholic schools were all of them in constant financial difficulties. They did much of their building by borrowing, often from the banks, and by incurring debts to their builders and suppliers. The schools thus blossomed 'in a spirit of crusade and revenge', and they were perhaps the greatest beneficiaries of inflation. In 1951 Catholics were estimated to have debts, from their educational work in the department of the Vendée alone, to the tune of 100 million francs. By that date they were spending, in the diocese of Paris, 560 m. a year on primary education, 800 m. a year on secondary education and 110 m. on technical schools.[2] The secondary schools were naturally by far the most expensive to build and to run. They were saved from bankruptcy by the Vichy government, which

---

[1] G. Jacquemart, *Catholicisme* (1956), 4. 235.

[2] Jean Pélissier, *Grandeurs et servitudes de l'enseignement libre* (1951), 51.

in 1941 allowed communes to subsidise private education and itself undertook to pay three-quarters of the expenses of private schools, though it calculated the salaries of their teachers at only 60 per cent of the level received by state teachers. In 1945 these subsidies were withdrawn, but it was obvious by then that, whatever the ideological objections, the Church was educating too large a proportion of the country's youth for it to be simply ignored; and the advent of de Gaulle led to the state paying the salaries of all approved and qualified teachers, and a proportion of running expenses (Loi Debré, 1959). As the church schools increasingly used lay and specialised teachers and as (after 1945) the clergy moved away from the schools back to pastoral work, their salary bill grew ceaselessly. It was not surprising that some people began questioning whether separate church schools were in fact the best means of advancing the cause of religion, for it meant cutting Catholics off from contacts where they could hope to exert influence.[1]

The new wave in Catholic education, which began in the 1920s and 1930s, was, on the whole, more modern and forward-looking than its first revival of the 1850s had been. The Catholics rewrote their textbooks. Their schools were expanding so fast that this was highly profitable, quite apart from anything else. The Alliance des Maisons d'Éducation Chrétienne, which brought the headmasters together, had a vigorous publisher in Joseph de Gigord, who specialised in producing Catholic secondary textbooks, written for the most part by highly qualified authors, some of them holding appointments in the University. Many other publishers joined in.[2] Following the pastoral letter by Archbishop Germain of Toulouse in 1919, urging that the social conflicts of the nineteenth century should be ended, and that a new relationship between workers and employers should be evolved, the headmasters drew up a syllabus of social morals —which they opposed to that of Durkheim sociology—involving

---

[1] Cercle Jean XXIII, *École Catholique: Aliénation*, ed. by Guy Goureaux *et al.* (1968), particularly instructive on the diocese of Nantes and the history of its church schools.

[2] Gigord died in 1947, when his son-in-law took over. The firm is still at 14 rue Cassette, Paris 6. Other major Catholic publishers included Mame (founded 1767), Lethielleux (1864), Beauchesne (1851 in Lyon, transferring to Paris in 1895), Bloud et Gay (1875), Casterman (1780 in Belgium, Paris branch 1857), Desclée de Brouwer (1877), Letouzy et Ané (1885), Alsatia (Colmar, 1897), Spes (1923), Seuil (1936), Éditions Ouvrières (1929), La Bonne Presse, etc.

the study of trade unions, wages, the organisation of companies and of labour relations, to be supplemented by practical work through pupil participation in charitable clubs. Abbé Renaud, almoner of the Collège Stanislas, undertook to write a textbook for this, and Gigord offered to publish it.[1] The articles in *L'Enseignement chrétien*, the Catholic headmasters' journal, gave prominence to moral education with a view to encouraging boys to enjoy taking risks, assuming responsibility and showing initiative: parents and teachers should aim at making themselves useless. They denied that schoolboys were overworked, saying their hours were no longer than those of their contemporaries who earned their livings. Far from locking themselves away in the contemplation of ancient authors, they regularly reviewed the latest novels, though it was significant that they condemned Proust as 'a failed genius' and believed that he had attacked homosexuality.[2] The claim that the Catholics were pioneers first in primary education, and then in technical and social education, had much truth in it. The child was no longer seen as an incomplete or evil being, but as an independent and whole personality.[3] Of course, there were many different tendencies among the headmasters: the large and flourishing schools in the cities had the resources to be more original.

How much of their attitudes penetrated to the pupils is difficult to assess, but certainly some fashionable schools left their boys plenty of freedom. At the Catholic boarding-school, Beaucamps, near Lille, run by the Marist order, the sermons in the 1920s were still based on those of Tronson (1622–1700), whose principal book, published in 1690, was reprinted at least fifty-two times in the course of the nineteenth and twentieth centuries. But this traditional approach was counterbalanced by the almoner's catechism class every morning between eight and nine, which in fact consisted of his reading out bits of political, economic or literary news from the paper, or reporting what he had heard on the radio, and discussing it with the boys; but then he had written a book and his ambition was to become a member of the French Academy, for whose members he had a great respect. Holy books were read aloud during breakfast, but

---

[1] *L'Enseignement chrétien* (1930), 26–38.
[2] Ibid. (1931), 39. Cf. Henri Pradel, *Comment donner le goût de l'effort* (1930).
[3] *L'Enseignement chrétien* (1931), 80.

history, travel or adventure ones at lunch—like Marbot's Napoleonic Memoirs.[1] The evolution of the attitudes of Catholics can be seen in the history of these Marists, who were one of the most successful teaching orders. Their founders, in the early nineteenth century, were inspired by the view that 'man has only one thing to do on earth, seek his salvation. All else is illusion and folly.' But the superior of the order from 1883 to 1907, Frère Théophane, was above all an administrator—he had become headmaster of one of their large boarding-schools at the age of twenty-six—who had other educational interests beyond improving the religion of the teachers, even though he made use of a bed of nails as an instrument of penance for himself: he saved half their schools through the period of anticlericalism. Frère Diogène (1920–42) not only expanded their already large boarding-schools, but also built a new one in Buenos Aires for 800 pupils, and one in Syria for 700. In 1940 this order had 10,000 teachers in forty-two countries.[2]

Side by side with these international chains of schools were purely local ones, which resulted from much humbler local efforts. In Roanne, where the *lycée* occupied the buildings of the old Jesuit college, a rival Institution Saint Joseph was founded in 1901 as a result of two benefactions. One was from the bishop, whose brother was a wealthy industrialist; the second was from a cotton wholesale merchant of Lyon who had settled in a château in the district; and in addition the Superior of the local convent and the Crédit Foncier provided sizeable loans. They started with 100 boys in 1903, rising to 150 in 1914; 250 in 1940 and 400 in 1962. Despite constant deficits, and an accumulated debt of nearly two million francs in 1931, they continued to buy more property, expand, build new dormitories and supply them with new furniture and linen. Their philosophy class had an average of a dozen boys in it between the wars, but the success rate was exceptional—between 68 and 77 per cent got through the *baccalauréat*. At first most of the teachers were priests, but in 1918 only seven out of thirty were. They provided a service designed above all to appeal to the parents who supported them.[3] This kind of school on the one hand offered teachers the

---

[1] Paul Dehondt, *Beaucamps ou la vie de collège* (Monte Carlo, 1970), 53.

[2] Institut des Petits Frères de Marie, *Nos Supérieurs* (St. Genis-Laval, 1954).

[3] Jean Canard, *L'Institution Saint Joseph de Roanne 1901–61* (Roanne, 1962).

opportunity to provide alternative types of education, stressing in particular the adaptation of methods to suit the individual child and service to the community, and on the other hand to 'enable pupils rejected by the *lycées* to appeal against a premature and precipitate judgement'.[1]

Privilege and Culture

The effect of secondary education on the relationships between social classes was, throughout this period, a subject of passionate debate and of contradictory interpretations. On the one hand the *lycées* were said to be the democratic instrument which made the rule of merit possible, by allowing intelligent boys to climb the social ladder. The function of secondary education, declared the chairman of the parliamentary inquiry into it in 1895, 'is to create a ruling élite'.[2] On the other hand, however, the *lycées* were denounced as bastions of class privilege, where the bourgeoisie segregated their children and had them stamped with distinctive characteristics, to differentiate them from the vulgar masses. Primary education effectively kept the masses, for which it catered exclusively, inferior to the small minority that enjoyed instead a separate training on its own. The radical party on the whole took the former view: so long as boys could win scholarships and work their way to the top, they believed democracy existed. The socialists, however, protested that the very existence of two kinds of school was divisive and unfair, that a complete education should be available for everybody, and that children should choose careers not on the basis of accident of birth, wealth or schooling, but in accord with their individual temperaments and gifts. The facts did not completely support any of these various assertions about the educational system. The satisfactions and animosities the schools produced were commented on in an atmosphere of much ignorance, prejudice and confusion. Even today, it is not easy to get at the facts, for the statistics

---

[1] P. Gerbod, 'Les Catholiques et l'enseignement secondaire, 1919–39', *Revue d'histoire moderne et contemporaine* (1971), 375–414; Jean Jaouen, *La Formation sociale dans l'enseignement secondaire* (1932). For an example of an old boys' association, see *Les 50 ans 1906–1956 de l'Amicale des anciens du collège St. Joseph Matzenheim* (1956). Memoirs, e.g., in Edward Mortier, *L'Âge enclos dans un collège libre* (1907); Abbé Léon Joly, *Quinze ans à la rue des Postes 1880–95. Souvenirs* (1909).

[2] A. Ribot, *La Réforme de l'enseignement secondaire* (1900), 60.

which would be needed to make defensible generalisations were never properly collected in this period, and what statistics there are remain difficult to use. The generalisations are well worth investigating, however, because they point to forces of great power in this society. Social mobility was a universal and constant preoccupation. The ambitions and the frustrations the schools produced often marked people for the whole of their lives. Quite apart from the knowledge the schools imparted, quite apart from the way they encouraged their pupils to talk and to think, they played a crucial role in the formation of their emotional attitudes, and of the view they had of their place in society.

That secondary education catered for a small minority is the starting-point of every discussion. The proportion of boys aged between 11 and 17 who went to state secondary schools was as follows (%):

1850	1·35		1930	3·58
1860	1·54	under 2%	1939	5·44
1871	1·81		1944	6·95
			1951	8·28
1881	2·35		1955	11·26
1890	2·40		1960	14·11
1900	2·59	under 3%	1964	19·65
1910	2·74			
1920	2·59			

These are the statistics for state schools. They therefore need to be, roughly, doubled to include the pupils of private schools. But they then need to be reduced because these schools did not give a full secondary education to all their pupils. Thus in 1843 it was calculated that only one boy in ninety-three in fact received a secondary education; in the 1860s, the amended figure would be under 2 per cent (for both public and private schools). In the course of the second half of the nineteenth century, the number of pupils doubled, but the largest rise occurred in the years 1850–80, and there was not much change in the total between 1880 and 1925. It was only in the 1930s that secondary education began to be an experience for more than a tiny number, and only after the 1960s that it ceased to be the preserve of a minority.[1]

[1] Statistics in Isambert-Jamati, op. cit. 377.

It was perfectly true that most of its pupils were, throughout this period, at least relatively well-to-do, if only for the obvious reason that the poor needed their children's wages simply to survive. Secondary education was, without doubt, a luxury, an investment and a status symbol. But, just as quite poor peasants were often landowners—a very diverse class—so there were many varieties of secondary education and many different types of people were able to get at least a smattering of it. In 1864 the minister of education asked headmasters of state secondary schools to produce a list of the occupations of the parents of their pupils. These showed that the rich were certainly vastly over-represented, but also that the poor formed a far from negligible proportion of the pupils. Thus even the Lycée Bonaparte (later Lycée Condorcet), which was situated in a fashionable quarter of Paris, had nearly one-third of its pupils who were sons of small shopkeepers (250), clerks (50) and teachers (50), almost as many, put together, as the sons of 'property owners and *rentiers*' (395), and as the sons of 'notable merchants' (150), bankers (55) and lawyers (90). It also had fifty sons of army officers, of unspecified rank, fifty artists and musicians, sixty doctors. Altogether therefore it was nowhere like a representative sample of society, but it did have representatives of all but the humblest levels of it. Almost every town had an individual mixture of these different elements, depending on its economic character and on the types of opportunity it offered. Thus the *lycée* of Marseille, for example, had fewer 'property owners' but more people from commerce, shipping and industry. The *lycée* of Lyon, with 852 pupils, had 291 sons of small shopkeepers, 17 workers, 2 peasants, in addition to 209 property owners, 106 merchants, industrialists and bankers, 97 members of the liberal professions, 89 civil servants and 39 soldiers. The small *collèges*, municipal secondary schools in the minor towns, were patronised very largely by the peasantry and some of them had a large falling-off in attendance during harvest time, just like the primary schools. In towns where there was no teacher-training college, there were *lycées* with pupils who became primary teachers. Over half of the pupils of the municipal college of the Meuse between 1850 and 1855 went into agriculture. In Paris, with its large variety of *lycées*, each had a distinctive social character: those on the right bank took only day-boys;

Charlemagne, near the Faubourg Saint-Antoine, was the least snobbish; Saint-Louis specialised in science; Louis-le-Grand and Napoléon (later Henri IV) were more literary; each appealed therefore to a slightly different clientele.[1]

However, with the passage of time, the *lycées'* social composition altered considerably. During the Second Empire they were almost comprehensive schools; not the least significant of their functions was that they also provided 'complementary courses', which were really of a primary nature and designed to prepare children for humbler careers: in some *lycées* as many as a quarter or even a third of the pupils followed these courses, and of course left long before they reached the age for taking the *baccalauréat*. One needs to distinguish between those who meant to stay for the full secondary course and those who did not. The rector of the academy of Douai wrote in 1864: 'There are boys from the countryside whose families "send them to town", as they put it, so that they should learn something more than the village school-master can teach them and so that they should develop a little through contact with children who are better brought up . . . They leave the *lycée* after one or two years to go back to their parents, to help in their farming.' But as the *lycée* became increasingly dominated by the *baccalauréat* and as a greater variety of specialised schools were established, the *lycée* pupils became more homogeneous. The *école primaire supérieure*, the technical school, the 'special' schools were invented to increase the educational opportunities open to the masses but their effect was to segregate the different classes for whom they were individually intended. So the Third Republic was to a considerable extent responsible for increasing social divisions by its nominally egalitarian educational policies. Thus by 1907–8 the Lycée Condorcet had a noticeably different social composition: only 5·58 per cent of its pupils were sons of artisans and shopkeepers; it had no sons of workers; 11·6 per cent were sons of clerks and supervisors, 1·59 were sons of primary teachers—altogether only 20 per cent were now from the lower and lower middle classes.[2]

The growth of the church schools increased the separation of

---

[1] R. D. Anderson, 'Some Developments in French Secondary Education during the Second Empire' (Oxford D.Phil. thesis, 1967), chapter 7, has analysed the replies of the headmasters to the minister's inquiry.

[2] G. Vincent, 'Les Professeurs du second degré au début du 20ᵉ siècle', *Le Mouvement social* (Apr.–June 1966), 60.

families of different tastes and aspirations. It has been seen that the church schools, though also involving fees, were in no way exclusively aristocratic or bourgeois, but it is clear that many parents with social pretensions preferred to send their children to church schools. The result was that, particularly in the smaller towns, the *lycées* became increasingly dominated by the sons of civil servants. The state catered for its own employees, reverting to the original purpose of the *lycées*, and it helped to

Social origins of candidates for the baccalauréat, *1932* (%)

		Private Schools	State Schools
Occupations favouring state education	Civil servants	13·69	25·23
	Executives (*employés dirigeants*)	8·55	10·83
	Clerks	4·56	13·54
	Workers	0·95	2·27
	Artisans	0·76	1·95
	Small shopkeepers	1·14	1·94
Occupations favouring private education	Liberal professions	19·22	14·33
	Businessmen	17·68	10·83
	Industrialists	13·12	6·92
	Property owners and *rentiers*	10·26	1·95
	Peasants	2·47	1·27
	Miscellaneous	7·60	8·94

Source: C. Bouglé, *Enquêtes sur le baccalauréat. Recherches statistiques sur les origines scolaires et sociales des candidats au baccalauréat dans l'académie de Paris* (1935).

build up a wall around its own small world. Thus in 1932, one-quarter of the state schools' pupils taking the *baccalauréat* were children of civil servants: in Paris only 21·8 per cent were, while in the provinces the proportion was as high as 37 per cent. Whereas in Paris state schools 15 per cent of *baccalauréat* candidates were children of the liberal professions, in the provinces only 10 per cent were. At this final point in the school careers of the pupils, very few members of the working class were left in the secondary system.

The industrial working class entered secondary education in significant numbers only in the late 1930s and during the Second World War. In 1936–7 only 2·6 per cent of pupils entering secondary schools were the children of workers (plus 4·47 per cent who were children of artisans). In 1943–4, 14·4 per cent were children of workers (plus 9·7 per cent children of artisans). The obstacles to the democratisation of the *lycées* were partly financial, but there was also strong reluctance by the workers to penetrate into institutions which they did not regard as their own, and in which they did not feel at ease. This was clearly revealed when fees were abolished. But long before then, it was not just fees that kept the workers out.

Social origins of pupils entering secondary school (%)

	1936–7	1943–4
Liberal professions	10·6	6·9
Heads of industrial and commercial firms	24·6	14·3
Civil servants and soldiers	28·5	24·47
Clerks	20·3	19·2
Artisans	4·47	9·7
Peasants	1·7	8·2
Workers	2·6	14·4
Miscellaneous	5·8	2·8

Source: Christiane Peyre, 'L'Origine sociale des élèves de l'enseignement secondaire en France', P. Naville *et al.*, *École et société* (1959), 6–33.

As has been shown, day-boys were offered tuition at a rate within the reach of perhaps half the country, that is all of those who were capable of saving something from their earnings. During the Second Empire, scholarships were still a means of rewarding loyal service to the government more than a form of assistance to bright children; and there were only about 1,300 of them in the 1850s. The ministry had no hesitation in awarding them to well-to-do civil servants in preference to junior ones. By the turn of the century the state was still awarding only 1,000 scholarships annually, but the departments and municipalities raised the total to 5,528. Of these, 1,586 were to boys going on from primary schools to secondary schools. Only about 20 per cent of scholarships were given to sons of peasants and workers. The decisive factor which brought the workers in was not the abolition of fees and the award of scholarships, but, first, the payment of wages (and family allowances) to parents which enabled them to support a family without the children having to go to work and, secondly, the development of attitudes which would encourage children in remaining idle up to their eighteenth year. This is bound up with the question of social aspirations and mobility, with the question, that is, of what people expected from the schools in career terms, how much the schools could advance them, and what difference the schools did in fact make to the jobs their pupils got.

It has been seen[1] that in the middle of the nineteenth century the desire to rise above the station into which one was born was still something of an exception. On the whole jobs were obtained through one's father and his connections; despite the French Revolution, professions and trades still had, to some degree, the character of corporations, in which family tradition and nepotism played an important part. At the same time as democrats talked of careers being open to talent, others (and sometimes democrats too) were worried by the dangers this could produce, and social mobility was still called *déclassement*. Thus the republican Vacherot lamented that when poor children tasted the educational fruits hitherto reserved for the aristocracy 'for the most part they rejected their fathers and made themselves noticed for the harshness and contempt in the ranks of society into which the exhausted hands of their heroic families have raised them'. In the inquiry of 1864, headmasters were asked to give not only the profession of their pupils' fathers, but also the profession which these pupils hoped to enter. In the department of the Seine-Inférieure, one-third of the pupils in the classical forms intended to follow in their fathers' footsteps, but in the 'special', i.e. modern forms, 54 per cent did. The sons of poor people, who predominated in these latter, clearly did not expect too much from the schools; while a classical education was by contrast more often seen as a means by which one could move into the liberal professions or the civil service. Far more statistics about the fate of schoolchildren in their later working life will be needed before firm statements can be made about the country as a whole. But it seems that the schools were not as active agents of social change as they were sometimes said to be.[2]

A survey carried out in the early 1960s showed that even then the family's influence was still more powerful than that of the

---

[1] See Zeldin, *Ambition and Love*, ch. 7.
[2] See Robert Gildea's doctoral thesis on education in the Ille-et-Vilaine (unpublished, Oxford, 1977).

school. Those who went on from school to university were predominantly from backgrounds which favoured this. Thirty years after the introduction of free secondary schooling, only 1 per cent of the sons of agricultural workers went to university, compared to 80 per cent of the sons of members of the liberal professions. The subjects which students chose for their university courses were clearly related to their fathers' profession. Fifteen per cent of sons of the liberal professions and of managers chose medicine, but only 3 to 5 per cent of sons of workers and peasants did: the long training and capital required to set oneself up as a doctor were clear deterrents. The class which chose science in a greater proportion than any other was that of the workers (52·5 per cent); and it was the agricultural workers who chose the faculty of letters most (37 per cent), presumably because it led to teaching jobs. (The daughters of agricultural workers also went in massively for this—65·6 per cent, but letters attracted all girls, even 48·6 per cent of daughters of managers and the liberal professions.) The law faculty was favoured most by the sons and daughters of clerks, aspiring to rise, and by the sons of liberal professions and management, inheriting their parents' firms or training for administrative jobs.[1]

A subtle difference remained between education and culture. The schools' diplomas were certainly highly valued. Positions of importance were controlled by holders of diplomas who insisted on diplomas as essential qualifications for those seeking jobs under them: the proliferation of examinations increasingly made the schools almost indispensable for anyone with ambition. In the 1960s, students of the lower classes obtained distinctions (*mentions*) twice as often as upper-class students. The schools rewarded perseverance, hard work and intelligence. But there were limits to what they could do. To be cultured meant to be more than educated, in the sense that it involved knowledge which had to be acquired outside the school—by going, for example, to the theatre, concerts and museums, by knowing about *avant-garde* art as opposed to the classical art taught in schools. Interest in exotic countries was found to be more frequent as one went up the social scale, as also were

---

[1] Pierre Bourdieu and J.-C. Passeron, *Les Héritiers, les étudiants et la culture* (1964), 16.

breadth of interest and dilettantism: it required a sense of security to be detached from the school syllabus, and it needed rich parents to enable one to cultivate unusual tastes. Significantly, the cinema was the only extra-curricular interest of which all classes had more or less equal knowledge. The schools sought to give their pupils general culture but, in the most sophisticated forms, they also had aristocratic ambitions beyond their capabilities: their best teachers despised syllabuses and pedantry and exalted what they could not really teach. They could not perform their whole task in a single generation, nor independently of the life-style parents adopted. The schools were on the road that children had to tread in order to acquire culture, but only the beginning of the road. That is why they were both praised as democratic and criticised as bastions of privilege. While opening new horizons for many, they also created privileges for those who passed successfully through them. They never discovered how to console their failures, for they were part of a society that punished stupidity, slowness and lack of competitiveness. They were not able to eliminate the advantages enjoyed by children from cultivated homes; and since they laid such stress on linguistic fluency, the upper classes usually had the advantage, not least in oral examinations. Economic inequality could not be eradicated simply by educational reforms.

But the schools, in the eyes of a great number of people, nevertheless seemed to be the pivot round which all other reforms would have to turn, and their democratisation became a mounting obsession during the twentieth century. Previously literacy had been the great goal; now it was the *école unique*, the comprehensive school. This was the answer to the fact that the primary and secondary systems were largely independent, so that in 1913 only three or four thousand pupils finishing their education in the former continued it in secondary schools. In the years 1880–1930, when the number of pupils in *lycées* was almost static, those in the *écoles primaires supérieures* increased fourfold. The contrast of the two systems thus gradually became more noticeable and the question of whether their existence and rivalry was desirable inevitably became important. However, the debate was initiated not by frustrated workers but by university professors. A group of them calling themselves Les Compagnons de l'université nouvelle, shaken by their experience of near-defeat in 1914–18, declared that this war had shown the failure of the bourgeois élite; they believed that the country must look to the common people, whose virtues had been 'the great revelation of the war', for its revitalisation. They protested that education had hitherto been 'the creed of a sect', proud of enjoying 'spiritual benefits unknown to the vulgar'; that its hero was the intellectual who sought truth in books rather than in life, and whose skill was his ability to imprison life in verbal formulae. Education, they said, produced intellectuals of narrow rationalism, unconstructive critical powers and selfish individualism. It must cease to be dilettante and must yield a more socially useful return, for, in its present form, it produced too much frustration, disillusionment, revolt, and dangerous errors in vocation; it diminished the vigour of the nation without increasing its idealism. Education must contribute to the country's resurrection: its reform was possible now because such a large proportion of the teachers had been killed in the war. It should turn its attention to training producers and industrialists, to rebuilding France's economic life. The schools should be practical and democratic in their objectives; they should be free and they should not insist on teaching Latin to everybody. There should be one school for children of all classes until the age of 13 or 14: the *école unique* required the abolition of the *petites classes*, the preparatory forms of the *lycées* which the snobs used, to avoid the primary schools. After that, the *école prolongée* should prepare children for a profession, but without neglecting to educate the whole personality—the mind, the body and the will. The syllabus should be adapted to the needs of each region; and the habit of teaching in order to produce teachers, of a uniform stamp, should be got rid of. The war on the church schools should be ended: these should receive state subsidies; but totally free education would ensure that parents would not prefer church schools for purely class reasons. The Compagnons condemned the teacher in almost unmeasured terms: 'The harm that these *fakirs* have done to France, without realising it, is great. They have led people to think that the educational system had a life outside that of the nation; they cultivated a

critical disposition among children at the expense of the will
and character which are the supreme faculties; they have
given them a distaste for action and so they have incurred
a heavy responsibility in the crisis we have suffered.' A few
teachers, it is true, had participated in national life, but then
only to go into politics and produce the 'very worst exaggerations'. The Compagnons said they wanted to stop the University being a church and they did not want to create a new
church to replace it; they did not want 'to model people's
consciences'. But they also said, rather contradictorily, that
the divisions of the teachers had made them weak, and that in
the new order the teachers must cast off the control of the
state and become an independent corporation, uniting teachers
—both lay and religious—of primary, secondary, higher and
professional education, in regional groupings. The political
implications of this programme—its anti-anticlericalism, its
opposition to state control, its regionalism and corporatism—
inevitably prevented it from being universally acceptable: the
école unique was not a simple summons to national unity.[1]

It was presented as democratic, but it was more truly meri-
tocratic, in that it wanted secondary education reserved for
'the élite', except that the élite would now be those judged fit
to belong to it, and it would be the teachers who would be
the judges. The *école unique* became a slogan which concealed
numerous and different aims. François Albert, the radical
minister of education in 1924, saw in it a means of destroying
the church schools. The more extreme left wing, interested in
a more thorough transformation of society, disliked the idea of
the *école unique* being the preparation for a qualitative selection:
they wanted not to pick out the bright children by this 'suction
device to extract the new spiritual forces from the people and
put them into the service of the bourgeoisie', but rather to
make mass education the basis of every individual finding the
career that suited him best. Some of them considered that the
école unique would by itself be powerless, and that the workers
should build their own educational system, teaching a workers'
culture. The problem of embourgeoisement by education was
never properly tackled by the advocates of the *école unique*.
The precise effect of the *école unique* on parental and individual

[1] Les Compagnons, *L'Université nouvelle* (1918).

freedom also remained confused. Léon Blum, speaking for the socialists, made it clear that they saw it as a 'national and social idea', opposed to 'the family idea': parents should not have the right to prefer church schools to it. It was denied that children would be obliged to adopt the career which the experts in selection and orientation declared suitable for them, but nevertheless the Catholics prophesied the 'seizure by a caste—the teachers—of the entire life of the nation'.[1] The formula *l'école unique* became fashionable, so that people of many persuasions claimed to be its partisans, but interpreted it to suit their own ends. Thus most secondary-school teachers, determined to uphold the superiority of their teaching over all others, paid lip-service to its egalitarian ideals but resisted it in practice, not least because those of them who taught in the junior forms of *lycées* would be reclassified as primary teachers.[2]

The Influence of Teachers

Many people seem to have hated their schooldays and yet very few disapproved of governments pouring increasing sums of money into the expansion of education. Many people despised teachers as a class and yet they allowed teachers to claim an essential role and a profound influence on the improvement of mankind. To understand these paradoxes, one must examine more closely the social status of the teachers and also the range of activities and ideas which were affected by them. For the teachers were at once disadvantaged inhabitants of a ghetto and upholders of the *status quo* in the world around them: they were unwavering admirers of classical traditions but they were also revolutionary or utopian reformers; they aspired to win acceptance as members of the bourgeoisie and yet they often despised bourgeois values, while continuing to inculcate them at school; they were both the champions of children and their enemies. Their equivocal position on many issues is the explanation of why such different roles have been attributed to them. In Germany in the 1840s, a secondary-school teacher would not have been indulging in a wild fantasy if he hoped to marry a

[1] Marc Dubruel, *Le Règne des pédagogues: l'école unique* (1926).
[2] There is an excellent discussion of education in the interwar period in John E. Talbott, *The Politics of Educational Reform in France 1918–40* (Princeton, 1969).

general's daughter: his salary was equal to that of a councillor of state (fifth class it is true) and if he rose to be a successful university professor he could hope to earn as much as a minister. The French teacher could have no dreams of such wealth, but far more French teachers actually became ministers. The contrast of France and Germany, two countries where education was highly valued but in very different ways, is a useful way of seeing the extent and the limits of the teachers' importance.

The secondary-school teachers who believed that they were shaping not just the minds of their pupils, but perpetuating and perfecting France's peculiar genius, were a small group, and one forgets just how few of them there were until quite recently. In 1840, there were only 670 *professeurs de lycée*. Altogether, including ushers and administrators, there were only 4,500 teachers in the state's secondary schools at that date. The number rose to 7,500 by 1877, 10,000 by 1887 and in 1945 it was still only 17,400. To this one needs to add teachers in private secondary schools. In 1854 there were 7,500 of these, in 1938 13,000. The great explosion in the number of secondary teachers occurred only after 1950, when they more than doubled over fifteen years, so that in 1965 there were altogether 67,000 secondary teachers. But in the last years of the reign of Louis-Philippe the total number of people living who had ever been to a secondary school was still only 80,000. In the nineteenth century, secondary education thus occupied a very small place in society. In 1848 there might be only ten secondary teachers in a whole department; in 1877 only nineteen departments had more than a hundred of them. The majority of these teachers, moreover, had a profound contempt for most of their fellows, because they were even more hierarchical than an army. At least military men got promotion of sorts by seniority, but teachers claimed superiority by virtue of their knowledge and the examinations they had passed to prove it; and they clearly had difficulty in passing examinations.

Theoretically, only *agrégés de l'université*, selected in an annual competition, were considered fit for the dignity of occupying teaching chairs in *lycées*; the more junior forms were supposed to be staffed by *licenciés*, i.e. university graduates. But in the 1840s only 10 per cent of the secondary teachers were *agrégés* (about 360 in all), another 20 per cent were *licenciés*, but over 50 per cent had no more than the *baccalauréat*. At the turn of the century the *agrégés* were still only 1,855 in number and in 1938 only 2,466. In 1966 the *agrégés* were still an élite comprising only 17 per cent of the secondary teaching body, even after a vast increase in the number admitted to their exalted ranks, following the expansion of education. The idea obstinately survived that to teach the senior forms was a task calling for such gifts and such knowledge that enough intelligent men could never be found of an adequate standard. Between 1866 and 1876 under 20 per cent of the 3,500 candidates offering themselves for the *agrégation* were successful. The schools were thus continuously staffed by teachers officially judged to be incompetent. In 1877 only 21 per cent of teachers in the *collèges communaux* were graduates (*licenciés*); in 1909 only 66 per cent were. In 1965 a quarter of all teachers in secondary schools were still unqualified. The Third Republic had conspired to maintain this situation almost as a tradition, while pretending to lament it, but obstinately refusing to increase the number of well-paid teaching posts. Instead it preferred to pay teachers overtime: in 1900 this expenditure amounted to a sum equivalent to the salaries of 270 chairs. The teachers accepted this system, because they wanted more money and because it increased their differentials, though they also complained that they were overworked and that their expectation of life was, as a result, below the national average. Inequality of merit was something they believed in as passionately as the principle of equality for equal merit. How else could they have continued to accept the enormous differences in salary they received for very similar work?

The *agrégés* were the privileged minority among them. During the early Second Empire, when a good Parisian carpenter could earn 1,300 francs a year, the *agrégés* started at 2,200 francs and they could hope to rise to 6,600 francs as senior teachers at the best Paris *lycées*. This latter salary was six times what a teacher in a communal college would earn; while a junior usher might earn even less, under 1,000 francs. Like labourers, teachers were expected to improve their incomes by extra work, and private lessons were therefore a minor industry, exploiting the anxiety of parents keen on getting their children through examinations. A headmaster who knew how to run a boarding-school efficiently and economically might reach 20,000 francs a year; and private schools were sold for large sums, as profitable ventures; but under Napoleon III only 5 per cent of teachers got salaries of over 4,500 francs a year; more than half got between 1,100 and 1,900 francs; while 13 per cent got less than 1,000 francs. In 1900 the salary range still started at 700–2,700 for ushers and rose to 7,500 for *agrégés* in Paris. An *agrégé* in a Paris *lycée* had a maximum salary which was higher than that of a provincial university professor, and it is this sort of person who, disdaining the pretensions of the faculties, gloried in his prestige as teacher of the élite of the élite. Between the world wars, the gaps in salaries between senior and junior teachers diminished very considerably, and between the different types of school. In theory this ought to have made the jealousies between provincials and Parisians, *lycée* teachers and municipal teachers, old and young, certified and unqualified less bitter, but they all continued to receive slightly different slaries which offended quite as much because movement from one category to another was not easy. The Parisian *agrégé* earned the same as a lieutenant-colonel in the army, the provincial one as much as a captain, while the average municipal college teacher got as much as a sub-lieutenant. The trouble of course was that these latter would remain sub-lieutenants all their lives. The dangerous men in this academic army were the captains and a few of the colonels. But these—the *agrégés*—clung tenaciously to their privileges, forming a society which watched over their special interests with fervour, publishing in their bulletin every individual promotion and transfer, so that all should know exactly how much their colleagues were earning.[1] Their power, inevitably, was limited by the fact that they were unable to unite their inferiors behind them. When the secondary teachers got round to forming trade unions, they divided up into four different ones: *lycée* ushers kept separate from municipal college ushers, and *lycée* teachers both from them and from municipal college teachers; and in addition all of them remained aloof from the primary teachers and from the Fédération des Fonctionnaires. Many teachers refused to join unions at all and preferred societies

[1] *L'Agrégation. Bulletin officiel de la société des agrégés de l'Université* (Bimonthly) (1938, 22nd year), 245, for debates about salaries.

catering for their individual specialities, between which there always remained rivalry if not contempt: like supporters of rival football teams, classicists despised scientists and modernising believers in pedagogic reforms ridiculed the traditionalists, and they could only with difficulty unite to look down on those who could not play football at all. The *agrégés* were barely on speaking terms with the ushers (*répétiteurs*), condemned to the status of non-commissioned officers; they seldom invited them to their weddings; they thought it right that a *professeur* should have a clean napkin twice a week, but a *répétiteur* only once a week. At the turn of the century, *répétiteurs* were complaining, more loudly now, that barely one *professeur* in twenty ever condescended to shake their hands, and, as for headmasters, it was unheard of for them to take off their hats to salute them. The Normalien in particular, they said, 'believed himself to be of a superior essence, rejoicing in the humiliating position in which he always keeps his subordinate'. There was a class struggle within the teaching profession itself. The pupils were well aware of it and reproduced their quarrels in the playground.[1]

But what distinguished the successful teacher was that he was a man on the move. Teaching was often an absorbing passion, a dearly loved profession, but from the social point of view it was often an escape and a step towards something better. The large majority of teachers had parents who were socially inferior to themselves. Artisans, small shopkeepers and clerks produced the largest proportion of teachers—about 40 per cent in 1850, about 33 per cent in 1910. Ten per cent of teachers in 1850 and 14 per cent in 1910 were sons of peasants. About one-fifth or one-quarter of teachers were always the sons of other teachers.[2] Only gradually did the liberal and managerial professions come to regard teaching as an acceptable career: in 1850 and 1910 only one-tenth of the teachers came from such families, but in the 1960s about one-third did. This was the great change stimulated by the creation of a new

[1] G. Vincent, 'Les Professeurs de l'enseignement secondaire dans la société de la belle époque', *Revue d'histoire moderne et contemporaine* (Jan.–Mar. 1966), 49–86.

[2] At one stage, these teachers were more often than not sons of primary teachers, doing one better; but in the 1870s as many as 16 per cent were sons of secondary teachers and only 11·5 per cent sons of primary teachers. In 1960, the proportions were 12 and 11 per cent respectively.

intellectual proletariat endowed with university degrees, fashionable labels but otherwise often useless, except for teaching. Previously, however, three-quarters of secondary teachers came from homes with virtually no traditions of culture, or sometimes even of literacy. The acquisition of culture was the great achievement of their lives, and that is why they were so deeply and so conservatively attached to the study of the classics, which made them what they were. They fought so passionately for the preservation of the old syllabus precisely because it was so new to them.[1]

The teachers were men on the move in another sense too, in that promotion was obtained by transfer to larger schools and more senior forms: they had so many grades to climb that they seldom stayed long in any one place. In the early years of the Third Republic one-third of the teachers and half the ushers were, on average, always new to the schools in which they served, either through appointment or transfer, though the municipal college staffs were more permanent—only one-fifth were moved around each year. They tolerated this even though three-quarters of them were now married (only 42 per cent had been in the 1840s). This meant that they could not build up influence and respect in their localities in the way of doctors and barristers, who seldom moved. They were dependent for their status on their minister and their inspectors, whom they cordially resented. But they could try to force themselves past these hurdles by study, research and examinations. In the July Monarchy, ambition was still moderate, even rare, amongst them. But as the century progressed, they seem to have grown more dissatisfied and restive. They enrolled in the faculties for higher degrees. They increasingly wrote books, abetted by the growing phalanx of publishers and printers. In 1877 the government invited teachers to send in copies of their works for an exhibition: an amazing total of 1,650 works arrived, suggesting that in the preceding decade two-thirds of teachers of senior forms had published something. It is true 70 per cent of these productions were textbooks, and that the rest were lectures at prize-givings, articles in learned periodicals and translations.

[1] Gérard Vincent, 'Les Professeurs du second degré au début du 20e siècle: essai sur la mobilité sociale et la mobilité géographique', *Le Mouvement social* (Apr.-June 1966), 47-73.

Originality was not their strong point, and they certainly pre-ferred literary criticism to novel writing. They did not there-fore make any large contribution to the movement of ideas. Combes, the radical prime minister who had started as a teacher, was right when he said in 1899 that the teachers were 'essentially conservatives . . . men who mistrust novelty'. In the 1870s, about 10 per cent of them were inscribed as students at the faculties, aiming to better themselves. Each year, about twenty-five teachers obtained doctorates, the crowning achieve-ment. This was the tiny minority that was successful in climb-ing out of the schoolroom, and on to a more national or public stage. The weakness of the profession was that the best in it moved out of it altogether, on G. B. Shaw's principle that 'those who can, do; those who cannot, teach'. But this became a serious problem only after 1945, when the universities expanded and the *agrégés*, originally specifically selected for secondary teaching, invaded the faculties.

It is impossible to say how frustrated teachers were before then, for lack of sufficiently detailed information about the silent majority. A sample survey conducted in the early 1960s is the only source available to answer this question, and its results cannot be read back into the prewar period; but it is suggestive. Roughly half the teachers questioned declared themselves to be satisfied with their profession and half dissatis-fied; but 87 per cent of those who had passed the secondary-school teachers' certificate examination[1] said they were satisfied. The latter were teachers who had been specifically trained for their jobs. Women teachers were distinctly more satisfied than male ones. The *agrégés* were the most frustrated of all, though they were also very satisfied with their training and had a good opinion of themselves. But altogether about a quarter of teachers said they had become teachers because they wanted to do something else, whether it was research or some other activity, political or literary. As many as 59 per cent indeed regretted that they had been unable to pursue a career in research. When asked what other jobs they would be willing to do, 62 per cent aspired to a career in the liberal professions (33 per cent as doctors, 20 per cent as pharmacists). None wanted to be civil

[1] C.A.P.E.S. (Certificat d'aptitude professionnel de l'enseignement secon-daire).

servants, because, as the historian Ch.-V. Langlois (1863–1929) had said in 1905, and as still seemed true, one became a teacher because it provided a decent living straight away, but it also gave one a great deal of liberty or independence. The liberal professions gave more liberty but one needed a private income to survive the early days without clients. That is why, at the turn of the century, four out of the seven senior ushers at the Lycée Montaigne in Paris were doctors of medicine, who lacked the capital to set up in practice. Beyond independence, teachers admired genius. 'Artists' were the occupation they selected as that for which they had the greatest admiration. These were the impractical, uncommercial values they upheld. No wonder, forced as they were to devote their lives to a perpetual routine, that they came at the top of the table for frequency of mental illness and that hypochondria constantly plagued them. Four-fifths of a sample of teachers retiring in 1958–64 were classified as 'psychologically abnormal, obsessional or hyperaesthesic'.[1] It would be wrong, however, to see the teachers of the Third Republic as sad or embittered. Far from it, they were probably on the whole men of enthusiasm, with an almost childish optimism which experience had much difficulty in abating. Francisque Sarcey, a Normalien who escaped into journalism, declared that 'twenty years of teaching kills a man. One goes to bed a wit, and one is amazed to find that one wakes up an old fogy.' But what the teachers felt they lacked in themselves, they made up for by their love of learning and their faith in its saving grace. Though they therefore suffered from the exclusiveness and self-righteousness of converts, their conversion had involved a rebellion against their own background. For all their obsession with never having enough money, they were ultimately not materialists. That is why they were simultaneously a challenge to and a pillar of a society that never lived up to their ideals.

Their place in society was therefore infinitely subtle, difficult both for themselves and for others to define. If one simply considered the monetary rewards they received, one would dismiss them as servants of the bourgeoisie, who sometimes forgot their place, but who were essentially servants. This would be as misleading as any similar judgement on the clergy would

[1] Gérard Vincent, *Les Professeurs du second degré* (1967).

be. If one read novels to discover what contemporaries thought of them, one might reach the conclusion that they were generally regarded as figures of fun, weak, ignorant of the world behind their pedantry, always at the mercy of their superiors, and therefore sometimes rebellious, but basically conscious of their own inferiority, of their modest origins, lacking in social grace and so kept at a distance by the smartest people, forced to make friends only with other teachers—a profession, in short, to be pitied, even though individual members of it very often had admirable qualities like generosity, intelligence and self-sacrifice. This portrait must not be accepted uncritically, because one must remember that novelists were too close to teachers to be impartial observers; they had often escaped from teaching into literature and they were describing in the teachers' lot all that they themselves wanted to avoid. One must add evidence from other sources and try to distinguish between the reputation teachers enjoyed—which contained much in-accurate representation of their situation—the view they had of themselves, and the real influence—less obviously discern-ible and seldom analysed—which they wielded despite their poverty.

Victor Laprade's book, *Education as Homicide* (1867), blamed the teachers for making the schools a combination of monas-teries, barracks and prisons. They ruined the health of children by their obsession with examinations. Their repetitive, mecha-nical teaching did more harm than good; the whole history of French pedagogy indeed was 'a monument of stupidity and harshness'.[1] The career guides warned that unless one was an *agrégé*, one was condemned to a life of 'modest simplicity', in which moreover one was in danger of suffocating intellectually, so narrowing and oppressive were the conditions of work. The men who innocently went into teaching were those who 'felt some attraction for letters or science, those who had failed to obtain admission to the state's *grandes écoles* [which led to better careers] and those who feared military service'.[2] Victor Duruy himself, who was a teacher and inspector before he became Napoleon III's minister of public instruction, was ambivalent towards the profession. He proclaimed, on taking

---

[1] V. Laprade, *L'Éducation homicide* (1867).
[2] V. Doublet, *Dictionnaire universel des professions* (1858), 303.

office, that the teachers were 'the Great Army of Peace . . . waging war without respite against all evil, against ignorance, against sloth, against the defects of the mind as against the vices of the heart'. They formed, he said, that 'great institution that Napoleon I hurled like a block of granite in the midst of the current of the century, to regularise its flow'—an analogy that in part contradicted the grander metaphor he had previously used. For he also admitted that 'if the French are the wittiest people on earth, it is not always to our teachers that we owe it'. He was well aware of the inertia, apathy and mediocrity that balanced the teachers' virtues and knowledge.[1] At the lower levels of the profession, there was indeed little pretentiousness. As the headmaster of the municipal college of Nantua said in 1861: 'We are rarely crowned with glory; our lives run their course laboriously, monotonously and obscurely in a narrow sphere; our exhausting duties come to an end only when we die. That does not matter . . . To prepare virtuous citizens and new generations of honourable men . . . that is our ambition. It is the love of this modest good that sustains us in our unprofitable careers.'[2]

The paradox was that the teachers seldom believed that they were succeeding in putting the world right. On the contrary, they were always lamenting that it was going to the dogs, that immorality, laziness, materialism were everywhere triumphing. Beauty and truth, as they saw it, were always being trampled on. They were essentially in love with the past, even if their whole lives were devoted to improving the future. They taught admiration for the classical traditions, just as the clergy urged men to turn their minds to the next world: both feared and disliked the present. The teachers' reputation as radicals was unjustified. In 1848 at most only a third of them were republicans, and these were largely concentrated in the *lycées*: the vast majority of municipal colleges had no republican sympathisers in them at all. Teachers were blamed for the spread of socialism, for instilling wild ideas into pupils 'inflamed with erudition and blown up with vanity'; they were told to shave off their beards, a sign of insubordination, by Napoleon III, who however thought his own became him; but only about

[1] P. Gerbod, *La Condition universitaire* (1965), 427, 447.
[2] Ibid. 389.

300 were actually sacked for strictly political reasons by his government. Less drastic persecution affected many more, and the teachers came to have the reputation of being hostile to Bonapartism, but this again is exaggerated: only a minority expressed strong views on the matter. In the early years of the Third Republic, very few teachers joined the freemasons; even fewer were freethinkers when that was a bold thing to be. In 1850 Émile Deschanel had been suspended from his teaching post for participating in politics: the council of the University rejected his view that a teacher could say and write what he pleased outside his class; it laid down that a teacher had 'special obligations' which 'diminish his liberty as a citizen'. This case had been used as a precedent for repressing inconvenient republicans under the empire, but, contrary to what might have been expected, under the Third Republic the secondary teachers' unions repeatedly refused to concern themselves with politics. They were far from all being radicals. They refused to vote an address of encouragement to Combes, drowning the motion with cries of 'No politics'.

One must distinguish between the teachers as a political pressure group—in which capacity they were as strong only as their numbers, which have only recently become large—and the teachers as an influence on children—in which case their ideas are multiplied many times over. But the teachers did not find it easy to modify their pupils' beliefs and behaviour. In the first place, they too often approached the children with hostile prejudices. Though they were infinitely well meaning, the teachers did generally regard their pupils as having evil propensities, a liability to laziness, perpetuating in effect the Catholic doctrine of original sin even when they formally rejected it, because it was artificiality, knowledge and morals that they tried to impose upon them. The teachers did not consider that they were being oppressive, for the acquisition of culture had liberated them: they were only forcing children to be free, in their wake. But it was inevitable that this should have aroused resistance among their pupils. The teachers' ideal was to be monarchs of their classes, even when they preached liberal doctrines. Those in secondary schools were the slowest to adopt 'modern' theories of education. The pupils replied by ragging—a kind of child's sabotage—and by forming what have been termed 'delinquent groups'—a miniature version of trade unions. Above all, they adopted special attitudes and a special language while in school, which lulled the teacher into thinking he had won his victory, so that his demands on them were reduced; but this could be as superficial a subservience as the workers taking off their caps to their employers. The independent culture of secondary-school children was, however, nowhere near as resistant to their teachers as was that of primary children. It is true that older children could sometimes penetrate the mask their teachers wore, realise that they were not monarchs so much as actors, discern the inferiority complex that lay behind the severity and seize on the self-denigration into which teachers lapsed intermittently. Secondary-school children mocked their teachers in an almost institutionalised way: except for the few children who succeeded, most of them resented the humiliations which the teachers' marking system regularly imposed on them; and they practised the war of generations against their teachers, before they took it into the outside world. But the central feature of the teachers' message and role was the belief in the importance of ideas, and secondary pupils did not wholly reject this, partly because they adopted it as an instrument to fight off the teacher's oppression: the most successful ragger was the wittiest one, who could turn the teachers' guns to fire back in their faces. The role of wit and taste was all-important.

The teachers' power came precisely from their modesty. This is what distinguished them from their German counterparts, whom they generally envied for the higher status these enjoyed. German teachers built up elaborate philosophical theories to bolster their self-importance, but this placed them in a fool's paradise. They developed an ideal of *Bildung* and *Kultur* which was far more ambitious than anything French teachers claimed to achieve. German idealism disdained French 'civilisation' which it condemned as frivolous polish, a superficial veneer of good manners. It saw the world as the product of consciousness, it attributed 'objective reality' to its intellectual constructions, it claimed that scholarship was capable of yielding not just knowledge, but also wisdom and virtue, and a whole *Weltanschauung* which was essentially a self-justification. The German academic tradition made its philosophising the highest goal. It cut itself off therefore from the rest of the country, despised the world of industry and commerce and put all its reliance on the state, which it tried to turn into a Kultur-state. In France this mistake was made not by the academics but by the Catholic Church, whose alliance with monarchy proved disastrous for it. Erudition was never valued so highly in France as in Germany, unless it was seasoned with elegance, precisely because French teachers never convinced either themselves or anybody else that they were the salt of the earth. Since the teacher did not have this philosophical justification of his own importance, he aimed to please society more, to make education an ornament more than an initiation, to seek out what was judged tasteful in the world at large and attempt to propagate it, rather than to oppose an alternative, Platonic or mystical ideal of perfection. The French teachers achieved their importance by trying to make themselves more immediately, even if less exaltedly, useful.

They too escaped from their sense of inferiority by cultivating speculation, though to a lesser degree than the Germans. They too lived in their own small world, bolstering their importance by professionalising themselves, by developing 'pedagogy' into a science. Their love of abstraction was also a roundabout way of protesting against new technical and commercial forces that they were unable to cope with. But the vast majority of them did not aspire to being more than intellectual tailors, who dressed up their contemporaries with the ideas and the forms of speech that they thought society valued. The clothes they made were almost always out of date, and in the depths of the provinces sometimes positively archaic; these were the clothes that they had learnt to admire from their teachers and it was by no means the case that society at large did consider them as becoming as the teachers imagined. Their achievement remained important, however, for three reaons. Even if their values were largely rejected by the people who passed through their schools, the forms of speech and of thought they cultivated seem to have had a permanent effect on a not inconsiderable portion of their pupils: so though the pedantic clothes they tailored were hardly ever seen being worn by adults (apart from teachers), they were often kept as underclothes, taken for granted, unmentioned and unnoticed. It is this substratum of life that the teachers were responsible for. In addition, apart from this general effect on the educated classes, the teachers were increasingly important as a force magnifying the virtues of literary and intellectual activity. It will be shown in due course how the writers, in their books, their reviews and their newspapers, blew up their own productions and rivalries into matters of national, even universal, significance. The teachers were a sort of chorus on the sidelines of this world of mutual congratulation and denigration; and they encouraged their older pupils to be spectators if not participants in it. They thus increased the size of the world that revolved around books, though one must always remember that this was only one of many worlds. Finally, the teaching profession was one of the most active vehicles of social ascension in France. The vast majority of its members came of humble backgrounds and it is not surprising that they therefore held examinations, which had recognised their merits, in such esteem. France was therefore a country in which it was relatively easy for poor families to rise, in the space of about three generations, to middle-class respectability, if not wealth; its character was certainly modified by the fact that this social climbing could be achieved simply through book-learning. The main alternative methods of ascension were the army and commerce. Each of these paths was taken by people of different temperament, different family tradition, or from different regions: the teachers (before 1914 at any rate) came very definitely from only some (mainly northern) parts of France. The worlds of education, commerce and the army always remained hostile to one another. But they had a common origin in their ambition, directed towards social ascension. They were three products of the same motivation, and their antipathy for each other should not be allowed to obscure the fact that together they represented a distinct segment in a society which did not always move in the same direction as the rest of France.

7. Universities

THE secondary schools were important instruments for the creation of national uniformity. The universities, by contrast, split the nation again. They did this in two ways, by breaking it up into specialist groups, and by enabling students to establish themselves as the leaders of the emergent new class that young people now came to form.

There is no higher education in France, said a work on 'The Ruling Classes' in 1875.[1] This statement was almost true. There were no universities in the nineteenth century until 1896. The twenty-two universities which had existed in 1789 were abolished by the Revolution. Decay and corruption had reduced them to a mere shadow of their original medieval selves.[2] For a large part, it was no longer a university education that they dispensed. The superior faculties of theology, law and medicine nominally provided professional training but their standards had fallen abysmally low, as had the number of students in them. Many professors had abandoned lecturing altogether, and confined themselves to the lucrative task of issuing degrees. On one occasion the students of Bordeaux even sued their professors to compel them to lecture, but their zeal was exceptional; in the faculty of law, less than 2 per cent of the students bothered to attend lectures. Examinations were more a financial than an academic matter, in fact the purchase of a privilege. General education in the humanities and the sciences was provided by the faculty of arts and the degree of master of arts was the normal preliminary for entry to the higher faculties. This M.A., however, was of secondary-school standard; children entered the faculty of arts at the age of 10 or even 9, stayed on till 17 or 18, and confined themselves

[1] Charles Bigot, *Les Classes dirigeantes* (1875), 129–35. Cf. the pessimistic view of Gabriel Hanotaux, *Du choix d'une carrière* (1902), 205-6, 219–20, and Jules Payot, *La Faillite de l'enseignement* (1937), 36–7.

[2] Louis Liard, *L'Enseignement supérieure en France 1789–1889* (1888–94), vol. 1; Stephen d'Irsay, *Histoire des universités françaises et étrangères* (1933–5), vol. 2; F. Ponteil, *Histoire de l'enseignement en France 1789–1964* (1966); and A. Prost, *Histoire de l'enseignement en France 1800–1967* (1968).

largely to the study of Latin. The universities had no connection, therefore, with the important scientific discoveries of the eighteenth century, and they taught virtually nothing about them: sixty years passed before Newton's *Principia* was lectured on in Paris.[1]

During the Revolution and Empire, the idea of universities dealing with the whole of human knowledge was abandoned. Instead specialised schools were founded to provide professional training in separate subjects. The former elements of the universities were fragmented into independent faculties, designed, like the *écoles spéciales*, to provide professional training, though rather less efficiently, because, unlike the schools, they were not residential. The use of the medieval word 'faculty' was confusing. They were no longer faculties, or parts, of universities, for these were abolished. They were faculties only in the sense that they had the right to issue degrees or licences to practise in certain professions, particularly medicine, law and teaching. Each faculty was entirely independent of the others. The situation in the mid-nineteenth century was that sixteen major towns had faculties, but only a few of these towns had the full range, since medicine and theology in particular were taught only in a few places. But all sixteen had at the very least faculties of sciences and letters (the medieval faculties of arts were now thus subdivided into two), because these were essential to the secondary-school system. They not only awarded degrees to school-teachers (the *licence* or teacher's diploma), but also examined for the *baccalauréat* (the school-leaving certificate). The old connection of the faculty of arts with secondary education was thus retained and the faculties of sciences and letters awarded most of their *grades* for work done in *lycées*. The syllabuses for the *baccalauréat* and the *licence* were much the same: *lycée* students sometimes attended university lectures and prospective teachers were principally required to learn how to teach this syllabus rather than to engage in higher studies.[2]

Most faculties were given only four to six professors, who between them had to cover all the subjects. Pluralism flourished:

---

[1] Strasbourg was an exception: the standard was higher and the outlook more international and modern.

[2] A. de Beauchamp and A. Générès, *Recueil des lois et règlements sur l'enseignement supérieur* (1880–1915) is the best source for the legislation on this subject.

at one period the Rector of the Academy of Pau was simultaneously also dean and professor of the faculty and headmaster of the *lycée*. There were few students: the faculty of letters
at Caen had only forty-two at one point during the Restoration: twenty-two of them were boys at the *lycée* and twenty
students of the faculty of law. Research was almost unknown.
The lectures at these faculties were open to the general public
and for the most part attracted retired or leisured people. They
tended to be rhetorical, elegant popularisations. Guizot, Cousin
and Villemain set the standard of the professor as a man of
the world rather than a scholar; moreover, they quickly left
the university for parliament; and nearly all the professors of
Paris got substitutes (*suppléants*) to lecture for them. Professors
at the faculties of law were often more interested in their practice at the bar than in their lectures. There was some discussion
during the July Monarchy about reducing the number of these
isolated small faculties and building up a few great provincial
centres of learning, but the need for the state to strengthen its
secondary schools against the competition of the Church
seemed to make this impossible. Louis-Philippe's ministers
confined themselves to creating some more faculties here and
there (very few towns had all four faculties). This cost the state
little, if anything; higher education paid for itself because of
the very substantial income received in examination fees. As
late as 1866 the state was spending only 221,000 francs (£9,046)
on the faculties—the total budget of 3,800,000 francs was
almost balanced by receipts of 3,597,000 francs.[1] When Nancy
petitioned for a faculty of law, it was granted one in 1864, on
condition that it would compensate the state if any expenditure was involved in the first ten years—and hardly any was.[2]
It was the municipalities themselves which, from civic pride,
supplied the buildings. Nancy was in fact the first to give its
faculties a new building: most towns did not do so till the
latter part of the century. Till then, nearly all the faculties had
only the most primitive and exiguous accommodation, frequently tucked away in some hidden corner of the city. In

[1] V. Duruy, *Rapport à S.M. l'Empereur sur l'enseignement supérieur 1865–8* (Dec.
1868), xxvii.
[2] Aline Logette, *Histoire de la Faculté de Droit de Nancy, 1768–1864–1914* (Nancy,
1964), 87, 95.

the 1870s the faculty of sciences at the Sorbonne was still housed in a few tiny rooms, formerly used as bedrooms and kitchens by students. An inquiry of 1885 revealed that the scientific equipment in the faculties was almost identical with that of 1847: they had hardly any money to spend. The law faculty of Paris in 1869–70 allocated 1,000 francs (£40) to its library—and took no foreign periodicals at all. Marseille spent nothing on books.[1] The faculty of letters of Clermont-Ferrand in 1855 used up virtually all its budget of 22,286 francs (£891) on paying its five professors 4,000 francs each. In 1876 it still had only seven regular students; in 1894–5 the rector proudly reported 'the imposing figure of seventy-eight students'.[2]

Dissatisfaction with this state of affairs in due course developed. There was little public feeling on the subject before 1945, since popular interest was concentrated on school education. Because school-teachers were regarded with suspicion by conservative governments, the faculties, responsible for the training of teachers, had to be carefully controlled. Fortoul (minister 1851–6) warned faculties against the dangers of too much knowledge. He restricted the syllabus in order to reduce controversy; he transformed the chair of the history of philosophy at the Sorbonne into a safer one of comparative classical grammar. The first man to undertake a serious study of the situation of the faculties was Victor Duruy, whose thorough inquiry, begun in 1865, revealed the appalling physical conditions in which they were working. 'All Paris has been rebuilt,' he wrote; 'the buildings for higher education have alone remained in a state of decay which contrasts painfully with the imposing grandeur of the edifices created for other departments.' Duruy wished to create a genuinely *higher* education, of whose function he gave a revolutionary definition: it should no longer concern itself with preparation for examinations but should teach the methods by which students might learn the sciences which these methods have created. He wanted specialisation, erudition, teaching in small groups, the study of subjects beyond those of the secondary syllabus, and university scholarships. There were already 408 professorial chairs in fifty-three

---

[1] Louis Liard, *Universités et facultés* (1890), 16–20.
[2] Pierre Janelle, 'Histoire de la Faculté des lettres de Clermont-Ferrand', *Revue d'Auvergne*, vol. 68 (1954). A good article based on archival sources.

faculties: it was not institutions that the country lacked but their right application. However, he despaired of changing the conservative faculties and set up instead, outside them, the École Pratique des Hautes Études, a research institute. Once again the university continued unreformed because progress could be achieved more easily outside it. As it was, Duruy had great difficulty in finding the money to pay even for his small creation. The reform of the faculties was too colossal and expensive a task.

The war of 1870 gave the reform movement a great stimulus. Renan declared that it was the German universities which had won the war. A group of French scholars, meeting at the Collège de France, lamented also that 'there is no higher education in France'. The isolation of the faculties meant they could not treat knowledge as a whole; they concerned themselves with only a limited range of subjects; their teaching was not disinterested, because it was primarily directed at professional examinations, and government control meant they were not free in the pursuit of knowledge. All their lectures could be abolished without altering very much the way in which students studied; they were incapable of stimulating a taste for research because they merely prepared men to be schoolmasters. Reporting their conclusions, Gabriel Monod (who was later to found the *Revue historique*) wrote that the purpose of higher education should be 'on the one hand to maintain the taste for and the tradition of disinterested research, and on the other to create the spiritual unity of the nation by being the centre of its intellectual life'. The first of these aims involved the total transformation of the faculties on the lines of the École Pratique des Hautes Études; the second meant giving them an entirely new place in society, and a very central one. Monod proposed that all secondary and primary teachers should spend three years at a faculty—so bringing unity to the educational system and at the same time giving the faculties real full-time pupils. They should be given scholarships, and the state could in this way compel them to go to provincial universities, rather than to overcrowded Paris. University degrees should be purely academic: entry into the civil service (including the teaching profession) should be by separate examination. Academic study would thus become more disinterested. The faculties should be given more freedom to decide what they would teach, but since they would need greater strength to sustain their increased responsibilities and independence, they should be united into provincial universities. They should absorb the *écoles spéciales*, which would cease to drain off the best pupils. They would need a lot more money, though they could economise somewhat by obtaining *privatim docentes* to give many of the new courses free of charge. Monod's pamphlet is particularly interesting because it raised most of the issues involved in the reorganisation of higher education.[1]

For the first years of the Third Republic, however, attention was taken up by the Catholics' demand for freedom in higher education, that is, the right to establish Catholic faculties. In 1875 the monarchist Assembly passed a law granting this, though in 1880 the republicans withdrew the right to award degrees. The Catholics' success was slight; they attracted few students and could never compete in prestige against the state faculties.[2] The 1875 law required the government to present a bill for the reform of the state faculties within a year—but the ministers did not find a propitious moment to do so. The budget for higher education was indeed substantially increased at this period. It had been 2,876,000 francs in 1847; the Second Empire had raised it to 4,200,000. Waddington in 1877 raised it from 5,100,000 to 7,799,000 and Ferry brought it up to 11,600,000, at which figure it remained for another ten years. This should be compared, however, with the 18 million francs spent on secondary and the 100 million on primary schools. The increased expenditure represented little real change: most of it was used to create eleven small new faculties of the old pattern. It is true that sixty-seven new chairs were created in the already existing faculties, so that for example the faculty of sciences at Lyon, which in 1870 had only seven chairs, had in 1890 ten, plus three 'supplementary courses' and five *conférences* or seminars. These were an innovation borrowed from the École Normale, which had long used seminars as a method of instruction. Keen faculty professors had begun to introduce

---

[1] Gabriel Monod, *De la possibilité d'une réforme de l'enseignement supérieur* (1876).
[2] Mgr J. Calvet, 'L'Institut Catholique de Paris', in L. Halphen *et al.*, *Aspects de l'Université de Paris* (1949); René Aigrain, *Les Universités catholiques* (1935).

them on their own initiative, in order to make contact with serious students, but they remained the exception. Another innovation was the introduction of scholarships for university students: 300 were established in 1877, and another 200 in 1881. These, it should be noted, were respectively for students for the *licence* and the *agrégation*, i.e. for prospective schoolmasters. But the idea of disinterested study by autonomous faculties was not yet accepted.[1]

The man who did most to stimulate higher education in this period was Louis Liard. A graduate of the École Normale, placed first in the competition for the *agrégation* in philosophy, while still a young lecturer at Bordeaux he became deputy mayor of the city and organised the rebuilding of the faculty. His reputation as an administrator got him appointed rector of the Academy of Caen at thirty-six, and in 1884 he became director of higher education in the ministry, where he remained for eighteen years. Even when he moved on to be vice-rector of Paris University (1902–17) he continued to dominate the administration, visiting his old offices every afternoon. In his final years his principal achievement for Paris University lay in the collection of a large number of benefactions from private individuals. He had a strong respect for vested interests and his ideas were never revolutionary. The professors of faculties with whom he had to deal were even more conservative and slow. It took twenty years for his principal reform to be passed into law. In 1883 Jules Ferry had invited the professors to give their opinion on a possible amalgamation of the faculties into provincial universities. Most had been favourable, though some feared for a loss of their independence. One man—Boutroux, the philosopher—with exceptional foresight thought such a reform would be bound to increase the administrative chores of the professors.[2] The republican politicians felt too weak to surrender any power or control over the state's faculties, at the height of their battle against the Church. In 1885 no more was done than to establish some liaison between faculties in the same town, which were to meet in a *conseil général des facultés* to discuss common problems and to

---

[1] Paul Gerbod, *La Condition universitaire en France au 19ᵉ siècle* (1965), 568; L. Liard, *Universités et facultés* (1890), 34–56.
[2] *Enquêtes et documents relatifs à l'enseignement supérieur*, vol. 16 (1885), 35.

share a common budget. In 1896 finally they were united and
the provincial universities were established.[1]

The new universities were not true copies of the German ideal
of the generation of 1870. Dissatisfaction remained, because
they were not really independent bodies simply devoted to
higher learning. The Rector continued to be the representative of the government, in charge also of primary and secondary education in the region. The faculties continued to be
examining bodies for the secondary schools, and the best
institutions of higher learning, the *grandes écoles*, remained
outside them. The amalgamation was largely superficial and
the real unit remained the faculty, to such an extent that
Monod in 1900 proposed the abolition of the faculties within
the universities—without success, of course. Right up to 1968,
professors usually referred to themselves as *professeurs à la
faculté* rather than *à l'université*. Ferdinand Lot, the medieval
historian and deputy director of the École des Hautes Études,
published a vigorous denunciation of the new system in 1905,
showing how far the new universities were from rivalling their
German counterparts. The Directeur de l'Enseignement
Supérieur, overwhelmed by paperwork and personal solicita-
tions, saw only the satisfied Paris professors who had enough
money and students, but provincial scholars were very unhappy.
Paris could stand comparison with Berlin: it had an income
(faculties and *écoles*) of 10 million francs, one-half of the whole
higher education budget of 21 million. But the German universities, apart from Berlin, had an income three times as large as
that of the French provincial universities (and this excluded
very considerable extraordinary expenditure by the Germans).
Since the establishment of the French provincial universities,
the state had done little for them, and they were in debt. The
German professor gave six to eight lectures or classes a week:
the French one was still required to give only three. His isolation from the students continued. The gaps in the courses
offered by provincial universities were so great as to make
it doubtful whether they could be called universities. The

---

[1] Texts of the laws and decrees of the various steps in this reform in *Enquêtes et
documents*, vol. 58 (1898), together with extracts from relevant parliamentary
debates; E. Lavisse, 'Louis Liard', *Revue internationale de l'enseignement* (1918),
vol. 72, 81–99.

traditional domination of the secondary syllabus continued. For example, in five provincial universities the professor of modern history had to teach geography as well; two universities had no professor of German, two had no professor of English, and in Montpellier English and Italian were combined in one chair. The history of the French language was studied more in Germany than in France: 'matters have reached such a stage that it is necessary to know German in order to study French.' There was not even a chair of Provençal in France—a subject better studied in Germany. Slavonic studies, Sanskrit, and oriental philosophy barely existed at all in the provinces. The teaching of economics, sociology and psychology was still rudimentary. The French science faculties were strong in zoology, anatomy and physiology, because they taught these subjects to prospective medical students; and they were also good on anthropology and botany; but the Germans had more than twice as many professors of chemistry. Lot estimated that two hundred more chairs were needed in the provinces. With few exceptions, the old methods of teaching by magisterial lectures continued. *Conférences* or discussion classes were organised for students preparing for the *agrégation*, but here a student would simply read an essay and the professor would say how it ought to be written in order to pass: there was no real discussion of the subject. The attitude was indistinguishable from that in secondary education. The standard of examinations was still absurdly low and to obtain a degree did not require any physical attendance at the university. The French universities had only half the number of students the Germans had.[1]

The war of 1914 postponed reform for a generation. Inflation produced acute financial difficulties in the universities, so that it was not even possible to maintain the standards of 1914. When in 1921 the faculty of sciences of Paris asked for 4·7 million francs it was allocated 800,000—as in 1914. With salaries lagging far behind prices, professors resorted even more to pluralism. Any idea of expanding the universities was shelved for two different reasons. On the one hand, the country's

[1] F. Lot, *De la situation faite à l'enseignement supérieur en France, Cahiers de la Quinzaine*, série 7, 9, 11 (1905); C. Seignobos, *Le Régime de l'enseignement supérieur des lettres* (1904).

economic problems made retrenchment a principal objective
of successive governments. The universities were quickly
picked on as particularly wasteful institutions, overgrown,
overlapping, capable of being pruned without harm; indeed
a definite hostility to them developed. On the other hand, reformers declared that the universities were based on outdated
principles. A reaction set in against Liard's work—or rather,
the demands which his partial reforms had barely satisfied now
made themselves heard. The Compagnons de l'Université
nouvelle, whose ideas were to dominate the debates on all
grades of education from the publication of their articles in 1919
until the Second World War, advocated a totally new system.
A number of faculties, they declared, had never really lived
except on paper. The dispersal of resources between them was
wasteful. The very idea of a faculty was in any case out of date.
The aim of making universities encyclopedic should be abandoned and instead the unit in higher education should be the
specialised institute, which could combine several linked
subjects.[1] Léon Bérard, minister of education in 1922, wished
to abolish a considerable number of faculties, to have only five
national universities and eight regional ones—the latter being
reduced in size and specialising in a few subjects only. The
faculties in general should lose their financial autonomy. They
should avoid too-much theoretical teaching 'expensive for the
state and the need for which is not always evident'; the laboratories and libraries of different faculties should be combined to
achieve economies. Professors must be made to work harder:
'it is indispensable to put an end to certain habits and traditions and to fix, at all levels, each one's duties so as to safeguard the interests of the students and of the state'.[2] Bérard
destroyed any chances of implementing this programme by his
unpopular attempt to revive Latin as a predominant subject in
secondary education, in the interests, as he claimed, of saving

[1] The Compagnons included Edmond Vermeil, later well known as professor
of German history, and a number of secondary-school masters. See J. M. Carré,
'L'Histoire des Compagnons', in *Les Compagnons de l'Université nouvelle* (1920); Les
Compagnons: *L'Université nouvelle* (2nd edition, 1919), 2. 147–96. For the place of
the Compagnons in the history of education reform, see Luc Decaunes, *Réformes et
projets de réforme de l'enseignement français de la Révolution à nos jours 1789–1960* (1962).
[2] Proposals of Léon Bérard, 29 May 1922, in *Revue internationale de l'enseignement*
(1923), vol. 77; for his ideas in general see Léon Bérard, *Au service de la pensée
française* (1925).

French culture from 'barbaric materialism'. His successor Anatole de Monzie in 1925 again brought up the suggestion of creating specialist universities, instead of expecting them all to cover the whole of knowledge.[1] He had a certain amount of support, but too many political considerations, rivalries and electoral interests were involved, and nothing was done. Attention was concentrated on primary and secondary education. Jean Zay, the most active reforming education minister of the century (1936–9), does not appear to have had a particular interest in the universities—or at least he did not give them a high priority. This was certainly justified from the social point of view which concerned him most—the universities could never be made democratic until the *lycées*, which supplied them with pupils, lost their class character. He said he did not propose to do anything for the universities until he saw how the reforms at the lower levels worked out.[2] The major achievement of the inter-war period was the establishment of the Caisse des Recherches, later the Centre National de la Recherche Scientifique—which, one professor wrote, 'saved French science'. But the C.N.R.S. still left unsolved the problem of making research an integral part of the universities' work, and of freeing more professors from the chores of administration; it had besides difficulty in its early years in obtaining the co-operation of industry and of the different ministries engaged in scientific research. A national programme of scientific research was far from achieved.

In 1939, therefore, the universities were still shackled by the outdated ambitions of Napoleon and still enslaved to the needs of the secondary schools. This can be seen with special force in the syllabuses, for despite the reforming zeal of some critical professors, few basic changes were made in this period. The most static subject of all was probably medicine. Until 1835 doctors trained in Paris went into practice without ever having seen a woman give birth or even without having examined a pregnant woman. There was for long a contempt by doctors for sciences called 'accessory', like chemistry or

[1] A. Audolent, 'Y a-t-il lieu de "spécialiser" et de "moderniser" nos universités provinciales?', *Revue internationale de l'enseignement* (1926), vol. 80; cf. A. de Monzie, *Discours en action* (1927), 193–220.

[2] Jean Zay and Henri Belliot, *La Réforme de l'enseignement* (1938), 93–4; Jean Zay, *Souvenirs et solitude* (1945), 271.

microscopy. It was only in the late nineteenth century that therapeutics aroused the same interest as diagnostics. What professors prided themselves on was the beauty of their diagnosis, rather than its practical consequences. In the early part of the century they went round the wards followed by as many as 200 students each, so few could see the patients that were talked about; later they abandoned all reference to the patients and gave 'magisterial lectures', in which each preached his pet theory. If one was more interested in actual treatment, one went to Germany.[1] Little provision was made for medical research, and laboratories were totally inadequate (Pasteur got more support from the personal benefaction of Napoleon III than from the state). The French could defend this on the ground that they were interested in turning out practical physicians, but they soon fell so far behind advances in the medical sciences that their degrees ceased to be recognised by a number of countries, including the United States. It was only in the late 1950s that universities and hospitals were at last united.[2] This conservatism did not prevent France from producing some of the world's most brilliant physicians and medical scientists; but their influence on students was not always evident.

The faculties of law throughout this period had the largest number of students: they had long been looked upon as a kind of finishing school for gentlemen, as well as providing professional training for many lucrative professions, including the civil service. But they were having increasing difficulty in fulfilling this dual role. They had too many students (their number doubled between 1900 and 1939); their libraries and lecture halls were quite inadequate to accommodate even a fraction of them. In Paris, where there were 14,000 law students in 1920 and 19,000 in 1930, the law library had only 765 seats. The professors were overwhelmed with examinations: one professor reported having read no fewer than 200 theses in one year.[3]

[1] Mireille Wirot, *L'Enseignement clinique dans les hôpitaux de Paris entre 1794 et 1848* (1970), 125, 140 ff.; C. D. O'Malley, *The History of Medical Education* (U.C.L.A., 1970).
[2] Abraham Flexner, *Medical Education, a comparative study* (New York, 1925), 15–27, 118, 166, 167, 170; J. L. Crémieux-Brilhac, *L'Éducation nationale* (1965), 183–93; *Enquêtes et documents relatifs à l'enseignement supérieur* (1883–1922), vol. 91.
[3] H. Berthélemy, *L'École de Droit* (1932), 28.

The Paris faculty pressed for higher standards to eliminate the weak, but it failed to lengthen the course from three to four years. The lawyers insisted, however, on dominating social studies and keeping these within their faculty. Their syllabus was from time to time widened to include politics, economics, statistics and administration. As early as 1877 economics was made a compulsory subject for second-year law students— though in the face of much opposition from some lawyers, who in 1889 succeeded in transferring it to the first year. In 1905 the amount of economics taught was doubled, but it always remained a subsidiary subject, without a complete under-graduate course; the standard therefore remained very low, even at the doctoral level. Only in 1960 was a fully independent *licence ès sciences économiques* established.[1]

In 1894 the faculty of letters of Paris complained that its *licence* was still 'expressly and exclusively an attestation of good secondary studies' and expressed the wish that it should become a mark of higher education.[2] Until 1880 the *licence ès lettres* involved no specialisation: it required two dissertations, one in Latin and one in French, and used to be prepared for in the *lycées* with as much success as in the faculties. In 1880 a timid effort was made to add a *partie spéciale* devoted to philosophy, history and languages, but in practice this was neglected and the examinations in these subjects were purely formal, because the candidates' time was absorbed by the *partie commune*, done by everybody, on French and classics. In 1894, when candidates were allowed the option of offering a short thesis in the *partie spéciale* instead of undergoing a written examination, some professors took the opportunity to create seminars for these students, with good results—but the vast majority of candidates continued to opt for the traditional examination. In 1907 the compulsory French and classics were abolished and students were allowed to choose their own subjects. For the first time specialisation at a respectable level became possible, but again in practice the standard remained low: most candidates still read only a few textbooks. A further reform in 1920

---

[1] M. Lefas, 'La Réforme des études juridiques' in *Les Cahiers de redressement français*, no. 4 (1927). For the failure of earlier reforms see *Enquêtes et documents*, vol. 26 (1888); C. Rist, G. Pirou *et al.*, *L'Enseignement économique* (1937).

[2] *Enquêtes et documents*, vol. 52 (1894), 3.

raised the level a little but the traditional methods continued. History students, for example, could hardly ever read works in foreign languages, and their knowledge of foreign history was elementary. Special classes were sometimes offered by professors but attended by only a tiny minority. The memorising of dogmatic lectures and textbooks remained the students' principal occupation. In 1932 French and classics were once again made compulsory for students wishing to become schoolmasters. The schools spent about half their time on these subjects, up to a quarter of their time on modern languages, but very much less on each of their other arts subjects, philosophy, history and geography. Nevertheless, out of every 100 *licenciés* the universities were producing 26·5 classicists, 17 philosophers, 26 historians and geographers, and 30 modern linguists. Historians, geographers, and philosophers were declared to be lacking in 'culture générale', and compelled to take one paper in French, Greek and Latin. The confusion between teacher training and university education remained a difficult obstacle in the way of improved standards.[1]

The same was true in the science faculties. The university course was in theory distinguished from the school syllabus by far more practical work, but lack of laboratories, overcrowding, and chronic shortage of funds made this impossible in practice. There was even no special allocation for scientific research by the professors, and the acknowledged need for more demonstrators and technicians was not met: indeed, the government talked of economising. There was great variety in the standard of students in the various subjects—which were also taken to very different levels in the schools. But even in mathematics, in which France had a very high international reputation around 1900, the standard fell between the wars, when the reform of the secondary syllabus reduced the amount of time allocated to science. The scientists bitterly complained that far less was spent on higher education than was still allocated to the feeding of horses in the French cavalry in 1927, in the age of the motor car.

This stagnation in university methods was all the more remarkable and unacceptable because it survived into a period

[1] Louis Villat, 'L'Agrégation et l'enseignement supérieur', *Revue internationale de l'enseignement* (1930), vol. 34, 19–29.

when the demand for higher education was greater than ever before. The increase in the number of students can be seen from the table:[1]

	1900	1910	1920	1930	1939	1968
Students in the Faculty of:						
Law	9,709	16,915	13,948	19,585	22,470	126,000
Letters	3,476	6,363	6,355	16,928	21,339	196,000
Sciences	3,857	6,287	10,517	14,781	12,822	123,000
Medicine	8,781	9,721	11,990	16,246	16,027	98,000
Pharmacy	3,395	1,758	2,128	5,737	6,023	20,000

The increase in science students, though considerable, was very much less than that of students of letters; in 1939 there were still fewer students of science than of medicine, and law was still the most popular subject. There were more students, that is, but they were of the traditional type. The distribution of resources between the faculties was thus not really challenged by public opinion. The increase moreover was quite slight. The explosion in university education was to come well after the war of 1939–45. In 1939 there were 80,000 university students; in 1955–6 the number was 157,000; in 1965 it was 357,000. The small place held by the universities in the nation's life can be seen even more clearly if the number of professors is compared:[2]

1867	1878	1945	1950	1960	1963	1970
678	942	2,090	2,853	10,967	24,798	35,679

The increase in the number of students was not generally viewed with approval, for though more teachers were required, there was also much talk about graduate unemployment. In 1933, for example, a single post of junior master in Rennes—a perfectly ordinary post—attracted 245 applications.[3] Many professors spoke contemptuously of incompetent students and demanded entrance examinations and a limitation of numbers. 'Those who have not the talent or who have

---

[1] *Receuil des statistiques scolaires et professionnelles de 1936 à 1942*, published by the Bureau Universitaire de Statistique (1943), 12, 28, 44, 60, 76; *Annuaire statistique 1969* (1971), vol. 76, 104.

[2] Crémieux-Brilhac, op. cit., 375; *Statistique de l'enseignement supérieur* (1878), xliv.

[3] The Rector of Rennes who reported this said the situation had changed by 1937 and unemployment had disappeared. Cf. Walter M. Kotschnig, *Unemployment in the Learned Professions: an International Study of Occupational and Educational Planning* (Oxford, 1937), 114–17.

not acquired the knowledge necessary for receiving higher education, should confine themselves to secondary education.'[1]

This is perhaps why so little was done for the material welfare of the students. The Cité Universitaire in Paris (mainly for foreigners) and that at Lille, built between the wars, were exceptions. Students were expected to look after themselves. Most of them were still supported by their parents; many worked part or even full time to keep themselves; a minority seem to have survived in great poverty. Medical examinations before 1914 revealed that 7 per cent of students were tubercular and 12 per cent syphilitic.[2] Students' unions and associations were still weak. Perhaps the best account of the students' life and attitude can be obtained from the speeches of the young Merleau-Ponty, representing France at an international conference of students in 1938. He protested against the German delegate's view that the universities were too intellectual, that they did not devote enough attention to the students and to their 'affective life'. 'I think', he said, 'that this state of affairs is quite satisfactory, and that the university has nothing to do with their affective life nor even with their individual conduct. It is not a church, nor a school of character, nor even a sanatorium for melancholy students.' His description of Paris university life was interesting. There were no relations between students and professors in most subjects, he said. 'The professor gives his course, assigns grades to the dissertations of the students when they write any, and asks questions in the examinations.' There was a total absence of corporate life or internal cohesion—and so no pressures were exerted. 'Certain currents of thought prevail, inevitably, but each individual is free to revolt against them. The spirit of conformity is practically unknown. Each member of the university feels himself so much a stranger to the others that the attacks directed against it leave him indifferent . . . There are, however, some exceptions. Within the faculty of letters there exist certain rather closely united groups where there is much greater cohesion than in the faculty as a whole. These are groups which are

[1] Société de l'Enseignement Supérieur, *Problèmes d'université* (1938), 216, 226.
[2] Achille Mestre, *Études et étudiants* (1928); Marcelle Risler, 'L'Évolution de la condition des étudiants de la seconde moitié du XIXᵉ siècle à 1959', in *Cahiers de Musée Social* (1960), no. 1, 11.

concerned with highly specialised questions and which have a sort of monopoly of their subjects. Here the professors know their students, direct their work, accept their collaboration, and train them to become their successors. Professors and students are bound by very close ties; and these groups are very exclusive. It is not always easy to enter them. But these groups are separated by watertight compartments. They have nothing to do with one another or with the mass of the students. By the narrowness of the aims pursued, by their strictly technical character, they are rather collaborative workshops than genuine communities. The same is true as regards the sciences. In that field the work is less scattered, and a certain unity is maintained by virtue of the predominance of mathematical training. Furthermore, through the necessities of experimental work, a close contact is maintained between professors and students. But here too, I think, we must speak of collaboration rather than community. One only of the branches of the university presents the character of a genuine community: the faculty of medicine. That institution exercises a real monopoly over medicine in France. Not only have all who practise medicine passed through it, but the élite of French doctors is composed of the professors of the faculty. Outside the faculty there is no salvation, either for the doctor or for the patient. Although rivalries between doctors reach a degree of intensity rarely seen elsewhere, and although each student who wishes to succeed must attach himself to a *patron* who will defend him with all his influence against the favourite of another *patron*, the medical community is very coherent and very conscious of its privileges.'[1]

It has been said that Liard's provincial universities were a complete failure.[2] At any rate they did not succeed in winning an influential or highly respected place in the nation's life in this period, and there are several reasons for this. The principal one is that the reform of the universities was tackled in a very piecemeal manner, so that they never became the true apex of the educational system. The scale of values established by Napoleon survived. It was the *lycées* which were considered to

[1] League of Nations: International Institute of Intellectual Co-operation (Paris), *Students in search of University* (1938), 125–7.
[2] Georges Gusdorf, *L'Université en question* (1964), 197.

provide *culture générale*, a complete education in itself, rather than a mere preparation. Their top forms, the *classes de philosophie* and *mathématiques spéciales*, and the preparatory classes for candidates for the *grandes écoles*, had very high standards, and worked to a level which could rival that of the *licence*. Some of the teachers in these higher forms, like Alain and Bellesort, provided what was virtually higher education in the *lycée*, and more effectively in their small classes than the professors of the faculties could do with their anonymous audiences. The *licence* remained depressed because it was a professional qualification for an ill-paid and still inferior school-teaching job. The revival of the universities took place long after an active cultural life had already been established in France and had found different ground in which to grow. The intellectual élite, men of letters, the world of the *salons*, continued more or less independent of the universities. The progress of knowledge took place largely outside them too. The most specialised forms of education were entrusted to *grandes écoles*, which became major institutions of higher learning outside the university. It is these very small institutions which produced the country's 'mandarins'.

In the eighteenth century two special schools were founded to train engineers for the Ponts et Chaussées and for the Mines, and others for army and naval officers. In 1794 another was established to train engineers for public works—extended in 1795, as the Polytechnique, to train all kinds of military and civil engineers. In 1795 also the École Normale Supérieure was founded to train senior schoolmasters. As new sciences and new public needs developed, further *grandes écoles* and *écoles d'application* were established to provide even more specialised and advanced education in different forms of engineering and applied science. Important social consequences followed. The *grandes écoles* were entered by competitive examination (unlike the universities, which were open to all who had very elementary paper qualifications) and they offered scholarships, long before the universities did. The École Normale and the Polytechnique particularly came to attract the very best students in the country, and the marked success their graduates had in public life and in industry gave them enormous and increasing prestige. Both were residential and developed a unique *esprit de corps*. The result was that sizeable groups within the ruling class and among the most influential people in the country's economic and intellectual life were graduates of a few institutions. The lawyers had always had a dominant position in politics. Many of them, trained in Paris, knew each other from their student days, when they won oratorical distinction in moots. (The conférence Molé, where Gambetta's generation met, is perhaps the most famous of these.) It would be too simple to say that their position was challenged first by the Normaliens, particularly powerful in the Socialist party, and then by the Polytechniciens, who came to dominate big business. But there is just a little truth in this.

Though originally a teacher training college, the École Normale quickly became, because of the distinction of its professors and its pupils, a leading institution of higher learning. It developed methods of instruction totally different from the dogmatic ex-cathedra lecturing of the faculties. The professors were called *maîtres de conférences*, the discussion class was given more emphasis than the lecture, and private reading in the large library replaced the memorising of textbooks. Unlike the faculties, here the students were in intimate contact with their teachers, and being boarders, living in dormitories and in shared studies, they taught one another too. They had no difficulty in getting the best jobs in the schools and increasingly in the universities also, to such an extent that the school was attacked for abandoning its original function of teacher training and becoming a rival of the Sorbonne. The hostility aroused by their success led to the idea that the Normaliens were moulded into a single type. Zola wrote of them as 'musty pedants . . . filled with the silent impotent envy of bachelors who had failed with women'. The idea that they generally had any one political or religious opinion was misconceived. The school produced men of totally opposed tendencies—Jaurès and Bergson in one year; Herriot but also Mgr Baudrillart, Tardieu, Déat, Giraudoux, Bellesort, Massigli, and Louis Bertrand. Its teachers were equally diverse and never even tried to impose a single dogma. One of its directors, Bersot, called it *un lieu de tolérance*.[1]

---

[1] Jules Lemaître, 'L'Esprit normalien', in *Le Centenaire de l'École Normale 1795–1895* (1895), 565–71; Alain Payrefitte, *Chroniques de la vie normalienne* (1950),

The École Normale's relations with successive regimes were chequered and its character was considerably modified by successive directors. It was suspect under the Restoration for its liberalism: it did not seem to Bishop Frayssinous to be a repository of the 'sound doctrines, good traditions and useful knowledge which it is called upon to spread among the various classes of society'. By contrast it enjoyed high favour under Louis-Philippe, and no less a man than Cousin became its head. He had a passion for discipline and maintained the full rigour of Napoleonic austerity. The students rose at five and spent long periods in silent study under supervision; only in their third year could they obtain private rooms. 'Dangerous or futile books', said his regulations, 'must not enter the school; the reading of newspapers is forbidden, being irrelevant to the syllabus.' Since there are records of students being punished for spending the morning in bed, the severity of the rules must have been mitigated in practice. However, provided he was obeyed, Cousin was a powerful patron who actively assisted the graduates of the school to the best jobs: he was perhaps the first to give them the consciousness of being an élite, as well as of belonging to an organised clientage. In 1847 the school was moved out of highly insalubrious slums (for it was still an appendage of the Lycée Louis-le-Grand) into new buildings in the rue d'Ulm, which it occupies to this day. But the Second Empire plunged it again into disgrace. For fear of political deviation, it was firmly restricted to training only 'modest teachers, not rhetoricians, more skilled at raising insoluble and dangerous problems than at transmitting useful knowledge'. The tough minister of education Fortoul halted its progress towards becoming an institution of higher learning by ending the specialisation which had gradually developed. The students were confined to learning how to teach the *lycée* syllabus: they had to choose between being teachers of science or teachers of the arts. The specialist philosophy course was abolished as producing only 'vanity and doubt'. Even geometry had now to be taught so as not to inspire 'the pride which

272–3; for brief and bitter sketches of many other graduates Hubert Bourgin, *De Jaurès à Léon Blum: l'École Normale et la politique* (1938). R. J. Smith, 'L'Atmosphère politique à l'E.N.S. à la fin du 19ᵉ siècle', *Revue d'histoire moderne et contemporaine* (Apr.–June 1973), 248–68.

leads to false ideas'; geography should be purely descriptive, so as to 'show man his smallness . . . and lead his thoughts towards the Creator'. The students were not completely cowed, however: a new rule that they should request loans from the library in writing produced a strike, and they abstained from using the library for a year. This governmental hostility led to a catastrophic decline in applications for admission. The second half of Napoleon III's reign was spent undoing the damage, and specialisation was gradually restored. Pasteur, who became head of the science department, did a great deal to get the school recognised as a research establishment: in 1864 he founded the *Annales scientifiques de l'ENS* in which its discoveries were published. His fame even won him an allocation for research assistants. But he did not treat his students as equals: he expected them to be as obedient to constituted authority as he was himself, and he became pretty unpopular. There is a solemn table and statistical analysis, written in his own hand, of punishments imposed in 1858–9: they include castigations 'for having read a novel', 'for having read a newspaper', 'for having introduced a periodical into the school'. On one occasion he threatened to expel anyone caught smoking: seventy-three students handed in their resignation in protest: the matter had to be settled by the minister. When one student refused to attend prayers on the ground that he had been converted to Protestantism, Pasteur refused to accept this unless he produced a certificate from a pastor and he declared that if the student 'had no religion recognised by the state', he would be expelled.[1] Only in 1867 were the students allowed to get up at six instead of five.

It was some time before the arts side made precise erudition its ideal. Nisard (director 1857–67) believed the 'admiration of the classics' to be the best occupation for an educated man and 'French commentary' to be superior to 'German philological explication', taste to be more important than industry. Bersot (director 1871–80) had not completely abandoned his master Cousin's view of philosophy as involving 'adherence to those compromise truths, consecrated both by the faith of centuries and by the spiritual witness of men's conscience'; he approved of inquiry but did not believe it could lead anywhere. However,

[1] Cf. V. Glachant, 'Pasteur disciplinaire', *Revue universitaire*, July 1938.

Fustel de Coulanges (professor of history 1870, director 1880–3) abhorred dilettantism and indifference; he incited his students to engage in controversy, to avoid generalisation, to make detailed studies of small subjects based on original sources. He never spoke to them about their examinations; his lectures did not contain long recitals of facts, but enthusiastic extempore arguments, propounding one or two ideas. He was never known to smile or tell a joke, but his appeal to their intellectual liberty filled them with confidence. His successor, the archaeologist Perrot (1883–1904), tried (unsuccessfully) to make the school a graduate one, admitting only *licenciés*, but he also defended the traditional syllabus, praising even the educational merits of writing Latin verse.

Hostility to the school developed; the faculties protested that it was stealing the best students from them, but not fulfilling its function of giving pedagogic training to secondary teachers. The success of its graduates aroused envy: in the history *agrégation* in 1903, all six of its candidates were successful, but only three out of the forty from the Sorbonne and one out of the thirty from the provincial universities. The spread of socialism in the school, largely through the influence of its librarian Lucien Herr (famous for helping to convert Jaurès), exacerbated the hostility to it. In 1903, as a result of parliamentary pressure, it was made part of the University of Paris; its professors were withdrawn and attached to the Sorbonne; its independent teaching was largely ended; it was turned into a hostel, whose students attended the university lectures; it was to become simply the pedagogical department of the university, and its students were to devote a considerable period (instead of a nominal fortnight as before) to teaching practice in *lycées*. Its budget was drastically cut, and deputies in parliament even demanded its abolition altogether.[1] It had just then reached the peak of its influence: Wallon, the father of the constitution, and at one stage the presidents of both chambers of parliament were graduates of it. Whereas in 1890 it had ten times as many applications as it could admit, by 1914 this ratio was halved. In science, its standing became distinctly inferior to the

---

[1] C. Bouglé, 'Rapport sur les réformes proposées', *Revue internationale de l'enseignement* (1904), vol. 47, 45–9; G. Monod, 'La Réforme de l'École Normale', *Revue historique* (1904), vol. 84, 79 n.

Polytechnique, and candidates for both schools almost invariably preferred the latter if elected to both: the École Normale was reduced to taking the Polytechnique's rejects. This was very different from the situation in the nineteenth century: in 1864 a man who came top in the entrance examination for the Polytechnique, and second in that for the École Normale, had chosen the latter.

The principal architect of this transformation was the historian Ernest Lavisse (director 1904–19), one of the most influential figures behind the reorganisation of French education during the first half of the Third Republic. He made some changes in almost every arts examination. He wrote history textbooks for every stage of the school and university curricula. He was a close friend of Du Mesnil, Dumont, and Liard (successively directors of higher education at the ministry) and, some said, the man really behind the creation of the provincial universities. He was determined to make the Sorbonne not only eminent but also an active teaching institution with real students—of which the Normaliens would be the nucleus. It was not promotion for Lavisse to be made director; he had held more senior jobs; and he did not even bother to take up his official residence in the school. His unwillingness to supervise it closely was conscious: his temperament and his system both led to a great relaxation of discipline.[1]

The very existence of the school seemed threatened. It was saved partly by the heroism of its students in the war: 50 per cent of them were killed and the school was awarded the Croix de Guerre. The inter-war period was an uneasy one. Lanson (director 1919–27), famous as the author of a standard textbook on French literature which had sold 350,000 copies in its first twenty-seven years, tried to preserve the school's independence within the university. In 1927 a scientist (Vessiot) was appointed director and began the building of new laboratories, though he was unable to prevent the students' meagre scholarships being reduced by a quarter in the national economy drive. Bouglé (director 1935–40), the sociologist and founder of the school's Centre de Documentation Sociale (of which he made

---

[1] E. Lavisse, *Questions d'enseignement national* (1885); *Études et étudiants* (1890); *A propos de nos écoles* (1895); *Souvenirs* (1912); Inaugural speech on becoming director of the ENS in *Revue internationale d'enseignement* (1904), vol. 48.

Raymond Aron secretary), broadened its relations with the outside world, encouraged travel abroad, at last introduced central heating and running water. New life was thus injected into the school. But it survived also because it moderated its pretensions. From being a training college, it had developed the ambition of providing the republic with its ruling class. 'Democracy', wrote its director Perrot in 1895, at the height of its prestige, 'needs an élite, to represent the only superiority it recognises, that of the mind. It is up to us to recruit this élite, or, to speak more modestly, to work to furnish some of the elements which will constitute it.'[1] Lanson in 1926 still regarded his task as the 'training of the élite . . . the discovery and education of individuals fit to become leaders'.[2] However, when Herriot wrote on the school in 1932, he was content to speak of it only as a nursery of wit, intelligence, and liberalism. Extreme left-wing graduates poured scorn on its 'esprit de corps reminiscent of the seminary and the regiment'.[3]

At the École Polytechnique the idea of forming an élite persisted more strongly. Placed under the ministry of war, this school, exclusively scientific, was designed to train officers for the technical corps of the army and engineers for the various departments of state such as the Mines and the Ponts et Chaussées. The great majority of the graduates used to go into the army, a tendency strengthened after the war of 1870. The military law of 1905 which required them to spend one year in the ranks before entering the school reduced the ardour of some when they saw the army from the private soldier's viewpoint. The proportion of soldiers diminished henceforth, probably even more because other careers appeared more attractive. In the 1914–18 war, many of the French commanders were Polytechniciens, including Marshals Fayolle, Foch, Joffre, Manoury, and General Nivelle. By 1924 only a quarter of the graduates went into the army; Pétain is said to have excluded them systematically from the highest posts; so they could maintain that the school had no responsibility for the débâcle of

---

[1] *Le Centenaire de L'École Normale 1795–1895* (1895), xlv.
[2] G. Lanson, 'L'École Normale Supérieure', in *Revue des Deux Mondes*, 1 Feb. 1926; cf. A. François-Poncet, *G. Lanson* (1958).
[3] E. Herriot, *Nos Grandes Écoles: Normale* (1932), 194–9; Pierre Jeannin, *École Normale Supérieure, Livre d'Or* (1963), 138.

1940.[1] Increasing numbers went into private companies. Many of the greatest names in the history of industry and applied science are those of Polytechniciens, from Talabot and Citroen to Louis Armand. The school produced only a few politicians—Freycinet, Sadi Carnot, Albert Lebrun, Jules Moch, but its influence in politics has nevertheless been considerable. In the early years it was a seminary of Saint-Simonians and other theorists—Comte, Enfantin, Michel Chevalier, Considérant, Le Play. Its graduates played a leading part in the acquisition of the French empire. Between the wars, the school produced numerous graduates who took an interest in economics and advised successive governments.[2] The Polytechniciens were an important link between government and industry. Their *esprit de corps* was, and is, legendary. The school indeed consciously sought to create this by its military organisation. Its students lived in groups of about eight, for the two years of their course, with one room in which there were eight desks, a bedroom with eight beds, and a bathroom with eight wash-basins. On the wall a time-table told them exactly how they would be spending every minute of the day.[3] Little more than 100 students were recruited annually in the first half of the nineteenth century; and usually between 200 and 250 after 1870. As freshmen they were subjected to initiation ceremonies, sometimes of considerable brutality. A strong respect for the traditions of the school was quickly established and the 'glorification of its past' flourished as 'a respectable rite of the community'. This is not to say all of them were turned into conservatives, even though the school remained military. The students opposed the Restoration and the July Monarchy (the school was closed four times by the government in this period), and played a popular part in the revolutions of 1830 and 1848. In 1855 they refused to shout 'Vive l'Empereur' at the review by Napoleon III, and in 1868 they greeted a visit from the Prince Imperial with stony silence.[4] Since then they have remained politically diverse, though they do not seem to have

[1] J. P. Callot, *Histoire de l'École Polytechnique* (1959), 238; Maurice d'Ocagne, 'L'École Polytechnique', *Revue des Deux Mondes*, 1 June 1926.

[2] See Zeldin, *Anxiety and Hypocrisy*, ch. 7 (forthcoming).

[3] I describe what I saw in 1965 in the buildings put up between the wars: these have since been abandoned and the school has moved to the outskirts of Paris.

[4] G. Pinet, *Histoire de l'École Polytechnique* (1887), 273.

produced any revolutionaries. The social origins of the students may partly explain this. Napoleon had established only thirty scholarships. In 1850 the number of scholarships was made unlimited but dependent on a means test; about a third of the students were given scholarships, and by 1881 one-half were; in 1926 two-thirds were; only in 1930 was the school made entirely free. A considerable proportion thus came from well-to-do families. The idea of the hierarchy of merit dominated the whole course. The students were perpetually examined, usually at short notice, in brief, surprise orals; they were placed in numbered order on entry and graduation. They used the library very little and were taught mainly by lectures. Half the Polytechnique's entrance examination was in mathematics, discouraging the schools from teaching more natural science. Special classes in the best *lycées* prepared able boys for it, but these boys spent two or three years repeating the same narrow syllabus, for it was usual to fail a few times before getting in. It has been claimed that the 'Polytechnic mentality' was in fact acquired in these classes, where lessons, in the 1960s, still lasted from eight in the morning to eight in the evening, after which there was 'homework' to do; and only some did not study on Sundays. Admission to the Polytechnique was based on *surmenage* (overwork), so that by the time the successful candidates were admitted, they were already distinguished by their 'exceptional industriousness, rapidity of reasoning, memory and suppleness of mind'; but by then, they were already exhausted and their 'curiosity' vanished for ever once they had won their place. In the 1960s it was claimed about 60 per cent of them did not worry about the rank they would achieve in their final examination; only a minority continued to be competitive.[1]

Only two small institutions were devoted exclusively to research. The Collège de France had been founded in 1530 with six professors to advance humane studies and the spirit of the Renaissance, for the university, hidebound by its privileges and traditions, already appeared incapable of reform. By 1798 the College had twenty professors; by 1930 it had forty-seven. New chairs were added to advance new sciences; when a chair fell

[1] Michel Ullmann, 'Formations et mentalité polytechniciennes. Causes et conséquences' (mémoire Institut d'Études Politiques, unpublished, 1963).

vacant, it was not necessarily filled with a specialist in the same subject; the professors met to decide freely which subject— and often a new one—was most in need of further research. The College was entirely independent of the university; its professors did not have to hold any degrees; they could lecture on any subject they pleased, without having any examinations in view; they were required only to make their lectures contributions to knowledge, rather than simply popularisations; and these lectures were open free to the general public. The College was served by the most distinguished scholars and it did a great deal to maintain France's prestige in the world of learning. But, in common with the universities, its premises and laboratories were seriously inadequate, and extensions never kept up with its growing needs.[1]

The École Pratique des Hautes Études was founded in 1868 to fulfil two functions which the faculties were neglecting: the pursuit of *higher* learning, and the training of scholars for this by the *practical* co-operation of pupil and teacher in seminars and laboratories, instead of the former simply listening to the lectures of the latter. Originally its principal activity was to have been scientific—the provision of laboratories, but these laboratories never had an independent life, being attached to other establishments such as the Museum, the Collège de France, or the faculties of science. Nothing came of the economic section, because the faculty of law expressed no interest. The section of historical and philological sciences alone developed as an independent body, though at first it had only a corner in the Sorbonne library to meet in. It did a great deal for oriental studies and for linguistics. Gabriel Monod, who had attended seminars at Göttingen, introduced the seminar system into the historical sections, recruiting his first pupils from the École des Chartes and later the École Normale. It was a great innovation for professors and students to sit at the same table and work together on the solution of a problem or the editing of a text. But the directors of studies (as they were called here, there were no professors) usually also had other jobs, for example at the

[1] *Le Collège de France 1530–1930, Livre jubilaire*, by A. Lefranc, P. Langevin *et al.* (1932); M. Croiset, 'Le Collège de France' in E. Durkheim, *La Vie universitaire à Paris* (1918); M. Croiset, 'Le Collège de France' in *Revue des Deux Mondes*, 1 May 1926.

Collège de France or the Sorbonne. A characteristic of many of the institutes and other similar establishments is that they were often simply a group of men, rather than a building, and of men who spent much of their time in other institutions: they were more clubs than schools, and the importance of their publications was out of all proportion to their physical size. In 1886, when the faculties of Catholic theology were abolished, a section of religious sciences was added to the École Pratique. This was again a remarkable novelty, the first body to study all religions, including primitive and oriental ones. The École des Hautes Études demanded no paper qualifications from its students and it had no examinations. In these exceptional conditions, it was able to do work of great interest, but again for only a tiny minority of scholars and only in a few subjects.

The École Libre des Sciences Politiques, established in 1872, under the influence of the defeat by Germany, represented another attempt to remedy the gaps in the faculty system. Émile Boutmy, its founder, intended it to fulfil two functions. *Culture générale* was offered only in the *lycées*: he proposed to provide it at university level, and by the study of modern subjects instead of the classics. This liberal education would be different from the traditional type because it would turn out not 'conversationalists with ornamental minds' but 'competent judges of political questions, capable of solid discussions on these and capable of leading opinion'. He wished, secondly, to train 'an élite . . . formed of men who by their family situation or special aptitudes had the right to aspire to exercise an influence on the masses in politics, in the service of the state, or in big business'.[1] It began with ninety-five pupils paying 70 francs each in fees; by 1882 it had 250; in the 1890s between 300 and 400; by 1938 over 1,750. Over a tenth of these came from other countries. It was indeed unique in its international outlook and its interest in foreign politics and institutions, particularly those of England and the United States. Nearly all its professors worked elsewhere most of the time (they were for long paid for their lectures by the hour), and so it had close links with the outside world of politics, business and the civil service. Two departments were established at first, for diplomatic and administrative

[1] Pierre Rain, *L'École Libre des Sciences Politiques* (1963), 13–15; E. d'Eichtal, *L'École Libre des Sciences Politiques* (1932), 73, 77.

studies; later three more were added—economic and financial, economic and social, and general. The most successful
was the financial, which in 1932 attracted 42 per cent of the
school's students. Leading companies sent trainees to it. Until
1931 anybody could join, no qualifications being required. A
large number of students of the faculty of law attended its
lectures as supplementary courses. It became highly influential
because it was in effect an administrative college, and in time
it gained a virtual monopoly of the best civil service jobs. In
the period 1901–35, of 117 successful candidates in the competition for entry into the Conseil d'État, 113 were from Sciences
Po., 202 out of 211 admissions to the Inspection des Finances,
82 out of 92 to the Cour des Comptes, and 246 out of 280 to the
ministry of foreign affairs.[1]

A sizeable proportion of the country's intellectual and technical leaders passed through the institutions of higher learning[2]—
it is of course impossible to review them all here—but perhaps
for this very reason, their general structure and organisation
remained largely unchanged. The *esprit de corps* of their graduates and the conservatism (in professional, as distinct from
political, matters) of most of their teachers, preserved their
privileged, almost oligarchical, character. They claimed they
were democratic because the élite they created was recruited by
examination, but there was no real equality of opportunity to
pass the examinations. They drew the vast majority of their
pupils from the middle classes, because secondary education
was not yet freely available to the poor. They offered some
scholarships, but very few in proportion to their total numbers.
They still made study in Paris an almost indispensable condition—and sign—of success. Their examinations, moreover, were
extremely old-fashioned and universally decried for rewarding
memory more than anything else. Nevertheless, the institutions
were not intolerable, precisely because of their defects. Their
limited ambitions allowed freedom, their decadence left room
for hope and for leisure. For all their theoretical stress on

[1] Rain, op. cit. 90.

[2] Nicole Delefortrie-Soubeyroux, *Les Dirigeants de l'industrie française* (1961),
57–8; Alain Girard, *La Réussite sociale en France* (1961), *passim*; Pierre Lalumière,
L'Inspection des Finances (1959), 30, 70; A. Odin, *Genèse des grands hommes: gens de
lettres français modernes* (1895).

uniformity, their chaotic disorganisation gave plenty of scope for individuality. Despite them and partly thanks to them, France was able to enjoy a century of cultural achievement as distinguished as any in its history. The significance of the expansion of higher education was not generally appreciated, partly because this expansion was moderate compared to that which took place in the 1960s, partly because the static population meant that there were proportionately fewer young people in the country, and partly because the best students were quickly absorbed by society and given a more or less privileged position. But the universities were already beginning to create a vast new *compagnonage*, and it was no accident that students played a major role in the revolution of 1968.

France, as a nation, was to a large extent created by an effort of will. These seven chapters have shown how politicians and intellectuals tried to make it much more than a conglomeration of neighbours, but also how their ideals were never quite realised. The French did not all come to think alike; the schools did not quite succeed in transforming their pupils. The elaborate hierarchical structure of examinations produced much more mediocrity and parody than anyone had bargained for. There were too many forces, regional, ideological, temperamental, which resisted uniformity. The conflicts of boys and girls, of young and old, of the primary and the secondary mentality, were paradoxically strengthened. To measure the success of the French nationalists, it is necessary to study this resistance further, to look at the parallel development of the non-intellectual sides of life, to assess the strength of other attractions and to investigate the emotional demands of the people out of school.[1] Only then will it be possible to judge the role of the intellectuals in a comprehensive context.[2]

[1] See Zeldin, *Taste and Corruption*.
[2] See Zeldin, *Anxiety and Hypocrisy*, ch. 9 (forthcoming).

GUIDE TO FURTHER READING

THIS volume has been concerned with almost timeless themes, and certainly with issues that are still topical and controversial. It is useful therefore to see the French case in its international context. One can begin with general works on national character and ideology like André Siegfried, *L'Âme des peuples* (1950); Salvador de Madariaga, *Englishmen, Frenchmen, Spaniards* (1928); Leonard Doob, *The Psychological Foundations of Nationalism and Patriotism* (New York, 1964); Boyd C. Shafer, *The Faces of Nationalism* (New York, 1972); Karl W. Deutsch, *Nationalism and Social Communication* (Cambridge, Mass., 1966); F. H. Hinsley, *Nationalism and the International System* (1973); E. Kedourie, *Nationalism* (1966); A. D. Smith, *Theories of Nationalism* (1971); and, finally, seek further guidance in Karl W. Deutsch and R. L. Merritt, *An Interdisciplinary Bibliography on Nationalism 1935–65* (Cambridge, Mass., 1966).

The history of French patriotism is studied in Carlton Hayes, *France, a Nation of Patriots* (New York, 1930); A. Aulard, *Le Patriotisme français de la Renaissance à la Révolution* (1921); Jean Lestocquoy, *Histoire du patriotisme en France* (1968); J. Y. Guiomar, *L'Idéologie nationale* (1974); Raoul Girardet, *Le Nationalisme français 1870–1914* (1966) and *L'Idée coloniale en France 1871–1962* (1972); Henri Guillemin, *Nationalistes et nationaux 1870–1914* (1974); Stanley Hoffmann, *Decline and Renewal: France since the 1930s* (1974) and *In Search of France* (New York, 1963), published in England under the title *France: Change and Tradition* (1963); Jean Plumyène, *Histoires du nationalisme* (1979); and Steven Englund *The Politics of the Nation Ideology in France 1780–1891* (forthcoming). On local civilisations see, e.g., Pierre Jakez Hélias, *The Horse of Pride: Life in a Breton Village* (Yale University Press, 1978), and C. Gras and G. Livet, *Régions et régionalisme en France du 18ᵉ siècle à nos jours* (1977).

Books pour out endlessly on the history of education, but the best starting-point is still Antoine Prost, *Histoire de l'Enseignement en France 1800–1967* (1968). To pursue special interests look at P. Juif and F. Dovero, *Manuel bibliographique des sciences de l'éducation* (1968), and their *Guide de l'étudiant en sciences pédagogiques* (1972); also Maurice Debesse and Gaston Mialaret, *Traité des Sciences pédagogiques* (1969 ff., 7 vols.), and F. Buisson, *Noveau Dictionnaire de pedagogie et d'instruction primaire* (1911 edition). E. Durkheim, *L'Evolution pédagogique en France* (1938, reprinted 1969) is stimulating. For the history of French educational thought, Maurice Chavardès, *Les Grands Maîtres de l'éducation* (1966), and J. Cambon, *Anthologie des pédagogues français contemporains* (1974). For solid detail, read Maurice Gontard, *L'Enseignement primaire en France de la Révolution à la loi Guizot* (1955) and *Les Écoles primaires de la France bourgeoise 1833–75* (n.d.); H. C. Rulon and Ph. Friot, *Un Siècle de pédagogie dans les écoles primaires 1820–1940* (1962), on the work of the religious teaching Orders; Louis Legrand, *L'Influence du positivisme dans l'œuvre scolaire de J. Ferry* (1961); C. Falcucci, *L'Humanisme dans l'enseignement secondaire au 19ᵉ siècle* (1939); P. Gerbod, *La Condition universitaire en France au 19ᵉ siècle* (1965), which deals with secondarys; teacher Gérard Vincent, *Les Professeurs du second degré* (1967), deals with them in the 1960s; Ida Berger and Roger Benjamin, *L'Univers des instituteurs* (1957); and Jacques Ozouf, *Nous les maîtres d'écoles* (1967). There is interesting discussion in the *Enquête sur l'enseignement secondaire* under the chairmanship of A. Ribot (1899). For examples of the reforming spirit, Alfred Binet, *Les Idées modernes sur les enfants* (1909), and Pauline Kergomard, *L'Éducation maternelle dans l'école* (1886–95). For the universities, Louis Liard, *Universités et facultés* (1890), and G. Antoine and J. C. Passeron, *La Réforme de l'Université* (1966). And there is now a good book on the peculiarities of girls' education: Françoise Mayeur, *L'Enseignement des jeunes filles sous la troisième république* (1977).

Recent works in English on French education inculde W. D. Halls, *Society, Schools and Progress in France* (Oxford, 1965) and *Education, Culture and Politics in Modern France* (Oxford, 1976); W. R. Fraser, *Reforms and Restraints in Modern French Education* (1971) and *Education and Society in Modern France* (1973); O. E. C. D., *Reviews of National Policies for Education: France* (Paris, 1971); J. Talbott, *The Politics of Educational Reform in France 1918–40* (Princeton, 1969); R. D. Anderson, *Education in France 1848–70* (Oxford, 1975); J. M. Clark, *Teachers and Politics in France* (Syracuse, 1967).

Finally, one should go and see Jean Vigo's film, *Zéro de Conduite* (1933), which was banned for being too authentic a description of the way boys were treated at school.

INDEX

D. THOMSON

DEMOCRACY IN FRANCE SINCE 1870

'a most valuable study of the fortunes of the democratic
idea in France'   *International Affairs*

Where does the Fifth Republic of de Gaulle stand in
relation to the two parliamentary republics which, in the
course of the last hundred years, have preceded it? Is the
pedigree of Gaullism monarchist or even Bonapartist, rather
than republican? These questions call for a sustained analysis
of the changes that have taken place in the economy and
social structure of France since 1870, as well as of its
democratic ideas and its organs of government.

Democracy in France since 1870, first published in 1946, has
established itself both in Britain and overseas as a standard
work on modern France, and the present edition for Oxford
Paperbacks has given the author a new opportunity to assess
the spirit and achievements of the Fifth Republic. Gaullism,
he maintains, stands within the authentic and continuous
tradition of French republicanism: but it brings to mind the
emergency regimes of a Gambetta and a Clemenceau and
the provisional authority of a Thiers or a Pétain, rather
than the more familiar modes of parliamentary government. This analysis of the Fifth Republic, covering events
down to the end of 1968, furthers the original purpose of the
book – to explore the special meaning and character of
democratic ideals and institutions in France.

A. J. P. TAYLOR

THE STRUGGLE FOR
MASTERY IN EUROPE 1848–1918

The international system of Metternich ended with his fall
in 1848. New ideals of internationalism reappeared with
Lenin and Wilson in 1918. Nationalism, tempered by the
Balance of Power, dominated Europe in the intervening
seventy years. This book describes the relations of the great
European powers, when Europe was still the centre of the
world. Though primarily diplomatic history, it seeks to
bring out the political ideas and economic forces which
shaped day-to-day diplomacy. The author has gone through
the many volumes of diplomatic documents which have
been published in the five great European languages; and
the story is based on these original records. By vivid
language and forceful characterization, the book aspires to
be a work of literature as well as a contribution to scientific
history.

'one of the glories of twentieth-century history writing'
Observer

PAGES FROM THE GONCOURT JOURNAL

Edited and translated by Robert Baldick

The literary partnership of Jules and Edmond de Goncourt was remarkable for its closeness, for its shared tastes, and for its suspicion and dislike of the outside world; but it is the brothers' *Journal*, in which they recorded in minutest detail the French literary scene of the nineteenth century, which has assured their immortality. The *Journal* begins on the day of Napoleon III's *coup d'état*, takes us through the Commune in 1870–1, and ends with Edmond's death in 1896. Characters great and small, works of art and literature, appear, are discussed, and are the subjects of often scurrilous anecdotes. Victor Hugo, Baudelaire, Maupassant, George Sand, Rodin, Degas, Flaubert, and Zola are just a few of the people who pass through the brothers' drawing-room.

THE CONCISE OXFORD
DICTIONARY OF FRENCH LITERATURE

Edited by Joyce M. H. Reid

This abridgement of the classic *Oxford Companion to French Literature* preserves the unique utility of the original work and at the same time extends its scope with the addition of some 150 new entries to bring it right up to date.

Abridgement has been effected by condensation rather than omission; the *Dictionary* thus retains such valuable and distinctive features of the *Companion* as its long general articles on genres, its coverage of a great many minor, as well as major, writers and movements, its generous lists of works in articles on individual authors, its wealth of plot-summaries and cross-references; and, like the *Companion*, the *Dictionary* ranges far beyond the strictly literary and artistic field to cover aspects of French history, philosophy, religion, language, politics, administration, and education, newspapers and reviews, a very wide variety of institutions, and many other facets of cultural and social life.

The new material includes articles on leading contemporary writers and literary reviews, and on topics ranging from the Resistance to the *nouveau roman* and from *Poujadisme* to Structuralism. Many other entries have been revised or expanded – to note deaths, to include a writer's later works, to reflect such developments as the reform of higher education, for example – making this the most widely ranging and up-to-date reference book in this field.